Future of Customer Engagement Through Marketing Intelligence

Mudita Sinha
Christ University, India

Arabinda Bhandari
Presidency University, India

Samant Shant Priya
Lal Bahadur Shastri Institute of Management, India

Sajal Kabiraj
Häme University of Applied Sciences, Finland

T0396640

A volume in the Advances in Marketing, Customer Relationship Management, and E-Services (AMCRMES) Book Series

Published in the United States of America by
IGI Global
Business Science Reference (an imprint of IGI Global)
701 E. Chocolate Avenue
Hershey PA, USA 17033
Tel: 717-533-8845
Fax: 717-533-8661
E-mail: cust@igi-global.com
Web site: http://www.igi-global.com

Library of Congress Cataloging-in-Publication Data

CIP DATA PROCESSING

ISBN(hc):9798369323670 I ISBN(sc):9798369346389 I eISBN:9798369323687

This book is published in the IGI Global book series Advances in Marketing, Customer Relationship Management, and E-Services (AMCRMES) (ISSN: 2327-5502; eISSN: 2327-5529)

British Cataloguing in Publication Data
A Cataloguing in Publication record for this book is available from the British Library.

All work contributed to this book is new, previously-unpublished material. The views expressed in this book are those of the authors, but not necessarily of the publisher.

For electronic access to this publication, please contact: eresources@igi-global.com.

Advances in Marketing, Customer Relationship Management, and E-Services (AMCRMES) Book Series

Eldon Y. Li
National Chengchi University, Taiwan & California Polytechnic State University, USA

ISSN:2327-5502
EISSN:2327-5529

MISSION

Business processes, services, and communications are important factors in the management of good customer relationship, which is the foundation of any well organized business. Technology continues to play a vital role in the organization and automation of business processes for marketing, sales, and customer service. These features aid in the attraction of new clients and maintaining existing relationships.

The Advances in Marketing, Customer Relationship Management, and E-Services (AMCRMES) Book Series

addresses success factors for customer relationship management, marketing, and electronic services and its performance outcomes. This collection of reference source covers aspects of consumer behavior and marketing business strategies aiming towards researchers, scholars, and practitioners in the fields of marketing management.

COVERAGE

- Cases on Electronic Services
- Database marketing
- Customer Relationship Management
- CRM and customer trust
- CRM strategies
- Ethical Considerations in E-Marketing
- Telemarketing
- Relationship Marketing
- Data mining and marketing
- Cases on CRM Implementation

IGI Global is currently accepting manuscripts for publication within this series. To submit a proposal for a volume in this series, please contact our Acquisition Editors at Acquisitions@igi-global.com or visit: http://www.igi-global.com/publish/.

Titles in this Series

701 East Chocolate Avenue, Hershey, PA 17033, USA
Tel: 717-533-8845 x100 • Fax: 717-533-8661
E-Mail: cust@igi-global.com • www.igi-global.com

Table of Contents

Detailed Table of Contents

The dynamic environment of the business world is full of uncertainty, complexity, and ambiguity. It is necessary to quickly understand market trends and customer needs, accurately position the market, and ensure an absolute advantage in the fierce market competition. The dynamic changes of Industry 4.0 have become an important alternative. Meanwhile, e-commerce is the leading representative of the Industry 4.0 transformation, using computing devices and communication platforms to conduct business online. Managers need to accurately understand the current high demand and dynamic market based on advanced technology, data analysis, and interconnected systems, with a primary customer orientation and do an excellent excellent job in customer relationship management to create a competitive advantage for organisations that can leverage the information at their disposal. However, the booming e-commerce also hides challenges. Organisations are responsible for keeping information secure, preventing unlawful use, maintaining customer trust, and using information competitively and strategically.

Chapter 2

Consumer behaviour and the nature of community-focused retail experiences are being shaped by social commerce, an amalgam of social media and e-commerce, revolutionising the business landscape. Changes in retail are being propelled by digital transformation, which is also spawning new business-social relationships. Businesses are facing a rapidly evolving market driven by technology and customer expectations as social commerce micro-moments and digital transformation come to light. In order to surpass expectations set by digital transformation and revolutionary moments, companies must embrace empathy and innovation. In order to deduce what drives consumers, sophisticated algorithms for demand prediction and real-time data analysis are required. To help organisations navigate this landscape, this study examines micro-moments related to digital transformation and social commerce. By leveraging these interactions, companies can take advantage of the dynamic digital world and offer guidance on adapting micro-moments in social commerce environment.

Nitesh Behare, Balaji Institute of International Business, Sri Balaji University, Pune, India
Rashmi D. Mahajan, Balaji Institute of International Business, Sri Balaji University, Pune, India
Ashish Mohture, Institute of Management and Research, Chatrapati Sambhaji Nagar, India
Shrikant Waghulkar, Arihant Institute of Business Management, India
Shubhada Nitesh Behare, Independent Researcher, India
Vinayak Shitole, Arihant Institute of Business Management, India
Anandrao Bhanudas Dadas, Neville Wadia Institute of Management Studies and Research, Pune, India

This chapter delves into the transformative influence of genetic information on precision marketing, exploring the opportunities and challenges it presents. Beginning with an overview of precision marketing and its evolution towards personalization, the chapter examines the types and methods of collecting genetic data for marketing purposes. It highlights the immense potential for personalized product recommendations, targeted advertising, and enhanced customer experiences. However, the exploration does not shy away from addressing the ethical considerations and challenges associated with privacy, consent, and the potential societal impact of genetic data usage. Best practices for responsible data management and compliance with evolving regulatory frameworks are discussed, ensuring a balanced approach between personalization and ethical considerations. The chapter concludes by peering into the future, exploring emerging technologies and anticipated trends that will further shape the landscape of precision marketing with genetic insights.

Muhammad Usman Tariq, Abu Dhabi University, UAE & University of Glasgow, UK

This chater delves into the synergistic convergence of two transformative technologies reshaping the business landscape. Commencing with an exploration of fundamental blockchain principles, the segment elucidates its decentralized nature, distributed ledger, and smart contract capabilities. Simultaneously, it navigates the intricacies of IoT, unraveling interconnected devices, data communication, and practical applications spanning diverse sectors. Acknowledging the challenges inherent in IoT, such as security concerns and data integrity, the chapter strategically positions blockchain as a viable solution to address these issues. A comprehensive examination of the fusion of blockchain and IoT is undertaken, emphasizing the heightened security, transparency, and efficiency resulting from their integration. Through a series of real-world applications, the segment illustrates how this amalgamation transforms supply chain management, legal and financial processes, healthcare, and the energy sector.

Mohammed Majeed, Tamale Technical University, Ghana

The hotel and tourism industry is undergoing significant changes due to the widespread adoption of digital technologies that enable instant client communication and data gathering. The aim of the chapter was to do a review to understand the AI technologies that influence value co-creation in the hospitality and tourism industry. The author found AI influencing VCC to include natural language processing, chatbot, intelligent agents, voice-activated digital support, personal digital assistants that aid online visitors, ML, etc. The DART model was selected as the primary framework due to its status as a prominent theory and its widespread application in the study of VCC. It was noticed that AI can facilitate dialogue, access, risk, and transparency, leading to customer/guests/visitor engagement. Future research should focus on AI for marketing and promotion. It was concluded that AI technology provides compelling prospects for engaging interactions and virtual gatherings.

Arabinda Bhandari, Sarala Birla University, Ranchi, India
Mudita Sinha, Christ University, Bangalore, India

Artificial intelligence (AI) has grabbed the attention of the extent of literature and customer engagement of many business organizations in the past decade, especially with the advancement of machine learning and deep learning. However, despite the great potential of AI to solve customer problems and engage customers, there are still many issues related to practical uses and lack of knowledge to create value through customer engagement. In this context, the present study aims to full fill the gap by providing a critical literature review based on 53 A* and A categories of Australian Business Deans Council (ABDC) journals (2011-2023) by highlighting the benefits, challenges, framework, and future research directions in theory, context, characteristic and methodology (TCCM) areas. These findings contribute to both theoretical and managerial perspectives for developing a future novel theory and new forms of management practices.

Yamijala Suryanarayana Murthy, Vardhaman College Engineering, India
Ravi Chandra B. S., Vardhaman College of Engineering, India

This study examines the growing role of AI chatbots in customer loyalty by examining digital experience preferences across age groups. The study examines AI chatbot features like availability, simplicity of use, accuracy, responsiveness, assurance, and empathy, which are thought to affect digital experience and loyalty. The research uses hybrid methodologies to capture a variety of user interactions and viewpoints. Quantitative data is collected by administering structured surveys to a demographically diverse sample to examine chatbot attributes' effects on behavioral and attitudinal customer loyalty. The expected results may show a complex relationship between AI chatbots and customer loyalty. Younger generations value simplicity and quickness, whereas older people value accuracy and confidence. The scholarly discussion on digital customer engagement benefits from this study. This study helps organizations optimize their AI chatbot strategy to serve a wide range of clients. It emphasizes the need to understand generational preferences in the digital ecosystem.

Chapter 8

The emergence of digitization, automation, and artificial intelligence has transformed service delivery, allowing businesses to increase productivity, tailor client experiences, and provide cutting-edge solutions. The delivery, use, and accessibility of services are changing in various service sectors due to innovations. Among them, healthcare, education, and finance have received considerable attention in recent years. To synthesize prior research on innovations in the service industry, the chapter attempts a thematic, sentiment, and bibliometric analysis of the research domain. For the analysis, data was extracted from the Scopus database and was filtered by application of inclusion-exclusion, with the use of NVivo and Bibliometric software VOS viewer. Most productive and influential articles, authors, journals, and affiliations were recognized. Thematic mapping and trend analysis revealed past and present research subdomains that were used for the prediction of future research agendas.

Chapter 9

Augmented reality (AR) is being used to transform the landscape of online retail by enhancing customer engagement and experience. This chapter delves into how AR's unique capabilities, such as virtual try-on and interactive product visualisation, can overcome the limitations of traditional online shopping and create deeper connections between brands and consumers. It explains how AR personalises the customer journey by providing customised product recommendations and immersive virtual experiences that drive purchase decisions. By analysing past implementations and future trends, this chapter demonstrates how ARM can usher in a new era of customer engagement and personalised experiences in online retail.

Chapter 10

This chapter explores the evolving phenomenon of webrooming in the retail landscape. It delves into how technological advancements and changing consumer behaviors are reshaping the way customers engage with both online and offline retail environments. It highlights the importance of a seamless omnichannel strategy, addressing the synergy between digital browsing and physical purchasing. The chapter also emphasizes the role of personalization, customer experience, and sustainable practices in appealing to webroomers. Through a comprehensive analysis, it offers insights into how retailers can effectively harness webrooming to enhance customer engagement and drive sales, navigating the complexities of modern retail.

The present study highlights the critical role that marketing plays in promoting sustainable consumption through eco-packaging. It does this by reviewing academic research in the fields of behavioral science and marketing that looks at the best practices for changing consumer behavior towards sustainability through eco-packaging. During the review process, the writers create a thorough framework for imagining and promoting long-term changes in customer behavior. The framework, which goes by the abbreviation SHIFT, suggests that when a message or context makes use of the psychological elements of social influence, habit formation, individual self, feelings and cognition, and tangibility, customers are more likely to act in ways that support the environment. In addition, the researchers list five major obstacles to promoting sustainable behavior, and they utilize them to formulate original theoretical ideas and suggest future lines of inquiry. Lastly, the authors describe how this paradigm might be applied by practitioners who want to promote ecological behaviour among consumers.

Chapter 12

The human mind is constantly being influenced by a vast number of external stimuli that are perceived consciously as well as unconsciously. The chapter attempts to explore how unconscious (subliminal) priming of known and unknown human faces could impact product selection and decision-making time of consumers. 2 (Known face X Unknown face) X 2 (Product selection X Decision-making time) within-subject design was used for the study. A pilot study was conducted to estimate the subliminal time threshold of the population. It was found to be 17ms. A stimulus-priming experiment designed in Opensesame software was used to subliminally expose the participants to both known and unknown human faces. They were then asked to select a product that they were willing to buy from an option of four products, of which one of the products was primed along with human face (known vs. unknown). The product selection rates as well as the time taken to select the product were recorded. A total of 100 participants falling in the age category of young adults (18-39) took part in the study.

Banks were forced to modernize their action plans and strategies in banking relationships so as not to lose their place in an increasingly competitive market due to the use of the internet. Relationship marketing arises in the banking context, due to the need to retain customers and not just because of the concern with attracting new customers. The sudden changes which affects society and the national and global economy mean that we must attribute increasing importance to relationships, loyalty and fidelity, and in the banking sector, the manager-client relationship requires some determinants such as loyalty, satisfaction, quality, and trust. The aim of this topic is to understand how the paradigm of relationship marketing in the banking sector has changed nowadays, considering the drastic change in the practices used by banks regarding their marketing and communication strategies, resulting of technological evolution. In order to achieve the proposed objectives, a qualitative methodology was used with semi-structured interviews.

Preface

In today's dynamic and fiercely competitive business landscape, effective marketing stands as a cornerstone of success. As editors, we recognize the imperative for businesses across all sectors to develop sustainable and efficient marketing strategies. The convergence of traditional and cutting-edge methodologies, such as leveraging alternative data and AI-based solutions, underscores the evolving nature of marketing in a world that straddles the physical and digital realms.

The question arises: How can businesses navigate this shifting terrain effectively? The answer lies in data. In the modern marketing milieu, data serves as the linchpin for addressing crucial challenges and unlocking new opportunities. Great marketing strategies, we contend, emerge from a deep understanding of market dynamics supported by rich, factual data. Enter marketing intelligence—a discipline explicitly designed to enhance all facets of modern marketing through the collection, analysis, and strategic utilization of information.

With this ethos in mind, we present *Future of Customer Engagement Through Marketing Intelligence*. This book serves as a comprehensive guide, offering readers a step-by-step roadmap for establishing, implementing, and harnessing the power of market intelligence to derive actionable insights.

Our objectives in compiling this edited volume are manifold. We aim to explore emerging trends, offer expert insights, highlight best practices, address ethical considerations, evaluate tools and technologies, glean cross-industry perspectives, forecast future developments, educate practitioners, embrace diverse viewpoints, tackle challenges head-on, foster innovation, encourage collaboration, engage our audience, delve into policy implications, and advocate for sustainable and responsible customer engagement strategies.

The intended audience for this book is broad and diverse. Marketing professionals, data analysts, and business leaders seeking practical insights into leveraging marketing intelligence for enhanced customer engagement will find valuable guidance within these pages. Likewise, academics and researchers in marketing and related fields will discover a wealth of contributions to inform their scholarly pursuits. Consultants, technology developers, and policymakers keen on staying abreast of industry trends and regulatory considerations will also benefit from the insights offered herein.

Furthermore, we extend our invitation to students studying marketing and business, as well as any curious individuals interested in understanding the evolving landscape of customer engagement and marketing intelligence, irrespective of their professional background.

In assembling this volume, our aim is not only to inform but also to inspire. We hope that the insights shared within these pages will catalyze transformative strategies, spark innovative approaches, and ultimately contribute to the ongoing evolution of customer engagement in the realm of marketing intelligence.

ORGANIZATION OF THE BOOK

Within the pages of this edited reference book, readers will embark on a journey through diverse chapters that collectively illuminate the evolving landscape of customer engagement through the lens of marketing intelligence. Each chapter offers unique insights, expert analyses, and practical perspectives, contributing to a comprehensive understanding of this dynamic field.

Chapter 1, titled "E-Commerce Revolution: Navigating Industry 4.0 for Competitive Advantage," authored by Zhang Jieyao and Jeetesh Kumar, navigates the complex terrain of the contemporary business environment. It explores the transformative impact of Industry 4.0 dynamics, particularly through the lens of e-commerce. Readers will delve into the essential strategies for leveraging advanced technology, data analysis, and customer relationship management to gain a competitive edge while navigating the challenges inherent in the burgeoning e-commerce landscape.

In Chapter 2, "Micro-Moments in Social Commerce: Impact, Triggers, and Digital Transformation," Abhay Grover and Nilesh Arora unravel the intricate interplay between social commerce, digital transformation, and consumer behavior. The chapter examines the profound implications of micro-moments and digital transformation on retail experiences, emphasizing the importance of empathy, innovation, and data-driven insights in surpassing customer expectations.

The third chapter, "Data-Driven Insights: The Power of Genetic Information in Precision Marketing," authored by Nitesh Behare, Rashmi Mahajan, Ashish Mohture, Shrikant Waghulkar, Shubhada Behare, Vinayak Shitole, and Anandrao Dadas, delves into the realm of precision marketing enhanced by genetic insights. From personalized product recommendations to targeted advertising, this chapter explores the vast opportunities and ethical considerations surrounding the utilization of genetic data in marketing, offering guidance on responsible data management and compliance.

Chapter 4, "Application of Blockchain and Internet of Things (IoT) in Modern Business," by Muhammad Usman Tariq, examines the synergistic convergence of Blockchain and IoT technologies. Readers will gain insights into the transformative potential of this integration across diverse sectors, from supply chain management to healthcare, highlighting enhanced security, transparency, and efficiency.

"Demystifying Artificial Intelligence and Customer Engagement: A Bibliometric Review Using TCCM Framework," penned by Arabinda Bhandari and Mudita Sinha, Chapter 6, provides a critical literature review of AI's impact on customer engagement. Through an exploration of theoretical frameworks, challenges, and future research directions, this chapter offers valuable insights for both scholars and practitioners seeking to harness the potential of AI in customer engagement strategies.

Continuing the exploration of digital innovation, Chapter 7, "AI Chatbots as a Catalyst for Customer Loyalty Investigating Digital Experience Preferences Across Age Groups," by Yamijala Murthy and Ravi Chandra BS, investigates the role of AI chatbots in fostering customer loyalty across generational divides. By analyzing digital experience preferences, this chapter sheds light on the complex relationship between AI chatbots and customer loyalty, offering practical implications for organizations aiming to optimize their digital engagement strategies.

In Chapter 8, "Service Industry Alchemy: A Symphony of Digital Innovations in Customer Engagement," by Shikha Bhagat, Rashmi Rai, K. Lakshmypriya, and Sunita Kumar, readers embark on a thematic, sentiment, and bibliometric analysis of digital innovations in the service industry. Through an examination of past research and future trends, this chapter offers valuable insights into harnessing digital innovations to enhance customer engagement across various service sectors.

The immersive capabilities of augmented reality in transforming online retail experiences take center stage in Chapter 9, "ARise to the Occasion: Elevating Customer Engagement," by Anagha Nair and Dinesh Kumar R. Readers will explore how augmented reality personalizes the customer journey, drives purchase decisions, and creates deeper connections between brands and consumers.

Chapter 10, "Webrooming: Bridging the Digital Divide in Customer Engagement," by Sahil Kohli, Rishi Shukla, and Piyush Samant, delves into the evolving phenomenon of webrooming in the retail landscape. Through an examination of technological advancements and consumer behaviors, this chapter offers insights into effectively harnessing webrooming to enhance customer engagement and drive sales in the modern retail landscape.

Chapter 11, "Shifting Consumer Behaviors Towards Sustainability Through Eco-Packaging," highlights the critical role that marketing plays in promoting sustainable consumption through eco-packaging. It does this by reviewing academic research in the fields of behavioral science and marketing that looks at the best practices for changing consumer behavior towards sustainability through eco-packaging. During the review process, the writers create a thorough framework for imagining and promoting long-term changes in customer behavior.

In Chapter 12, "A Study Exploring the Effect of Subliminally Priming Known Human Faces vs. Unknown Human Faces on Consumers' Product Selection Decisions: Unseen Motivators," by Rabia Abhay and Sibin Mathew Nesin, readers are immersed in an exploration of the unconscious influence of human faces on consumer product selection. Through experimental research, this chapter sheds light on the subtle yet profound impact of subliminal priming on consumer decision-making processes.

Lastly, Chapter 13, "Relational Marketing Applied to the Banking Sector in Portuguese Context," by Cátia Rodrigues, Bruno Sousa, Alexandrino Ribeiro, and Manuel Fonseca, offers a qualitative exploration of the evolving paradigm of relationship marketing in the banking sector. Through semi-structured interviews, this chapter unveils the shifting dynamics of customer relationships, loyalty, and trust in response to technological evolution and changing marketing strategies.

Collectively, these chapters offer a rich tapestry of insights, analyses, and practical implications for marketing professionals, researchers, students, and anyone curious about the evolving landscape of customer engagement driven by marketing intelligence. We invite readers to embark on this enlightening journey and explore the myriad dimensions of the future of customer engagement through marketing intelligence.

IN CONCLUSION

As editors of this edited reference book, we stand at the culmination of a journey through the intricate landscape of customer engagement driven by marketing intelligence. Across the diverse array of chapters presented within these pages, we have traversed the realms of e-commerce revolution, social commerce micro-moments, precision marketing with genetic insights, blockchain and IoT applications, AI-driven customer engagement, augmented reality in online retail, and beyond.

Through the collective wisdom of esteemed authors and researchers, we have delved into the transformative power of data-driven insights, digital innovations, and emerging technologies in shaping the future of customer engagement. Each chapter has offered unique perspectives, expert analyses, and practical implications, contributing to a comprehensive understanding of this dynamic field.

As we reflect on the insights gleaned from these chapters, several key themes emerge. The imperative for businesses to leverage advanced technology, data analytics, and customer-centric approaches to gain a competitive edge in today's dynamic marketplace is unmistakable. Moreover, the ethical considerations inherent in the responsible use of data and emerging technologies underscore the importance of maintaining trust and transparency in customer relationships.

Furthermore, the evolution of customer engagement extends beyond traditional boundaries, encompassing seamless omnichannel experiences, personalized interactions, and empathetic engagement across diverse demographics. As we navigate this evolving landscape, it becomes increasingly evident that successful customer engagement strategies must embrace innovation, adaptability, and a deep understanding of evolving consumer behaviors and preferences.

In closing, we extend our gratitude to the authors whose contributions have enriched this volume with valuable insights and perspectives. We also express our appreciation to the readers who embark on this journey with us, seeking to deepen their understanding of the future of customer engagement through marketing intelligence. May the knowledge shared within these pages inspire innovation, foster collaboration, and pave the way for sustainable and responsible practices in the realm of customer engagement.

Mudita Sinha
Christ University, India

Arabinda Bhandari
Presidency University, India

Samant Shant Priya
Lal Bahadur Shastri Institute of Management, India

Sajal Kabiraj
Häme University of Applied Sciences, Finland

Chapter 1
E–Commerce Revolution:
Navigating Industry 4.0 for Competitive Advantage

Zhang Jieyao
https://orcid.org/0009-0004-3562-0389
School of Management and Economics, Chuxiong Normal University, China

Jeetesh Kumar
https://orcid.org/0000-0001-9878-1228
School of Hospitality, Tourism, and Events, Taylor's University, Malaysia

ABSTRACT

The dynamic environment of the business world is full of uncertainty, complexity, and ambiguity. It is necessary to quickly understand market trends and customer needs, accurately position the market, and ensure an absolute advantage in the fierce market competition. The dynamic changes of Industry 4.0 have become an important alternative. Meanwhile, e-commerce is the leading representative of the Industry 4.0 transformation, using computing devices and communication platforms to conduct business online. Managers need to accurately understand the current high demand and dynamic market based on advanced technology, data analysis, and interconnected systems, with a primary customer orientation and do an excellent excellent job in customer relationship management to create a competitive advantage for organisations that can leverage the information at their disposal. However, the booming e-commerce also hides challenges. Organisations are responsible for keeping information secure, preventing unlawful use, maintaining customer trust, and using information competitively and strategically.

INTRODUCTION

The world economy is transforming physicalisation to information digitisation (den Hond & Moser, 2023). All business organisations are being turned into information-based operations by adopting web technologies. The speed of technological transformation is increasing exponentially, and modern e-commerce is causing significant changes in the economic environment, affecting all areas of industry.

DOI: 10.4018/979-8-3693-2367-0.ch001

E-commerce refers to electronic commerce or business conducted using electronic technology. According to Rahman (2014), e-commerce is seeing a daily increase in the use of technology. Networks expand the scope of corporate organisation and operations. The internet's platform independence and widespread reach enable businesses to create new buyer-seller communities, expand their revenue streams, and improve their bottom line. The earliest stages of e-commerce occurred in the 1970s when it was limited to activities conducted by large corporations that set up private communication networks and used electronic fund transfer systems to conduct financial transactions and document exchanges electronically (Galinari et al., 2015). Since the 1990s, e-commerce has grown, and the development of this industry is closely related to the progress of information technology. The earliest forms of e-commerce involved the straightforward distribution of goods and services through digital channels. This progressed from order issuance and product delivery to facilitating online transactions between vendors and buyers. With specific e-commerce solutions, consumers may purchase and pay their bills without leaving their house's comforts. This can be done on the weekends and holidays as well, round the clock. The primary drivers of customers' growing use of electronic commerce are their need for convenience and even privacy. Chinese business and commerce have been impacted by the Internet, which arrived in the nation in 1994 and has grown over the last 20 years.

Traditional industry markets now operate differently, owing to fundamental changes from the Internet. The E-commerce industry in China has shown tremendous growth velocity in the last few years. Enterprises have benefited from the increased entrepreneurship resulting from the use of E-commerce technologies. Simultaneously, China's international e-commerce is expanding under the open strategy of "Going global strategy and bringing in," which has emerged as a new catalyst for economic growth. E-commerce in Brazil reportedly started about eight years ago, and it is now home to a growing number of new businesses and a clientele that is expanding daily. The main factor pushing more people to adopt this new mode of commerce was the ease with which they could now access the Internet. E-commerce is spreading throughout developing nations and is thought to contribute to achieving the global development agenda. Together with many others, the BRICS countries—Brazil, Russia, India, China, and South Africa—view e-commerce as a tool for promoting inclusive, fast, and sustainable economic growth that will raise living standards and reduce poverty (Karine, 2021).

According to Albertin (2012), there are four stages in the evolution of EC. During Phase One, companies disclosed information about their products and services using the Internet's features. That was the original impetus behind the invention of EC. Phase Two still took orders and provided information and guidance on using their goods and services. At this stage, logistics started to affect businesses. The distribution of goods and services through information technology (IT) constituted phase three of the progression. This stage began the digital commercialisation of various products, such as software and music. Phase Two involved taking orders, providing information, and giving directions on how to use their goods and services. During this stage, logistics had its initial effect on businesses. The use of information technology (IT) for the distribution of goods and services was the third phase of the progress. During this stage, certain things, such as software and music, started to be sold online. The last stage involves combining electronic commerce with exchanging information between the vendor and the customer; data transmission and product delivery are no longer the sole options. Given the possibilities of EC, such engagement allowed the average Internet user to become a prospective consumer with the advancement of IT and the widespread usage of the Internet. The desire to innovate, grow more competitive, and meet rising customer expectations—all of globalisation's effects— led to more contemporary business management techniques. In 2012, 3G and 4G technologies emerged in Brazil, enabling mobile devices like smartphones and tablet PCs to access high-speed Internet. With such technologies, consumers may more easily compare prices across different places. Some customers utilise that resource even in actual stores to interact with the merchandise and select the sales channel that best suits their needs.

In the recent COVID-19 pandemic, technology-enabled e-commerce sustainability witnessed tremendous growth (Stalmachova et al., 2021). Companies immediately adopt technology to reach customers and gain market share (Kramer, 2022). In practically every industry, there is constant competition between businesses (Wall, 2022). All products, including books, medications, and hotel and ticket bookings, are now accessible online. Customers also seek comfort and satisfaction through trustworthy purchases (Khan et al., 2019). The e-commerce platform offers goods and services based on what the consumer requires. With just a few clicks, a customer may easily navigate the market in an e-commerce setting, comparing prices, delivery times, and product quality with those of other service providers. As a result, the customers benefit from a win-win situation. E-commerce is one of the most critical activities that influence consumer purchase decisions. E-commerce is essential to the phases and procedures of purchase (Li & Liu, 2021). Because of this, e-commerce has become a problem that demands attention since it makes people's decisions and purchases more significant every day. E-commerce brings things to the business community and consumers that were previously impossible. However, it appeared with others; it brought some difficulties, including the cyber security issue.

Hence, this chapter aims to explore the transformative impact of Industry 4.0, explicitly focusing on the pivotal role of e-commerce in dynamic business environments. It investigates how e-commerce leverages advanced technology, data analysis, and interconnected systems to meet customer preferences, understand market trends, and establish a competitive edge. Further, this chapter demonstrates how business organisations can harness this technological revolution to navigate uncertainty and cyber crises, adapt to changing market dynamics, and effectively cater to the evolving needs of their customers—adapting and implementing e-commerce strategies in the context of Industry 4.0, providing a more comprehensive global perspective. Discuss the challenges and strategies of cross-cultural e-commerce and how specific emerging technologies are used in e-commerce. Discuss sustainability challenges in e-commerce and make appropriate ethical considerations around consumer data privacy.

Cross-Cultural and Global E-Commerce

E-commerce offers a fresh approach to conducting business. It builds a complicated yet effective system with the potential to save money and time. However, for multinational enterprises, the main issue is how to develop comprehensive strategies and new processes to successfully develop e-commerce strategies, which depends on their understanding of customers in a global environment and the secure transmission of customer information. The enterprises must modify their business practices to focus on locating sources of CRM, including segmentation, needs and capabilities, benefits, values, purchasing patterns, and trust factors. Businesses must set themselves apart from the competition to facilitate and encourage the shift to an online system. Electrolux Professional Laundry Group, a multinational company, interviewed customers and sales offices across Europe to determine their understanding and perception of closing warehouses to focus on in-house e-commerce. Electrolux's results strategy demonstrates the need to clarify the system's role, customer data security, and the relationship between these issues and the duties of the relevant sales offices.

Furthermore, thorough research on clients is necessary to ensure that the new system aligns with their capabilities and purchasing preferences. After they are developed, a precise model is produced to ascertain how they impact building an effective e-commerce strategy. The necessity to have a thorough e-commerce strategy is essential because of the growing e-commerce rivalry in Electrolux's business. Although they have some of the best reviews in the business for their goods and services, their e-commerce platform has to be enhanced to live up to the expectations of their well-known brand. As a result, thorough consideration of each step of the strategy process will be necessary to develop their e-commerce operations.

Cross-border e-commerce (CBEC) has increased due to economic globalisation, which has expanded trade across nations worldwide. Unlike traditional e-commerce, CBEC connects buyers and merchants from various nations or areas. To fully utilise the global market, create an open and multifaceted model of multilateral economic and trade cooperation, and share experiences with one another, CBEC platforms should strive for these goals (Cheng et al., 2019). Given the continent's distinctive economic and cultural background, it makes sense that African customers may behave differently from consumers in other regions regarding CBEC platforms. How consumers travel, shop, and eat can all be significantly impacted by differing levels of acculturation (Ibarra-Cantu & Cheetham, 2021). Acculturation can affect how customers feel about accepting e-commerce when they shop online. Regarding cross-border consumer electronics commerce (CBEC), customers are regularly exposed to cultures from various geographical locations as they make cross-border purchases. Higher levels of acculturation confer greater familiarity with product details and market dynamics on consumers, enabling them to assess products independently.

Technology, Innovations and E-Commerce

Testa, Luciano, and Freitas (2004) state that because the Internet is constantly being enhanced, new applications frequently surface that aim to use better the services provided by electronic commerce. E-procurement is the automation of goods and service purchases. In addition to promoting purchasing dynamism, it significantly reduces costs and shortens decision-making times. E-learning is another crucial tool that reduces distances between teachers and students and allows them to access training sessions and courses from anywhere. Notable instances could include online universities and language schools. E-banking is a valuable and effective instrument that benefits financial institutions and their customers. It lets customers perform things from the comfort of their homes that they previously had to do by visiting a bank location. In addition to making things more practical for customers, banks save a significant amount of money. E-gambling is how individuals in any country—including those that forbid traditional casinos—can access Internet casinos and place bets with real money. Online auctions, or "e-auctioning," lower transportation expenses and improve accessibility and speed over traditional auctions. Despite their lesser expression, many other instruments are just as crucial to the growth of electronic commerce. As an illustration, consider e-trade, the online buying and selling of stock shares, and e-drugs, virtual pharmacies that complement physical pharmacies (Whig et al., 2024). For goods and services distributed through the Internet, such as software, music, news, banking services, online ticketing and reservation, and consulting services, among others, delivery costs can be minimised, and goods can be made instantly available (Li et al., 2023).

Over the past few years, augmented reality (AR) has become increasingly popular as an emerging technology. AR is a core technology in shifting from desktop-based interaction to ubiquitous computing, enabling "anytime, anywhere" innovative services (Rane et al., 2023). When mixed with other technologies like wearables, gesture recognition, and the Internet of Things (IoT), augmented reality (AR) has the potential to enhance product innovation, boost operational effectiveness, and shed light on customer behaviour (Nair & Tyagi, 2023). One such sector where AR has enormous promise is e-commerce. Prominent online shops such as Tobi, J. C. Penney, Barbie, Zawara, and others have recently included and evaluated virtual changing room software into their web applications to provide online buyers with an in-store experience. In the comfort of their homes, consumers may browse the selection, virtually try on clothing and accessories, and make purchases thanks to the virtual dressing room. The largest furniture retailer in the world, IKEA, has also included mobile augmented reality in its smartphone app. In addition to making online shopping more accessible, it enables users to determine how well furniture or bed lamps will fit into their home design.

Mobile Commerce

Mobile commerce (m-commerce) is a subset of e-commerce that refers to any monetary transaction carried out over a mobile network (Ngai & Gunasekaran, 2007). Indeed, they can execute various e-commerce activities using mobile handheld devices such as Personal Digital Assistants (PDAs) and smartphones. M-commerce is a technology frontier that is an appealing field for research due to its novelty, quick expansion, and possible applications. M-commerce applications have two main characteristics: mobility and broad reach. Mobility means portability; for example, mobile devices allow consumers to do business in real-time. M-commerce allows customers to be contacted at any time using a mobile device. M-commerce is best suited for accommodating consumers' impulse buying, as early experience with B2C m-commerce has taught us. It also prioritises the relevance of an offer to the user's current position (e.g., location, time, and mission) over price. M-commerce can be implemented using a variety of standards and methods, such as wireless application protocol (WAP), short message service (SMS), multimedia message service (MMS), enhanced message service (EMS), and satellite-based global positioning system (GPS).

Social Media and E-Commerce

A recent advancement in e-commerce, known as "social commerce", is the result of using social media to enable online client interaction. New social platforms have emerged due to recent ICT breakthroughs, the rise of Web 2.0 technologies, the popularity of social media and social networking sites, and other factors. The usage of social commerce is made more accessible by these platforms. These developments create a postmodern consumer in which people interact, exchange experiences, participate in forums, evaluate and rate other items, and suggest goods and services. One benefit of the social commerce era is that customers can influence one another through social interaction. For customers, trust in e-commerce can be a challenge. Since social commerce involves customer interactions that boost trust, trust can now be supported by social commerce.

The Changing Business Dynamics: The Transformative Impact of Industry 4.0

The dynamic environment of the business world is full of uncertainty, complexity, and ambiguity. It is necessary to quickly understand market trends and customer needs, accurately position the market, meet customer preferences, and ensure an absolute advantage in the fierce market competition. The dynamic changes of Industry 4.0 have become an important alternative. The term Industry 4.0 originates from the concept of the fourth industrial revolution. Rapid advances in sensor technology, interconnectivity and data analytics have given rise to integrating all these technologies into various industry domains. Schlechtendahl et al. (2015) emphasise the speed element of information availability, an industrial environment where all entities are always connected and can communicate information. Kagermann et al. (2013) proposed a more technical understanding that Industry 4.0 is the integration of cyber-physical systems (CPS) and the Internet of Things and Services (IoT and IoS) into industrial processes, such as manufacturing and logistics, among other processes.

Exploration of E-Commerce Development in the Context of Industry 4.0

Technological advancements have contributed significantly to our daily lives. Applications of technology to business processes are among its significant accomplishments (Wang et al., 2022). It has elevated conventional commercial practices to new heights. The quality, cost, and business methods of goods and services are all impacted by new technology (Thomson et al., 2022). The world is transitioning away from in-store buying and towards online shopping. As a result of this transformation, technical advances are being made to improve online business processes (Hooks et al., 2022). Customers may purchase products more quickly, thanks to e-commerce, which has also shown to be one of the most influential forces for corporate transformation (Thomson et al., 2022).

Business activities involving the application of electronic technology are known as e-commerce. E-commerce activities are completed online through the internet using websites. The three main e-commerce segments are e-marketplaces, online retail, and online auctions. Customers can purchase products or services remotely using the application or technology that offers the product (Khurana, 2019). Choosing a particular product, money transfers, and data exchanges are essential e-commerce activities (Ahmadian, 2021). Other activities include internet-based marketing, online management, and automated data collection systems. E-commerce benefits companies by expanding their market reach and scale, lowering operating expenses, and removing obstacles (Lorette, 2013). In e-commerce, customers purchase directly from online stores using websites and mobile apps. Live chat, chatbots, and voice assistants can all be used to communicate. Purchasing products and services through e-commerce allows customers to choose when and where to purchase and research merchandise, suppliers, and other options. The capacity to obtain information online has completely changed the purchasing process. E-commerce has already impacted all aspects of the industry, from providing services to customers to the design of new products (Kalia et al., 2017). E-commerce provides fresh ways for businesses to interact and interact with customers, like online commercialisation and advertising, online order fulfilment, and online customer service.

The most significant contributor to e-commerce is information technology, the field of buying and selling in cyberspace formed due to the millions of computers connected to the internet. In the e-commerce process, the first step is to provide consumers with information services that determine their choices. Through e-commerce, a company's reach becomes wider as interested parties can sell its products and services worldwide without geographic restrictions (Hussien et al., 2022). Similarly, companies can directly deal with their customers, understand customer needs first, and create a time difference to cater to the market faster. Economic e-commerce is the trigger for the formation of the digital economy. In this economic concept, all resources that can be digitised are unlimited, and information and knowledge are also decisive resources for economic participants to carry out their activities successfully. We can take the initiative in the fierce market competition only with more data resources and the ability to integrate resources. Electronic linkage is an essential electronic relationship mechanism between e-commerce

(Metalidou et al., 2014). Both departments can work together efficiently through electronic data exchange. It is an essential driving force for business organisations, effectively establishing direct contact with customers and efficiently expanding their influence on customers. This technological revolution is disruptive because e-commerce transforms traditional business models into new business methods. This development is primarily due to the quick evolution of information and communication technologies. Businesses must consider strategic actions to ensure that the new business processes they are implementing are sustainable as they move from traditional to digital forms of operation.

Challenges and Opportunities in the Changing Dynamics of Customer Relationships

Connectivity and access to information are causing the balance of power to shift from suppliers to consumers. In the context of changes in customer relationships in Industry 4.0, business leaders are leveraging the internet to boost customer value and create closer bonds with partners and customers. Business homeostasis and technical constraints hampered corporate relationships, procedures, and business model changes. The technological revolution changed all that. The internet's capacity to connect everyone led to the development of new business procedures that disintermediated old partners while including new ones. The disruptive nature of business models can significantly inspire established companies to try innovation and develop novel collaborative ideas. The foundation of the present information revolution is premised on the fact that business success requires a comprehensive understanding and management of the business. However, it was challenging to efficiently manage organisations where finance and personnel data was dispersed across numerous business units or disparate, disconnected platforms.

Determining the timing of entering new markets or adopting technologies such as the Internet is a critical strategic decision for businesses. Business organisations with early mover advantage (EMA) who enter a new market first may gain certain advantages over later entrants, thereby gaining a significant competitive advantage that can be expressed as a large market share or returns. E-commerce platforms are online marketplaces that offer technology solutions to a large number of small vendors, for example, Taobao and Amazon. These electronic platforms enjoy EMA, immune to network effects and entry barriers posed by advanced IT infrastructure. To win a stable customer base, network operators must have customer relationship management (CRM) capabilities, which is the ability to build and integrate the required resources, activities and processes for the company to manage customer relationships while creating company and customer value. Coltman, Devinney, and Midgley (2011) indicate that CRM functionality has proven profitable for businesses. CRM operations directly improve the quality of customer relationships; as a result, they raise the non-contractual switching costs for customers and contribute to a rise in the customer lifetime value for businesses. CRM objectives are divided into three primary dimensions: customer attraction, conversion, and retention. Internet technology creates new marketing strategies and tools to assist businesses in bringing in, converting, and keeping clients. The first requirement is that commercial organisations have customer attraction, which refers to the capacity of e-retailers to attract online traffic to e-commerce platform-powered web storefronts.

E-retailers can use various online marketing tools to attract and acquire new customers and adequate customer resources, including online advertising, social marketing, email marketing, search engine marketing, and affiliate marketing platforms. While attracting customer groups, they also need to convert potential purchasing customers. E-tailers need to be able to convert potential visitors into buyers to increase their market share. E-retailers can take advantage of sticky features, such as online consumer preference systems and customer feedback information, which have the potential to raise the frequency, duration, and average purchases per visit; these features can also raise the possibility of turning visitors into buyers (Ludwig et al., 2013). E-tailers can retain customers by building close relationships with them and securing goods and services while ensuring customer loyalty. Product or service customisation, caring blessings, contact interactivity, website ease of use, variety of product categories, and creativity in user interface design are methods used to enhance online client loyalty and keep existing customers. These strategies require companies to learn new network operations skills and transform their customer relationship management capabilities on the Internet to enhance customer satisfaction. The Industry 4.0 revolution has brought about the development of IT and the Internet. With the explosive growth of customer data, enterprises have been able to conduct data analysis based on large-capacity data and realise customer resource management. The ability to discover, attract and retain customers are two specific manifestations of the company's customer management capabilities: tracking, analysing and managing compelling customer and clickstream data (Ludwig et al., 2013). Customer conversion is a fine-grained metric that connects acquisition and retention in customer management. This is an important capability that can turn potential customers into loyal customers. Therefore, the ability to attract, convert, and retain customers has been included in the customer management goals of enterprises. The effective customer management capabilities thus formed are essential for companies with e-commerce channels.

With the popularity of live streaming, many customers are attracted to online retail because e-stores usually provide them with corresponding services and products based on their preferences. Convenience, flexible pricing, discounts, round-the-clock availability, and free door-to-door delivery are the advantages of e-commerce. One of the main benefits of Internet commerce for customers is convenience, which also increases client loyalty. Consumers can consume via the Internet regardless of time and location. An e-commerce platform that offers a smooth functioning system and multiple payment options is essential for any customer and offers more features that can be accessed online. An increasing number of online retailers are experiencing growing customer demand for products and services (Singh & Rana, 2018), making customer-centricity a catalyst for competitive advantage for e-commerce platforms. Because of the increasing rivalry in online retail, e-tailers have shifted their attention from enticing consumers to motivating them for recurring purchases. However, compared to typical offline environments, e-retail has substantially greater client acquisition costs (Purani et al., 2019). Therefore, the most critical aspect determining the profitability and competitive advantage of an online business in the market is the e-loyalty of customers. The success of e-commerce depends on the quality of its system and how much consumer incentive value is gained through shopping. The amount of user satisfaction with a system's technical and functional components is determined by criteria such as usability, availability, response time, reliability, and adaptability. The customer retention model suggests that for customers to be loyal to an online retail brand, satisfaction is necessary, and customer satisfaction occurs when an e-retailer has an e-quality system supported by an appropriate set of values. Suppose e-commerce platforms want to improve customer satisfaction. In that case, they need to meet customers' practical value and psychological expectations, including utilitarian value (function-oriented) or hedonic value (fantasy and multi-sensory based on emotions) (Hepola, Leppäniemi, & Karjaluoto, 2020). Customer satisfaction is considered a key driver of purchases, repeat purchase intentions, and customer loyalty, making it one of the most essential variables in ensuring the success of an online company. Chen and Cheng (2009) indicated that a consumer's desire to repurchase can be influenced by perceived usefulness, customer satisfaction, and past online buying experience.

Problem and Challenges of E-Commerce in Complex Market Environments

The market for electronic commerce is not growing in tandem with commercial and public enterprises. Developing the e-commerce industry requires the help of private and public cooperation. Working together gives consumers the credibility they need to thrive in e-commerce. Regarding the expansion of e-commerce, financial institutions and intermediaries are hesitant to assist the developed world's e-commerce business actively. However, retail e-commerce needs the support of banks to expand the scope and visibility of e-commerce operations and reduce theft and potential losses due to credit card fraud. However, financial service providers face threats outside their payment card strategy in places with no standard credit card offerings or substitute methods for making secure and quick online transactions. In online e-commerce, there is a cultural phenomenon of purchasing goods by bargaining with suppliers, which is a challenge to formulating e-commerce standards. One of the biggest challenges facing e-commerce is price wars, which are lower prices for goods and services on the internet. When low-price competition occurs on the internet, it will disrupt the inherent business order and standards and may cause chaos in some markets. Regulators are working to regulate the market. However, due to the massive network delivery and service volume, the Internet has not maintained commodity price and market competition norms. The most critical factor in e-commerce is the test of trust in electronic settlement (Liu et al., 2022). Standard documents on basic laws and rules might include the veracity and correctness of online transactions. Trust in developed countries is based on modern legislation and the fairness of electronic transactions. Although the legislative and judicial systems do not cover a system where e-commerce transactions are not established, there are real and perceived disadvantages (Team, 2022).

The present era's hyper-connectedness of technology and the reliance of industry and commerce on these hyper-connected systems are two significant causes of cybersecurity problems (Abdel et al., 2022). It refers to the interconnectivity of an organisation's massive record-keeping information system with the external world in e-business or e-commerce. Because of its connectivity, it can be used by cybercriminals. Cybercriminals and cyber-attacks always target e-commerce corporate organisations and customers (D'Adamo et al., 2021). Attackers typically target customers' personal information, the most critical asset in e-commerce. Cybercriminals discover vulnerabilities in existing e-commerce systems and exploit them (Jang-Jaccard & Nepal, 2014). They might launch an attack to steal an organisation's sales records and client information. These records are crucial to the e-commerce company and are the foundation of strategic planning (Hepfer & Powell, 2020). Business organisations embrace and invest in cutting-edge information technologies to gain a competitive edge and seize a sizable portion of the market. However, this frequently results in increased human error when utilising the technology.

Regarding risk and security management, clients and staff constitute the weakest link (Alavi et al., 2016). Apart from implementing cutting-edge technologies to mitigate potential dangers, it is imperative to reduce human behavioural risk through appropriate training and developing their comprehension of interacting with the organisation's information systems (Metalidou et al., 2014). Both consumers and online retailers must be aware of the dangers posed by client data breaches and the accompanying expenses (Martin & Murphy, 2017). Organisations are responsible for keeping information secure, preventing unlawful use, maintaining customer trust, and using information competitively and strategically.

Regulatory and Compliance Issues

The Chinese government highly values the growth of e-commerce and sees it as a crucial tool for the country's economic opening up and change. The government, ministries, and regions have implemented rules and regulations in response to the quickly evolving trade environment, and a system of retail e-commerce regulation has been progressively formed. The government is actively encouraging the development of e-commerce platforms. It is streamlining capital registration processes, lowering obstacles to entry, and resolving preapproval concerns in the e-commerce sector. The authorities are supporting the building of transregional and cross-industry logistical platforms, establishing logistical terminals and intelligent logistical platforms, and encouraging community management systems, village information service stations and retail establishments to offer express delivery services.

The government mandates that e-commerce businesses adhere to technical requirements and information security protection laws. Establishing a mechanism for managing the security of online transactions is essential to clarify each party's obligations. The government has encouraged digital certificate application and cross-recognition across electronic certifying authorities in an effort to lower risk. Electronic contracts were designed using a standardised administration structure to enhance data security further. A risk monitoring body may perform online spot inspections, and a supervising regulatory body could oversee various government sectors and locations. The government also intends to take decisive action against network theft, other illicit online trading operations, and the production of phoney and subpar goods. Given the quickly evolving business climate, the government is modifying current regulations in response to public input. The necessities of e-commerce have led to revisions to the government's legislation, including the Consumer's Interest Protection and Advertising Law. Concurrently, the government has elucidated the lawful entitlements of electronic invoices, electronic contracts, electronic inspection reports, and further electronic transaction documentation.

Consumer Privacy and Data Security

Before e-commerce can be fully established, several hurdles must be met by all parties involved. It remains challenging to predict the future development of these emerging sectors. Specific recently formed markets are already evolving, especially the Internet provider market, where smaller players are finding it harder and harder to compete with more prominent players who can provide their customers with a more excellent choice of services (cable or modem connections, ADSL [Asymmetric Digital Subscriber Line] technology, satellite links, etc.) (Zhou et al., 2024). The Internet still needs help in balancing privacy concerns with high-quality services. Delivery is another difficulty for commerce since EC clients need more confidence that things will be delivered of the desired quality and that refunds will only be impeded if the quality is met. For example, the website must adhere to the program's guiding principles and the TRUSTe's oversight and resolution processes to be TRUST compliant. According to the program's guiding principles, a website must have a privacy policy that explains precisely what personally identifiable information is gathered. According to the principles, users must agree to use and share the data. Sufficient security measures must also be in place on the website to protect user data. To determine whether websites are adhering to their declared standards, one of the oversight techniques involves "seeding" user information. Resolving complaints is done through a procedure that may go from TRUST e-mediation to in-person compliance audits by official auditors like PricewaterhouseCoopers and finally to referral to the relevant government body (Moores, 2005).

Due to the widespread use of the Internet, regulation is another crucial issue that has to be addressed. It needs to be more effective and explicit to ensure that business transactions occur at a price consistent with more conventional forms of trade. With the expansion of e-commerce in Brazil, there are pertinent logistical issues for the practice of e-commerce. Logistics managers must adopt varied operational procedures to satisfy their customers' evolving needs. Customers who shop online are typically pickier than those who shop in person. The operationalisation dynamics of online businesses have had to alter significantly due to these additional demands, and new solutions for customer satisfaction have also been introduced. The features of the online shopping experience positively impact the emotional and cognitive states of the customer. Customers become more absorbed in and focused on their shopping experience when the virtual environment is more appealing.

E-Commerce Post Pandemic

COVID-19 had a significant psychological and behavioural impact on consumers, as seen in shifts in purchasing patterns and social behaviours. Retail establishments have suffered due to online retailers' successful increase in sales. The COVID-19 epidemic and its aftermath on healthcare, society, and the economy are causing a shift in consumers' purchasing behaviours. The development in the widespread use of e-commerce demonstrates an enormous predisposition towards online purchasing among consumers, especially amongst people who would not ordinarily use these kinds of shopping. Just 38.7% of Portuguese adults between 16 and 74 made online purchases in 2019. This is significantly less than the 63% European average, or nearly 60% in the case of Spain.

In contrast to 2019, the pandemic's effects resulted in a 40%–60% surge in e-commerce, particularly for food-related goods. Online retail sales in Europe increased by an average of 31% in 2020, the year of the pandemic, excluding food. With a growth of 38%, Spain had the second-highest increase of any nation (Higueras-Castillo et al., 2023). Due to the growing consumer confidence in online shopping, physical distributors are forced to include online features in their products to make them more appealing as they become more and more integrated into offline environments.

Sustainability in E-Commerce

According to studies comparing the environmental effects of traditional in-store purchasing with e-commerce, brick-and-mortar retailing or shopping at physical stores can reduce CO_2 emissions by as much as 70% (Van Loon et al., 2015). E-commerce is a good option for long-distance, non-urban distribution since it eliminates the need for private transportation to get to cities, where malls are typically found (Bibri et al., 2024). The "last mile," where various elements, including package design, material and size, and consumer behaviour, are all substantial contributors to carbon emissions, is where most delivery issues in metropolitan areas occur (Manerba et al., 2018). Indeed, many customers were prepared to shell out an extra 10% above the standard cost for a sustainable container. However, consumers who made purchases online needed to be made aware of the importance of sustainability and instead prioritised other, more alluring factors like cost, quantity, and delivery time (Monnot et al., 2019). One way to achieve sustainability in e-commerce is to prioritise packaging made of paper and paperboard materials. Mirjam de Bruijn has created the unique package known as "Twenty" in this vein. By reducing the water content of beauty, personal care, and home care products by 80%, this product makes it possible to use smaller cardboard packaging. Twenty uses less packing material and eliminates the need for plastic bottles, which lowers shipping costs to the point where it might influence consumer behaviour (Solanki, 2018).

Trend of E-Commerce

Essential aspects of e-commerce that require improvement are technological know-how, practical logistics, and maintaining a positive relationship with the consumer throughout the entire sales cycle in a virtual setting. Along with overcoming the obstacles of offering increased security for payments and purchases, an easy-to-navigate layout with a higher degree of entertainment and interaction, and other improvements that could improve the shopping experience, it is recognised that e-commerce is likely to continue developing and evolving due to the introduction of new technologies like virtual 3D experimentation. Access to all product dimensions in a 3D model can benefit customers by increasing their product knowledge, increasing the likelihood that they will find a more assertive product or alternative, saving time, and ultimately increasing their satisfaction and dependability when shopping online (Ferreira et al., 2015). E-commerce encompasses integrating various technologies, including virtual intelligence, language translation, globalisation, adaptive interfaces that consider the unique characteristics of user groups, and mobile commerce to enhance the online shopping experience for customers and improve the purchasing environment (Nienow et al., 2017).

Electronic channels are among the newest types of interactive marketing. The client initiates and increasingly controls the process in this new type of client-company interaction. Considering how simple it is to compare costs online, customers are the ones who determine what information they require, what offers they are interested in, and what prices they are ready to pay. To attract new customers to their online stores, businesses must analyse their websites' context (design) and content. After all, users judge a virtual company's performance based on how user-friendly and visually appealing their website is. Considering intense competition and rising customer expectations, electronic commerce businesses are becoming increasingly focused on locating, gaining the trust of, caring for, and retaining their lucrative current clientele. To remain competitive, a business must constantly strive to meet the client's specified value and deter him from switching to a rival. Establishing trusting relationships is a difficult task for businesses, to the point that some have even given up a portion of their earnings to stand out from the competition. By doing this, businesses demonstrate to their clients that they value them and want to support them regardless of the short-term financial implications. These build or strengthen the kind of trust that leads to customer loyalty.

Trust may be crucial when it comes to business-to-consumer (B2C) e-commerce. Customers are encouraged to purchase goods and services even if they need clarification on the e-trader. It promotes the increased use of e-commerce technologies, facilitates e-transactions, raises the degree of e-commerce acceptance and adoption, improves consumer commitment, raises customer satisfaction, introduces the idea of loyalty, maintains enduring relationships with customers, and helps acquire a competitive advantage. Price increases can be accepted and used as motivation for future purchases. It eases clients' concerns over the privacy of their information and makes it easier for them to put up with the sporadic errors that the e-trader makes. Trust has many facets and is a complex idea that requires attention.

Information distribution technologies and content are changing the fundamental basis of competitiveness in electronic commerce or activities that directly support commerce through electronic (networked) connections. Information flows over international networks have established an electronic marketplace of businesses that are learning to take advantage of commercial opportunities. Companies require a suitable classification scheme for the e-commerce sector, its products, and services to compete effectively. Industries are frequently segmented to study the complexities of how a market works. One of the most well-known industry classification schemes is the Standard Industrial Classification (SIC). The proposed e-commerce industry classification follows the same logic: the e-commerce industry will be defined by substructures or units that share specific features. E-commerce is a dynamic, fast-evolving industry. In such a situation, managers must quickly predict the sector's direction, develop competitive strategies, forge strategic partnerships, and establish and disband virtual organisations. Providers of e-commerce goods and services should find information about how to categorise this developing market to be helpful.

DISCUSSION AND CONCLUSION

Industry 4.0 Transformation: Close Link Between E-Commerce and Customers

Amid the frenzy surrounding e-commerce and the recent collapse of several dot-com companies, it holds real promise for small businesses in developing countries. Suppose the internet's ability to lower transaction costs is sufficient to catalyse a broad change in the global economy. Electronic commerce holds excellent promise for small-scale manufacturers who need help to break into overseas markets. New trends in the e-commerce industry have expanded in many directions. As technology advances rapidly, consumers' perspectives are on the verge of a complete shift. However, e-commerce platforms will increasingly centre on the customer's mind, focusing on consumer services enhanced through the hyper-local space of the Internet of Things (IoT), data processing, artificial intelligence, logistics, personalisation, and next-generation e-commerce models. The primary factors in Internet transactions are the payment method, including debit cards, credit cards, online banking purchases and electronic funds transfers. Therefore, future e-commerce will require payment gates as the world moves away from cash and digital currencies. Analytics in e-commerce are empirical methods that transform data into decisions. Data analysis helps organisations collect, organise, review and comment on their customers. The information explosion has significantly increased data, making business organisations dependent on research and analytical data to understand customer purchasing intentions and behaviour. Online retailers must be able to obtain and analyse real-time data to calculate the return on Internet investment and channel mix to ensure market share. Basic analytics that can be used include basket size measurements, average order size, and conversion rates for customer insights, and more in-depth analytics are needed. E-commerce companies can track customers' search and shopping trends to help companies develop marketing strategies that satisfy consumers. To promote their products, business organisations can use social media to achieve brand promotion and expand influence and visibility. Social media can be effectively used involving computer applications and blogs that allow connections and exchange of information over the internet using a computer or mobile phone. Social networks are critical in product creation for e-commerce, and they serve as a brand-building tool for cultivating a loyal customer base and spreading word of mouth.

With the impact of the industry 4.0 technological revolution, the e-commerce industry will become one of the leading industries in the business field. The electronic commerce revolution has quickly opened up new markets and crossed boundaries, hugely favourably impacting the transaction business. It has dramatically affected the world's traditional market system and order, improving people's lives and consumption patterns. Although e-commerce provides convenience to customers and sellers, it hinders the sustainable development of traditional business models. E-commerce is still evolving because of new technology and its applications. To improve the process and make it more advantageous and profitable, e-commerce has drawn scholars from various fields, including business and technology. However, the industry has also faced significant hurdles due to these advances (Post, 2023). One of the most common issues it faces is the "cybersecurity issue" in e-commerce (Mishra et al., 2022). Businesses involved in e-commerce are constantly investing to handle the growing issue of cybersecurity (Vinoth et al., 2022). Concerning this matter, governments are also enacting laws and policies (Luo & Choi, 2022). However, as technology advances, fraudsters also develop new ways to target clients or businesses. Likewise, businesses encourage using cutting-edge and reliable website tools and technologies to stay competitive and uphold client confidence (Gull et al., 2022).

On the other hand, researchers are also continually improving technology. For example, efforts have been made to increase false alarm detection's effectiveness and subsequently more precisely identify genuine alarms (Li et al., 2022), and several techniques for phishing detection have been suggested (Gupta et al., 2021). Additionally, researchers are creating new methods and frameworks to identify vulnerabilities (Cvitić et al., 2021). Blockchain technology is an alternative for e-commerce trust and security (Centobelli et al., 2021) and digitalisation (Cerchione et al., 2022).

The opportunities and challenges of online marketing communication have led to product or service marketing breakthroughs. E-commerce platforms are now used as a starting point for product launches and building customer loyalty. Under such conditions, the design of online business strategies in the current digital media era is undoubtedly a way for corporate organisations to conduct online marketing to meet the various needs of customers and guide changes in customer needs, thereby ensuring the success of a robust marketing position. Network operators must have customer relationship management (CRM) capabilities to win a stable customer base. While creating a company, they can build and integrate the resources, activities and processes required by the company to manage customer relationships. Internet technology has created new marketing strategies and tools to help companies introduce, convert and retain customers to improve the quality of customer relationships and help increase the company's customer lifetime value. Business organisations need to master technology to keep up with the business trends of this era. As the convenience of technology increases, potential customers are more willing and inclined to shop and use services through devices. There are many forecasts in technology about "paradigm" shifts that will rock the globe. However, recent shifts (e.g., client/server, business rules, distributed object computing) have yet to live up to the hype. Although many business organisations have become accustomed to the digital age, there still needs to be an improvement in the operation of advanced technologies, the accuracy of current market data control and analysis, and the effectiveness of interconnected systems at all levels.

Particularly concerning enhancing marketing through e-commerce productivity, it is imperative to develop digital-era e-commerce strategies that can adjust to the evolving competitive landscape of Industry 4.0, which has become a new opportunity for business organisations. Now, e-commerce has entered the e-commerce 4.0 stage, involving the development of various technologies such as artificial intelligence (AI) and the Internet of Things (IoT) (Anwar et al., 2024). In dynamic business scenarios, understanding customers' decision-making processes must be supported by discovering information. Managers need to accurately understand the current high demand and dynamic market based on advanced technology, data analysis, and interconnected systems, with a primary customer orientation, and satisfy customer needs to create a competitive advantage for organisations that can leverage the information at their disposal. Marketing managers must also adapt to business model changes and focus on using media and technology in digital/e-marketing to understand and cater to the target market to cope with uncertain market dynamics and stay at an advantage in the fierce competition. The purpose is to improve industrial competitiveness in a dynamic global market. Essential aspects of e-commerce that require improvement are technological know-how, practical logistics, and maintaining a positive relationship with the consumer throughout the entire sales cycle in a virtual setting. Trust promotes the increased use of e-commerce technologies, facilitates e-transactions, raises the degree of e-commerce acceptance and adoption, improves consumer commitment, raises customer satisfaction, introduces the idea of loyalty, maintains enduring relationships with customers, and helps acquire a competitive advantage.

REFERENCES

Abdel Hakeem, S. A., Hussein, H. H., & Kim, H. (2022). Security requirements and challenges of 6G technologies and applications. *Sensors (Basel)*, *22*(5), 1969. doi:10.3390/s22051969 PMID:35271113

Ahmadian, S. (2021). Review of e-commerce service delivery models. *Arman Process Journal*, *2*(3), 14–20.

Ahn, T., Ryu, S., & Han, I. (2007). The impact of Web quality and playfulness on user acceptance of online retailing. *Information & Management*, *44*(3), 263–275. doi:10.1016/j.im.2006.12.008

Alavi, R., Islam, S., & Mouratidis, H. (2016). An information security risk-driven investment model for analysing human factors. *Information and Computer Security*, *24*(2), 205–227. doi:10.1108/ICS-01-2016-0006

Albertin, A. L. (2012). Comércio eletrônico: da evolução para as novas oportunidades. Academic Press.

Anwar, T., Khan, G. A., Ashraf, Z., Ansari, Z. A., Ahmed, R., & Azrour, M. (2024). The Combination of Blockchain and the Internet of Things (IoT): Applications, Opportunities, and Challenges for Industry. *Blockchain and Machine Learning for IoT Security*, 56-76.

Becker, J. U., Greve, G., & Albers, S. (2009). The impact of technological and organisational implementation of CRM on customer acquisition, maintenance, and retention. *International Journal of Research in Marketing*, *26*(3), 207–215. doi:10.1016/j.ijresmar.2009.03.006

Bibri, S. E., Krogstie, J., Kaboli, A., & Alahi, A. (2024). Smarter eco-cities and their leading-edge artificial intelligence of things solutions for environmental sustainability: A comprehensive systematic review. *Environmental Science and Ecotechnology*, *19*, 100330. doi:10.1016/j.ese.2023.100330 PMID:38021367

Centobelli, P., Cerchione, R., Esposito, E., & Oropallo, E. (2021). Surfing blockchain wave, or drowning? Shaping the future of distributed ledgers and decentralised technologies. *Technological Forecasting and Social Change*, *165*, 120463. doi:10.1016/j.techfore.2020.120463

Cerchione, R., Centobelli, P., Riccio, E., Abbate, S., & Oropallo, E. (2023). Blockchain's coming to hospital to digitalise healthcare services: Designing a distributed electronic health record ecosystem. *Technovation*, *120*, 102480. doi:10.1016/j.technovation.2022.102480

Chen, C. W. D., & Cheng, C. Y. J. (2009). Understanding consumer intention in online shopping: A respecification and validation of the DeLone and McLean model. *Behaviour & Information Technology*, *28*(4), 335–345. doi:10.1080/01449290701850111

Cheng, X., Su, L., & Zarifis, A. (2019). Designing a talents training model for cross-border e-commerce: A mixed approach of problem-based learning with social media. *Electronic Commerce Research*, *19*(4), 801–822. doi:10.1007/s10660-019-09341-y

Coltman, T., Devinney, T. M., & Midgley, D. F. (2011). Customer relationship management and firm performance. *Journal of Information Technology*, *26*(3), 205–219. doi:10.1057/jit.2010.39

Cvitić, I., Peraković, D., Periša, M., & Gupta, B. (2021). Ensemble machine learning approach for classification of IoT devices in smart home. *International Journal of Machine Learning and Cybernetics*, *12*(11), 3179–3202. doi:10.1007/s13042-020-01241-0

D'Adamo, I., González-Sánchez, R., Medina-Salgado, M. S., & Settembre-Blundo, D. (2021). E-commerce calls for cyber-security and sustainability: How european citizens look for a trusted online environment. *Sustainability (Basel)*, *13*(12), 6752. doi:10.3390/su13126752

DeLone, W. H., & McLean, E. R. (2003). The DeLone and McLean model of information systems success: A ten-year update. *Journal of Management Information Systems*, *19*(4), 9–30. doi:10.1080/0742 1222.2003.11045748

den Hond, F., & Moser, C. (2023). Useful servant or dangerous master? Technology in business and society debates. *Business & Society*, *62*(1), 87–116. doi:10.1177/00076503211068029

Ferreira, J. B., de Freitas, A. S., Giovannini, C. J., Kurtz, R., & Pina, F. (2015). Tecnologias Interativas: Efeitos no Varejo de Vestuário Online. *Revista Eletrônica de Estratégia & Negócios*, *8*(2), 241–265. doi:10.19177/reen.v8e22015241-265

Frawley, T., & Fahy, J. (2006). Revisiting the First-Mover Advantage Theory: A Resource-Based Perspective. *Irish Journal of Management*, *27*(1).

Galinari, R., Cervieri Júnior, O., Teixeira Júnior, J. R., & Rawet, E. L. (2015). Comércio eletrônico, tecnologias móveis e mídias sociais no Brasil. Academic Press.

Gefen, D. (2000). E-commerce: The role of familiarity and trust. *Omega*, *28*(6), 725–737. doi:10.1016/S0305-0483(00)00021-9

Grandon, E. E., & Pearson, J. M. (2004). Electronic commerce adoption: An empirical study of small and medium US businesses. *Information & Management*, *42*(1), 197–216. doi:10.1016/j.im.2003.12.010

Gull, H., Saeed, S., Iqbal, S. Z., Bamarouf, Y. A., Alqahtani, M. A., Alabbad, D. A., Saqib, M., Al Qahtani, S. H., & Alamer, A. (2022). An empirical study of mobile commerce and customers security perception in Saudi Arabia. *Electronics (Basel)*, *11*(3), 293. doi:10.3390/electronics11030293

Gupta, B. B., Yadav, K., Razzak, I., Psannis, K., Castiglione, A., & Chang, X. (2021). A novel approach for phishing URLs detection using lexical based machine learning in a real-time environment. *Computer Communications*, *175*, 47–57. doi:10.1016/j.comcom.2021.04.023

Hepfer, M., & Powell, T. C. (2020). Make cybersecurity a strategic asset. *MIT Sloan Management Review*, *62*(1), 40–45.

Hepola, J., Leppäniemi, M., & Karjaluoto, H. (2020). Is it all about consumer engagement? Explaining continuance intention for utilitarian and hedonic service consumption. *Journal of Retailing and Consumer Services*, *57*, 102232. doi:10.1016/j.jretconser.2020.102232

Higueras-Castillo, E., Alves, H., Liébana-Cabanillas, F., & Villarejo-Ramos, Á. F. (2023). The consumer intention to use e-commerce applications in the post-pandemic era: a predictive approach study using a CHAID tree-based algorithm. *European Journal of Management and Business Economics*.

Hooks, D., Davis, Z., Agrawal, V., & Li, Z. (2022). Exploring factors influencing technology adoption rate at the macro level: A predictive model. *Technology in Society*, *68*, 101826. doi:10.1016/j.techsoc.2021.101826

Hussien, F. T. A., Rahma, A. M. S., & Wahab, H. B. A. (2022). Design and implement a new secure prototype structure of e-commerce system. *Iranian Journal of Electrical and Computer Engineering*, *12*(1), 560–571.

Ibarra-Cantu, C., & Cheetham, F. (2021). Consumer multiculturation in multicultural marketplaces: Mexican immigrants' responses to the global consumer culture construction of Tex-Mex as Mexican food. *Journal of Business Research*, *134*, 70–77. doi:10.1016/j.jbusres.2021.05.012

Jang-Jaccard, J., & Nepal, S. (2014). A survey of emerging threats in cybersecurity. *Journal of Computer and System Sciences*, *80*(5), 973–993. doi:10.1016/j.jcss.2014.02.005

Kagermann, H., Lukas, W. D., & Wahlster, W. (2013). Final report: Recommendations for implementing the strategic initiative INDUSTRIE 4.0. Industrie 4.0 Working Group. *Forschung Union: Frankfurt*.

Kalia, P., Kaur, N., & Singh, T. (2017). *E-Commerce in India*.

Karine, H. A. J. I. (2021). E-commerce development in rural and remote areas of BRICS countries. *Journal of Integrative Agriculture*, *20*(4), 979–997. doi:10.1016/S2095-3119(20)63451-7

Khan, W. Z., Aalsalem, M. Y., Khan, M. K., & Arshad, Q. (2019). Data and privacy: Getting consumers to trust products enabled by the Internet of Things. *IEEE Consumer Electronics Magazine*, *8*(2), 35–38. doi:10.1109/MCE.2018.2880807

Khurana, A. (2019). *Did You Know That There Are 4 Types Of Ecommerce?* The Balance Small Business.

Kramer, L. (2022). What strategies do companies employ to increase market share. Academic Press.

Li, J., Herdem, M. S., Nathwani, J., & Wen, J. Z. (2023). Methods and applications for Artificial Intelligence, Big Data, Internet of Things, and Blockchain in smart energy management. *Energy and AI*, *11*, 100208. doi:10.1016/j.egyai.2022.100208

Li, S., Qin, D., Wu, X., Li, J., Li, B., & Han, W. (2022). False alert detection based on deep learning and machine learning. *International Journal on Semantic Web and Information Systems*, *18*(1), 1–21. doi:10.4018/IJSWIS.313190

Li, Y., & Liu, Q. (2021). A comprehensive review study of cyber-attacks and cyber security; Emerging trends and recent developments. *Energy Reports*, *7*, 8176–8186. doi:10.1016/j.egyr.2021.08.126

Lieberman, M. B. (2005). Did first-mover advantage survive the dot-com crash. *Unpublished working paper, UCLA*.

Liu, X., Ahmad, S. F., Anser, M. K., Ke, J., Irshad, M., Ul-Haq, J., & Abbas, S. (2022). Cyber security threats: A never-ending challenge for e-commerce. *Frontiers in Psychology*, *13*, 927398. doi:10.3389/fpsyg.2022.927398 PMID:36337532

Lorette, K. (2013). *How ecommerce can reduce business transaction costs*. Chron Small Business by Demand Media.

Ludwig, S., De Ruyter, K., Friedman, M., Brüggen, E. C., Wetzels, M., & Pfann, G. (2013). More than words: The influence of affective content and linguistic style matches in online reviews on conversion rates. *Journal of Marketing*, *77*(1), 87–103. doi:10.1509/jm.11.0560

Luo, S., & Choi, T. M. (2022). E-commerce supply chains with considerations of cyber-security: Should governments play a role? *Production and Operations Management*, *31*(5), 2107–2126. doi:10.1111/poms.13666

Maddox, K., & Blankenhorn, D. (1998). Web Commerce: Building a Digital Business. John Wiley and Sons.

Manerba, D., Mansini, R., & Zanotti, R. (2018). Attended Home Delivery: Reducing last-mile environmental impact by changing customer habits. *IFAC-PapersOnLine*, *51*(5), 55–60. doi:10.1016/j.ifacol.2018.06.199

Martin, K. D., & Murphy, P. E. (2017). The role of data privacy in marketing. *Journal of the Academy of Marketing Science*, *45*(2), 135–155. doi:10.1007/s11747-016-0495-4

Metalidou, E., Marinagi, C., Trivellas, P., Eberhagen, N., Skourlas, C., & Giannakopoulos, G. (2014). The human factor of information security: Unintentional damage perspective. *Procedia: Social and Behavioral Sciences*, *147*, 424–428. doi:10.1016/j.sbspro.2014.07.133

Mishra, A., Alzoubi, Y. I., Gill, A. Q., & Anwar, M. J. (2022). Cybersecurity enterprises policies: A comparative study. *Sensors (Basel)*, *22*(2), 538. doi:10.3390/s22020538 PMID:35062504

Monnot, E., Reniou, F., Parguel, B., & Elgaaied-Gambier, L. (2019). "Thinking outside the packaging box": Should brands consider store shelf context when eliminating overpackaging? *Journal of Business Ethics*, *154*(2), 355–370. doi:10.1007/s10551-017-3439-0

Moores, T. (2005). Do consumers understand the role of privacy seals in e-commerce? *Communications of the ACM*, *48*(3), 86–91. doi:10.1145/1047671.1047674

Nair, M. M., & Tyagi, A. K. (2023). AI, IoT, blockchain, and cloud computing: The necessity of the future. In *Distributed Computing to Blockchain* (pp. 189–206). Academic Press. doi:10.1016/B978-0-323-96146-2.00001-2

Ngai, E. W., & Gunasekaran, A. (2007). A review for mobile commerce research and applications. *Decision Support Systems, 43*(1), 3–15. doi:10.1016/j.dss.2005.05.003

Nikolaeva, R. (2005). Strategic determinants of web site traffic in online retailing. *International Journal of Electronic Commerce, 9*(4), 113–132. doi:10.1080/10864415.2003.11044344

Padmanabhan, B., Zheng, Z., & Kimbrough, S. O. (2006). An empirical analysis of the value of complete information for eCRM models. *Management Information Systems Quarterly, 30*(2), 247–267. doi:10.2307/25148730

Payne, A., & Frow, P. (2005). A strategic framework for customer relationship management. *Journal of Marketing, 69*(4), 167–176. doi:10.1509/jmkg.2005.69.4.167

Polo, Y., & Sesé, F. J. (2009). How to make switching costly: The role of marketing and relationship characteristics. *Journal of Service Research, 12*(2), 119–137. doi:10.1177/1094670509335771

Post, J. (2023). Top e-commerce challenges facing SMBs. Academic Press.

Purani, K., Kumar, D. S., & Sahadev, S. (2019). e-Loyalty among millennials: Personal characteristics and social influences. *Journal of Retailing and Consumer Services, 48*, 215–223. doi:10.1016/j.jretconser.2019.02.006

Rahman, S. (2014). *Introduction to E-commerce technology in business.* GRIN Verlag.

Rane, N., Choudhary, S., & Rane, J. (2023). Sustainable tourism development using leading-edge Artificial Intelligence (AI), Blockchain, Internet of Things (IoT), Augmented Reality (AR) and Virtual Reality (VR) technologies. Academic Press.

Reynolds, J. (2000). eCommerce: A critical review. *International Journal of Retail & Distribution Management, 28*(10), 417–444. doi:10.1108/09590550010349253

Ryals, L. (2005). Making customer relationship management work: The measurement and profitable management of customer relationships. *Journal of Marketing, 69*(4), 252–261. doi:10.1509/jmkg.2005.69.4.252

Ryan, S. D., & Harrison, D. A. (2000). Considering social subsystem costs and benefits in information technology investment decisions: A view from the field on anticipated payoffs. *Journal of Management Information Systems, 16*(4), 11–40. doi:10.1080/07421222.2000.11518264

Schlechtendahl, J., Keinert, M., Kretschmer, F., Lechler, A., & Verl, A. (2015). Making existing production systems Industry 4.0-ready: Holistic approach to the integration of existing production systems in Industry 4.0 environments. *Production Engineering, 9*(1), 143–148. doi:10.1007/s11740-014-0586-3

Singh, S., & Rana, R. (2018). Effect of demographic factors on consumers' perception of online shopping. *Global Journal of Management and Business Research, 18*(6), 27–38.

Solanki, S. (2018). *Why materials matter: responsible design for a better world.* No Title.

Soltanmohammadi, S., Asadi, S., & Ithnin, N. (2013). Main human factors affecting information system security. *Interdisciplinary Journal of Contemporary Research in Business, 5*(7), 329–354.

Srinivasan, S. S., Anderson, R., & Ponnavolu, K. (2002). Customer loyalty in e-commerce: An exploration of its antecedents and consequences. *Journal of Retailing, 78*(1), 41–50. doi:10.1016/S0022-4359(01)00065-3

Stalmachova, K., Chinoracky, R., & Strenitzerova, M. (2021). Changes in business models caused by digital transformation and the COVID-19 pandemic and possibilities of their measurement—Case study. *Sustainability (Basel), 14*(1), 127. doi:10.3390/su14010127

Team, E. (2021). Must-Know Cyber Attack Statistics, and Trends. Academic Press.

Testa, M. G., Luciano, E. M., & Freitas, H. M. R. D. (2004). Management information systems and technologies: analysing research topics in France and Brazil. Read: revista eletrônica de administracão, 10(6).

Thomson, L., Kamalaldin, A., Sjödin, D., & Parida, V. (2022). A maturity framework for autonomous solutions in manufacturing firms: The interplay of technology, ecosystem, and business model. *The International Entrepreneurship and Management Journal, 18*(1), 125–152. doi:10.1007/s11365-020-00717-3

Trotti, F., Burgos, G., Júnior, G., Pavão, M. D. O. P. D., & Pavão, O. (2017). Comércio eletrônico: como conquistar clientes e aumentar o faturamento em um ambiente virtual. *Revista IT-Inovação & Tecnologia, 1*(1).

Van Loon, P., Deketele, L., Dewaele, J., McKinnon, A., & Rutherford, C. (2015). A comparative analysis of carbon emissions from online retailing of fast moving consumer goods. *Journal of Cleaner Production, 106*, 478–486. doi:10.1016/j.jclepro.2014.06.060

Vinoth, S., Vemula, H. L., Haralayya, B., Mamgain, P., Hasan, M. F., & Naved, M. (2022). Application of cloud computing in banking and e-commerce and related security threats. *Materials Today: Proceedings, 51*, 2172–2175. doi:10.1016/j.matpr.2021.11.121

Wall, W. P., & Wall, W. P. (2022). Global Competition—The Battlefield. *Global Competitiveness: Ten Things Thai Businesspeople Should Know*, 1-6.

Wang, Z., Li, M., Lu, J., & Cheng, X. (2022). Business Innovation based on artificial intelligence and Blockchain technology. *Information Processing & Management, 59*(1), 102759. doi:10.1016/j.ipm.2021.102759

Wendler, M., Tremml, B., & Buecker, B. J. (Eds.). (2008). *Key aspects of German business law: a practical manual*. Springer Science & Business Media.

Whig, P., Velu, A., Nadikattu, R. R., & Alkali, Y. J. (2024). Role of AI and IoT in Intelligent Transportation. In *Artificial Intelligence for Future Intelligent Transportation* (pp. 199–220). Apple Academic Press.

Winer, R. S. (2001). *Customer relationship management: a framework, research directions, and the future*. Haas School of Business.

Zhou, X., Huang, W., Liang, W., Yan, Z., Ma, J., Pan, Y., ... Wang, K. (2024). Federated Distillation and Blockchain Empowered Secure Knowledge Sharing for Internet of Medical Things. *Information Sciences, 662*, 120217. doi:10.1016/j.ins.2024.120217

Chapter 2
Micro–Moments in Social Commerce:
Impact, Triggers, and Digital Transformation

Abhay Grover
https://orcid.org/0000-0003-1013-9746
Chandigarh University, India & Lovely Professional University, India

Nilesh Arora
https://orcid.org/0000-0002-8901-2205
Chandigarh University, India

ABSTRACT

Consumer behaviour and the nature of community-focused retail experiences are being shaped by social commerce, an amalgam of social media and e-commerce, revolutionising the business landscape. Changes in retail are being propelled by digital transformation, which is also spawning new business-social relationships. Businesses are facing a rapidly evolving market driven by technology and customer expectations as social commerce micro-moments and digital transformation come to light. In order to surpass expectations set by digital transformation and revolutionary moments, companies must embrace empathy and innovation. In order to deduce what drives consumers, sophisticated algorithms for demand prediction and real-time data analysis are required. To help organisations navigate this landscape, this study examines micro-moments related to digital transformation and social commerce. By leveraging these interactions, companies can take advantage of the dynamic digital world and offer guidance on adapting micro-moments in social commerce environment.

DOI: 10.4018/979-8-3693-2367-0.ch002

1. INTRODUCTION

In the realm of commerce, which is undergoing rapid change, the combination of social media and e-commerce, which is referred to as "social commerce" (Dwivedi et al., 2021), holds a prominent position at the dynamic intersection of business and communication inside the realm of digital technology. Using the built-in social features of platforms like Instagram, Facebook, and TikTok, a dynamic shift occurs in consumer behaviour, which goes beyond a simple convergence. This crucial paradigm leverages complex social connections to influence consumer choices and create community-focused retail experiences (Chakraborty & Jain, 2022). The egalitarian nature of this convergence, in which social discourse and commerce are inseparable, is its defining feature. In this context, consumers navigate the realms of discovery, participate in vibrant discussions, and make purchases without ever leaving their familiar social feeds (Busalim & Hussin, 2016). There is a meteoric rise in the visibility of social commerce all across the world, and it is not a passing fad. The exponential rise of mobile connectivity has blurred the boundaries between entertainment, communication, and business (Luna-Nevarez & McGovern, 2021). This crossroads is ripe with the opportunity to reshape the antiquated boundaries of conventional retail formats, and its significance is immense.

A spectacular transformation is on the horizon for consumer dynamics and strategic business evolution, spurred by the confluence of micro-moments (AIContentfy team, 2023a) and the dogged advance of digital transformation in the social commerce domain (Attar et al., 2022). In these brief but significant times, consumers are compelled to seek out digital platforms in their relentless pursuit of instant satisfaction or answers, reiterating the observations made by (Sanyal, 2022). On the one hand, the foundation of today's business landscape is laid by the seismic transformations being wrought by the ongoing digital transformation tale. These significant shifts mark the beginning of a period in which companies must change direction and adjust to meet the demands of a market driven by fast technology development and changing customer expectations. These forces are coming together in a way that goes beyond just following trends; it is like a symphony that is changing the fundamental nature of business.

As we navigate this hyper-connected digital era, it is essential to remember that micro-moments are like a crossroads where customer intent and the digital domain meet. These moments go beyond being isolated incidents; they can drastically affect consumers' buying decisions and their loyalty to a brand, as highlighted in the groundbreaking research of (Laura Adams et al., 2015). The present digital landscape is rife with micro-moments, which are brief yet profound contacts with customers. Businesses run the danger of falling behind in the digital race if they do not masterfully use these moments (Arora et al., 2019; Bruce, 2019). Intricate algorithms for real-time data analysis and predicting individual demands are required to decipher the reasons that drive shoppers in these moments (Sarker, 2021). The foundation for creating unique user experiences, essential for promoting relevant and timely interactions in the ever-changing digital world, lies in these immediate insights.

The purpose of this study is to probe the interdependent nature of social commerce's micro-moments and digital transformation. It aspires to shed light on the complex interaction, providing essential insights for organisations navigating this complex landscape. Businesses are given powerful tools to harness micro-moments effectively when these complicated relationships are revealed. The overarching goal of this research is to help businesses better engage their customers and strengthen their marketing strategies to withstand the onslaught of digital disruption. It aims to strengthen organisations by providing a thorough understanding and strategic counsel, enabling them to manage the always-changing landscape skilfully.

The following are some of the research questions that will be investigated in this study:

RQ 1: How do Micro-Moments in Social Commerce Influence Consumer Behaviour?
RQ 2: What Role Digital Transformation can play in Intensifying Micro-Moments?
RQ 3: How can Businesses Effectively Leverage Micro-Moments for Enhanced Customer Engagement Amidst Digital Transformation?

2. MICRO-MOMENTS IN SOCIAL COMMERCE

2.1. Micro-Moments

Micro-moments are transitory yet seismic occasions that occur in the vast digital platform. They are the point at which the purpose of consumers converges with the expansive domain of digital possibilities (Sela, 2023). These brief moments, condensed into a single pulse, represent the critical crossroads where people naturally go to their phones to satisfy an urgent need—whether it is to get answers, make a purchase, or just look into potential options. This phenomenon, which has profoundly reshaped the contours of consumer involvement, has been brought about by the ubiquitous presence of cell phones and the all-encompassing and all-encompassing reach of social media platforms. These micro-moments are no longer occasional occurrences; instead, they are woven into the every aspect of our lives that are intertwined with technology (Atterby, 2023). They can appear at any moment, regardless of the time or place.

Imagine a buyer who is considering making a purchase; a fleeting notion causes them to instinctively grab their smartphone, which then proceeds to unfold a complex web of micro-interactions. In digital technology, these micro-moments weave together a narrative of decision-making that is changing in real time (Dalal, 2023). This narrative includes activities such as reading reviews, studying product descriptions, and analysing costs across various platforms. This contextualisation of micro-moments within the digital paradigm sheds light on the delicate relationship that they have with consumer behaviour and the tremendous influence that they exert.

2.2. Categorization of Micro-Moments

Micro-moments, despite their transience, reveal a complex web of consumer-digital interactions (*Micro-Moments: The Rising Trend in Digital Marketing*, 2023). These categorizations assess customer activity in the context of exploration and transactions and shape the complex fabric of digital engagements in social commerce. Micromoments have many purposes and capacities as they move along a spectrum. Pioneering micro-moments involve customers exploring products and services and seeking knowledge. These moments represent that initial spark, the digital need to explore a topic or something. However, transformative micro-moments are the embodiment of intent (Lineer, 2021). Customers make important decisions like adding items to a shopping basket or paying at them.

Revolutionary micro-moments occur when customers carefully analyse and evaluate options before making a decision. Post-purchase service micro-moments occur when customers want help with debugging, product inquiries, or after-sales support (AbouElgheit, 2022). Each stroke in these micro-moment tapestries generates a unique customer contact tableau, illustrating the complexity of digital interactions. These micro-moment typologies thrive in social commerce and are strongly ingrained in online consumer behaviour. When Instagram users see an influencer post, pioneering micro-moments occur. The post inspires them to examine the items tagged. This spark starts an adventurous adventure that may lead to transformative transactions.

Imagine a consumer sees a Facebook ad that promises a limited-time discount and clicks on it (Majid et al., 2019). This is a social commerce transactional micro-moment. In that time, the focus turns from discovery to action, whether it's a quick shopping cart insertion or a smooth transaction spurred by an approaching offer. While browsing Pinterest, organising their Wishlist, or evaluating products based on visuals and social media, consumers might reflect (Scolere, 2023). Customers experience a series of service micro-moments after buying. Tagging companies on Twitter, they ask for help or leave remarks. These social interactions illuminate the post-purchase landscape and the importance of consumer-brand engagements beyond transactional partnerships. Social commerce micro-moments are a sophisticated work of art woven with endless shades of human desire, intent, and action, leaving an eternal mark on the virtual canvas.

2.3. Triggers and Duration of Micro-Moments

The core of micro-moments is not only their ephemeral character; instead, it is the invisible triggers that spark these instant encounters and the temporal tapestry that defines their existence. Getting to the bottom of these triggers and gaining a knowledge of where they came from sheds light on a complicated engagement within the intricate digital world involving customer requirements, external cues, and purposeful actions.

2.3.1 Identifying Triggers: Needs, Stimuli, Consumer Intent

The origin of micro-moments may be traced back to triggers resulting from a confluence of customer demands, external nudges, and intent (PALMER, 2021). Individuals are driven to seek explanations, solutions, or a rapid sensation of fulfilment when they are confronted with consumer wants, regardless of whether they are dormant or explicit. External cues, such as nudges from social media or ambient stimuli, provide the spark that ignites these micro-moments, amplifying consumers' responses. These triggers are channelled into speedy actions by the consumer intent, which acts as a catalyst. This transforms an urge into a digital connection that has significant consequences. The world of social commerce is entirely of different ways that triggers might present themselves. Consider the scenario in which a consumer suddenly develops a need for a product due to an Instagram influencer's recommendation (Bertini et al., 2020). This is an example of a latent demand that is fuelled by external stimuli, resulting in a micro-moment that requires rapid satisfaction.

2.3.2 Duration and Timeline of Micro-Moments

Micro-moments are carefully intertwined with elegance and purpose. They are fleeting, yet their impact lasts. Depending on the consumer's needs and the complexity of the launched actions, they can last from a split second to an extended engagement. The intention to buy triggers transactional micro-moments in a blink (PALMER, 2021). These seconds are dedicated to adding an item to a cart or buying. However, exploratory micro-moments are long-lasting and include substantial research or information gathering, stretching engagement. Due to their interconnectedness throughout the customer journey, these micro-moments often have non-linear timelines (Snegirjova & Tuomisto, 2017). The seamless integration of informative and transactional micro-moments shows the non-sequential nature of this digital rendezvous. In a constantly changing environment, micro-moments are transient but crucial threads that weave customer interaction and reshape digital narratives.

2.4. Significance in Consumer Behaviour

The influence that micro-moments have on consumer behaviour within the complex arena of social commerce is significant and frequently overstated despite the fact that they may appear to be transient. These moments are more than just interactions; they shape the very core of purchasing decisions, the ways in which consumers perceive brands, and the basis upon which they build their loyalty.

2.4.1 Influence on Purchasing Decisions

Micro-moments have revolutionised the customer decision-making in social commerce (Grover et al., 2023b). Brief contacts with intent and relevance set the course for customer purchases. Consumers prefer resolutions, recommendations, and validations in micro-moments because they require rapid pleasure (Bottary, 2019). These moments are especially influential at important periods in the buying process. Imagine a buyer discovering a tailored Facebook campaign. These speedy interactions provide instant gratification and relevancy, which motivates people to engage and buy. These micro-moments also switch clients from thinking to acting (PALMER, 2021). They become crucial triggers for the purchase rather than just useful snippets. This shows how micro-engagements can change consumer behaviour.

2.4.2 Impact on Brand Perception and Loyalty

In online commerce, micro-moments affect brand perception and loyalty (Mocanu, 2020). Every micro-interaction can shape opinions, affinity, and allegiance. Brands that are capable of scheduling important micro-moments leave a lasting impression, build emotional resonance, and connect (Casemajor, 2023). Consider a situation where a customer makes a purchase and then receives prompt, helpful support from a company on X (formerly known as Twitter) (Porter, 2023). This quick micro-moment not only addresses a problem but also leaves an indelible impression, which influences how the company is seen in terms of its commitment to ensuring that the consumer is satisfied.

More than that, these moments have a cumulative effect that goes beyond short-term deals, fostering long-term associations. Through the continual delivery of relevance and value throughout these micro-moments, brands are able to embed themselves in the psyche of consumers, so planting the seeds for subsequent loyalty and advocacy. Every micro-moment contributes to the rich tapestry, which is the relationship between the brand and the consumer, which helps cultivate long-term loyalty and advocacy. Micro-moments, which are frequently short but have a significant influence, are responsible for weaving an intricate story beyond individual interactions. They are responsible for moulding perceptions, guiding decisions, and cultivating lasting connections within the ever-changing social commerce environment.

3. DIGITAL TRANSFORMATION AND INTENSIFICATION OF MICRO-MOMENTS

3.1. Digital Transformation in Online Commerce

The unrelenting advancements in digital technology are the driving force behind the ongoing transformation that the commercial landscape is undergoing. In particular, social commerce is undergoing a transformational evolution, which is redefining the ways in which customers communicate with one another, engage with one another, and traverse purchasing decisions.

3.1.1 Evolution of Digital Landscape in Social Commerce

In the early 2000s, as online communities grew in popularity and started to have a bigger impact on consumers' buying decisions, social commerce was born (Gibreel et al., 2018). The widespread use of social media platforms facilitated the merging of online and offline worlds, bringing together e-commerce and interpersonal connections. The traditional, transaction-based model of online business is giving way to a more community-driven, relationship-oriented strategy in social commerce (Dwivedi et al., 2021). This development is intricately related to the broader context of the Digital Transformation, which has mandated that businesses become more customer-centric and linked in various ways. An essential idea in social commerce, "micro-moments" highlight the significance of real-time, brief interactions that influence consumer behaviour. The authenticity and spontaneity of these micro-moments give social commerce an advantage over traditional e-commerce models, creating a more engaging and sustainable setting for consumers to shop (Baykal, 2020). Businesses venturing into the unexplored realm of digital transformation and social commerce must give careful consideration to these occasions and how to make the most of them if they want to keep up with the constantly evolving expectations of their consumers.

The trajectory of social commerce represents a substantial change away from websites that are static and towards ecosystems that are dynamic and participatory (Grover et al., 2023a). Through the seamless integration of social contact and commercial transactions, social media platforms are transforming into bustling retail channels, thereby altering the behaviour of consumers. Consumers actively participate in these digital arenas, looking for affirmation, endorsements from their peers, and instant gratification (Lăzăroiu et al., 2020). When it comes to social commerce, the digital landscape is evolving into a complex arena that seamlessly integrates consumer interactions, brand engagements, and transactions. Various social media platforms, like Instagram, Facebook, and TikTok, have evolved into virtual markets, which have enabled a convergence of social connections and economic opportunities (Stafford & Duong, 2023). These digital storefronts create immersive, personalised experiences tailored to each customer's tastes, hence increasing the intensity of micro-moments that serve as the driving force behind consumer decisions.

3.1.2 Role of Technological Advancements

Within the realm of social commerce, the dynamics of micro-moments are substantially influenced by technological advancements. The combination of artificial intelligence (AI) and data analytics revolutionises how consumer insights and customisation are handled (Ifekanandu et al., 2023). Micro-moments' value is elevated due to the use of artificial intelligence algorithms that decode consumer behaviour, anticipate preferences, and dynamically adapt experiences. The widespread availability of mobile technology emerges as a critical factor that propels micro-moments to the forefront of the industry of consumer involvement (Matr, 2022). The lines between the online and physical worlds are becoming increasingly blurry owing to the fact that mobile devices serve as portals for quick connections. Because of the immediacy and accessibility that mobile technology provides, micro-moments can occur more frequently and have a more significant impact. This allows customers to interact spontaneously, creating an atmosphere that encourages quick decision-making.

Furthermore, the integration of augmented reality (AR) and virtual reality (VR) into social commerce enhances the fact that micro-moments are more immersive than they were before (Flavián et al., 2019). Consumers can visualise things inside real-world surroundings thanks to these technologies, which bridge the gap between digital and physical environments and give them additional influence over their purchasing decisions. Micro-moments are becoming increasingly important in driving purchasing decisions within an ever-changing landscape as a result of the unrelenting advancements in technology that are constantly reshaping social commerce. These advancements are integrating digital experiences with consumer behaviour.

3.1.3 Challenges in Social Commerce (Micro-Moments)

Businesses have an unprecedented opportunity to connect with customers at the precise moment they need it, influence their purchase decision, and cultivate brand loyalty thanks to the exponential growth of micro-moments in social commerce, which is being driven by digital transformation. However, certain issues, such as consumer information overload and market saturation, are getting worse as the number of micro-moments increases (Kahn, 2017). When a market is oversaturated with a large number of identical products or services, it leads to intense competition and lowers the effectiveness of marketing campaigns (Korenkova et al., 2020). Particularly for businesses that strive to capture and hold the transient interest of consumers in micro-moments, market saturation becomes a difficult nut to crack. The potential for less effective campaigns and weaker contextual messaging arises when numerous brands choose to attend to the same micro-moment (Goldberg & Gustafson, 2023).

Consumers may experience information overload if there is an abundance of personalised content that targets them during micro-moments (Palalas, 2017). In order to provide hyper-targeted content, businesses leverage algorithms that can analyse data in real-time. The result will be an overwhelming amount of data being sent to consumers. When consumers are overwhelmed with choices and unable to make rational judgements, a condition known as decision fatigue, sets in (Hirshleifer et al., 2019). To overcome these challenges, companies should develop a strategy for micro-moment marketing that prioritises quality over quantity. Businesses should stop trying to please everyone with their vast amounts of content and instead focus on reaching out to specific people with tailored messages that meet their needs. To further ensure that micro-moments continue to have an impact and be effective in maintaining consumer engagement and conversion, it is possible to use strategies such as frequency capping and content optimisation to keep the market from becoming saturated.

3.2. Impact of Digital Transformation on Micro-Moments

The rise of digital transformation dramatically impacts the frequency and type of micro-moments in the dynamic realm of social commerce. This has the effect of radically altering how customers connect and engage with companies.

3.2.1 Proliferation of Micro-Moments

Micro-moments are becoming increasingly prevalent and broad within the areas of social commerce, and digital transformation is acting as a catalyst to accelerate this growth and integration. Digital transformation is driving social commerce micro-moments growth and integration. These formerly rare moments now saturate the consumer journey and intricately weave themselves into multiple touchpoints. Digital platforms becoming dynamic market ecosystems increase these rapid contacts. On social commerce platforms, micro-moments are expanding and permeating numerous elements (David, 2023). Customers easily navigate many of these micro-interactions, from exploratory to transactional to significant. Technological advances enable continuous solidarity, which exponentially increases micro-moments and enriches the customer experience with fast, purposeful interactions.

3.2.2 Triggers and Opportunities for Engagement

The frequency of customer engagement inside micro-moments is not only increased by digital transformation, but it also increases the triggers and chances for such engagement. Modern innovations in fields like AI and ML have made it possible for platforms to predict user intent with startling accuracy, leading to better triggers for key occasions. Digital transformation also creates a data-rich environment that gives companies deep insights into individual behaviour, allowing them to tailor customer experiences (Verhoef et al., 2021). These insights enable firms to strategically capitalise on micro-moments by providing relevant, timely, and consumer-relevant engagements by amplifying triggers.

In addition, digital revolution is changing the social commerce business environment, creating various opportunities for micro-moments involvement (Dwivedi et al., 2021). These occasions allow brands to execute transactions, build relationships, and reinforce their brand identity. Micro-moments offer interactive information, customised recommendations, and real-time reactions. Customers and companies form deep bonds with these shifts. The paradigm change caused by digital transformation transforms micro-moments into widespread, meaningful encounters that reimagine consumer-brand engagements in social commerce.

3.2.3 Ethical and Privacy Issues

Ethical and privacy issues are heightened by the meteoric rise of social commerce, a byproduct of digital transformation and micro-moments centred on data analytics and artificial intelligence (X. Wang et al., 2020). Concerns about data security, privacy, and the possible abuse of personal information may arise as a result of the integration of complex algorithms for demand prediction with real-time data analysis (Chen et al., 2021). As businesses try to decipher customer behaviour, ethical questions regarding data collection and use emerge as central concerns. Finally, it's important to remember that cultural norms and consumer behaviours are part of the global context. When considering non-Western markets, it's important to take their diverse cultural norms into consideration (AIContentfy team, 2023b). Because people have different moral standards, it's hard to use analytics and AI with any degree of accuracy. When it comes to social commerce, it's just as important to respect people's privacy as it is to make sure your strategies are in line with local sensitivities (Attar et al., 2021). It follows that in order to promote ethical innovation and strike a healthy balance between technical advancement and ethics, a comprehensive examination of these ethical dimensions, taking a global view, is required.

3.3. AI and Data Analytics in Shaping Micro-Moments

In the ever-changing landscape of social commerce, the incorporation of Artificial Intelligence (AI) and Data Analytics has emerged as a crucial driving force, delicately shaping the dynamics and strengthening the micro-moments that occur.

3.3.1 Role of AI in Personalization and Contextual Targeting

In micro-moments, AI transcends its technical side to arrange customised, context-focused interactions that elevate customer experiences. AI can analyse massive databases to discover people's preferences and behaviours (Dwivedi et al., 2023). Imagine yourself as a social commerce customer. AI systems use historical data and real-time interactions to customise feeds. This personalised feed matches the user's choices and forecasts their needs to create a micro-moment when they feel deeply connected to the content (K.B, 2021). In addition to predictive personalisation, AI can enable contextual targeting during micro-moments. Artificial intelligence analyses user behaviour and contextual cues to strategically position content that matches the user's context and intent. Refined targeting boosts conversion and emphasises micro-moments during the transaction (AIContentfy team, 2023c).

3.3.2 Data Analytics for Optimizing Micro-Moment Interactions

Recognising data analytics' revolutionary impact in social commerce is crucial to understanding digital transformation and micro-moments. Data analytics optimises micro-moment interactions by mining, filtering, and transforming massive information into actionable insights (Ajah & Nweke, 2019). As they use social commerce platforms, customers create digital footprints. Data analytics processes these breadcrumbs to discover patterns and preferences that illuminate consumer behaviour and provide organisations ways to improve. Data analytics becomes a strategic tool for identifying consumer engagement triggers as micro-moments proliferate. It deconstructs the actions leading to a transactional micro-moment or the exploratory routes customers take before making judgements. With this insight, companies may tailor their strategies to customer decision-making in micro-moments. Data analytics also lets companies evaluate micro-moment interactions through a retrospective lens. Because of this feedback loop, organisations may constantly refine and improve their strategy.

3.4. Mobile Technology and Micro-Moments

Within the complex framework of social commerce, mobile technology is the fulcrum that is serving as the linchpin of an unparalleled paradigm change. This shift is redefining the tapestry of consumer interactions and experiences.

3.4.1 Mobile's Contribution to Real-Time Micro-Engagements

Within the realm of social commerce, the popularity and significance of micro-moments have been exponentially magnified as a result of the widespread availability and mobility of mobile devices, which have ushered in a new era that is characterised by instantaneous connections and interactions that take place in real-time. Customers are given the ability to interact seamlessly with brands and content through the use of handheld devices such as smartphones, which creates an environment that is conducive to making rapid micro-engagements (Verhoef et al., 2021). Consider the following scenario: a customer is suddenly motivated to shop and quickly visit a social commerce platform using their mobile device after feeling the urge to do so. As a result of the immediacy that mobile technology provides, rapid inquiry, comparison, and definite action are made possible, ultimately resulting in a transactional micro-moment.

As a result of mobile devices acting as catalysts, temporal barriers between consumer intent and action are eliminated, which results in an increase in the frequency of these ephemeral yet important engagements (Glay, 2019). Additionally, mobile technology fosters a culture of continuous connectedness, which makes it possible to engage in a continuous stream of micro-interactions between individuals. Every touch, slide, or press on a mobile screen represents a possible micro-moment. This includes the ability to effortlessly scroll through product feeds as well as engage with material that facilitates interaction. The seamless nature of these engagements not only increases the frequency with which they occur but also magnifies the significance that they play in influencing the decisions that consumers make (Sheikh et al., 2019).

3.4.2 Location-Based Services and Their Impact on Micro-Moments

Regarding the progression of micro-moments within social commerce, location-based services (LBS) are an essential component that plays a crucial role in enhancing the contextual relevance of consumer engagements. Taking advantage of the geospatial capabilities of mobile devices, location-based services (LBS) flawlessly link the experiences of consumers with their immediate physical context, thereby shaping micro-moments with an unprecedented level of precision (Huang et al., 2018). Consider the following scenario: a customer is strolling through a retail area at a leisurely pace, and they are receiving notifications from a social commerce app that are triggered by their position. The consumer's location in relation to particular brands or stores is considered when these notifications, which LBS, present individualised product recommendations or unique offers drive. In order to capitalise on the immediacy of customer intent, this combination of physical proximity and digital interaction generates a micro-moment that is ready for quick action (Flavián et al., 2021).

Furthermore, LBS not only improves the relevancy of micro-moment engagements but also speeds up the timeliness of activities. They make it possible for companies to distribute hyper-targeted material or incentives at precisely the moment when consumers are ready to take action, capitalising on immediate settings to push individuals to interact quickly. This combination of the digital and physical worlds amplifies the effect of micro-moments, converting them from simple online interactions into seamless extensions of the offline experiences that customers have (Arora et al., 2022; Flavián et al., 2021). Exemplifying the potential for real-time, location-driven encounters within the area of social commerce, the combination of location-based services (LBS) and micro-moments serves as a testament to the convergence of technology and consumer behaviour.

4. BUSINESSES LEVERAGING MICRO-MOMENTS

4.1. Real-World Examples of Businesses Leveraging Micro-Moments

Implementing micro-moments has emerged as a crucial tactic for companies within a wide range of industries striving to improve the quality of their interactions with customers. Let us take a more in-depth look at two prominent companies that have successfully capitalised on micro-moments:

4.1.1 Starbucks

Artificial intelligence is utilised by Starbucks in order to personalise the experience of its customers. Customers are likelier to remain loyal to a brand when they feel valued and appreciated. Artificial intelligence systems can learn a customer's likes, dislikes, purchasing history, and other preferences in order to provide personalised product and promotion recommendations. The business has seen an uptick in revenue and client happiness thanks to this tailored strategy (Moon, 2017). Starbucks has also benefited from AI's ability to forecast customer behaviour, which has allowed them to manage workforce and inventory levels better.

Starbucks' groundbreaking use of mobile technology positions them as a model for capitalising on micro-moments. The company's mobile app integrates users' tastes, purchasing history, and current location to provide instant, tailored suggestions—the backbone of its customer interaction strategy. Customers get location-based push notifications from the app when they get close to a Starbucks or navigate nearby (Some, 2019). The app then suggests favoured or new options based on individual interests. Starbucks is very good at capturing micro-moments to create relevant, immediate, and engaging interactions. This is evidenced by the seamless integration of user preferences and contextual data.

4.1.2 Instagram

Even though many companies have changed their business structures in response to the COVID-19 pandemic, online sales remain a significant obstacle for many. To sustain businesses and simplify purchasing for consumers, we are launching a new shopping experience today. Businesses can create a story around their brand and encourage product discovery through Shops and immersive full-screen storefronts that offer a native shopping experience. Customers can shop directly from a company's Instagram page, as well as through the feed and Stories (Gibreel et al., 2018). Shoppers may peruse inventory, investigate collections, and make purchases via our in-app browser or with in-app checkout without ever leaving the app. We hope that by opening stores, people will be able to enjoy shopping for pleasure rather than dread it. Retailers can personalise customers' shopping experiences by showcasing curated product collections that tell their company's story.

As an early innovator in s-commerce, Instagram is changing the game for micro-moments with its simplified buying process. Brand dedication to optimising transactional micro-moments is exemplified by the strategically placed "Buy Now" button on its platform. This function shortens the time it takes from finding a product to paying for it with only one click. Reducing consumer effort and appealing to the impulsive nature of micro-moments is Instagram's strategy, and it dramatically boosts conversion rates. The platform's seamless user experience showcases the brand's keen awareness of how consumers make quick decisions and micro-moments' importance in motivating immediate actions (Jin & Ryu, 2020).

4.2. Success Stories and Strategies for Engaging Consumers Through Micro-Moments

In the process of analysing successful strategies for engaging customers through micro-moments, we uncover the complex methods that companies use to maximise the effectiveness of these transitory transactions that have a significant impact:

4.2.1 Content Personalization and Timely Responses

Sephora's mobile app exemplifies successful micro-moment engagement by utilising content techniques made just for the app. In order to cater to the specific interests of each individual customer, the brand creates individualised makeup tutorials, product recommendations, and bespoke beauty advice. Sephora creates a profound connection between its brand and its customers by providing them with meaningful and relevant content when they are looking for knowledge or inspiration. Underscoring the brand's mastery of micro-moment utilisation is the commitment to provide personalised content at crucial moments, which helps to cultivate a strong rapport with customers (Bilos et al., 2018).

4.2.2 Seamless Cross-Channel Experiences

Integration of micro-moments across numerous touchpoints is demonstrated by Domino's Pizza's "AnyWare" approach, which demonstrates the significance of this integration. Customers are allowed to place orders effortlessly across various platforms, including the company's website, mobile app, voice assistants, and social media channels, which is a convenient service offered by the brand. Regardless of the platform or device that is being utilised, this cross-channel integration emphasises convenience and instant gratification. Domino's Pizza caters to multidimensional micro-moments by providing simple interactions across various platforms (NCR, 2021). This enhances the convenience and engagement of the customer.

4.2.3 Contextual Targeting and Location-Based Offers

The "McDelivery" service offered by McDonald's uses location-based services and contextual targeting to provide customers with relevant offers prompted by their proximity to the restaurant's locations. By utilising location data, the company is able to ensure that promotions are timely and relevant, thereby capitalising on the moment when customers are most likely to engage with the brand. This intelligent strategy converts micro-moments into opportunities that may be taken advantage of, hence strengthening interactions between consumers and brands through the alignment of offers with immediate context (FasterCapital, 2023).

5. FUTURE TRENDS AND IMPLICATIONS

5.1. Predictions on the Evolution of Micro-Moments

Micro-moments weave a story of transformative transformations inside the sphere of social commerce, which is a tapestry that is constantly evolving. In order to envision the future tendencies of these moments, it is necessary to conduct a holistic investigation of the interaction between technology innovation, evolving consumer behaviours, and dynamic market forces. A close relationship exists between the development of Artificial Intelligence (AI) and Machine Learning (ML) and the path that micro-moments will take in the future (Sarker, 2021). With the help of these technical foundations, micro-moments will reach levels of hyper-personalization that have never been known before. In the future, artificial intelligence algorithms will go beyond simply comprehending consumers' preferences; they will also investigate feelings and intentions, enabling the creation of micro-interactions that are both finely tailored and emotionally resonant (Dwivedi et al., 2021). Micro-moment interactions will be elevated as a result of the continuous refining of machine learning models, which will ensure significantly improved accuracy, predictiveness, and contextual relevance.

The incorporation of technologies that fall under the Extended Reality (XR) umbrella, such as augmented reality (AR) and virtual reality (VR), holds the potential to reshape the structure of microcomments. These immersive solutions will easily bridge the gap between the digital and physical domains, bringing customers into lifelike situations where they may virtually try on items or sample products in simulated surroundings if they choose to do so. These kinds of immersive experiences will revolutionise micro-moments, giving customers the ability to make decisions that are both well-informed and emotionally resonant.

Technologies that are activated by voice and commerce that are conducted through conversation will transform the dynamics of micro-moments. Voice-enabled technology will be the driving force behind interfaces that will bring spontaneous micro-moments through interactions based on natural language. These conversational micro-moments will be presented by providing personalised recommendations, responding to inquiries, and smoothly facilitating transactions. Voice commerce is about to change the game regarding micro-interactions, making them more accessible and more convenient for users (Boland, 2018). A paradigm change is heralded by the development of micro-moments inside the fabric of social commerce. Technical advancements and the dynamic evolution of customer expectations are driving this shift. In the future, the landscape of micro-moments will revolve around hyper-personalisation, immersive experiences, contextual triggers, and conversational commerce. This is because artificial intelligence, augmented reality, the Internet of Things, and speech technologies continue their ascent. Not only will businesses that can accept these transformative waves be able to adapt to the constantly shifting landscape of social commerce, but they will also prosper in this environment.

5.2. Implications for Researchers

Theoretically, micro-moments in social commerce have far-reaching implications that encourage interdisciplinary study of consumer behaviour, digital transformation, and social connections, demonstrating the phenomenon's multidisciplinary character. How individual micro-moments shape the shared identity of online groups is a topic of sociological inquiry (Alsalemi et al., 2019). Scholars can deduce how fleeting moments of engagement impact the development of social relationships and the shape of virtual groups by analysing the structure of interactions within these communities. Future research can reveals the hidden mechanisms that cause micro-moments to either bring virtual communities together or drive them apart. From a psychological perspective, studying micro-moment-related triggers and cognition processes provides a wealth of interesting data for understanding decision-making behaviours in digital settings. Researchers investigate users' emotional reactions, cognitive heuristics, and attentional biases to understand how they react to micro-moments. Understanding how people engage with information and make decisions in the face of overwhelming stimuli can be solved by identifying these processes, which in turn improve our visibility into user engagement and satisfaction (Alistair Sutcliffe, 2022). Better campaign performance through micro-moment marketing and user-based experiences are both helped along by this psychological approach.

5.3. Implications for Businesses and Marketers

As a result of the proliferation of micro-moments inside social commerce, firms and marketers are experiencing a seismic upheaval in their mode of operation. Understanding these consequences is essential for organisations working towards the goal of releasing the unrealised potential of micro-moments to achieve sustained growth and acquire a competitive advantage. In order to accommodate the emergence of micro-moments, traditional consumer interaction paradigms will need to undergo a comprehensive reconstruction (PALMER, 2021). Businesses must shift away from rigid and predetermined campaigns to accommodate interactions driven by context and occur in real time (X. Wang et al., 2020). In order to cater to the specific whims and wishes revealed within these ephemeral seconds, marketers need to adopt a nimble mindset and modify their content and experiences to meet those specifications. When it comes to capitalising on the potential that micro-moments bring, achieving a seamless integration of customer intent and brand resonance is of the utmost importance.

The essence of hyper-personalisation becomes accentuated within the context of micro-moments. In order to orchestrate micro-interactions that are precisely tuned and personalised micro-interactions, businesses and marketers need to harness the power of data derived from consumer behaviour (Zhang et al., 2021). One of the most essential aspects of effective engagement tactics is the creation of content tightly aligned with specific targets' preferences and intentions. When it comes to the intensely competitive field of social commerce, pioneering firms will stand out from the crowd by providing personalised replies, context-driven triggers, and individualised recommendations. Due to advancements in micro-moments, businesses and marketers are about to see a paradigm shift in their customer engagement methods. It is necessary to take a flexible approach while developing omnichannel experiences to maintain the highest standards of ethical data practices. This is because the emphasis is placed on real-time, hyper-personalised interactions powered by artificial intelligence. Through adopting these implications, businesses are strengthened to negotiate the complexities of micro-moments, assuring their continued relevance and resonance in an era in which ephemeral interactions affect consumers' decisions. When it comes to social commerce, success consists of recognising and skillfully capitalising on these fleeting moments that have a significant influence.

5.4. Implications for Society and Individual Privacy

Many people and communities have been influenced by social e-commerce micro-moments and the overall digital revolution (Lysik et al., 2017). Due to these technological advancements, businesses and consumers can now interact in new and exciting ways, with the potential for targeted marketing campaigns and individualised customer experiences (Appel et al., 2020). Privacy and security of customer information are still major worries as businesses try to profile customers' habits by using state-of-the-art algorithms that analyse data instantly (Himeur et al., 2022). Broadly speaking, mainstream privacy standards and expectations are significantly impacted by the wide dissemination of micro-moments in social commerce. Interception and improper use of personally identifiable information are becoming more likely as the amount of consumer data provided by individuals continues to rise. This sparks a debate about the ethics of data use and the extent to which individuals can manage their digital footprint.

Social commerce's incorporation of micro-moments further blurs the lines between virtual and physical purchasing, destroying the original idea of privacy (Dwivedi et al., 2022). The more consumers' online and offline lives become intertwined, the more intrinsic the correlation between their brand interactions on social media and their offline lives becomes (C. L. Wang, 2021). The acquisition raises concerns about the surveillance economy and the commercialization of individual data. Businesses, lawmakers, and the general public must work together to establish robust regulatory frameworks that safeguard personal information while encouraging new ideas in order to address these issues. Initiatives aimed at increasing digital literacy and giving consumers more agency over their data will also contribute to a more equitable and open digital landscape (Pérez-Escolar & Canet, 2022).

REFERENCES

AbouElgheit, E. (2022). A 2020s Marketing Taxonomy for Augmented Reality Customer Experience. In *Transdisciplinarity*. Springer. doi:10.1007/978-3-030-94651-7_13

Adams, L., Burkholder, E., & Hamilton, K. (2015). Micro-Moments: Your Guide to Winning the Shift to Mobile. *Google*. https://www.thinkwithgoogle.com/marketing-strategies/micro-moments/micromoments-guide//micromoments- guide-pdf-download/

AIContentfy team. (2023a). *Micro-Moments and Your Marketing Strategy*. AIContentfy. https://aicontentfy.com/en/blog/micro-moments-and-marketing-strategy

AIContentfy team. (2023b). *The importance of considering cultural differences in global customer acquisition*. AIContentfy. https://aicontentfy.com/en/blog/importance-of-considering-cultural-differences-in-global-customer-acquisition

AIContentfy team. (2023c). *The Role of Micro-Moments in Your Marketing Strategy*. AIContentfy. https://aicontentfy.com/en/blog/role-of-micro-moments-in-marketing-strategy

Ajah, I. A., & Nweke, H. F. (2019). Big data and business analytics: Trends, platforms, success factors and applications. *Big Data and Cognitive Computing*, *3*(2), 1–30. doi:10.3390/bdcc3020032

Alsalemi, A., Sardianos, C., Bensaali, F., Varlamis, I., Amira, A., & Dimitrakopoulos, G. (2019). The Role of Micro-Moments: A Survey of Habitual Behavior Change and Recommender Systems for Energy Saving. *IEEE Systems Journal*, *13*(3), 3376–3387. doi:10.1109/JSYST.2019.2899832

Appel, G., Grewal, L., Hadi, R., & Stephen, A. T. (2020). The future of social media in marketing. *Journal of the Academy of Marketing Science*, *48*(1), 79–95. doi:10.1007/s11747-019-00695-1 PMID:32431463

Arora, N., Prashar, S., Parsad, C., & Tata, S. V. (2019). Influence of celebrity factors, consumer attitude and involvement on shoppers' purchase intention using hierarchical regression. *Decision (Washington, D.C.), 46*(3), 179–195. doi:10.1007/s40622-019-00208-7

Arora, N., Prashar, S., Vijay, T. S., & Parsad, C. (2022). A Consumer Typology Based on Celebrity Endorsement Factors. *FIIB Business Review*. https://doi.org/https://doi.org/10.1177/23197145221112749

Attar, R. W., Almusharraf, A., Alfawaz, A., & Hajli, N. (2022). New Trends in E-Commerce Research: Linking Social Commerce and Sharing Commerce: A Systematic Literature Review. *Sustainability (Basel), 14*(23), 16024. Advance online publication. doi:10.3390/su142316024

Attar, R. W., Shanmugam, M., & Hajli, N. (2021). Investigating the antecedents of e-commerce satisfaction in social commerce context. *British Food Journal, 123*(3), 849–868. doi:10.1108/BFJ-08-2020-0755

Atterby, M. (2023). Harnessing the power of micro-moments. *CXFOCUS*. https://www.cxfocus.com.au/marketing/harnessing-the-power-of-micro-moments/

Baykal, B. (2020). Generational Differences in Omnichannel Experience: Rising New Segment: Gen Z. In Managing Customer Experiences in an Omnichannel World: Melody of Online and Offline Environments in the Customer Journey (pp. 117–132). doi:10.1108/978-1-80043-388-520201011

Bertini, M., Ferracani, A., Papucci, R., & Del Bimbo, A. (2020). Keeping up with the Influencers: Improving User Recommendation in Instagram using Visual Content. *UMAP '20 Adjunct: Adjunct Publication of the 28th ACM Conference on User Modeling, Adaptation and Personalization*, 29–34. https://doi.org/https://doi.org/10.1145/3386392.3397594

Bilos, A., Turkalj, D., & Kelic, I. (2018). Micro-Moments of User Experience: An Approach To Understanding Online User Intentions and Behavior. *International Journal of Marketing Science, 1*(1), 57–67.

Boland, M. (2018). *Is Voice the Future of Local AR?* The VR/AR Association. https://www.thevrara.com/blog2/2018/4/3/is-voice-the-future-of-local-ar-voice-alexa-google-apple-siri-augmentedreality-streetfight

Bottary, L. (2019). *What Anyone Can Do How Surrounding Yourself with the Right People Will Drive Change, Opportunity, and Personal Growth*. https://www.routledge.com/What-Anyone-Can-Do-How-Surrounding-Yourself-with-the-Right-People-Will/Bottary/p/book/9781138558205

Bruce, J. (2019). *How Healthcare Marketers Can Leverage Micro-Moments*. Media Space Solutions. https://www.mediaspacesolutions.com/blog/how-healthcare-marketers-can-leverage-micro-moments

Busalim, A. H., & Hussin, A. R. C. (2016). Understanding social commerce: A systematic literature review and directions for further research. *International Journal of Information Management, 36*(6), 1075–1088. doi:10.1016/j.ijinfomgt.2016.06.005

Casemajor, C. (2023). *Strategies for Building Brand Awareness and a Competitive Edge in Social Media in a Cross-Field Industry*. Seinäjoki University of Applied Sciences. https://www.theseus.fi/bitstream/handle/10024/816469/Casemajor_Charline.pdf?sequence=2&isAllowed=y

Chakraborty, A., & Jain, V. (2022). Leveraging Digital Marketing and Integrated Marketing Communications for Brand Building in Emerging Markets. In O. Adeola, R. E. Hinson, & A. M. Sakkthivel (Eds.), *Marketing Communications and Brand Development in Emerging Economies* (Vol. I). Palgrave Macmillan. doi:10.1007/978-3-030-88678-3_13

Chen, J., Ramanathan, L., & Alazab, M. (2021). Holistic big data integrated artificial intelligent modeling to improve privacy and security in data management of smart cities. *Microprocessors and Microsystems, 81*(September 2020), 103722. doi:10.1016/j.micpro.2020.103722

Dalal, M. (2023). *Micro-moments: Key to winning customers in the digital age.* Yourstory. https://yourstory.com/2023/10/micro-moments-digital-success

David, S. (2023). *2023: How social commerce bridged the gap between brands and consumers.* Exchange4media. https://www.exchange4media.com/digital-news/2023-how-social-commerce-bridged-the-gap-between-brands-and-consumers-131335.html

Dwivedi, Y. K., Hughes, L., Baabdullah, A. M., Ribeiro-Navarrete, S., Giannakis, M., Al-Debei, M. M., Dennehy, D., Metri, B., Buhalis, D., Cheung, C. M. K., Conboy, K., Doyle, R., Dubey, R., Dutot, V., Felix, R., Goyal, D. P., Gustafsson, A., Hinsch, C., Jebabli, I., ... Wamba, S. F. (2022). Metaverse beyond the hype: Multidisciplinary perspectives on emerging challenges, opportunities, and agenda for research, practice and policy. *International Journal of Information Management, 66*(July), 102542. doi:10.1016/j.ijinfomgt.2022.102542

Dwivedi, Y. K., Ismagilova, E., Hughes, D. L., Carlson, J., Filieri, R., Jacobson, J., Jain, V., Karjaluoto, H., Kefi, H., Krishen, A. S., Kumar, V., Rahman, M. M., Raman, R., Rauschnabel, P. A., Rowley, J., Salo, J., Tran, G. A., & Wang, Y. (2021). Setting the future of digital and social media marketing research: Perspectives and research propositions. *International Journal of Information Management, 59*(May), 102168. doi:10.1016/j.ijinfomgt.2020.102168

Dwivedi, Y. K., Kshetri, N., Hughes, L., Slade, E. L., Jeyaraj, A., Kar, A. K., Baabdullah, A. M., Koohang, A., Raghavan, V., Ahuja, M., Albanna, H., Albashrawi, M. A., Al-Busaidi, A. S., Balakrishnan, J., Barlette, Y., Basu, S., Bose, I., Brooks, L., Buhalis, D., ... Wright, R. (2023). "So what if ChatGPT wrote it?" Multidisciplinary perspectives on opportunities, challenges and implications of generative conversational AI for research, practice and policy. *International Journal of Information Management, 71*(March), 102642. Advance online publication. doi:10.1016/j.ijinfomgt.2023.102642

FasterCapital. (2023). *Geographic segmentation: Targeting Local Markets: Enhancing Sales with Geographic Segmentation Software.* FasterCapital. https://fastercapital.com/content/Geographic-segmentation--Targeting-Local-Markets--Enhancing-Sales-with-Geographic-Segmentation-Software.html

Flavián, C., Ibáñez-Sánchez, S., & Orús, C. (2019). The impact of virtual, augmented and mixed reality technologies on the customer experience. *Journal of Business Research, 100*(November), 547–560. doi:10.1016/j.jbusres.2018.10.050

Flavián, C., Ibáñez-Sánchez, S., & Orús, C. (2021). Integrating virtual reality devices into the body: effects of technological embodiment on customer engagement and behavioral intentions toward the destination. In Future of Tourism Marketing. Routledge, Taylor & Francis Group. doi:10.4324/9781003176039-8

Gibreel, O., AlOtaibi, D. A., & Altmann, J. (2018). Social commerce development in emerging markets. *Electronic Commerce Research and Applications*, *27*(December), 152–162. doi:10.1016/j. elerap.2017.12.008

Glay, A. (2019). Real-Time Push Mobile Marketing Strategy: To What Extent does Time and Relevance Matter? *Proceedings of the Ninth International Conference on Engaged Management Scholarship*. https:// papers.ssrn.com/sol3/papers.cfm?abstract_id=3454052

Goldberg, M. H., & Gustafson, A. (2023). A Framework for Understanding the Effects of Strategic Communication Campaigns. *International Journal of Strategic Communication*, *17*(1), 1–20. Advance online publication. doi:10.1080/1553118X.2022.2137674

Grover, A., Arora, N., & Sharma, P. (2023a). Examining the Influence of HEXACO Personality Traits on Impulse Buying Tendency, Perceived Enjoyment, and Impulse Buying Behaviour in the Context of Instagram Commerce. *International Journal of Electronic Marketing and Retailing*. doi:10.1504/ IJEMR.2023.10054386

Grover, A., Arora, N., & Sharma, P. (2023b). Social Commerce and Metaverse in a New Virtual World: Exploring Women's Adoption Intentions. In Cultural Marketing and Metaverse for Consumer Engagement (p. 25). Academic Press.

Himeur, Y., Sohail, S. S., Bensaali, F., Amira, A., & Alazab, M. (2022). Latest trends of security and privacy in recommender systems: A comprehensive review and future perspectives. *Computers & Security*, *118*, 102746. doi:10.1016/j.cose.2022.102746

Hirshleifer, D., Levi, Y., Lourie, B., & Teoh, S. H. (2019). Decision fatigue and heuristic analyst forecasts. *Journal of Financial Economics*, *133*(1), 83–98. doi:10.1016/j.jfineco.2019.01.005

Huang, H., Gartner, G., Krisp, J. M., Raubal, M., & Van de Weghe, N. (2018). Location based services: Ongoing evolution and research agenda. *Journal of Location Based Services*, *12*(2), 63–93. doi:10.10 80/17489725.2018.1508763

Ifekanandu, C. C., Anene, J. N., & Iloka, C. B., & Ewuzie, C. O. (2023). Influence of Artificial Intelligence (Ai) on Customer Experience and Loyalty: Mediating Role of Personalization. *Journal of Data Acquisition and Processing*, *38*(3). Advance online publication. doi:10.5281/zenodo.98549423

Jin, S. V., & Ryu, E. (2020). "I'll buy what she's #wearing": The roles of envy toward and parasocial interaction with influencers in Instagram celebrity-based brand endorsement and social commerce. *Journal of Retailing and Consumer Services*, *55*(March), 102121. doi:10.1016/j.jretconser.2020.102121

Kahn, B. E. (2017). Using Visual Design to Improve Customer Perceptions of Online Assortments. *Journal of Retailing*, *93*(1), 29–42. doi:10.1016/j.jretai.2016.11.004

K.B. B. (2021). *Micro-Moment Marketing Using a Customer Data Platform*. Lemnisk. https://www. lemnisk.co/blog/micro-moment-marketing/

Korenkova, M., Maros, M., Levicky, M., & Fila, M. (2020). Consumer perception of modern and traditional forms of advertising. *Sustainability (Basel)*, *12*(23), 1–25. doi:10.3390/su12239996

Lăzăroiu, G., Neguriţă, O., Grecu, I., Grecu, G., & Mitran, P. C. (2020). Consumers' Decision-Making Process on Social Commerce Platforms: Online Trust, Perceived Risk, and Purchase Intentions. In Frontiers in Psychology (Vol. 11). doi:10.3389/fpsyg.2020.00890

Lineer, K. (2021). The transformative power of micro-moments. Norwegian University of Science and Technology. https://doi.org/ doi:10.1071/HCv10n2-ED1

Luna-Nevarez, C., & McGovern, E. (2021). The Rise of the Virtual Reality (VR) Marketplace: Exploring the Antecedents and Consequences of Consumer Attitudes toward V-Commerce. *Journal of Internet Commerce*, *20*(2), 167–194. doi:10.1080/15332861.2021.1875766

Lysik, L., Lopacinski, K., Kutera, R., & Machura, P. (2017). Strategic Role of Consumer Moments of Truth: A Marketing Challenge in Mobile Communities. In *Analyzing the Strategic Role of Social Networking in Firm Growth and Productivity*. IGI Global. doi:10.4018/978-1-5225-0559-4.ch002

Majid, S., Lopez, C., Megicks, P., & Lim, W. M. (2019). Developing effective social media messages: Insights from an exploratory study of industry experts. *Psychology and Marketing*, *36*(6), 551–564. doi:10.1002/mar.21196

Matr, C. A. (2022). *An empirical study of customer satisfaction in the Italian railway industry: a focus on IBM case study*. LUISS.

Micro-Moments: The Rising Trend in Digital Marketing. (2023). Talking Stick Digital. https://talking-stickdigital.com/micro-moments-the-rising-trend-in-digital-marketing/

Mocanu, R. (2020). The Expanding Role of Customer Knowledge Management and Brand Experience during the Pandemic Crisis. *Management Dynamics in the Knowledge Economy*, *8*(4), 357–369. https://www.ceeol.com/search/article-detail?id=943533. doi:10.2478/mdke-2020-0023

Moon, S. (2017). *Starbuck AI-powered customer experience*. The Data Hunt. https://www.thedatahunt.com/en-insight/starbucks-ai-customer-experience

NCR. (2021). *The digital innovations that took Domino's from pizza place to tech titan*. NCR VOYIX. https://www.ncr.com/blogs/restaurants/digital-innovations-dominos

Palalas, A. (2017). Mindfulness in Mobile and Ubiquitous Learning: Harnessing the Power of Attention. *Perspectives on Rethinking and Reforming Education*. https://doi.org/https://doi.org/10.1007/978-981-10-6144-8_2

Palmer, M. (2021). *What Your Customer Wants and Can't Tell You: Unlocking Consumer Brains with the Science of Behavioral Economics Library*. Mango Publishing Group.

Pérez-Escolar, M., & Canet, F. (2022). Research on vulnerable people and digital inclusion: Toward a consolidated taxonomical framework. *Universal Access in the Information Society*, *22*(3), 1059–1072. doi:10.1007/s10209-022-00867-x PMID:35125988

Porter, S. (2023). *How X has become a key customer support channel*. https://business.twitter.com/en/blog/how-twitter-has-become-a-key-customer-support-channel.html

Sanyal, A. (2022). *Micro-Moment Engagement: A sure way to creating "Aha!" moments and winning customers.* ETBrandEquity. https://brandequity.economictimes.indiatimes.com/blog/micro-moment-engagement-a-sure-way-to-creating-aha-moments-and-winning-customers/90480802

Sarker, I. H. (2021). Machine Learning: Algorithms, Real-World Applications and Research Directions. *SN Computer Science, 2*(3), 1–21. doi:10.1007/s42979-021-00592-x PMID:33778771

Scolere, L. (2023). Connected Design Learning: Aspiring Designers, Pinterest, and Social Media Literacy. *Journal of Interior Design, 48*(3), 191–206. doi:10.1177/10717641231184214

Sela, R. (2023). *What Are Micro-Moments, and How to Leverage Them for Conversion?* https://www.ronsela.com/micro-moments/

Sheikh, Z., Yezheng, L., Islam, T., Hameed, Z., & Khan, I. U. (2019). Impact of social commerce constructs and social support on social commerce intentions. *Information Technology & People, 32*(1), 68–93. doi:10.1108/ITP-04-2018-0195

Snegirjova, M., & Tuomisto, F. (2017). *Micro-Moments: New Context in Information System Success Theory.* Norwegian School of Economics. https://openaccess.nhh.no/nhh-xmlui/bitstream/handle/11250/2456061/masterthesis.PDF?sequence=1

Some, K. (2019). *Starbucks Relies on AI Powered Customer Insights to Drive Growth.* Analytics Insight. https://www.analyticsinsight.net/starbucks-relies-on-ai-powered-customer-insights-to-drive-growth/

Stafford, T. F., & Duong, B. Q. (2023). Social Media in Emerging Economies: A Cross-Cultural Comparison. *IEEE Transactions on Computational Social Systems, 10*(3), 1160–1178. doi:10.1109/TCSS.2022.3169412

Sutcliffe, A. (2022). *Designing for User Engagement Aesthetic and Attractive User Interfaces.* Morgan & Claypool Publishers.

Verhoef, P. C., Broekhuizen, T., Bart, Y., Bhattacharya, A., & Dong, Q. (2019, November). Digital transformation: A multidisciplinary reflection and research agenda. *Journal of Business Research, 122*, 889–901. doi:10.1016/j.jbusres.2019.09.022

Wang, C. L. (2021). New frontiers and future directions in interactive marketing: Inaugural Editorial. *Journal of Research in Interactive Marketing, 15*(1), 1–9. doi:10.1108/JRIM-03-2021-270

Wang, X., Tajvidi, M., Lin, X., & Hajli, N. (2020). Towards an Ethical and Trustworthy Social Commerce Community for Brand Value Co-creation: A trust-Commitment Perspective. *Journal of Business Ethics, 167*(1), 137–152. doi:10.1007/s10551-019-04182-z

Zhang, Q., Lu, J., & Jin, Y. (2021). Artificial intelligence in recommender systems. *Complex & Intelligent Systems, 7*(1), 439–457. doi:10.1007/s40747-020-00212-w

Chapter 3
Data–Driven Insights:
The Power of Genetic Information in Precision Marketing

Nitesh Behare

https://orcid.org/0000-0002-9338-8563

Balaji Institute of International Business, Sri Balaji University, Pune, India

Rashmi D. Mahajan

https://orcid.org/0000-0001-9082-6874

Balaji Institute of International Business, Sri Balaji University, Pune, India

Ashish Mohture

https://orcid.org/0000-0002-5123-0880

Institute of Management and Research, Chatrapati Sambhaji Nagar, India

Shrikant Waghulkar

https://orcid.org/0000-0002-3767-3765

Arihant Institute of Business Management, India

Shubhada Nitesh Behare

Independent Researcher, India

Vinayak Shitole

https://orcid.org/0000-0002-5488-6543

Arihant Institute of Business Management, India

Anandrao Bhanudas Dadas

https://orcid.org/0009-0000-0647-5953

Neville Wadia Institute of Management Studies and Research, Pune, India

ABSTRACT

This chapter delves into the transformative influence of genetic information on precision marketing, exploring the opportunities and challenges it presents. Beginning with an overview of precision marketing and its evolution towards personalization, the chapter examines the types and methods of collecting genetic data for marketing purposes. It highlights the immense potential for personalized product recommendations, targeted advertising, and enhanced customer experiences. However, the exploration does not shy away from addressing the ethical considerations and challenges associated with privacy, consent, and the potential societal impact of genetic data usage. Best practices for responsible data management and compliance with evolving regulatory frameworks are discussed, ensuring a balanced approach between personalization and ethical considerations. The chapter concludes by peering into the future, exploring emerging technologies and anticipated trends that will further shape the landscape of precision marketing with genetic insights.

DOI: 10.4018/979-8-3693-2367-0.ch003

1. INTRODUCTION

In the dynamic landscape of contemporary marketing, the fusion of advanced technologies and data-driven insights has ushered in a new era known as precision marketing. Precision marketing, at its core, is a strategic approach that leverages data and technology to precisely target and engage specific audiences (Porter, 2022). By understanding the unique attributes, behaviours, and preferences of individual consumers, companies can tailor their marketing efforts with unprecedented precision. This precision not only enhances the efficiency of marketing campaigns but also fosters a more personalized and meaningful connection between brands and consumers (Dunham, 2023). The foundation of precision marketing rests on data-driven insights, where vast amounts of information are analysed to discern patterns, trends, and correlations. This analytical prowess allows marketers to move beyond traditional demographics and delve into the realm of psychographics, understanding the intricate motivations and aspirations that drive consumer behaviour. With the advent of sophisticated data analytics tools, marketers can now harness the power of big data to gain a nuanced understanding of their target audience (Porter, 2022).

The evolution of marketing strategies toward personalization is a key aspect driving the ascendancy of precision marketing (Pedersen, 2023). In the not-so-distant past, marketing efforts primarily relied on broad strokes, catering to general audience segments based on age, gender, and location (Belliappa, 2023). However, as consumers became increasingly inundated with a barrage of generic messages, the need for a more personalized approach became evident. This shift is underscored by the recognition that consumers, now more than ever, seek relevance and authenticity in their interactions with brands (Park, et al., 24). As marketing strategies evolve, the focus has shifted from mass communication to individualized engagement. Personalization is no longer just a buzzword; it is a strategic imperative. Genetic information, with its unique ability to unravel the intricacies of an individual's predispositions and susceptibilities, emerges as a potent tool in this pursuit of personalization. By integrating genetic data into the precision marketing framework, businesses can unlock a deeper understanding of consumer preferences and tailor their messaging with unparalleled precision (Daviet, Wind, & Nave, Genetic Data: Potential Uses and Misuses in Marketing, 2020).

2. GENETIC INFORMATION IN MARKETING

2.1. Definition and Roll of Genetic Information in Marketing

Genetic information in marketing refers to data derived from an individual's genetic code, encompassing traits, predispositions, and susceptibilities (Commission, 2022). This information plays a pivotal role in precision marketing by offering unprecedented insights into consumer behaviors, preferences, and health considerations (Retailer, 2021). By leveraging genetic data, marketers can tailor their strategies with unparalleled precision, delivering personalized messages that resonate on a deeper level with consumers. Understanding genetic predispositions allows for targeted product recommendations, health-related offerings, and lifestyle suggestions, enhancing the relevance and effectiveness of marketing campaigns (Reversedout, 2023). However, the integration of genetic information raises ethical considerations, requiring careful navigation of privacy concerns and transparent communication with consumers (Kisselburgh & Beever, 2022). As technology advances, the roll-out of genetic information in marketing signifies a transformative shift towards a more individualized and ethical approach, aiming to forge meaningful connections between brands and consumers.

Genetic information includes information about an individual's genetic tests and the genetic tests of an individual's family members, as well as information about the manifestation of a disease or disorder in an individual's family members (i.e. family medical history) (Commission, 2022).

2.2. Types of Genetic Information Used in Targeted Marketing

Genetic information used in marketing comprises of different types of data, each offering give insights into individual characteristics and preferences. This significant genetic information serves as the base for personalized marketing strategies, enabling brands to customize their products, services and marketing communications to reverberate more profoundly with consumers on a highly personalized level. In the targeted marketing campaigns, the integration of varied genetic information offers a chance to the marketers to personalize their offerings, strategies and communication methods, eventually enhancing efficacy, relevance and customer engagement. However, it is important for marketers to prioritize user consent, ethical considerations and data protection when integrating genetic data into marketing initiatives. These principles are derived from observations within the direct-to-consumer genetic testing industry and the fusion of genetic insights into marketing strategies.

Among the common types of genetic information used in marketing are:

2.2.1. Health-Related Genetic Data

This includes information about an individual's genetic predispositions to certain health conditions, such as susceptibility to heart disease, diabetes, or cancer. Marketers may use this data to promote products or services tailored to specific health concerns, such as wellness programs, health insurance plans, or preventive healthcare screenings (Lefebre, Salgaonkar, Willwerth-Pascutiu, & Zimmerman, 2019).

2.2.2. Nutritional Genetics

Nutritional genetic data provides insights into how individuals metabolize nutrients, their dietary preferences, and potential sensitivities or intolerances. Marketers can leverage this information to promote personalized nutrition plans, dietary supplements, or food products tailored to individuals' genetic profiles (Accardi & Aiello, 2021).

2.2.3. Fitness-Related Genetic Data

Genetic data related to fitness and exercise includes information about muscle composition, metabolism, and injury risk. Marketers may use this data to tailor fitness programs, workout routines, or sports equipment recommendations to match individuals' genetic predispositions and fitness goals (Bouchard, Rankinen, & Timmons, 2011).

2.2.4. Skin and Beauty Genetics

Genetic information related to skin characteristics, aging, and sensitivity can inform personalized skincare and beauty recommendations. Marketers may promote skincare products, cosmetics, or aesthetic treatments tailored to individuals' genetic profiles, addressing specific skin concerns or preferences (Makrantonaki, Bekou, & Zouboulis, 2012).

2.2.5. Behavioral Genetics

Behavioral genetic data provides insights into personality traits, cognitive abilities, and preferences for certain activities or experiences. Marketers can use this information to customize advertising messages, product recommendations, or experiential offerings that resonate with individuals' genetic predispositions and lifestyle preferences (Vedantu, 2022).

2.2.6. Ancestry and Heritage Genetics

Ancestry genetic data reveals insights into individuals' ethnic origins, ancestral migrations, and genetic heritage. Marketers may incorporate ancestry information into advertising campaigns, cultural events, or heritage-based products that celebrate diversity and cultural connections (Jorde & Bamshad, 2020).

2.2.7. Pharmacogenetics

Pharmacogenetic data relates to how individuals respond to medications based on their genetic makeup. Marketers in the pharmaceutical industry may utilize pharmacogenetic insights to promote personalized medicine or targeted drug therapies tailored to individuals' genetic profiles and medical histories (CDC, 2022).

2.2.8. Genetic Variants for Segmentation and Targeting

Businesses leverage genetic variants as foundational elements for segmentation and targeting within their marketing strategies. By identifying specific genetic markers, companies can tailor their campaigns to reach distinct consumer segments more effectively (Daviet, Wind, & Nave, Genetic Data: Potential Uses and Misuses in Marketing, 2020)..

2.2.9. Community and Personalization

Through innovative applications of genetic data, marketers aim to cultivate a sense of community and personalize consumer experiences. By incorporating genetic information into their messaging, brands seek to establish deeper connections with their target audience, enhancing brand loyalty and engagement (Daviet, Wind, & Nave, Genetic Data: Potential Uses and Misuses in Marketing, 2020).

2.2.10. Genetically Informed Study Designs

Genetic data plays a pivotal role in designing research studies aimed at testing causal relationships and refining consumer theories. By analyzing genetic factors underlying behavior, marketers gain valuable insights into consumer preferences and decision-making processes, enabling them to develop more targeted and effective marketing strategies (Daviet, Wind, & Nave, Genetic Data: Potential Uses and Misuses in Marketing, 2020).

2.2.11. Environmental and Functional Information

Marketers categorize genetic information into functional and environmental cues to align with consumers' diverse information-processing mechanisms. By tailoring marketing messages to match consumers' specific preferences and needs, companies can influence purchase intentions and drive sales more effectively (Jiang & Zhang, 2021).

Overall, the integration of genetic information into marketing campaigns underscores the importance of personalized targeting and consumer engagement. However, this practice also raises ethical concerns surrounding privacy, consent, and potential misuse of genetic data, highlighting the need for robust regulatory frameworks to safeguard consumer rights and interests.

2.3. Methods of Collecting and Analysing Genetic Data for Marketing Purposes

Collecting and analysing genetic data for marketing purposes involves several methods, each with its own set of considerations. It's crucial to approach these methods ethically and ensure compliance with privacy regulations.

Methods of collecting Genetic Data

2.3.1. Here Are Common Methods Used to Collect Genetic Data for Marketing

Direct-to-Consumer Genetic Testing (DTC): Companies offer genetic testing kits directly to consumers, allowing them to submit DNA samples for analysis. These kits typically focus on ancestry, health traits, or both. Marketers may partner with DTC genetic testing companies to access aggregated and anonymized data for targeted campaigns (Remi, Gideon, & Wind, 2022) (Bermseok, 2019).

Partnerships with Genetic Testing Services: Marketers may collaborate with established genetic testing services to access aggregated data. These partnerships can be structured to ensure data privacy and compliance with relevant regulations (Kayte, Amanda, Chris, Erica, & Scott, 2019).

Customer Surveys and Questionnaires: Gathering genetic information through surveys and questionnaires allows marketers to collect self-reported data on traits, health history, and preferences. While this method relies on individuals' willingness to share information, it may provide valuable insights (Buiten, 2021).

Integration with Health and Wellness Apps: Marketers can collaborate with health and wellness applications that incorporate genetic data into their platforms. Users willingly share genetic information for personalized health and lifestyle recommendations, offering marketers a targeted audience for relevant products (Katelyn, Stephen, & Walker, 2023).

Research Collaborations: Marketing teams may partner with scientific research initiatives focused on genetics. By participating in or sponsoring studies, marketers can gain access to valuable insights while contributing to scientific advancements (Kayte, Amanda, Chris, Erica, & Scott, 2019).

Social Media Analysis: Analysing publicly available genetic information shared on social media platforms can offer marketers insights into trends, preferences, and behaviours. However, privacy concerns and ethical considerations must be carefully navigated (Ruhl, Hazel, Clayton, & Malin, 2019) (Buiten, 2021).

In-House Genetic Testing Initiatives: Some companies may opt to conduct their own genetic testing initiatives, either through partnerships with genetic testing laboratories or by building in-house capabilities. This approach requires careful adherence to privacy and ethical standards (Kelly, Wyatt, & Anna, 2018).

2.3.2. Analysing Genetic Data for Marketing Strategies

For data analysis, innovative approaches like 'fuzzy techniques', have been proposed in genetic research, signifying probable applications in marketing practices. When integrating genetic into consumer behaviour theory, offers opportunities for filtering marketing strategies, segmentation and targeting based on genetic variants, and introducing biological mechanisms driving consumer behaviour.

Utilization of Genetic Algorithms: Employing genetic algorithms for market basket analysis has facilitated a more precise mapping of product preferences among consumers, aiding retailers in optimizing merchandising and category management for heightened profitability. By analysing patterns in consumer purchasing behaviour derived from genetic data, businesses can tailor their product offerings and promotional strategies to better meet the needs and preferences of specific customer segments (Daviet, Wind, & Nave, Genetic Data: Potential Uses and Misuses in Marketing, 2020)..

Segmentation and Targeting: Genetic data serves as a foundation for segmentation and targeting within marketing strategies, allowing for customization of products and services tailored to specific consumer groups based on genetic variants. This targeted approach enables businesses to create more personalized marketing campaigns that resonate with consumers on a deeper level, increasing the likelihood of engagement and conversion (Daviet, Wind, & Nave, Genetic Data: Potential Uses and Misuses in Marketing, 2020).

Creative Personalization: Genetic insights enable the development of personalized marketing approaches, fostering a sense of community and individualized experiences for consumers. By leveraging genetic data to understand consumer preferences and behaviors, brands can create marketing content and experiences that speak directly to the unique characteristics of their target audience, strengthening brand loyalty and customer satisfaction (Daviet, Wind, & Nave, Genetic Data: Potential Uses and Misuses in Marketing, 2020)..

Genetically Informed Study Designs: By informing study designs, genetic data aids in exploring causal relationships in marketing research, providing invaluable insights into consumer behavior and preferences. By incorporating genetic variables into research methodologies, marketers can gain a deeper understanding of the underlying biological factors that influence consumer decision-making, allowing for more accurate predictions and informed marketing strategies (Daviet, Wind, & Nave, Genetic Data: Potential Uses and Misuses in Marketing, 2020).

Figure 1. Genetic data analysis (ScopusAI generated)

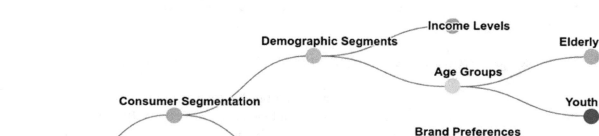

Integrating genetic data into marketing strategies not only improve logical understanding but also advances ethical considerations concerning privacy and discrimination. There are many potential challenges in this integration which include concern over potential misuse of consumer health data and the ethical implications of consent and privacy. Nonetheless, the potential benefits incorporate enhanced community building, personalization and scientific progress across diverse communities (Daviet, Nave, & Wind, 2020). As business navigate the intricacies of including genetic data into their strategies, it is crucial to highlight ethical considerations and obey regulatory guidelines to ensure consumer trust and protection of privacy rights.

Once genetic data is collected, by using advanced data analytics techniques, such as machine learning and statistical modelling, relevant meaningful insights can be drawn. The purpose of this analysis is to identify patterns, correlations and trends that can inform targeted marketing strategies while respecting individuals' privacy and adhering to legal and ethical guidelines. It is essential for marketers to be transparent about data usage, obtain informed consent, and prioritize the security of genetic information to build and maintain trust with consumers (Farmer, 2022).

3. OPPORTUNITIES IN PRECISION MARKETING WITH GENETIC INSIGHTS

Unlocking a new frontier in marketing, precision marketing fuelled by genetic insights presents unparalleled opportunities for businesses. By delving into the intricacies of individual genetic codes, marketers can tailor strategies with unprecedented precision, offering personalized products and experiences that resonate on a deeply individual level. From health and wellness recommendations to curated lifestyle offerings, the fusion of genetic insights and precision marketing opens doors to a realm where campaigns are not just targeted but anticipatory (CDC, 2022). Following are some of the opportunities that arise when businesses harness the power of genetic information for a more nuanced and effective approach to precision marketing.

3.1. Personalized Product Recommendations Based on Genetic Traits

The era of precision marketing has ushered in a ground-breaking approach to personalized product recommendations, leveraging insights derived from an individual's genetic traits. By analysing genetic data, businesses can discern unique characteristics and preferences, enabling them to curate offerings that align seamlessly with a consumer's biological predispositions. For instance, in the beauty industry, personalized skincare formulations can be tailored to address specific genetic factors such as skin type and aging markers (Xiaoran, Chih-Han, & Maria, 2020). In the realm of nutrition, food products can be recommended based on genetic metabolism traits, ensuring a personalized dietary experience (Szakály, et al., 2021).

This hyper-personalization extends beyond conventional demographics, offering consumers a bespoke shopping journey that resonates with their intrinsic attributes. The intersection of genetic insights and product recommendations (Bushra, Yousef, & Ayoub, 2020) not only enhances customer satisfaction but also fosters brand loyalty by demonstrating a commitment to individual well-being and preferences. As technology advances, the potential for even more refined and anticipatory recommendations grows, marking a paradigm shift towards a future where each product suggestion is uniquely crafted based on the intricate details encoded in an individual's genetic makeup. The amalgamation of genetic insights and personalized recommendations is not just a marketing strategy; it represents a transformative approach that elevates the consumer experience to unprecedented heights (Pérez-Beltrán, et al., 2022).

3.2. Tailored Advertising and Messaging for Specific Consumer Segments

Tailored advertising and messaging for specific consumer segments represents the pinnacle of precision marketing, where communication transcends the generic and resonates intimately with individual audiences (Červenka, Naščakova, Bednarova, Daneshjo, & Dudaš-Pajerska, 2018). By leveraging sophisticated data analytics, businesses can dissect consumer behaviour, preferences, and demographics to create highly targeted campaigns. This approach ensures that each message is meticulously crafted to appeal to the unique characteristics and interests of a specific segment, whether defined by age, location, lifestyle, or other parameters (Okolnishnikova, Greyz, Yulia, & Katochkov, 2018).

In the age of personalized advertising, content becomes a personalized experience, addressing the specific needs and desires of the intended audience. From personalized product recommendations to location-based promotions, tailored advertising goes beyond a one-size-fits-all approach, fostering a deeper connection between the brand and the consumer. This precision not only enhances the effectiveness of marketing efforts but also cultivates a sense of individual recognition and relevance (Okolnishnikova, Greyz, Yulia, & Katochkov, 2018), (Adogy, 2023).

The evolution of technology, including artificial intelligence and machine learning, further refines this process, allowing for real-time adjustments and dynamic personalization based on user interactions. As businesses continue to navigate the landscape of tailored advertising, the emphasis on understanding and adapting to the diverse needs of distinct consumer segments remains paramount, ushering in an era where each advertisement becomes a bespoke message tailored to resonate uniquely with its intended audience.

3.3. Enhancing Customer Experience Through Targeted Promotions

Enhancing customer experience through targeted promotions has become a cornerstone of successful marketing strategies. By leveraging data analytics and consumer insights, businesses can craft promotions that resonate specifically with their target audience, creating a more personalized and engaging experience. Targeted promotions go beyond generic offers, tailoring discounts, incentives, and product recommendations to align seamlessly with individual preferences and behaviours (Schindler, Lala, & Taylor, 2021).

This approach not only captures the attention of consumers but also fosters a sense of appreciation and relevance. When customers receive promotions that align with their needs and interests, it creates a positive and memorable interaction with the brand (Mommejat, 2020). For instance, e-commerce platforms can employ targeted promotions based on previous purchase history, offering discounts on complementary products or exclusive deals to loyal customers. Moreover, the advent of technology allows for real-time personalization, enabling businesses to adjust promotions dynamically based on user interactions and feedback. By delivering timely and relevant promotions, companies not only drive customer loyalty but also increase the likelihood of conversion (Masood & Hasyagar, 2020). The emphasis on enhancing the customer experience through targeted promotions reflects a strategic commitment to understanding and addressing the unique needs of individual consumers, fostering lasting connections and brand affinity in an increasingly competitive market (Cervenka., Naščáková, Bednarova, Daneshjo, & Dudas-Pajerska, 2018).

4. CHALLENGES AND ETHICAL CONSIDERATIONS

Navigating the landscape of precision marketing with genetic insights brings forth a myriad of challenges and ethical considerations. As businesses delve into the intricacies of consumer genetic data, questions arise about privacy, consent, and responsible use (Vries, et al., 2011). Balancing the quest for personalized marketing with safeguarding individual rights requires a delicate approach. Striking the right ethical chord is crucial to building trust with consumers, ensuring transparency in data practices, and addressing potential biases (Daviet, Wind, & Nave, Genetic Data: Potential Uses and Misuses in Marketing, 2020).

4.1. Privacy Concerns Associated With Genetic Data

The integration of genetic data in precision marketing raises profound privacy concerns, stemming from the uniquely personal and sensitive nature of this information. Genetic data encompasses an individual's predispositions, health markers, and familial connections, making it exceptionally private. As businesses delve into personalized marketing strategies, the risk of unauthorized access, data breaches, or inadvertent disclosure amplifies, posing a threat to the confidentiality of genetic profiles (Johanna, Genetic data are not always personal - disaggregating the identifiability and sensitivity of genetic data, 2023).

Privacy concerns extend beyond mere data security. The potential for unintended consequences, such as identity theft or misuse of genetic information for discriminatory purposes, further intensifies the ethical implications (Buiten, 2021). Consumers are rightfully apprehensive about the prospect of their genetic data being exploited without their knowledge or consent, necessitating stringent safeguards and transparent practices (Daviet, Wind, & Nave, Genetic Data: Potential Uses and Misuses in Marketing, 2020).

Striking a delicate balance between leveraging genetic data for targeted marketing and ensuring the privacy of individuals demands comprehensive legal frameworks, robust encryption measures, and a commitment to ethical data handling practices. As the marketing landscape evolves, addressing these privacy concerns becomes imperative for businesses seeking to harness the transformative power of genetic insights while respecting the fundamental right to privacy (Martinez-Martin & Magnus, 2020).

4.2. Informed Consent and Transparency in Genetic Information Usage

In the domain of precision marketing with genetic information, the ethical principles of informed consent and transparency emerge as foundational pillars. Informed consent involves obtaining explicit permission from individuals before collecting, analysing, or utilizing their genetic data for marketing purposes (Matt, Doug, & Severiche, 2023). This process requires businesses to communicate clearly, providing comprehensive information about the nature of data usage, potential risks, and the specific purposes for which the data will be employed (Bunnik, Janssens, & Schermer, 2014).

Transparency, on the other hand, emphasizes open communication about how genetic information will be used in marketing strategies. This includes disclosing the mechanisms of data analysis, the types of personalized marketing initiatives planned, and the measures in place to ensure data security. Transparent practices build trust between businesses and consumers, empowering individuals to make informed decisions about sharing their genetic data (Alan, Lee, & S.VanDyke, 2022).

Respecting informed consent and transparency is not only an ethical imperative but also a strategic necessity. Establishing clear communication channels and ethical guidelines ensures that consumers feel confident in sharing their genetic information, fostering a positive and trusting relationship (Arianna & Gabriele, 2020). This ethical framework is essential in navigating the intricate landscape where personalized marketing intersects with the sensitive realm of genetic insights (Niemie, Howard, Sterckx, Cockbain, & Prainsack, 2020).

4.3. Potential for Discrimination and Societal Implications

As precision marketing integrates genetic insights, a critical concern emerges regarding the potential for discrimination and its broader societal implications. Targeted advertising based on genetic data has the inherent risk of exacerbating societal divisions, reinforcing biases, and fostering discrimination on various fronts (LB, JE, & Holtzman, 1994).

a) *Discrimination in Marketing:* Precision marketing runs the risk of inadvertently perpetuating stereotypes or biases based on genetic traits. Targeted advertisements, if not carefully curated, could lead to exclusionary practices, limiting opportunities for certain segments of the population (Daviet, Wind, & Nave, Genetic Data: Potential Uses and Misuses in Marketing, 2020). This raises ethical questions about fairness, inclusivity, and the unintended consequences of personalized marketing strategies (Cowart & Darke, 2014).

b) ***Health Discrimination:*** Utilizing genetic data for health-related marketing may inadvertently result in discrimination based on predispositions to certain medical conditions (Daviet, Wind, & Nave, Genetic Data: Potential Uses and Misuses in Marketing, 2020). Individuals could face differential treatment in areas such as insurance coverage, employment opportunities, or even social interactions, amplifying ethical concerns around the potential stigmatization of individuals with specific genetic traits (Emilia, Kalokairinou, & Carmen, 2017).

c) ***Reinforcing Socioeconomic Divides:*** Precision marketing, if not ethically managed, might reinforce existing socioeconomic divides. Affluent individuals with access to genetic testing may receive more tailored and advantageous marketing offers, further marginalizing those without such access (Dinulos & Vallee, 2020). This exacerbates inequality and raises questions about the ethical implications of catering marketing efforts primarily to certain demographics (Daviet, Wind, & Nave, Genetic Data: Potential Uses and Misuses in Marketing, 2020).

d) ***Inclusivity and Ethical Guidelines:*** To mitigate the potential for discrimination, it is imperative for businesses to establish ethical guidelines that prioritize inclusivity (Daviet, Wind, & Nave, 2020). This involves a proactive approach in ensuring that precision marketing efforts contribute positively to societal well-being without inadvertently perpetuating biases or exacerbating existing inequalities.

5. BEST PRACTICES IN PRECISION MARKETING WITH GENETIC DATA

In the dynamic landscape of precision marketing, the integration of genetic data has opened new frontiers, offering businesses unprecedented opportunities to tailor their strategies with unparalleled precision. However, as this intersection evolves, the need for best practices in navigating the complexities of genetic data becomes paramount (Nasr, 2024). From ensuring informed consent and prioritizing privacy to addressing the potential for discrimination, businesses must adopt a principled approach. We explore the best practices that empower marketers to harness the transformative potential of genetic information responsibly, fostering trust, transparency, and meaningful connections with consumers (Kadiri, 2022).

5.1. Responsible Data Management and Protection

In the realm of precision marketing with genetic data, responsible data management and protection form the cornerstone of ethical practices. To navigate this intricate landscape, businesses must prioritize stringent measures to safeguard the confidentiality and integrity of genetic information (Chakraborty, 2021).

Data Encryption and Security Protocols: Implementing robust encryption techniques and security protocols is paramount to shield genetic data from unauthorized access. By adopting state-of-the-art technologies, businesses can fortify their databases, ensuring that sensitive genetic information remains confidential and protected against cyber threats (Sila, 2023).

Compliance with Privacy Regulations: Responsible data management involves unwavering compliance with privacy regulations and legal frameworks. Businesses must stay abreast of evolving laws related to genetic data and precision marketing, ensuring that their practices align with the highest standards of privacy protection and legal compliance (Tamrakar, 2023).

Limited Access and Transparent Usage Policies: Limiting access to genetic data strictly to individuals involved in precision marketing initiatives is essential. Establishing transparent usage policies ensures that only authorized personnel handle this sensitive information, minimizing the risk of data breaches or misuse. Clear communication with consumers about how their data will be utilized fosters trust and reinforces responsible practices (Clayton, Evans, Hazel, & Rothstein, 2019).

Regular Audits and Monitoring: Conducting regular audits and monitoring procedures allows businesses to proactively identify and address any vulnerabilities in their data management systems. This continuous evaluation ensures that security measures remain robust, providing a proactive defence against potential threats to genetic data integrity (Clayton, Evans, Hazel, & Rothstein, 2019).

Ethical Use of Data Analytics: Businesses should embrace ethical principles in the use of data analytics, employing methodologies that prioritize the anonymization and aggregation of genetic data. This approach minimizes the risk of individual identification while still extracting valuable insights for precision marketing strategies (Clayton, Evans, Hazel, & Rothstein, 2019).

By adhering to these best practices in responsible data management and protection, businesses can navigate the ethical considerations surrounding genetic data in precision marketing, fostering a secure environment that upholds consumer trust and privacy.

5.2. Strategies for Building and Maintaining Consumer Trust

In the emerging field of precision marketing with genetic data, building and maintaining consumer trust is essential for ethical and sustainable business practices. Employing transparent strategies that prioritize the well-being and privacy of individuals strengthens the bond between businesses and consumers. To ensure the secure storage and responsible handling of genetic data collected for precision marketing purposes, companies can implement the following measures, supported by insights from the provided abstracts:

Clear Communication and Informed Consent: Initiate trust-building through clear and transparent communication. Prioritize comprehensive explanations about the collection and use of genetic data, ensuring that consumers provide informed consent willingly. By fostering understanding, businesses empower individuals to make informed decisions about sharing their genetic information for personalized marketing (McGuire, 2023).

Data Security Assurance: Assure consumers of robust data security measures in place to protect their genetic information. Clearly communicate encryption protocols, security practices, and compliance with relevant privacy regulations. This assurance reinforces the commitment to safeguarding sensitive data, fostering confidence in consumers regarding the responsible handling of their genetic insights (Theodore & Schoop, 2015).

Education and Empowerment: Educate consumers about the benefits and potential risks associated with precision marketing. Provide resources and information to empower individuals in understanding how their genetic data contributes to personalized experiences. Transparently showcase how data-driven insights enhance the relevance and value of marketing interactions, emphasizing the consumer's control over their data (FasterCapital, Understanding Personalized Experiences In Marketing, 2021).

Anonymization and Aggregate Reporting: Emphasize the use of anonymization and aggregate reporting in data analytics practices. Highlight how these methods protect individual identities while still contributing to valuable insights (Xu & Zhang, 2022). Demonstrating a commitment to responsible data handling practices reinforces trust by mitigating concerns related to privacy breaches or misuse (FasterCapital, 2023).

Responsive Customer Support: Establish responsive customer support channels dedicated to addressing queries and concerns related to genetic data usage. A proactive and approachable customer support system demonstrates a commitment to consumer well-being, offering reassurance and assistance whenever needed (Krishna, 2023).

Ethical Considerations in Genetic Data Storage and Handling: Direct-to-consumer (DTC) genetic testing companies aggressively inspire their consumers to share their genetic data for research purposes, mainly targeting revenue generation by selling such data to research institution and pharmaceutical companies. Concerns arise regarding the lack of truly 'informed' consent, stemming from consumers' limited contractual knowledge, misunderstanding of potential benefits and risks, and low genetic literacy levels. Moreover, ethical dilemmas emerge concerning the access of genetic testing companies to individuals' genome data, exacerbated by issues surrounding insufficient, hidden, or misleading informed consent practices. These ethical concerns underscore the imperative to safeguard the legitimate rights and interests of consumers in the realm of genetic data utilization for marketing purposes (Buiten, 2021)..

By incorporating these strategies, businesses can not only build initial trust but also maintain a positive and enduring relationship with consumers. Upholding ethical standards and prioritizing transparency in genetic data practices are integral to cultivating a consumer-centric approach in precision marketing.

5.3. Balancing Personalization With Ethical Considerations

As businesses delve into precision marketing with genetic data, striking a delicate balance between personalization and ethical considerations becomes paramount. While personalization enhances the effectiveness of marketing strategies, ethical frameworks must guide these endeavours to ensure responsible practices.

Informed Consent and Opt-In Mechanisms: Prioritize obtaining informed consent from consumers before utilizing their genetic data for personalization. Implement clear opt-in mechanisms that allow individuals to willingly participate, fostering a sense of control over the use of their sensitive information (Mediline, 2020) (Siala & Wang, 2022).

Granular Data Anonymization: Anonymize genetic data at a granular level to protect individual identities. Implement robust data anonymization techniques that preserve privacy while still allowing for meaningful insights. This ensures that personalization efforts are rooted in aggregated trends rather than individual profiles (Krishna, 2023)..

Preference Customization without Intrusion: Tailor marketing efforts based on genetic insights without intruding on personal boundaries. Strive for a balance where personalized recommendations enhance the consumer experience without crossing into overly intrusive practices that may compromise privacy or make individuals uncomfortable (Alexander, Arne, & Katrien, 2018).

Regular Ethical Audits and Compliance Checks: Conduct regular ethical audits to evaluate the impact of personalization strategies on consumers. Ensure compliance with privacy regulations and ethical standards, adapting practices as needed to align with evolving societal expectations and legal frameworks.

Transparent Communication on Data Usage: Transparently communicate how genetic data is utilized for personalization. Provide clear explanations about the specific ways in which insights are applied to enhance the consumer experience. This open communication builds trust and reinforces the ethical foundation of precision marketing practices (Theodore & Schoop, 2015).

Continuous Consumer Education: Promote ongoing consumer education on the benefits and ethical considerations of personalized marketing. Empower individuals with information about how their genetic data contributes to tailored experiences, fostering a shared understanding that supports ethical practices (FasterCapital, Understanding Personalized Experiences In Marketing, 2021).

By navigating the intersection of personalization and ethical considerations with care and transparency, businesses can create a marketing landscape where tailored strategies not only captivate consumers but also adhere to principles of privacy, consent, and responsible data usage. This balance ensures that precision marketing remains a powerful tool for engagement while respecting the ethical boundaries that safeguard consumer trust.

6. REGULATORY FRAMEWORKS AND COMPLIANCE

In the rapidly evolving landscape of precision marketing with genetic data, navigating regulatory frameworks is paramount. As laws evolve to address the ethical complexities surrounding genetic information, businesses must stay informed, adapting their strategies to align with legal standards. Understanding and adhering to regulatory frameworks ensure that precision marketing initiatives remain ethically sound, respecting privacy, consent, and consumer rights in an ever-changing legal landscape.

6.1. Overview of Existing and Emerging Regulations Related to Genetic Data in Marketing

The regulatory landscape governing the use of genetic data in marketing is dynamic, reflecting society's evolving understanding and concerns regarding privacy and ethical practices. Existing regulations, such as the General Data Protection Regulation (GDPR) in the European Union and the Health Insurance Portability and Accountability Act (HIPAA) in the United States, lay the foundation for protecting individuals' genetic information (Johanna, 2023) (Buiten, 2021)..

Emerging regulations are responding to the unique challenges posed by the intersection of genetics and marketing. Countries and regions are exploring specific legislation to address the responsible use of genetic data in personalized advertising, emphasizing the need for transparent communication, informed consent, and stringent data protection measures. As businesses navigate this evolving regulatory landscape, a comprehensive understanding of existing and emerging frameworks is imperative to ensure ethical compliance and foster trust among consumers. Several countries have implemented or proposed regulations related to genetic data, often within the broader context of data protection and privacy laws. Here are examples from some jurisdictions:

European Union (EU): The General Data Protection Regulation (GDPR) is a comprehensive data protection regulation that applies to all member states of the European Union. It includes provisions related to the processing of genetic data, categorizing it as sensitive data that requires specific protections. Consent, transparency, and strict security measures are emphasized (Rahnasto, 2023).

United States: In the U.S., there isn't a comprehensive federal law specifically addressing genetic data in marketing. However, laws such as the Genetic Information Nondiscrimination Act (GINA) prohibit the use of genetic information in employment and health insurance contexts. Privacy concerns related to genetic data may also fall under broader data protection laws and regulations (USEEOC, 2024).

Canada: Canada's privacy laws, including the Personal Information Protection and Electronic Documents Act (PIPEDA), govern the use of personal information, which may encompass genetic data (Adrian, 2018). The federal Genetic Non-Discrimination Act (Bill S-201) prohibits genetic discrimination in the provision of goods and services, including the use of genetic information in marketing (OPCC, 2019).

Australia: Australia's Privacy Act 1988 regulates the handling of personal information, including genetic information. The Australian Genetic Non-Discrimination Act 2019 addresses concerns related to genetic discrimination, although it primarily focuses on areas outside marketing (Tiller, Lacaze, & Otlowski, 2022) (FRL, 2022).

These examples highlight the global trend toward recognizing the sensitivity of genetic data and implementing measures to protect individuals from discrimination and privacy infringements. It's essential to stay updated on the specific regulations and legal developments in each jurisdiction, as laws may evolve over time.

6.2. Compliance Strategies for Marketers to Ensure Legal and Ethical Practices

Marketers imposed with utilizing genetic data for precision marketing must embrace proactive strategies to assure legal and ethical compliance. This requires instigating vigorous compliance measures that prioritize consumer privacy, consent and transparency. By safeguarding against potential pitfalls and adhering to rigorous privacy norms, marketers can uphold the reliability of their data-driven marketing initiatives while fostering trust and accountability among consumers.

6.2.1. Legal Considerations for Marketers

Genetic data, classified as a special category of data, demands heightened privacy protection in both the EU and the USA. The General Data Protection Regulation (GDPR) in the EU holds significant relevance, establishing stringent requirements for consent, transparency, and data protection in the processing of genetic information (Buiten, 2021) (Rahnasto, 2023). Despite the GDPR's recognition of the sensitivity of genetic data, challenges persist in balancing legitimate interests with privacy concerns. In the USA, the Genetic Information Non-discrimination Act of 2008 provides safeguards against genetic discrimination, yet existing gaps underscore the need for comprehensive data protection laws to address emerging challenges (Hallinan, Friedewald, & Hert, 2013), (Spiller, 2016).

6.2.2. Ethical Guidelines for Marketers

Ethical considerations in genetic data marketing encompass autonomy, privacy, misinformation, and discrimination, given the personal and sensitive nature of genetic information (Daviet, Wind, & Nave, Genetic Data: Potential Uses and Misuses in Marketing, 2020). Challenges arise from inadequate informed consent processes, insufficient privacy protections, and low levels of genetic literacy among consumers (Matt, Doug, & Severiche, 2023). Direct-to-consumer genetic testing (DTC GT) poses specific ethical dilemmas, such as test validity, consent adequacy, and potential misleading advertising. Marketers must navigate these complexities to ensure transparency, respect for autonomy, and protection of consumer rights (Emilia, Kalokairinou, & Carmen, 2017).

6.2.3. Compliance Strategies

Robust compliance strategies are essential for marketers to uphold legal and ethical standards in genetic data marketing. This entails obtaining explicit informed consent, implementing strong data protection measures, and promoting genetic literacy and awareness (Matt, Doug, & Severiche, 2023). Compliance efforts should prioritize credibility, risk management, and consumer protection. Collaboration with regulatory authorities ensures alignment with evolving legal requirements and industry standards, promoting responsible use of genetic data in marketing (Nan & Lizhi, 2022).

6.2.4. Implications of Non-Compliance

Non-compliance with legal and ethical standards can lead to reputational damage, legal liabilities, and loss of consumer trust for marketers. Instances of genetic discrimination, privacy breaches, or misinformation can cause significant harm to individuals and communities. The commercialization of de-identified genetic health information raises ethical concerns, as genetic data possess inherent identifiability and may compromise privacy and confidentiality. Marketers must address these risks and uphold ethical principles in their genetic data marketing practices (Seward, 2018), (Daviet, Wind, & Nave, Genetic Data: Potential Uses and Misuses in Marketing, 2020).

By adopting these compliance strategies, marketers can navigate the intricate landscape of genetic data in marketing responsibly, aligning their practices with legal requirements and ethical standards. This not only mitigates risks but also contributes to the establishment of trustful and enduring relationships with consumers.

7. FUTURE TRENDS AND INNOVATIONS

7.1. Emerging Technologies in Genetic Data Analysis for Marketing

As precision marketing continues to evolve, emerging technologies are revolutionizing the landscape of genetic data analysis, offering marketers unprecedented insights for tailored strategies.

Artificial Intelligence (AI) and Machine Learning (ML): AI and ML algorithms are at the forefront, enabling advanced analysis of vast genetic datasets. These technologies can identify intricate patterns, predict consumer behaviour, and dynamically adjust marketing approaches based on real-time data, fostering hyper-personalized campaigns (Alam, Israr, & Kumar, 2024).

Predictive Analytics: Predictive analytics leverages historical genetic data and consumer behaviors to forecast future trends and preferences. Marketers can anticipate the needs and desires of individuals, allowing for proactive and anticipatory marketing strategies.

Blockchain Technology: Blockchain enhances data security and transparency. By utilizing decentralized and tamper-resistant ledgers, marketers can instill greater trust among consumers, assuring them that their genetic data is handled with the utmost integrity and privacy (Alam, Israr, & Kumar, 2024).

Augmented Reality (AR) and Virtual Reality (VR): AR and VR technologies offer immersive experiences in marketing. Businesses can use genetic insights to personalize virtual shopping experiences or showcase how products align with individual preferences, creating interactive and engaging consumer journeys (Alam, Israr, & Kumar, 2024).

Quantum Computing: Quantum computing, with its unparalleled processing capabilities, holds the potential to expedite complex genetic data analyses. This technology may unlock new dimensions in precision marketing, enabling marketers to decipher intricate genetic patterns more efficiently (Turk, 2023).

Internet of Things (IoT): IoT devices provide a wealth of real-time data, enabling marketers to integrate genetic insights into personalized experiences seamlessly. From smart wearables to connected home devices, IoT enhances the granularity of consumer information for more tailored campaigns.

Edge Computing: Edge computing allows for decentralized data processing, enabling faster and more efficient analysis of genetic data. This real-time processing capability is particularly valuable for delivering instant and personalized marketing interactions.

Privacy-Preserving Technologies: Innovations in privacy-preserving technologies focus on protecting individual identities while still extracting valuable insights. Homomorphic encryption and federated learning are examples that allow for secure data analysis without compromising individual privacy.

Embracing these emerging technologies in genetic data analysis heralds a new era in precision marketing. However, with these innovations come ethical considerations, necessitating a careful balance between leveraging cutting-edge tools and ensuring the responsible and transparent use of genetic insights in marketing practices.

7.2. Anticipated Trends in Precision Marketing With Advancements in Genomics

Enormous developments in the field of genomics is anticipated to revolutionize the future of precision marketing. These innovations have potential to transform the landscape, ushering in an era characterized by heightened personalization, unparalleled innovation and a keen focus on ethical considerations. Genomic insights provide marketers exceptional opportunities to deep dive into the complexities of individual traits and their preferences, creating a way forward for hyper-targeted campaigns that reverberate with consumers on extremely personal level. Conversely, amongst this wave of innovation, it's critical for marketers to navigate the ethical complexities of applying genomic data responsibly, safeguarding that the quest of personalization is matched with a firm commitment to customer privacy and permission. Anticipated trends in precision marketing, driven by genomics, include:

Genomic Health and Wellness Marketing: Precision marketing will increasingly focus on health and wellness, with genetic insights guiding personalized recommendations for nutrition, fitness, and preventive care. Brands in the health industry will tailor their products and services based on individual genetic predispositions, promoting a holistic approach to well-being (Schneider, 2023).

Pharmacogenomics in Pharmaceutical Marketing: Pharmaceutical companies will leverage genomic data to personalize drug recommendations. Targeted pharmaceutical marketing will emerge, providing individuals with medications tailored to their genetic makeup, improving treatment efficacy and minimizing adverse effects (Al-Worafi, 2023).

Lifestyle and Leisure Experiences: Genomic data will shape personalized lifestyle and leisure experiences. From travel and entertainment to fashion and recreation, marketing campaigns will be curated based on individuals' genetic traits and preferences, offering bespoke and memorable experiences (Forecast, 2023).

Inclusive and Ethical Marketing Practices: With the integration of genomic insights, marketers will prioritize inclusivity and ethical considerations. Campaigns will be crafted with sensitivity to diverse genetic backgrounds, avoiding discriminatory practices and fostering a more inclusive marketing landscape (Rivera, 2023).

Genetic Ancestry and Heritage Marketing: Genetic ancestry information will inspire marketing campaigns celebrating diversity and heritage. Brands will create tailored experiences that resonate with consumers' genetic backgrounds, emphasizing cultural connections and promoting products aligned with diverse lifestyles (Scodari, 2017).

Personalized Beauty and Fashion: In the beauty and fashion industry, genetic data will guide personalized recommendations for skincare, cosmetics, and fashion choices. Marketing efforts will focus on enhancing individual features based on genetic traits, creating a more tailored and authentic consumer experience (SiaPartner, 2023), (Insights, 2021).

Genomic Data Privacy Assurance: Anticipated trends include a heightened emphasis on genomic data privacy. Marketers will proactively communicate transparent data usage policies, employing secure technologies and ethical practices to build and maintain consumer trust (LLC, 2023).

DIY Genomic Testing and Direct-to-Consumer Marketing: The rise of do-it-yourself (DIY) genomic testing will contribute to a surge in direct-to-consumer marketing. Brands will forge partnerships with genetic testing companies, offering personalized products and services directly to consumers based on their genetic profiles (Sakhre, 2024) (Friend, O'Neill, Rivlin, & Browne, 2023).

As these anticipated trends unfold, marketers will need to navigate ethical considerations, ensuring responsible use of genomic insights while delivering meaningful and personalized experiences. The convergence of genomics and precision marketing promises a future where campaigns are not just targeted but are deeply attuned to the individual, marking a transformative era in consumer engagement.

8. CONCLUSION

This chapter will unpack the dynamic interplay between genetic information and precision marketing, revealing landscape rich in possibilities and complexities. The opportunities for tailored marketing strategies based on genetic insights are vast, offering businesses the potential to revolutionize consumer engagement. However, the ethical considerations and challenges, particularly those related to privacy and consent, demand careful navigation. Through the examination of case studies, we observed that successful campaigns strike a delicate balance between personalization and responsible data practices. As the field continues to evolve, marketers are urged to remain vigilant in adhering to ethical standards, incorporating lessons learned from both successes and challenges. Looking ahead, the future of precision marketing with genetic data holds promises of innovative technologies and trends, underscoring the continued importance of research, responsible practices, and ethical considerations in this rapidly advancing domain.

REFERENCES

Accardi, G., & Aiello, A. (2021). Ways to become old: Role of lifestyle in modulation of the hallmarks of aging. In H. F. Willard & H. F. Willard (Eds.), *Genomic and Personalized Medicine* (Vol. I & II, pp. 273–293). AAP. doi:10.1016/B978-0-12-822569-1.00009-3

Adogy. (2023, Sept 18). *Genomic Marketing*. Retrieved Jan 11, 2024, from https://www.adogy.com: https://www.adogy.com/terms/genomic-marketing/

Adrian, T. (2018, August 1). Canada: Will privacy rules continue to favour open science? *Human Genetics, 137*(8), 595–602. doi:10.1007/s00439-018-1905-0 PMID:30014188

Al-Worafi, Y. M. (2023). *Pharmacogenomics in Developing Countries* (Vol. 1). Springer. doi:10.1007/978-3-030-74786-2_294-1

Alam, S., Israr, J., & Kumar, A. (2024, Feb 06). Artificial Intelligence and Machine Learning in Bioinformatics. In V. Singh, & A. Kumar, *Advances in Bioinformatics* (Vol. 1, pp. 321-345). Springer. Retrieved from https://link.springer.com/chapter/10.1007/978-981-99-8401-5_16

Alan, A., Lee, N. M., Van, S., & Dyke, M. (2022, August 02). Examining the perceived transparency of DTC genetic testing company communication and its impact on consumer trust, attitude and behavioral intentions. *Journal of Communication Management (London)*, 26(03), 315–330. doi:10.1108/JCOM-01-2022-0006

Alexander, B., Arne, D. K., & Katrien, V. (2018). Customer Engagement Through Personalization and Customization. In Customer Engagement Marketing (Vol. 1, pp. 75-94). Palgrave Macmillan. doi:10.1007/978-3-319-61985-9_4

Arianna, R., & Gabriele, L. (2020, July). Transparency by design in data-informed research: A collection of information design patterns. *Computer Law & Security Report*, 37, 105402. Advance online publication. doi:10.1016/j.clsr.2020.105402

Belliappa, B. P. (2023, Sept 11). *Unleashing the Power of Personalized Marketing: Strategies, Examples, and Ethical Considerations*. Retrieved Jan 11, 2024, from https://www.moengage.com: https://www.moengage.com/blog/personalized-marketing-strategies-and-examples/

Bermseok, O. (2019, September 26). Direct-to-consumer genetic testing: Advantages and pitfalls. *Genomics & Informatics*, 17(3), e33. Advance online publication. doi:10.5808/GI.2019.17.3.e33 PMID:31610629

Bouchard, C., Rankinen, T., & Timmons, J. A. (2011, July). Genomics and Genetics in the Biology of Adaptation to Exercise. *HHS Author Manuscripts*, 1(3), 1603–1648. doi:10.1002/cphy.c100059 PMID:23733655

Buiten, M. C. (2021). 'Your DNA Is One Click Away': The GDPR and Direct-to-Consumer Genetic Testing. In *Economic Analysis of Law in European Legal Scholarship* (Vol. 9, pp. 205–223). Springer Nature. doi:10.1007/978-3-030-49028-7_10

Bunnik, E. M., Janssens, A. C., & Schermer, M. H. (2014, September). Informed consent in direct-to-consumer personal genome testing: The outline of a model between specific and generic consent. *Bioethics*, 28(07), 343–351. doi:10.1111/bioe.12004 PMID:23137034

Bushra, A., Yousef, K., & Ayoub, A. (2020). Improving recommendation quality and performance of genetic-based recommender system. *International Journal of Advanced Intelligence Paradigms*, 15(1), 77–88. doi:10.1504/IJAIP.2020.104108

CDC. (2022, May 20). *Pharmacogenomics: What does it mean for your health?* Retrieved Jan 05, 2024, from https://www.cdc.gov: https://www.cdc.gov/genomics/disease/pharma.htm#:~:text=Pharmacogenomics%20is%20an%20important%20example,way%20you%20respond%20to%20drugs

Červenka, P., Naščakova, J., Bednarova, L., Daneshjo, N., & Dudaš-Pajerska, E. (2018). Development Tendency Testing and Success of Marketing Communications. *ICETA 2018 - 16th IEEE International Conference on Emerging eLearning Technologies and Applications, Proceedings* (pp. 87-92). Institute of Electrical and Electronics Engineers Inc. 10.1109/ICETA.2018.8572144

Cervenka, P., Naščáková, J., Bednarova, L., Daneshjo, N., & Dudas-Pajerska, E. (2018). (2018). Development Tendency Testing and Success of Marketing Communications. *International Conference on Emerging eLearning Technologies and Applications (ICETA)* (pp. 87-92). IEEE. 10.1109/ICETA.2018.8572144

Chakraborty, P. (2021). *The Ethical and Legal Aspects of Data Collection in Digital Marketing.* Retrieved Jan 23, 2024, from https://www.winsavvy.com: https://www.winsavvy.com/the-ethical-and-legal-aspects-of-data-collection/

Clayton, E. W., Evans, B. J., Hazel, J. W., & Rothstein, M. A. (2019, October). The law of genetic privacy: Applications, implications, and limitations. *Journal of Law and the Biosciences, 6*(1), 1–36. doi:10.1093/jlb/lsz007 PMID:31666963

Commission, U. E. (2022). *Genetic Information - FAQs.* Retrieved Jan 13, 2024, from https://www.eeoc.gov/youth/genetic-information-faqs#:~:text=to%20genetic%20information%3F-,What%20is%20genetic%20information%3F,(your%20family%20medical%20history)

Cowart, K. O., & Darke, P. (2014, March). Targeting Miss Daisy: Using age and gender to target unethical sales tactics. *Marketing Letters, 25*(1), 67–75. doi:10.1007/s11002-013-9242-5

Daviet, R., Nave, G., & Wind, J. (2020, Dec 16). *Genetic Data and Marketing: Challenges, Opportunities, and Ethics.* Retrieved Mar 29, 2024, from American Marketing Association (AMA): https://www.ama.org/2020/12/16/genetic-data-and-marketing-challenges-opportunities-and-ethics/

Daviet, R., Wind, Y. J., & Nave, G. (2020, Nov 03). Genetic Data: Potential Uses and Misuses in Marketing. SSRN *Electronic Journal.* doi:10.2139/ssrn.3724241

Dinulos, M. B., & Vallee, S. E. (2020, March). The Impact of Direct-to-Consumer Genetic Testing on Patient and Provider. *Clinics in Laboratory Medicine, 40*(1), 61–67. doi:10.1016/j.cll.2019.11.003 PMID:32008640

Dunham, C. (2023, Aug 28). *Precision Marketing: Hitting the Bullseye with Target Audience Effectiveness.* Retrieved Jan 11, 2024, from https://www.linkedin.com: https://www.linkedin.com/pulse/precision-marketing-hitting-bullseye-target-audience-cory-dunham-/

Emilia, N., Kalokairinou, L., & Carmen, H. H. (2017, September). Current ethical and legal issues in health-related direct-to-consumer genetic testing. *Personalized Medicine, 14*(5), 433–445. doi:10.2217/pme-2017-0029 PMID:29754566

Farmer, D. (2022). *advanced analytics.* Retrieved Jan 01, 2024, from https://www.techtarget.com: https://www.techtarget.com/searchbusinessanalytics/definition/advanced-analytics

FasterCapital. (2021). *Understanding Personalized Experiences In Marketing.* Retrieved Jan 12, 2024, from https://fastercapital.com: https://fastercapital.com/topics/understanding-personalized-experiences-in-marketing.html

FasterCapital. (2023, Dec 17). *Ethical Data Handling: Responsible Practices in Data Anonymization*. Retrieved Jan 25, 2024, from https://fastercapital.com: https://fastercapital.com/content/Ethical-Data-Handling--Responsible-Practices-in-Data-Anonymization.html

Forecast, M. (2023, Aug 07). *Genomics Personalized Health Market Size, Share, Growth Statistics, Leading Players and Forecast 2028*. Retrieved Mar 11, 2024, from https://www.linkedin.com: https://www.linkedin.com/pulse/genomics-personalized-health-market-size-share/

Friend, D. L., O'Neill, D. J., Rivlin, D. A., & Browne, R. (2023). *Direct-to- consumer genetic testing-Opportunities and risks in a rapidly evolving market*. Retrieved Mar 08, 2024, from https://assets.kpmg.com: https://assets.kpmg.com/content/dam/kpmg/xx/pdf/2018/08/direct-to-consumer-genetic-testing.pdf

FRL. (2022, Nov 14). *Privacy Act 1988*. Retrieved Jan 26, 2024, from https://www.legislation.gov.au: https://www.legislation.gov.au/C2004A03712/2022-11-14/text

Hallinan, D., Friedewald, M., & Hert, P. D. (2013, August). Genetic Data and the Data Protection Regulation: Anonymity, multiple subjects, sensitivity and a prohibitionary logic regarding genetic data? *Computer Law & Security Report*, *29*(4), 317–319. doi:10.1016/j.clsr.2013.05.013

Insights, C. (2021, May 25). *14 Trends Changing The Face Of The Beauty Industry In 2021*. Retrieved Mar 10, 2024, from https://www.cbinsights.com: https://www.cbinsights.com/research/report/beauty-trends-2021/

Jiang, D., & Zhang, G. (2021, September 6). Marketing Clues on the Label Raise the Purchase Intention of Genetically Modified Food. *Sustainability (Basel)*, *13*(17), 9970. Advance online publication. doi:10.3390/su13179970

Johanna, R. (2023, July 1). Genetic data are not always personal - disaggregating the identifiability and sensitivity of genetic data. *Journal of Law and the Biosciences*, *10*(2), lsad029. Advance online publication. doi:10.1093/jlb/lsad029

Jorde, L. B., & Bamshad, M. J. (2020, March 17). Genetic Ancestry Testing What Is It and Why Is It Important? *Journal of the American Medical Association*, *323*(11), 1089–1090. doi:10.1001/jama.2020.0517 PMID:32058561

Kadiri, I. (2022). Genetic marketing: (R)evolution in customer segmentation. In *Remarketing The Reality* (pp. 322-329). Retrieved Jan 12, 2024, from https://www.researchgate.net/publication/369261477_GE-NETIC_MARKETING_REVOLUTION_IN_CUSTOMER_SEGMENTATION

Katelyn, E., Stephen, R., & Walker, A. (2023, August). A social and ethical framework for providing health information obtained from combining genetics and fitness tracking data. *Technology in Society*, *74*, 102297. Advance online publication. doi:10.1016/j.techsoc.2023.102297 PMID:37521714

Kayte, S.-B., Amanda, F., Chris, K., Erica, M., & Scott, R. J. (2019, December 01). Genetic data partnerships: Academic publications with privately owned or generated genetic data. *Genetics in Medicine*, *21*(12), 2827–2829. doi:10.1038/s41436-019-0569-z PMID:31204388

Kelly, S. E., Wyatt, S., & Anna, H. (2018). Mainstreaming genomics and personal genetic testing. In Routledge Handbook of Genomics, Health and Society (pp. 32-38). Taylor and Francis. doi:10.4324/9781315451695

Kisselburgh, L., & Beever, J. (2022). *The Ethics of Privacy in Research and Design: Principles, Practices, and Potential* (Vol. 1). Springer. doi:10.1007/978-3-030-82786-1_17

Krishna, B. (2023, Jun 16). *Understanding Data Anonymization: Protecting Privacy and Enabling Insights*. Retrieved Jan 25, 2024, from https://www.linkedin.com: https://www.linkedin.com/pulse/understanding-data-anonymization-protecting-privacy-enabling-tidhi/

LB, A., JE, F., & Holtzman. (1994). *Assessing Genetic Risks: Implications for Health and Social Policy*. Institute of Medicine (US) Committee on Assessing Genetic Risks.

Lefebre, D. J., Salgaonkar, D. S., Willwerth-Pascutiu, D. G., & Zimmerman, D. D. (2019, Apr). *Genetics and Insurance: Challenges and Opportunities II*. Retrieved Jan 10, 2024, from https://www.rgare.com/knowledge-center/article/genetics-and-insurance-challenges-and-opportunities-ii

LLC, M. (2023, Nov 8). *Data Privacy and Digital Marketing: What You Need to Know in 2023*. Retrieved Mar 11, 2024, from https://www.linkedin.com/pulse/data-privacy-digital-marketing-what-you-need-know-2023-metaweb3llc-p4f0c/

Makrantonaki, E., Bekou, V., & Zouboulis, C. C. (2012, July 1). Genetics and skin aging. *Dermato-Endocrinology*, *4*(3), 280–284. doi:10.4161/derm.22372 PMID:23467395

Martinez-Martin, N., & Magnus, D. (2020, August 7). Privacy and ethical challenges in next-generation sequencing. *Expert Review of Precision Medicine and Drug Development*, *4*(2), 95–104. doi:10.1080/23808993.2019.1599685 PMID:32775691

Masood, S., & Hasyagar, R. (2020, Mar 2). *Creating Unique User Experiences Through Hyper-Personalization*. Retrieved Jan 05, 2024, from https://www.infosys.com/iki/perspectives/creating-unique-user-experiences.html

Matt, A., Doug, H., & Severiche, M. C. (2023, December). Consumer genetics: What about informed consent? *Human Organization*, *82*(4), 394–403. doi:10.17730/1938-3525-82.4.394

McGuire, J. (2023, May 31). *The Power of Transparency: Building Trust and Accountability in Business*. Retrieved Jan 21, 2024, from https://www.linkedin.com: https://www.linkedin.com/pulse/power-transparency-building-trust-accountability-business-mcguire/

Mediline. (2020, Jan). *What is informed consent?* Retrieved Jan 25, 2024, from https://medlineplus.gov: https://medlineplus.gov/genetics/understanding/testing/informedconsent/

Mommejat, M. (2020, Nov 1). *Driving engagement in consumer genomics and research across Asia*. Retrieved Jan 01, 2024, from https://www.linkedin.com: https://www.linkedin.com/pulse/driving-engagement-consumer-genomics-research-across-asia-mommejat/

Nan, L., & Lizhi, L. (2022). Research on the Ethical Issues of Obtaining Genome Data in Direct-to-consumer Genetic Testing. *Chinese Medical Ethics*, *35*(12), 1329–1334. doi:10.12026/j.issn.1001-8565.2022.12.07

Nasr, F. (2024, Jan 23). *Molecular Aspects of Biotechnology: Exploring Experimental Approaches, Applications, and Ethical Considerations.* Retrieved Feb 01, 2024, from https://yeastwonderfulworld. wordpress.com: https://yeastwonderfulworld.wordpress.com/page/2/

Niemie, E., Howard, H. C., Sterckx, S., Cockbain, J., & Prainsack, B. (2020, May 15). Transparency, consent and trust in the use of customers' data by an online genetic testing company: An Exploratory survey among 23andMe users. *New Genetics & Society, 39*(4), 459–482. doi:10.1080/14636778.2020 .1755636

Okolnishnikova, I. Y., Greyz, G. M. Y. G., & Katochkov, V. M. (2018). Formation and development of marketing communications in the context of consumer demand individualization. *Proceedings of the 32nd International Business Information Management Association Conference, IBIMA 2018 - Vision 2020: Sustainable Economic Development and Application of Innovation Management from Regional expansion to Global Growth* (pp. 7401 - 7406). International Business Information Management Association, IBIMA. Retrieved Mar 10, 2024, from https://www.scopus.com/record/display.uri?eid=2-s2.0-85063066671&origin=scopusAI

OPCC. (2019, May). *PIPEDA in brief.* Retrieved Jan 12, 2024, from https://www.priv.gc.ca/en/privacy-topics/privacy-laws-in-canada/the-personal-information-protection-and-electronic-documents-act-pipeda/ pipeda_brief/

Park, J., Kim, J., Lee, D. C., Kim, S. S., Voyer, B. G., Kim, C., ... Yoon, S. (2022). *Why consumers seek refuge in products branded as authentic in the pandemic and post-pandemic era.* Retrieved Jan 11, 2024, from https://escp.eu/news/why-consumers-seek-refuge-products-branded-authentic-pandemic-and-post-pandemic-era

Pedersen, B. (2023, Sept 28). *The Power of Personalization: Revolutionizing Marketing Strategies.* Retrieved Jan 11, 2024, from https://www.linkedin.com/pulse/power-personalization-revolutionizing-marketing-bo-lund-pedersen/

Pérez-Beltrán, Y. E., Rivera-Iñiguez, I., Gonzalez-Becerra, K., Pérez-Naitoh, N., Tovar, J., Sáyago-Ayerdi, S. G., & Mendivil, E. J. (2022, March 21). Personalized Dietary Recommendations Based on Lipid-Related Genetic Variants: A Systematic Review. *Frontiers in Nutrition, 9*(1), 830283. Advance online publication. doi:10.3389/fnut.2022.830283 PMID:35387194

Porter, K. S. (2022, Sept 19). *Precision Marketing: What it is and Why You Need it.* Retrieved Jan 10, 2024, from https://www.marinsoftware.com/blog/precision-marketing-what-it-is-and-why-you-need-it#:~:text=Precision%20marketing%20uses%20data%20and,in%20a%20more%20relevant%20way

Rahnasto, J. (2023, July-December). Genetic data are not always personal—Disaggregating the identifiability and sensitivity of genetic data. *Journal of Law and the Biosciences, 10*(2), lsad029. Advance online publication. doi:10.1093/jlb/lsad029 PMID:38023689

Remi, D., Gideon, N., & Wind, J. (2022, January). Genetic Data: Potential Uses and Misuses in Marketing. *Journal of Marketing, 86*(1), 7–26. doi:10.1177/0022242920980767

Retailer, I. (2021, Dec 10). *The Emergence of Experiential Marketing and its Relevance in the New Normal.* Retrieved Jan 11, 2024, from https://www.indianretailer.com/article/whats-hot/consumer-trends/the-emergence-of-experiential-marketing-and-its-relevance-in-the-new-normal.a7591

Reversedout. (2023, Jul). *9 Key Insights: The Future of Marketing with Genetic-Based Consumer Targeting.* Retrieved Jan 20, 2024, from https://reversedout.com/genetic-marketing-consumer-targeting/

Rivera, M. (2023, Sept 01). *Inclusive Marketing for a Better Tomorrow.* Retrieved Mar 09, 2024, from https://www.linkedin.com/pulse/inclusive-marketing-better-tomorrow-maribel-rivera/

Ruhl, G. L., Hazel, J. W., Clayton, E. W., & Malin, B. A. (2019). Public Attitudes Toward Direct to Consumer Genetic Testing. *AMIA ... Annual Symposium proceedings / AMIA Symposium. AMIA Symposium. 2019*, 774-783. Retrieved Mar 08, 2024, from https://www.scopus.com/record/display.uri?eid=2-s2.0-85083872580&origin=scopusAI

Sakhre, P. (2024, Feb 26). *Consumer Genomics Market is Slated to Witness Tremendous Growth in Coming Years.* Retrieved Mar 09, 2024, from https://www.linkedin.com/pulse/consumer-genomics-market-slated-witness-tremendous-growth-sakhre-zeqnf/

Schindler, R. M., Lala, V., & Taylor, J. E. (2021, January). Born to shop? A genetic component of deal proneness. *Journal of the Association for Consumer Research*, 6(1), 48–53. doi:10.1086/710244

Schneider, M. (2023, Oct 17). *Impact and Potential of Personalized Medicine Market on Healthcare Industry.* Retrieved Jan 30, 2024, from https://www.linkedin.com/pulse/impact-potential-personalized-medicine-market-mira-schneider/

Scodari, C. (2017, December 5). When Markers Meet Marketing: Ethnicity, Race, Hybridity, and Kinship in Genetic Genealogy Television Advertising. *Genealogy*, 1(4), 22. Advance online publication. doi:10.3390/genealogy1040022

Seward, B. (2018, July 1). Direct-to-Consumer Genetic Testing: Finding a Clear Path Forward. *Therapeutic Innovation & Regulatory Science*, 52(4), 482–488. doi:10.1177/2168479017744774 PMID:29714553

Siala, H., & Wang, Y. (2022, March). SHIFTing artificial intelligence to be responsible in healthcare: A systematic review. *Social Science & Medicine*, 296(1), 114782. Advance online publication. doi:10.1016/j.socscimed.2022.114782 PMID:35152047

SiaPartner. (2023, Oct 2). *Hyper-personalization in the Beauty Industry-How Customization is Reshaping the Cosmetics Industry.* Retrieved mar 09, 2024, from https://www.sia-partners.com/en/insights/publications/hyper-personalization-beauty-industry

Sila, K. (2023, Sept 12). *Ethical Data Management: Navigating Responsible Practices in Business Intelligence.* Retrieved Jan 02, 2024, from https://www.linkedin.com/pulse/ethical-data-management-navigating-responsible-practices-kevin-sila/

Spiller, E. (2016). Legal implications associated with genetic research. Considerations on the Genetic Information Nondiscrimination Act. *BioLaw Journal, 2016*(2), 301-320. doi:10.15168/blj.v0i2.168

Szakály, Z., Kovács, B., Szakály, M., Nagy-Pető, D. T., Popovics, P., & Kiss, M. (2021, March 01). Consumer acceptance of genetic-based personalized nutrition in Hungary. *Genes & Nutrition, 16*(3). Advance online publication. doi:10.1186/s12263-021-00683-7 PMID:33648454

Tamrakar, A. (2023, Oct 03). *Data Privacy: Ensuring Compliance and Building Trust.* Retrieved Jan 20, 2024, from https://www.linkedin.com/pulse/data-privacy-ensuring-compliance-building-trust-ayush-tamrakar/

Theodore, M., & Schoop, A. (2015, May). *Customer Data: Designing for Transparency and Trust.* Retrieved Jan 23, 2024, from https://hbr.org/2015/05/customer-data-designing-for-transparency-and-trust

Tiller, J., Lacaze, P., & Otlowski, M. (2022, December). The Australian moratorium on genetics and life insurance: Evaluating policy compared to Parliamentary recommendations regarding genetic discrimination. *Public Health Research & Practice, 32*(4). Advance online publication. doi:10.17061/phrp3242235 PMID:36509687

Turk, K. (2023, Aug 30). *Quantum Computing: A Futuristic Answer to Healthcare Complexities.* Retrieved Jan 26, 2024, from https://www.linkedin.com/pulse/quantum-computing-futuristic-answer-healthcare-khalid-turk/

USEEOC. (2024). *The Genetic Information Nondiscrimination Act of 2008.* Retrieved Jan 25, 2024, from https://www.eeoc.gov/statutes/genetic-information-nondiscrimination-act-2008

Vedantu. (2022). *Behavioral Genetics.* Retrieved Jan 12, 2024, from https://www.vedantu.com/biology/behavioral-genetics

Vries, J., Bull, S. J., Doumbo, O., Ibrahim, M., Mercereau-Puijalon, O., Kwiatkowski, D., & Parker, M. (2011). Ethical issues in human genomics research in developing countries. *BMC Medical Ethics, 12*(5), 5. Advance online publication. doi:10.1186/1472-6939-12-5 PMID:21418562

Xiaoran, L., Chih-Han, C., & Maria, K. (2020, November). A DNA-Based Intelligent Expert System for Personalised Skin-Health Recommendations. *IEEE Journal of Biomedical and Health Informatics, 24*(11), 3276–3284. doi:10.1109/JBHI.2020.2978667 PMID:32149660

Xu, H., & Zhang, N. (2022, April). Implications of Data Anonymization on the Statistical Evidence of Disparity. *Management Science, 68*(4), 2600–2618. doi:10.1287/mnsc.2021.4028

Chapter 4
Application of Blockchain and Internet of Things (IoT) in Modern Business

Muhammad Usman Tariq

iD https://orcid.org/0000-0002-7605-3040

Abu Dhabi University, UAE & University of Glasgow, UK

ABSTRACT

This chater delves into the synergistic convergence of two transformative technologies reshaping the business landscape. Commencing with an exploration of fundamental blockchain principles, the segment elucidates its decentralized nature, distributed ledger, and smart contract capabilities. Simultaneously, it navigates the intricacies of IoT, unraveling interconnected devices, data communication, and practical applications spanning diverse sectors. Acknowledging the challenges inherent in IoT, such as security concerns and data integrity, the chapter strategically positions blockchain as a viable solution to address these issues. A comprehensive examination of the fusion of blockchain and IoT is undertaken, emphasizing the heightened security, transparency, and efficiency resulting from their integration. Through a series of real-world applications, the segment illustrates how this amalgamation transforms supply chain management, legal and financial processes, healthcare, and the energy sector.

INTRODUCTION

The current business environment is undergoing a significant transformation, driven by the integration of cutting-edge technologies that redefine traditional practices and propel innovation to unprecedented heights. Two such technological pillars, Blockchain and the Internet of Things (IoT), have emerged as formidable forces in this dynamic landscape, reshaping the very fabric of contemporary business operations. The focal point of this section is the symbiotic relationship between these technologies, as we delve into the intricate realm of possibilities they individually and collectively present.

Blockchain, initially synonymous with cryptocurrencies, has transcended its origins to become a disruptive force with broad implications across diverse industries (Narayanan et al., 2016). Its decen-

DOI: 10.4018/979-8-3693-2367-0.ch004

tralized and distributed ledger architecture, underpinned by cryptographic principles, ensures enhanced security, immutability, and transparency in data transactions (Swan, 2015). Unpacking the complexities of Blockchain reveals its evolution beyond digital currencies, finding applications in supply chain management, finance, healthcare, and beyond (Mougayar, 2016).

Concurrently, the Internet of Things (IoT) has played a pivotal role in fostering a connected ecosystem of devices, sensors, and systems, ushering in a new era of data-driven guidance (Atzori, Iera, and Morabito, 2010). The proliferation of IoT devices in everyday life, from smart homes to industrial equipment, underscores its transformative impact (Ashton, 2009). However, the rapid growth of IoT has introduced challenges, particularly regarding security, privacy, and interoperability (Zanella et al., 2014). The convergence of Blockchain and IoT emerges as a crucial response to address these challenges and unlock additional opportunities. By combining the security and transparency of Blockchain with the connectivity and data-sharing capabilities of IoT, businesses can establish a robust foundation for innovative applications across sectors (Dorri, Kanhere, Jurdak, and Gauravaram, 2017).

This section aims to unravel the complexities of this convergence, shedding light on the distinctive contributions of each technology and their collective impact on contemporary business. Exploring the individual contributions of Blockchain and IoT reveals that Blockchain's decentralized ledger brings a paradigm shift to data management and security. The immutability of records ensures trust in transactions, mitigating fraud and tampering concerns (Swan, 2015). For instance, companies like IBM have implemented Blockchain to enhance supply chain transparency, enabling stakeholders to trace the journey of products from manufacturing to delivery (IBM, 2018).

In the realm of IoT, the continuous data generated by interconnected devices serves as a catalyst for innovation in various domains. In healthcare, wearable IoT devices monitor vital signs and transmit data to healthcare providers, enabling remote patient monitoring and timely interventions (Hussain, Javaid, Ahmad, and Hayat, 2020). The potential benefits are equally evident in smart cities, where IoT sensors facilitate efficient traffic management, waste disposal, and energy consumption (Al-Fuqaha et al., 2015). However, the proliferation of IoT devices has raised concerns about data security and privacy. Blockchain, with its cryptographic foundations, offers a potential solution by securing data at the transactional level (Zhang, Wen, Knottenbelt, and Tschorsch, 2018). The decentralized nature of Blockchain reduces the risk of a single point of failure, enhancing the overall robustness of IoT ecosystems (Dorri et al., 2017).

These complementary features set the stage for a seamless integration that can redefine the landscape of contemporary business. The application of Blockchain and IoT in supply chain management serves as a compelling case study for their synergistic potential. Traditional supply chains often grapple with inefficiencies, lack of transparency, and vulnerability to fraud (Ivanov and Dolgui, 2020). Blockchain's ability to create an immutable record of transactions addresses these challenges by providing a transparent and traceable supply chain. The integration of IoT devices further enhances this transparency by continuously updating the Blockchain with real-time data on the movement and condition of goods (Beck et al., 2018). Smart contracts, a key feature of Blockchain, play a crucial role in streamlining and automating processes within supply chains. These self-executing contracts facilitate trustless transactions, reducing the need for intermediaries and minimizing the risk of disputes (Swan, 2015). Consequently, stakeholders across the supply chain stand to benefit from increased efficiency, reduced costs, and improved reliability in transactions (Mougayar, 2016).

In the financial sector, the collaboration between Blockchain and IoT is reshaping traditional practices and paving the way for decentralized finance (DeFi) applications. Blockchain's role in enabling secure and transparent financial transactions is well-established (Narayanan et al., 2016). When integrated with

IoT, this capability extends to the realm of smart banking, where interconnected devices facilitate seamless and secure financial transactions. Smart contracts in the financial sector automate processes such as credit approvals, insurance claims, and asset transfers. This automation not only reduces the time and cost associated with these processes but also minimizes the risk of errors and fraud (Mougayar, 2016). Decentralized applications (DApps) built on Blockchain provide a foundation for innovative financial services, from peer-to-peer lending to automated investment platforms (Swan, 2015).

Healthcare emerges as a domain where the combined power of Blockchain and IoT holds significant promise. The security and integrity of patient data are paramount in healthcare, and Blockchain's cryptographic features address these concerns (Hussain et al., 2020). Electronic health records (EHRs) stored on a Blockchain are not only secure but also accessible to authorized individuals in real-time. The integration of IoT devices in healthcare extends beyond wearables to include medical equipment and sensors. These devices continuously generate data, ranging from vital signs to treatment adherence, creating a comprehensive picture of patient health (Hussain et al., 2020). Blockchain ensures the integrity and confidentiality of this data, allowing healthcare providers to make informed decisions based on accurate and up-to-date information. In addition to data security, Blockchain and IoT contribute to drug traceability and authenticity in the pharmaceutical industry. Counterfeit drugs pose a significant risk to public health, and the ability to trace the entire journey of a drug product through the supply chain is crucial (Dorri et al., 2017). By leveraging Blockchain's transparent and tamper-proof ledger, stakeholders can verify the authenticity of drugs, ensuring the safety and effectiveness of medications (Mettler, 2017).

The energy and utilities sector is undergoing a transformation fueled by the integration of Blockchain and IoT. Traditional energy grids are evolving into smart grids, where IoT devices monitor energy consumption, production, and distribution in real-time (Conoscenti, Vetro, and De Martin, 2016). Blockchain's decentralized nature ensures the security and transparency of energy transactions in these complex environments. One notable application is decentralized energy trading platforms, where Blockchain facilitates peer-to-peer energy transactions. Prosumers, individuals who both consume and produce energy through renewable sources, can sell excess energy directly to other consumers without the need for intermediaries (Zhang et al., 2018). This promotes sustainability and creates a more resilient and adaptable energy system.

As we envision the future trajectory of Blockchain and IoT in contemporary business, several trends and challenges come to the forefront. Tokenization, the process of representing real assets on a Blockchain as digital tokens, is gaining momentum as a disruptive force in various industries (Swan, 2015). Real estate, art, and even intellectual property can be tokenized, enabling fractional ownership and new avenues for investment (Mougayar, 2016). Decentralized autonomous organizations (DAOs) represent another innovative trend facilitated by Blockchain technology. DAOs are organizations manifested through smart contracts on a Blockchain, where decision-making processes are automated and governed by code (Tapscott and Tapscott, 2016). This shift toward decentralized governance structures has the potential to redefine organizational models, fostering greater inclusivity and transparency (Tariq, 2024; Raimi et al. 2022).

However, amid these promising trends, challenges persist on the path to widespread adoption of Blockchain and IoT in modern business. Scalability remains a critical concern, particularly as the volume of transactions and data in Blockchain and IoT ecosystems continues to grow (Zhang et al., 2018). The energy consumption associated with certain Blockchain consensus mechanisms, such as Proof of Work, also raises sustainability issues (Narayanan et al., 2016). Regulatory and legal frameworks present another layer of complexity. The evolving nature of these technologies often outpaces regulatory developments, creating uncertainties and hindering broader adoption (Swan, 2015). Standardization efforts to ensure interoperability between different Blockchain platforms and IoT devices are crucial for creating a robust and integrated technological landscape (Zanella et al., 2014).

In summary, the integration of Blockchain and the Internet of Things (IoT) into contemporary business signifies a profound shift with extensive consequences. As these technologies progress and intersect, enterprises are tasked with navigating intricate landscapes, capitalizing on synergies, and addressing challenges to fully unlock their potential. Whether it be the overhaul of supply chains, the restructuring of financial services, or the transformation of healthcare, the pervasive influence of Blockchain and IoT is fundamentally altering the landscape of how we engage in and perceive business within the digital era. The ongoing journey toward this technological amalgamation holds the promise of a future where transparency, security, and efficiency cease to be mere aspirations and instead become foundational principles of modern business operations.

1. UNDERSTANDING BLOCKCHAIN INNOVATION

1.1 Fundamentals and Basics

Blockchain technology has emerged as a revolutionary force, disrupting conventional norms of data management and transactional processes. In this segment, we delve into the fundamentals and basics of Blockchain, examining its definition, the core principle of decentralization, the concept of a distributed ledger, and the consensus mechanisms that underpin its functionality. Additionally, we explore the innovative concept of smart contracts, a pivotal feature that extends the utility of Blockchain beyond a mere record-keeping system.

Definition and Fundamentals

At its core, Blockchain is a decentralized and distributed ledger technology that facilitates secure, transparent, and tamper-resistant record-keeping of digital transactions (Narayanan et al., 2016). It is not confined to a single location or controlled by a central authority, starkly contrasting with traditional centralized databases. Instead, Blockchain operates as a chain of interconnected blocks, with each block containing a list of transactions. The fundamental principle of Blockchain revolves around the notion of blocks linked through cryptographic hashes. Each block carries a unique identifier (hash) based on the information within it and the hash of the preceding block. This interlinking creates a chain of blocks, forming a chronological and immutable record of transactions (Swan, 2015; Tariq, 2024).

Decentralization and Distributed Ledger

Decentralization is a characteristic intrinsic to Blockchain technology. Unlike traditional systems where a central authority governs data and transactions, Blockchain operates on a peer-to-peer network of nodes. Each node maintains a copy of the entire Blockchain, ensuring the absence of a single point of control or failure. This decentralized architecture enhances security, transparency, and resilience, as there is no central entity vulnerable to hacking or manipulation (Swan, 2015). The distributed ledger aspect of Blockchain contributes to its reliability and transparency. Every participant in the network possesses an identical copy of the ledger, continuously updated as new transactions are added. This shared ledger eliminates the need for intermediaries and provides all participants with a consistent view of the data, fostering trust in the system (Mougayar, 2016).

Consensus Mechanisms

Consensus mechanisms are crucial for maintaining the integrity of the Blockchain, ensuring that all nodes agree on the validity of transactions. Two prominent consensus mechanisms are Proof of Work (PoW) and Proof of Stake (PoS).

Proof of Work (PoW)

PoW is the original consensus mechanism introduced by Satoshi Nakamoto in the Bitcoin whitepaper (Nakamoto, 2008). In a PoW system, participants (miners) compete to solve complex mathematical puzzles. The first miner to solve the puzzle broadcasts the solution to the network, and once validated, the new block is added to the Blockchain. This process requires substantial computational power and energy, making the Blockchain secure but energy-intensive (Narayanan et al., 2016).

Proof of Stake (PoS)

PoS is an alternative consensus mechanism designed to address environmental concerns associated with PoW. In a PoS system, validators (participants with a stake in the cryptocurrency) are chosen to create new blocks based on the amount of cryptocurrency they hold and are willing to "stake" as collateral. This mechanism aims to achieve consensus while minimizing energy consumption, as it eliminates the need for resource-intensive mining (Swan, 2015; Raimi et al. 2022).

Smart Contracts

Smart contracts represent a paradigm shift in the capabilities of Blockchain technology. Coined by Nick Szabo in 1994, smart contracts are self-executing contracts with the terms of the agreement directly written into code (Szabo, 1994). These contracts automatically execute and enforce the agreed-upon terms when predefined conditions are met. Smart contracts operate on the "if-then" logic, providing an automated and trustless means of executing agreements without the need for intermediaries. The implementation of smart contracts extends the functionality of Blockchain beyond a simple record-keeping system. They find applications in various domains, including finance, supply chain management, and legal processes. For instance, in financial transactions, smart contracts automate the execution of agreements, reducing the time and cost associated with traditional contract processes (Swan, 2015). In supply chain management, they enable transparent and automated execution of contractual obligations, enhancing efficiency and reducing the risk of disputes (Mougayar, 2016). Thus, the basics and fundamentals of Blockchain technology lay the groundwork for its transformative capabilities. The decentralized and distributed nature, consensus mechanisms, and the innovative concept of smart contracts collectively contribute to the robustness, security, and flexibility of Blockchain. As we delve further into specific applications and industries, these foundational principles become the building blocks for a new era of transparent, secure, and efficient digital transactions (Tariq, 2024).

1.2 Key Elements and Advantages of Blockchain Innovation

Blockchain technology, characterized by its decentralized and transparent nature, offers a plethora of key features and benefits that revolutionize the landscape of digital transactions. This section delves into the core attributes, emphasizing data security and immutability, transparency and traceability in transactions, and the significant reduction in fraud and tampering, ultimately fostering enhanced trust in blockchain-enabled processes.

Security and Immutability

One of the fundamental strengths of blockchain technology lies in its ability to provide robust security and immutability to digital transactions. Each block in the blockchain is cryptographically linked to the preceding block, forming a chain that is resistant to tampering or unauthorized alterations (Swan, 2015). The decentralized and distributed ledger ensures that any attempt to manipulate a single block requires altering every subsequent block, a computationally infeasible task that enhances the security of the entire system (Narayanan et al., 2016). Moreover, the consensus mechanisms used in blockchain, such as Proof of Work (PoW) or Proof of Stake (PoS), contribute to the security by establishing a common agreement on the validity of transactions across the network (Swan, 2015). This level of cryptographic security and consensus establishes a highly secure environment for sensitive data, making blockchain technology particularly appealing in industries where data integrity and confidentiality are paramount, such as finance and healthcare. In financial applications, for instance, the immutability of blockchain records ensures that once a transaction is recorded, it cannot be altered or deleted. This feature mitigates the risk of fraudulent activities, ensuring the integrity of financial transactions and reducing the likelihood of unauthorized modifications (Narayanan et al., 2016).

Transparency and Traceability

Transparency is one of the cornerstone of blockchain technology, providing participants in the network with an unhindered view of all transactions recorded on the blockchain. Each participant holds an identical copy of the distributed ledger, eliminating the need for intermediaries and creating a shared reality where all parties have access to the same information in real-time (Mougayar, 2016). This transparency is particularly beneficial in industries where accountability and visibility into transactional records are critical.

In supply chain management, blockchain's transparency and traceability features address challenges associated with accountability and authenticity. Every stage of the supply chain, from manufacturing to distribution, can be recorded on the blockchain, allowing stakeholders to trace the origin and journey of products (Beck et al., 2018). This reduces the risk of counterfeit goods and improves overall supply chain visibility, reducing inefficiencies and ensuring the authenticity of products reaching the end consumer.

The transparent nature of blockchain also plays a crucial role in enhancing accountability and trust in public sector applications. Government agencies can use blockchain to maintain transparent records of transactions, expenditures, and regulatory compliance, fostering public trust in the integrity of governance processes (Swan, 2015).

Reduced Fraud and Tampering

The combination of security, immutability, and transparency in blockchain technology leads to a significant reduction in fraud and tampering. The cryptographic principles underlying blockchain ensure that once a block is added to the chain, the information within it is secure and resistant to alterations (Swan, 2015). Attempts to tamper with the data would require the consensus of the majority of the network, making fraudulent activities highly improbable. In financial transactions, blockchain's resistance to tampering significantly mitigates the risk of fraudulent activities such as double spending and identity theft. The decentralized and consensus-driven nature of blockchain makes it inherently more secure than traditional centralized databases, where a single breach could compromise the entire system (Narayanan et al., 2016). Moreover, the reduction of intermediaries in blockchain transactions minimizes the opportunities for fraudulent activities. Smart contracts, a key feature of blockchain, automate and enforce contractual agreements without the need for intermediaries, eliminating the associated risks of fraud and human error (Swan, 2015).

Enhanced Confidence in Transactions

Blockchain technology fundamentally transforms the trust dynamics in digital transactions. Through its combination of security, transparency, and reduced fraud, blockchain instills a higher level of trust among participants in various ecosystems. The decentralized nature of blockchain eliminates the need for a central authority, fostering trust in a trustless environment (Narayanan et al., 2016). In financial sectors, blockchain's ability to provide a secure and transparent ledger builds trust among participants who may not have a direct relationship. The immutable and auditable nature of blockchain records enhances the credibility of financial transactions, fostering confidence among users and reducing reliance on traditional financial intermediaries (Swan, 2015).

Smart contracts, by automating and self-executing contractual agreements, further contribute to trust-building in transactions. The predefined rules and conditions encoded in smart contracts ensure that contractual obligations are met automatically, reducing the need for trust in intermediaries and minimizing the risk of disputes (Mougayar, 2016). In industries like healthcare, where the security and privacy of patient data are paramount, blockchain's ability to provide a transparent yet secure platform builds trust among patients, healthcare providers, and other stakeholders. Patients can trust that their medical records are accurate, secure, and accessible only to authorized individuals, fostering a more collaborative and reliable healthcare environment (Hussain et al., 2020).

In conclusion, the key features and benefits of blockchain technology redefine the way we approach digital transactions. The combination of security, immutability, transparency, and reduced fraud establishes a foundation for trust in various industries. As blockchain continues to evolve and find applications in diverse sectors, its profound impact on enhancing the integrity and reliability of digital transactions becomes increasingly apparent.

2. UNRAVELING THE INTERNET OF THINGS (IOT)

2.1 Core Concepts of IoT

The Internet of Things (IoT) stands as a transformative paradigm, weaving together an extensive network of interconnected devices and sensors to create a dynamic and intelligent environment. In this section, we delve into the fundamental concepts of IoT, exploring the intricacies of interconnected devices, the nuances of data collection and communication, the significance of IoT protocols such as MQTT and CoAP, and the emerging role of edge computing in enhancing its' capabilities.

Interconnected Devices and Sensors

At the heart of the Internet of Things is the concept of interconnected devices, forming a network where physical objects communicate and exchange data seamlessly. These devices, ranging from everyday items like refrigerators and thermostats to industrial machinery and wearable devices, are embedded with sensors and actuators that enable them to collect and transmit data (Atzori, Iera, and Morabito, 2010). The interconnectivity of these devices fosters a web of information exchange, resulting in an environment where the physical and digital realms converge. The proliferation of interconnected devices has permeated various facets of daily life, giving rise to the vision of smart homes, smart cities, and smart industries. In smart homes, for instance, IoT-enabled devices like smart thermostats and lighting systems communicate with each other to optimize energy consumption based on user preferences and environmental conditions (Atzori et al., 2010). This interconnectedness extends to industries, where IoT devices in manufacturing plants monitor equipment health, streamline processes, and enable predictive maintenance (Al-Fuqaha et al., 2015; Tariq, 2024).

Data Collection and Communication

The core functionality of IoT relies on the seamless collection and communication of data among interconnected devices. Sensors embedded in these devices capture various types of data, ranging from environmental parameters such as temperature and humidity to more complex information like biometric data from wearable devices (Al-Fuqaha et al., 2015). This data is then sent to other devices or integrated systems for processing and analysis. The data generated by IoT devices not only provides real-time insights into the status and conditions of the physical world but also serves as a foundation for informed decision-making. In healthcare, for example, wearable IoT devices continuously collect patient data, allowing healthcare providers to monitor vital signs remotely and intervene promptly if abnormalities are detected (Hussain, Javaid, Ahmad, and Hayat, 2020). This data-driven approach enhances the efficiency of healthcare delivery and improves patient outcomes. Communication protocols play a crucial role in facilitating the exchange of data between IoT devices. MQTT (Message Queuing Telemetry Transport) and CoAP (Constrained Application Protocol) are two prominent IoT protocols designed to enable efficient and lightweight communication between devices (Shelby and Hartke, 2014). These protocols enhance bandwidth utilization, ensuring that data transmission is both fast and resource-efficient, making them suitable for IoT environments where devices may have limited computational capabilities and network bandwidth (Atzori et al., 2010).

IoT Protocols: MQTT and CoAP

MQTT (Message Queuing Telemetry Transport): Developed by IBM in the late 1990s, MQTT has emerged as a widely adopted IoT protocol due to its lightweight and efficient design. It operates on a publish/subscribe model, where devices can publish messages to specific topics, and other devices subscribe to receive messages on those topics (Shelby and Hartke, 2014). This decoupled architecture enables flexible and scalable communication between devices, making MQTT suitable for scenarios where multiple devices need to exchange information without establishing direct, point-to-point connections.

CoAP (Constrained Application Protocol): CoAP, designed specifically for constrained devices and networks, is an open standard IoT protocol aiming to provide a simple yet efficient communication mechanism (Shelby and Hartke, 2014). CoAP is RESTful, reflecting the principles of HTTP but with optimizations for low-power, lossy networks commonly found in IoT solutions. It is particularly suitable for applications where resource constraints and energy efficiency are critical, such as in sensor networks and IoT devices operating on battery power. The adoption of standardized protocols like MQTT and CoAP contributes to the interoperability and seamless communication between a diverse array of IoT devices, facilitating a robust and integrated IoT ecosystem.

Edge Computing in IoT

The advent of Edge Computing represents a paradigm shift in how IoT data is processed and analyzed. Traditionally, IoT devices sent data to centralized cloud servers for processing, analysis, and storage. However, this approach poses latency and bandwidth challenges, especially in applications demanding real-time or near-real-time responses. Edge computing addresses these challenges by bringing computational capabilities closer to the source of data generation, i.e., the IoT devices themselves (Shi, Dustdar, and Nastic, 2016). This decentralized computing paradigm enables data processing at the edge of the network, reducing latency and bandwidth consumption (Tariq, 2024).

In an edge computing architecture, IoT devices process and analyze data locally, generating meaningful insights without the need for constant communication with centralized servers. This is particularly valuable in scenarios where real-time guidance is critical, such as in autonomous vehicles, industrial automation, and healthcare applications (Shi et al., 2016). Edge computing not only improves the speed of data processing but also addresses concerns associated with data privacy and security by keeping sensitive information closer to its source. The integration of edge computing and IoT empowers businesses to make data-driven decisions on the spot, enhancing operational efficiency and responsiveness. In smart cities, for example, edge computing enables local processing of data from sensors monitoring traffic, air quality, and public safety, allowing for immediate adjustments and interventions without relying solely on centralized data centers (Al-Fuqaha et al., 2015).

Thus, unraveling the core concepts of IoT reveals a landscape where interconnected devices, efficient data collection and communication, and standardized protocols form the foundation of a dynamic and intelligent ecosystem. As IoT continues to evolve, the adoption of protocols like MQTT and CoAP enhances interoperability, while the integration of edge computing reshapes the paradigm of data processing. These fundamental concepts pave the way for the transformative impact of IoT across various industries, heralding a future of smarter, more connected, and efficient systems.

2.2 Practical Applications of the Internet of Things (IoT)

The Internet of Things (IoT) has transcended its conceptual origins and evolved into a tangible force reshaping industries and enhancing daily life. This section delves into real-world applications of IoT, exploring how smart cities and infrastructure, Industrial IoT (IIoT) in manufacturing, healthcare and wearables, and precision farming in agriculture are leveraging IoT technologies to drive innovation and efficiency.

Smart Cities and Infrastructure

Smart cities leverage IoT to enhance the efficiency and sustainability of urban environments, addressing challenges such as traffic congestion, energy consumption, and public safety (Al-Fuqaha et al., 2015). In transportation, IoT-enabled sensors and devices monitor traffic patterns, parking availability, and public transit usage, providing real-time data to traffic management systems. For instance, in Barcelona, the implementation of smart parking solutions using IoT sensors enables citizens to locate available parking spaces through a mobile app, reducing congestion and emissions (Zanella et al., 2014). Furthermore, IoT contributes to public safety through applications like smart street lighting, where connected sensors can detect unusual activities or emergencies and automatically adjust lighting levels to improve visibility. In Chicago, IoT-based gunshot detection systems use sensors to identify and locate gunfire, aiding law enforcement in responding to incidents promptly (Al-Fuqaha et al., 2015). In the realm of environmental sustainability, IoT technologies monitor air and water quality, waste management, and energy consumption. For example, in Singapore, IoT sensors are deployed to monitor air quality, enabling authorities to take proactive measures to address pollution and safeguard public health (Zanella et al., 2014).

Industrial IoT (IIoT) in Manufacturing

The Industrial Internet of Things (IIoT) has revolutionized the manufacturing sector by introducing connectivity, automation, and data analytics into industrial processes (Lee, Bagheri, and Kao, 2015). In smart factories, IoT sensors are integrated into machinery to collect real-time data on equipment performance, enabling predictive maintenance and minimizing downtime. This approach improves operational efficiency and reduces maintenance costs. For instance, General Electric (GE) has adopted IIoT to enhance aircraft engine manufacturing. IoT sensors embedded in airplane engines gather data on various parameters, allowing engineers to monitor engine health, predict maintenance needs, and optimize performance (Lee et al., 2015). This predictive maintenance approach prevents unscheduled downtime, reduces maintenance costs, and extends the lifespan of critical assets. The concept of Digital Twins, a crucial component of IIoT, involves creating virtual simulations of physical assets. These virtual models enable manufacturers to simulate and analyze various scenarios, optimizing production processes and facilitating informed decision-making. Siemens, in its Amberg plant, uses Digital Twin technology to streamline production, reduce errors, and improve overall manufacturing efficiency (Lee et al., 2015).

Healthcare and Wearables

IoT applications in healthcare are transforming patient care, enabling remote monitoring, personalized treatment plans, and improved overall health management (Hussain et al., 2020). Wearable devices, equipped with sensors to measure vital signs, physical activity, and other health-related metrics, provide real-time continuous data to both patients and healthcare providers. For example, smartwatches and fitness trackers monitor heart rate, sleep patterns, and physical activity, empowering individuals to proactively manage their health. In healthcare settings, wearable devices play a crucial role in remote patient monitoring, allowing healthcare providers to track real-time conditions and intervene promptly in case of anomalies (Hussain et al., 2020). IoT technologies extend beyond wearables to enhance hospital operations. Connected medical devices, such as infusion pumps and patient monitors, enable healthcare professionals to monitor patients more closely and streamline workflows. Additionally, IoT solutions facilitate the management of medical assets and inventory, ensuring the availability of essential equipment and reducing operational costs.

Agriculture and Precision Farming

Precision farming, facilitated by IoT technologies, is transforming agriculture by optimizing resource use, increasing yields, and minimizing environmental impact (Gubbi et al., 2013). IoT sensors, robots, and satellite technology provide farmers with valuable data on soil health, weather conditions, and crop status, enabling data-driven decision-making. In precision agriculture, IoT-enabled devices monitor soil moisture levels, allowing farmers to optimize irrigation and conserve water resources. For example, the use of soil moisture sensors in vineyards enables precise watering, resulting in better crops and efficient resource utilization (Gubbi et al., 2013). Drones equipped with cameras and sensors contribute to crop monitoring and pest control. In large agricultural fields, drones capture high-resolution images, helping farmers identify areas that require attention, such as nutrient deficiencies or pest infestations. This targeted approach enables farmers to apply fertilizers and pesticides selectively, minimizing environmental impact and reducing costs. Moreover, IoT technologies assist in livestock management. Wearable devices for animals, equipped with GPS and health monitoring sensors, provide farmers with real-time information on the location and well-being of livestock. This data-driven approach enhances animal welfare, improves breeding practices, and contributes to overall farm productivity. Thus, the real-world applications of the Internet of Things span various sectors, each harnessing the transformative power of IoT to enhance efficiency, productivity, and sustainability. From the smart infrastructure of cities to precision farming practices in agriculture, IoT technologies continue to reshape industries and improve the quality of life. As IoT adoption continues to grow, the potential for innovation and positive impact on various aspects of human life remains substantial.

3. CONVERGENCE OF BLOCKCHAIN AND IOT

3.1 Addressing Challenges and Fostering Collaborations

The convergence of Blockchain and the Internet of Things (IoT) signifies a pivotal moment in the evolution of digital technologies. This section delves into how this fusion addresses inherent challenges in IoT, encompassing security concerns, data integrity, privacy issues, and the interoperability of diverse IoT devices. The amalgamation of Blockchain and IoT not only alleviates these challenges but also unlocks synergies that enhance the overall efficiency and reliability of interconnected environments.

Addressing Security Concerns in IoT

Security has long been a fundamental concern in the realm of IoT, given the proliferation of interconnected devices and the potential vulnerabilities arising from this extensive network. Traditional centralized security models encounter difficulties in securing distributed and heterogeneous IoT environments (Zhang, Wen, Knottenbelt, and Tschorsch, 2018). Blockchain, with its decentralized and cryptographic foundation, emerges as a robust solution to fortify the security posture of IoT ecosystems. In a Blockchain-IoT integration, every transaction or data exchange within the IoT network is recorded in a tamper-proof and immutable ledger. The decentralized nature of Blockchain eliminates the vulnerability associated with a single weak link, making it significantly more challenging for malicious actors to compromise the entire system (Dorri, Kanhere, Jurdak, and Gauravaram, 2017). The cryptographic principles underlying Blockchain enhance the authentication and validation processes within the IoT network, ensuring that only authorized devices can participate in transactions. For example, in a smart home scenario where IoT devices control various aspects of household management, Blockchain ensures that only authorized devices can execute commands. Unauthorized attempts to manipulate smart devices are promptly detected and rejected, fortifying the security and integrity of the IoT ecosystem (Zhang et al., 2018). This decentralized approach not only reduces the risk of unauthorized access and cyber attacks but also enhances the overall resilience of IoT systems.

Ensuring Data Integrity and Security

The integrity and security of data generated by IoT devices are critical considerations, particularly in applications where sensitive information, such as personal health data or industrial processes, is involved. Blockchain addresses these concerns by providing a transparent, tamper-proof, and auditable record of all transactions and data exchanges within the IoT network (Dorri et al., 2017). The decentralized ledger ensures that once data is recorded, it cannot be altered, ensuring data integrity. Consider a scenario in healthcare where wearable devices continuously monitor and transmit patient health data. By integrating Blockchain into the IoT framework, this sensitive health information is stored securely and permanently. Patients and healthcare providers can trust that the data recorded on the Blockchain is accurate, and any changes to the information are transparent and traceable. This not only protects patient privacy but also instills confidence in the reliability of IoT-generated data (Hussain et al., 2020). Furthermore, Blockchain's cryptographic techniques enable secure data sharing and selective disclosure. Using private keys, individuals or entities have some control over access to specific data on the Blockchain, allowing for granular permissions and safeguarding the privacy of sensitive information. In a supply chain scenario, for instance, where multiple stakeholders share information about the journey of products, Blockchain ensures that only authorized parties can access relevant data, mitigating concerns about data security and unauthorized disclosures (Zhang et al., 2018).

Interoperability of IoT Devices

Interoperability challenges have historically hindered the seamless integration of diverse IoT devices, each operating on different protocols and standards. The convergence of Blockchain and IoT introduces a standardized and interoperable layer, streamlining communication and data exchange among heterogeneous devices. Blockchain's role in fostering interoperability is particularly evident in scenarios where devices from various manufacturers or with varied functionalities need to collaborate. By providing a common and decentralized platform for communication, Blockchain eliminates the need for extensive middleware or complex integration processes (Dorri et al., 2017). Smart contracts, a crucial feature of Blockchain, facilitate automated and trustless interactions between devices, reducing dependencies on proprietary systems and enhancing overall interoperability. Consider a smart city system where various IoT devices, ranging from traffic sensors to environmental monitors, need to collaborate for effective urban management. Blockchain ensures that these devices can seamlessly exchange data and execute transactions through smart contracts, creating a unified and interoperable environment. The decentralized and standardized nature of Blockchain improves the integration of new devices into the network, fostering a more robust and scalable IoT environment (Zhang et al., 2018). Moreover, the convergence of Blockchain and IoT lays the groundwork for the development of decentralized applications (DApps) that operate on a common infrastructure. These DApps can leverage the decentralized and interoperable nature of Blockchain to create innovative solutions across various industries. For instance, in the healthcare sector, DApps could facilitate secure and interoperable sharing of patient data among different healthcare providers, enhancing collaboration and improving patient care (Hussain et al., 2020).

In conclusion, the integration of Blockchain and IoT addresses key challenges in the realm of IoT, providing solutions to enhance security, ensure data integrity and privacy, and foster interoperability. By combining the strengths of these technologies, businesses and industries can unlock collaborations that go beyond addressing challenges, ultimately reshaping the landscape of interconnected ecosystems. As the integration of Blockchain and IoT continues to evolve, the potential for innovative applications and transformative impact across different sectors remains substantial.

3.2 Advantages of Integrating Blockchain With IoT

The fusion of Blockchain with the Internet of Things (IoT) heralds a new era of technological collaboration, offering a plethora of benefits that extend beyond addressing challenges. This section explores the distinct advantages of blending Blockchain and IoT, emphasizing enhanced security through cryptographic techniques, the immutability and transparency of data records, efficient and trustless transactions, and the decentralized control and consensus mechanisms inherent in this integration.

Enhanced Security Through Cryptographic Techniques

A standout benefit of integrating Blockchain with IoT is the reinforcement of security through the utilization of cryptographic methods. In traditional IoT ecosystems, centralized security models are susceptible to weak links and potential breaches (Zhang, Wen, Knottenbelt, and Tschorsch, 2018). Blockchain, with its decentralized architecture and cryptographic foundations, presents a paradigm shift in securing IoT environments. Cryptographic techniques, such as public-key cryptography, bolster the security aspects in Blockchain-IoT integrations. Each device within the IoT network possesses a unique cryptographic key pair, comprising a public key for identification and a private key for secure communication (Dorri, Kanhere, Jurdak, and Gauravaram, 2017). This cryptographic approach ensures secure authentication and authorization, mitigating the risk of unauthorized access and data manipulation. For instance, in Industrial IoT (IIoT) scenarios where sensors monitor critical equipment in a manufacturing plant, Blockchain's cryptographic security measures ensure that only authorized devices can communicate with and control the machinery. Attempts by malicious entities to compromise the system are thwarted by the cryptographic protocols, enhancing the overall integrity and security of the IIoT environment (Zhang et al., 2018). Additionally, cryptographic methods play a crucial role in securing the identity and integrity of data generated by IoT devices. Each transaction or data entry on the Blockchain is cryptographically hashed, creating a robust and tamper-proof record. This not only safeguards the authenticity of data but also establishes a formidable defense against cyber threats in IoT applications ranging from smart homes to healthcare (Hussain et al., 2020).

Immutable and Transparent Data Records

The integration of Blockchain with IoT introduces the concept of immutable and transparent data records, addressing concerns associated with data integrity and providing a reliable foundation for digital transactions. In a Blockchain-IoT environment, each data transaction is recorded as a block, and these blocks are linked sequentially through cryptographic hashes, forming an unalterable chain of data (Dorri et al., 2017). The immutability of data records on the Blockchain ensures that once a transaction is added to the ledger, it cannot be changed or deleted. This feature is particularly significant in scenarios where the integrity and accuracy of data are paramount, such as in supply chain management or healthcare (Hussain et al., 2020). For instance, in supply chain applications, Blockchain ensures that the entire journey of a product, from manufacturing to distribution, is transparent and tamper-proof. Any attempt to alter the information recorded on the Blockchain is immediately detected, preserving the integrity of the supply chain data (Zhang et al., 2018). Transparency is an inherent characteristic of the Blockchain, where all participants in the network have access to the same data records. Each participant holds a copy of the entire ledger, and any changes or additions to the data are visible in real-time (Dorri et al., 2017). This transparency fosters trust among stakeholders, as they can independently verify the validity of data without relying on centralized authorities or intermediaries.

Efficient and Trustless Transactions

The integration of Blockchain with IoT streamlines transactions within interconnected environments, bringing efficiency and trustlessness?? into the process. Smart contracts, a crucial feature of Blockchain, are self-executing contracts with predefined rules encoded in code. These contracts automate and enforce the terms of an agreement when specified conditions are met, eliminating the need for intermediaries and enhancing transaction efficiency (Zhang et al., 2018). Consider financial transactions in a connected environment, where IoT devices facilitate seamless payments or microtransactions. Blockchain's smart contracts enable automatic and secure execution of these transactions based on predefined rules. For example, in a smart home, IoT devices can autonomously execute transactions for energy consumption or payment for shared resources, ensuring efficiency and reducing reliance on centralized systems (Dorri et al., 2017). The trustless nature of transactions in a Blockchain-IoT environment is particularly crucial.

Traditionally, transactions require trust in intermediaries, such as banks or payment processors, to facilitate and validate the exchange of value. Blockchain's decentralized and transparent ledger eliminates the need for trust in a centralized entity. Participants can trust the veracity of transactions recorded on the Blockchain, knowing that the system operates based on predefined rules and cryptographic security measures (Hussain et al., 2020). Furthermore, Blockchain's efficiency in handling microtransactions, facilitated by its ability to tokenize assets, opens additional opportunities in various industries. For instance, in the realm of intellectual property, artists can tokenize their work on the Blockchain, enabling fractional ownership and streamlined micropayments for the use of their creations (Zhang et al., 2018). This efficient and trustless transaction model democratizes access to and value exchange in creative industries.

Decentralized Control and Consensus

Decentralized control and consensus mechanisms are fundamental elements of Blockchain that contribute significantly to the advantages of integrating Blockchain with IoT. In traditional centralized IoT environments, a single authority or entity often controls the network, making it susceptible to failures or manipulation. Blockchain's decentralized architecture distributes control across the network, enhancing resilience and reducing the risk of weak links (Dorri et al., 2017). Consensus mechanisms, such as Proof of Work (PoW) or Proof of Stake (PoS), ensure that all nodes in the Blockchain network agree on the validity of transactions. This consensus is crucial in scenarios where multiple entities need to collaborate, and trust is established through the verification of a shared ledger. For example, in a consortium of companies involved in a supply chain, Blockchain's consensus mechanisms ensure that all participants have a consistent and agreed-upon record of transactions, fostering trust and collaboration (Zhang et al., 2018). Decentralized control and consensus are particularly valuable in addressing the challenges of scalability and interoperability in IoT environments. As the number of IoT devices proliferates, traditional centralized systems might struggle to handle the volume of transactions and data exchanges. Blockchain's decentralized nature allows for a more scalable and adaptable architecture, where the burden of processing and validating transactions is distributed across the network (Dorri et al., 2017).

In conclusion, the integration of Blockchain with IoT delivers a host of benefits that transcend the individual capabilities of each technology. Enhanced security through cryptographic methods, immutable and transparent data records, efficient and trustless transactions, and decentralized control and consensus mechanisms collectively redefine the landscape of interconnected environments. As industries continue to explore and implement Blockchain-IoT integration, the transformative potential in terms of efficiency, security, and trust sets the groundwork for a future where decentralized, transparent, and efficient systems become the norm.

4. APPLICATIONS IN MODERN BUSINESS

The fusion of Blockchain and the Internet of Things (IoT) has permeated various facets of modern business, ushering in a wave of innovative applications that redefine processes, enhance efficiency, and foster growth. This section delves into key applications in supply chain management, focusing on product traceability, counterfeit reduction, and the streamlining of operations through smart contracts. Additionally, it explores the implementation of smart contracts in legal and finance domains, showcasing the automation of contract execution, improved transparency in financial transactions, and the rise of decentralized finance (DeFi) applications.

4.1 Supply Chain Management

Traceability of Products

In the realm of supply chain management, the integration of Blockchain and IoT brings unparalleled benefits, with product traceability emerging as a foundational application. Conventional supply chains often grapple with challenges related to transparency and traceability, facing difficulties in tracking the origin, journey, and handling of products. Blockchain technology, with its transparent and immutable ledger, tackles these challenges by creating a meticulously structured record of every transaction and movement within the supply chain (Ivanov, Das, and Choi, 2020).

Imagine a global supply chain where numerous stakeholders, from manufacturers to distributors and retailers, are involved. Through the implementation of Blockchain and IoT, each product can be assigned a unique identifier or a digital twin equipped with IoT sensors.

These sensors record and transmit real-time data about the product's location, condition, and handling. This information is securely stored on the Blockchain, providing an auditable and transparent history of the product's journey through the supply chain (Ivanov et al., 2020). Product traceability is particularly crucial in industries like food and pharmaceuticals, where ensuring the authenticity and quality of products is essential. In the event of a recall, Blockchain enables swift and accurate identification of affected products, reducing the impact on consumers and minimizing financial losses for companies. The transparency introduced by Blockchain instills confidence in consumers, allowing them to trace the entire lifecycle of a product, from its origin to the point of sale, ensuring ethical purchasing and adherence to quality standards (Ivanov et al., 2020).

Reduction of Counterfeit Merchandise

Counterfeit goods pose a significant challenge to businesses and consumers alike, leading to financial losses and potential harm to consumers. The integration of Blockchain and IoT provides a robust solution to mitigate the proliferation of counterfeit goods by ensuring the authenticity and provenance of products. Each product within the supply chain is assigned a unique digital identity on the Blockchain, linked to physical items through IoT devices (Swan, 2015). As products traverse the supply chain, IoT sensors capture and record pertinent information, such as manufacturing date, transportation conditions, and storage history.

This data is then securely stored on the Blockchain, creating an unforgeable and transparent history of the product. Consumers can verify the authenticity of a product by scanning a QR code or using a mobile app to access the Blockchain and view the entire journey of the item from its origin to the point of checkout (Ivanov et al., 2020). The reduction of counterfeit products is not only a boon for consumers but also a competitive advantage for businesses. With Blockchain and IoT, brands can safeguard their reputation and build trust with consumers by ensuring the authenticity of their products. Moreover, the transparency provided by the technology aids in identifying and eliminating counterfeit products swiftly, protecting both consumers and businesses from the adverse effects of fraudulent activities (Swan, 2015).

Streamlining Operations With Smart Contracts

The implementation of smart contracts within the supply chain ecosystem is a transformative application that streamlines processes, enhances efficiency, and reduces dependence on intermediaries. Smart contracts, self-executing contracts with predefined rules encoded in code, automate and enforce contractual agreements when specified conditions are met (Ivanov et al., 2020).

Consider the intricate web of agreements and transactions involved in global trade. By utilizing smart contracts on the Blockchain, various processes, such as customs clearance, payments, and documentation, can be automated based on predefined rules. For instance, when a shipment reaches a specific geographical location, the smart contract can automatically trigger the release of payment to the supplier and update relevant documentation on the Blockchain. This automation accelerates the operations process and minimizes the risk of errors and disputes associated with manual processes (Ivanov et al., 2020).

The efficiency gains from smart contracts extend to the optimization of inventory management and order fulfillment. In a smart supply chain, IoT sensors continuously monitor inventory levels, and smart contracts automatically trigger reorder processes when predefined thresholds are reached. This proactive approach ensures that businesses maintain optimal stock levels, reduce carrying costs, and prevent stockouts or excess inventory situations (Ivanov et al., 2020).

In summary, the integration of Blockchain and IoT in supply chain management revolutionizes traditional processes, offering traceability of products, reducing counterfeit goods, and streamlining operations through the automation capabilities of smart contracts. These applications not only enhance efficiency but also contribute to increased transparency, trust, and sustainability in modern supply chain ecosystems.

4.2 Smart Contracts in Legal and Finance

Automation of Contract Execution

Smart contracts, a significant feature of Blockchain technology, find extensive applications in legal and financial domains, disrupting how contracts are executed and enforced. The automation of contract execution through smart contracts eliminates the need for intermediaries, streamlining processes, reducing costs, and improving the efficiency of legal and financial transactions (Mougayar, 2016). In legal settings, smart contracts automate the execution of predefined agreements without the need for traditional legal intermediaries. For example, in real estate transactions, smart contracts can facilitate the automatic transfer of ownership once predefined criteria, such as payment and verification of property title, are met. This eliminates the need for escrow services and expedites the entire process while ensuring the security and transparency of the transaction (Swan, 2015). Financial transactions, ranging from simple payments to complex derivatives contracts, benefit immensely from the automation capabilities of smart contracts. Cross-border transactions, typically requiring the involvement of multiple financial intermediaries and complex documentation, can be streamlined through smart contracts. The self-executing nature of these contracts ensures that payments are automatically triggered upon the fulfillment of predetermined conditions, reducing settlement times and mitigating the risk of errors (Mougayar, 2016).

Enhanced Transparency in Financial Transactions

The transparency inherent in Blockchain technology contributes to increased trust and visibility in financial transactions. In traditional financial systems, the lack of transparency can lead to challenges such as delayed settlement times, disputes, and difficulties in tracking the flow of funds. Blockchain's decentralized and transparent ledger resolves these issues by providing a real-time, immutable record of financial transactions (Swan, 2015). Imagine a scenario where a company issues bonds on a Blockchain platform. Every transaction, from the issuance of bonds to interest payments and bondholder transfers, is recorded on the Blockchain. Investors can access this transparent ledger to verify the authenticity of transactions, track the flow of funds, and ensure compliance with contractual agreements. This level of transparency instills confidence in investors, reduces the risk of fraudulent activities, and improves the overall integrity of financial markets (Mougayar, 2016). Moreover, the transparency of Blockchain extends to auditing and regulatory compliance. Regulatory authorities can access the Blockchain to conduct real-time audits, ensuring that financial institutions adhere to compliance regulations and reporting requirements. This streamlines the auditing process and reduces the likelihood of fraud and non-compliance by providing a tamper-proof and verifiable record of financial activities (Swan, 2015).

Decentralized Finance (DeFi) Applications

The integration of Blockchain and smart contracts has given rise to the phenomenon of decentralized finance (DeFi), a paradigm shift in the traditional financial landscape. DeFi applications leverage Blockchain technology to create decentralized and permissionless financial services, offering opportunities for lending, borrowing, trading, and asset management without the need for traditional financial intermediaries (Mougayar, 2016).

Decentralized lending platforms, built on Blockchain and smart contracts, enable users to lend or borrow funds directly from each other. Smart contracts automate the lending and repayment processes, eliminating the need for banks or intermediaries. Borrowers provide collateral in the form of digital assets, and smart contracts automatically execute transactions based on predefined terms, ensuring the security and efficiency of the lending ecosystem (Swan, 2015).

Thus, the integration of smart contracts into legal and financial processes, coupled with the emergence of decentralized finance (DeFi) applications, exemplifies the transformative potential of Blockchain technology. The automation of contract execution, improved transparency in financial transactions, and the growth of decentralized financial services contribute to a future where traditional intermediaries are gradually being replaced by efficient, transparent, and user-centric decentralized systems. As these applications continue to evolve, they are restructuring the landscape of contemporary business, paving the way for a more inclusive, efficient, and decentralized financial environment.

4.3 Healthcare and Patient Data Management

The integration of Blockchain and the Internet of Things (IoT) in the healthcare sector has ushered in a new era of innovation, particularly in the secure sharing of medical records, monitoring and tracking of medical devices, and ensuring the traceability and authenticity of medications. These applications not only enhance the efficiency of healthcare processes but also address critical challenges related to data security, interoperability, and patient care.

Secure Sharing of Clinical Records

Securing the sharing of medical records is a paramount concern in healthcare, where patient data's privacy and integrity are crucial. Blockchain, with its decentralized and cryptographic structure, offers a robust solution to challenges associated with medical record management. Each patient's medical history, diagnostic reports, and treatment plans can be securely stored on the Blockchain, ensuring that the data is tamper-proof and accessible only to authorized healthcare providers (Hussain et al., 2020).

Imagine a scenario where a patient seeks medical care from a different healthcare facility than their primary care provider. Through Blockchain and IoT, with the patient's consent, medical records can be securely shared with the new healthcare provider in real-time. The decentralized nature of Blockchain ensures that the patient retains control over their data, granting access only to authorized personnel. This streamlines healthcare delivery and eliminates the need for redundant diagnostic tests, reducing the risk of medical errors due to incomplete information (Linn, Koo, and Nicol, 2017).

Secure sharing of medical records is particularly critical in emergency situations, where quick access to accurate patient information can be a matter of life and death. Blockchain ensures that emergency responders and healthcare providers have real-time access to a patient's medical history, allergies, and ongoing treatments, facilitating timely and informed decision-making. This application significantly contributes to improving patient outcomes and the overall efficiency of healthcare delivery (Linn et al., 2017).

Monitoring and Tracking of Medical Devices

Monitoring and tracking of medical devices are essential components of healthcare management, ensuring the proper functioning and maintenance of critical equipment. IoT sensors integrated with medical devices, combined with Blockchain, create a transparent and traceable system for monitoring the lifecycle of these devices. Every interaction, from manufacturing to deployment and maintenance, is recorded on the Blockchain, providing a comprehensive and immutable history of the device (Hussain et al., 2020).

Consider the case of a medical imaging device equipped with IoT sensors. These sensors can capture data on usage patterns, performance metrics, and maintenance requirements.

The data is securely recorded on the Blockchain, allowing healthcare facilities to monitor the device's status in real-time. Automated smart contracts can be used to trigger maintenance requests or updates based on predefined conditions, ensuring that the devices are consistently operating optimally (Linn et al., 2017).Tracking of medical devices is crucial for regulatory compliance, quality control, and patient safety. Blockchain's transparency and immutability enable healthcare providers, regulatory bodies, and manufacturers to trace the entire lifecycle of a medical device. In the event of audits or safety concerns, this technology facilitates rapid identification and notification, minimizing potential risks to patients and maintaining the integrity of healthcare processes (Hussain et al., 2020).

Drug Traceability and Legitimacy

Ensuring the traceability and authenticity of drugs is a significant challenge in the healthcare industry, with counterfeiting and supply chain issues posing risks to patient safety. Blockchain, integrated with IoT, provides a comprehensive solution to address these challenges by creating a transparent and unalterable record of the pharmaceutical supply chain. Each stage of the drug's journey, from manufacturing to distribution and retail, is recorded on the Blockchain, providing a tamper-proof history of the medication (Linn et al., 2017).

Imagine a scenario where a patient receives a prescribed medication. Through Blockchain and IoT, the patient can verify the authenticity and origin of the medication by scanning a QR code or accessing the Blockchain. This transparency instills confidence in patients, ensuring that they receive genuine and safe medications. Additionally, healthcare providers can use this technology to verify the authenticity of drugs in their inventory, reducing the risk of dealing with counterfeit or substandard medications (Hussain et al., 2020).

Blockchain's role in drug traceability extends to regulatory compliance, particularly in addressing stringent requirements for drug supply chains. The decentralized nature of Blockchain ensures that all stakeholders, including manufacturers, distributors, and regulatory authorities, have real-time access to a shared and verifiable record. This facilitates seamless auditing, regulatory reporting, and compliance verification, contributing to the overall integrity and safety of drug supply chains (Linn et al., 2017).

In conclusion, the integration of Blockchain and IoT in healthcare and patient information management presents innovative applications that enhance the security, efficiency, and transparency of healthcare processes. From secure sharing of medical records to monitoring and tracking of medical devices, and ensuring drug traceability and authenticity, these applications contribute to improved patient care, reduced costs, and streamlined healthcare operations.

4.4 Energy and Utilities

The energy and utilities sector has undergone a paradigm shift with the integration of Blockchain and the Internet of Things (IoT), offering remarkable applications in smart grids, efficient energy distribution, monitoring and maintenance of infrastructure, and the emergence of decentralized energy trading platforms. These applications transform the traditional energy landscape, providing opportunities for increased efficiency, sustainability, and decentralized energy management.

Smart Grids and Efficient Energy Distribution

Smart grids, powered by the integration of Blockchain and IoT, represent a significant advancement in the energy and utilities sector. Traditional energy grids face challenges related to reliability, lack of real-time data, and vulnerability to issues. The implementation of IoT sensors and Blockchain technology addresses these issues by creating intelligent, self-monitoring networks that enhance energy distribution and consumption (Swan, 2015).

Imagine a smart grid scenario where IoT sensors are integrated into power lines, transformers, and distribution points. These sensors continuously collect real-time data on energy consumption, grid performance, and equipment health. The data is securely recorded on the Blockchain, creating a transparent and immutable record of the entire energy system. Smart contracts embedded in the Blockchain can automate processes such as load balancing, issue detection, and response to peak demand, improving energy distribution in real-time (Zhang, 2018).

The efficiency gains from smart grids extend to renewable energy integration and demand-side management. Through Blockchain and IoT, energy producers can track the generation of renewable energy, such as solar or wind power, and efficiently distribute it across the network. Consumers, equipped with IoT-enabled devices, can actively participate in demand response programs, adjusting their energy consumption based on real-time pricing or grid conditions. This bidirectional communication facilitated by smart grids enhances overall energy efficiency and sustainability (Zhang, 2018).

Monitoring and Maintenance of Infrastructure

The monitoring and maintenance of the energy infrastructure are critical aspects of ensuring the reliability and longevity of energy assets. IoT sensors, combined with Blockchain technology, create a robust system for continuous monitoring and predictive maintenance. Sensors installed on equipment, such as turbines, transformers, and substations, collect data on performance metrics, temperature, and wear and tear. This data is securely recorded on the Blockchain, providing a transparent and tamper-proof history of the system (Swan, 2015).

Consider a wind farm equipped with IoT sensors on each turbine. These sensors monitor the health and performance of the turbines, collecting data on parameters such as blade rotation speed, vibration levels, and energy output. This real-time data is securely stored on the Blockchain, enabling predictive maintenance through automated smart contracts. When predefined conditions indicative of potential issues are met, smart contracts can trigger maintenance alerts, ensuring timely intervention to prevent equipment failures and improve the lifespan of the energy infrastructure (Zhang, 2018).

Decentralized Energy Trading Platforms

One of the most remarkable applications of Blockchain and the Internet of Things (IoT) in the energy sector is the emergence of decentralized energy trading platforms. These platforms utilize Blockchain's smart contracts to facilitate peer-to-peer energy trading among consumers, producers, and prosumers (consumers who also generate energy). Through IoT-enabled smart meters, data on energy consumption and production are securely recorded on the Blockchain, enabling transparent and automated energy transactions (Zhang, 2018). Imagine a residential area equipped with solar chargers on several rooftops. The energy generated by these solar chargers is logged on the Blockchain through IoT-enabled smart meters. Residents can then engage in peer-to-peer energy trading, exchanging excess energy directly with their neighbors. Smart contracts automatically execute transactions based on predefined pricing and usage agreements, creating a decentralized and efficient energy marketplace (Swan, 2015).

Decentralized energy trading platforms offer numerous advantages, including increased energy efficiency, reduced reliance on centralized utilities, and potential opportunities for renewable energy producers to monetize surplus generation. Consumers, in turn, can benefit from lower costs, enhanced transparency, and the ability to support local and sustainable energy sources. The decentralized nature of these platforms aligns with the broader trend of energy democratization, empowering individuals and communities to actively participate in and shape the future of the energy landscape (Zhang, 2018).

In conclusion, the integration of Blockchain and IoT in the energy and utilities sector introduces innovative applications that redefine traditional energy systems. From smart grids optimizing energy distribution to real-time monitoring and predictive maintenance of infrastructure, and the emergence of decentralized energy trading platforms, these applications contribute to increased efficiency, sustainability, and decentralization in the energy landscape. As the energy sector continues to embrace these advancements, the potential for a more resilient, efficient, and consumer-centric energy environment becomes increasingly tangible.

5. FUTURE TRENDS AND CHALLENGES

The convergence of Blockchain and the Internet of Things (IoT) has ushered in an unprecedented era in modern business, introducing novel applications and reshaping existing paradigms. As we look ahead, several trends and challenges emerge, influencing the trajectory of this technological fusion. This section delves into the evolving business models facilitated by tokenization and Decentralized Autonomous Organizations (DAOs), offering new revenue streams and organizational structures. Additionally, it explores the challenges and considerations that must be addressed for the widespread adoption of Blockchain and IoT, including scalability issues, regulatory hurdles, and the need for standardization to ensure interoperability.

5.1 Evolving Business Models

Tokenization and New Revenue Streams

One of the most compelling trends shaping the future of businesses utilizing Blockchain and IoT is the advent of tokenization. Tokens, digital representations of real or virtual assets, are created and managed on Blockchain platforms, providing numerous opportunities for companies to tokenize assets, products, or services. This opens up new avenues for revenue generation and innovative business models (Mougayar, 2016).

Imagine a scenario where a manufacturing company decides to tokenize its production processes. Each stage of the manufacturing lifecycle, from raw material acquisition to final product assembly, can be represented by tokens on the Blockchain. These tokens could be traded or exchanged within the ecosystem, allowing stakeholders like suppliers, distributors, and even end consumers to participate in and benefit from the value chain. Tokenization transforms traditionally illiquid assets into easily tradable and divisible units, unlocking liquidity and democratizing access to investment opportunities (Swan, 2015).

Furthermore, tokenization extends beyond tangible assets to include digital goods, intellectual property, and even services. Content creators, for instance, can tokenize their digital art, music, or written content on Blockchain platforms. Consumers can then purchase or trade these tokens, providing artists with direct monetization opportunities and a more equitable distribution of revenue. Tokenized digital goods also pave the way for new business models in the gaming industry, where in-game assets can be tokenized and seamlessly traded across different gaming platforms (Mougayar, 2016).

The tokenization of assets aligns with the broader trend of fractional ownership and decentralized finance (DeFi). Companies can issue security tokens representing ownership in real assets, offering investors the ability to hold fractional shares. This democratization of ownership increases liquidity in traditionally illiquid markets and expands access to investment opportunities. As Blockchain technology continues to evolve, the tokenization of various assets is expected to become a cornerstone of emerging business models, reshaping how value is created, exchanged, and distributed in the digital economy (Tariq, 2024).

Decentralized Autonomous Organizations (DAOs)

Decentralized Autonomous Organizations (DAOs) represent another frontier in emerging business models, leveraging Blockchain's smart contract capabilities to create autonomous, self-governing entities.

DAOs are organizations run by code, with decision-making processes and governance rules encoded in smart contracts. This enables stakeholders to collectively manage and govern the organization without the need for traditional hierarchical structures (Zhang, 2018).

Imagine a venture that chooses to operate as a DAO. The rules governing navigation, resource allocation, and profit distribution are entirely encoded in smart contracts on the Blockchain. Stakeholders, who hold governance tokens, participate in the decision-making process by voting on proposals. Smart contracts automatically execute decisions based on the outcome of these votes, providing a transparent and trustless mechanism for organizational governance. This decentralized approach to decision-making reduces the need for centralized authority and enhances transparency and inclusivity within the organization (Mougayar, 2016). DAOs offer a paradigm shift in organizational structures, fostering greater collaboration, efficiency, and scalability. Traditional companies often grapple with issues of transparency, accountability, and decision-making bottlenecks. DAOs address these challenges by providing a transparent and auditable record of all decisions and transactions on the Blockchain. The elimination of intermediaries and centralized control mitigates the risk of corruption, fraud, and power imbalances within organizations (Zhang, 2018).

Moreover, DAOs extend beyond traditional corporate structures to govern decentralized networks, protocols, and even communities. For example, a blockchain protocol could be governed by a DAO, with token holders collectively deciding on protocol upgrades, parameter changes, and ecosystem development initiatives. This decentralized governance model enhances the resilience and sustainability of blockchain communities, ensuring that the community has a direct say in the evolution of the technology (Mougayar, 2016). As businesses and organizations explore the potential of DAOs, challenges related to legal frameworks, accountability, and decision-making processes need to be navigated. Nevertheless, the contribution of decentralized, transparent, and autonomous organizational structures positions DAOs as a pivotal trend in shaping the future landscape of business models (Yan et al., 2021).

5.2 Challenges and Considerations

Scalability Issues in Both Blockchain and IoT

While the integration of Blockchain and IoT offers great possibilities, scalability remains a critical challenge that must be addressed for widespread adoption. In the context of Blockchain, scalability refers to the ability of a network to handle a growing number of transactions without compromising performance. Traditional blockchain networks, especially those using Proof of Work (PoW) consensus mechanisms, face limitations in transaction throughput and latency (Swan, 2015).

The scalability challenge is exacerbated when it comes to IoT, where a large number of devices generate and exchange data in real-time. Current blockchain architectures might struggle to accommodate the sheer volume of transactions generated by IoT devices, leading to congestion, delays, and increased transaction costs. As companies plan to deploy large-scale IoT applications integrated with blockchain, finding scalable solutions becomes crucial (Dorri et al., 2017).

Several scalability solutions are being explored within the blockchain space. The adoption of alternative consensus mechanisms, such as Proof of Stake (PoS) or Directed Acyclic Graphs (DAGs), aims to improve transaction throughput and reduce latency. Layer 2 scaling solutions, such as state channels and sidechains, enable off-chain processing of transactions, alleviating the burden on the main blockchain network. Furthermore, ongoing research and development focus on optimizing blockchain protocols and architecture to enhance scalability without compromising decentralization and security (Zhang, 2018).

In the realm of IoT, scalability challenges manifest as device interoperability, data management, and network congestion. As the number of IoT devices proliferates, the existing infrastructure might struggle to handle the massive data influx, leading to bottlenecks and failures. Ensuring seamless communication and data exchange among diverse IoT devices, each with its own specifications and protocols, poses a significant interoperability challenge (Dorri et al., 2017).

To address these challenges, the integration of edge computing with IoT emerges as a promising solution. Edge computing involves processing data closer to the source, reducing latency and alleviating the burden on centralized cloud servers. Combining edge computing with blockchain can enhance the scalability and efficiency of IoT applications by distributing computational tasks and data storage across a decentralized network. This distributed approach not only improves scalability but also enhances the overall reliability and responsiveness of IoT ecosystems (Zhang, 2018; Bayanati, 2023).

Regulatory and Legal Obstacles

The integration of Blockchain and IoT presents novel challenges in the regulatory and legal landscape, requiring careful navigation to ensure compliance and facilitate innovation. Regulatory frameworks for blockchain and IoT applications vary significantly across regions, posing complexities for companies operating in a global context. Issues like data privacy, security, intellectual property, and consumer protection demand clear legal frameworks to provide certainty for businesses and safeguard the rights of users (Kshetri, 2017). Concerning IoT, data privacy emerges as a distinct concern. The vast amount of personal and sensitive data generated by IoT devices raises questions about how this data is collected, stored, and shared. Traditional data protection regulations may not fully address the unique challenges posed by the decentralized and interconnected nature of IoT ecosystems. Compliance with regulations like the General Data Protection Regulation (GDPR) in the European Union becomes crucial, necessitating transparent data practices, user consent mechanisms, and robust security measures (Bil, Hossain, and Kang, 2018).

Blockchain, despite providing enhanced security and transparency, introduces a set of regulatory challenges. The pseudonymous and immutable nature of blockchain transactions may clash with traditional financial regulations, particularly concerning anti-money laundering (AML) and know your customer (KYC) requirements. Regulators grapple with the need to strike a balance between preserving the privacy and security benefits of blockchain while ensuring adherence to established legal frameworks (Kshetri, 2017). Smart contracts, a crucial element of blockchain technology, further complicate the regulatory landscape. The enforceability and legal status of smart contracts vary across jurisdictions, necessitating legal clarity to validate their use in business processes. Clear definitions, regulations, and legal precedents are essential to ensure that smart contracts align with existing legal structures and provide a reliable basis for contractual agreements (Bil et al., 2018).

Moreover, the evolution of tokenized assets and decentralized finance (DeFi) applications introduces new dimensions to regulatory challenges. The issuance of tokens, the regulatory status of decentralized exchanges, and the oversight of decentralized financial instruments all require careful consideration. Regulatory bodies worldwide are grappling with the need to adjust existing frameworks or create new ones to accommodate the decentralized and innovative nature of blockchain-based financial services (Kshetri, 2017).

Normalization for Interoperability

Interoperability, or the seamless exchange of data and transactions across different systems and platforms, is a central consideration for the successful integration of Blockchain and IoT. The diverse and evolving nature of both technologies requires standardized protocols and frameworks to ensure compatibility and interoperability. Lack of standardization can lead to fragmented ecosystems, limiting the potential benefits of blockchain and IoT integration (Dorri et al., 2017). In the context of blockchain, normalization involves agreeing upon common protocols, data formats, and technical procedures. Various blockchain platforms may use unique consensus mechanisms, smart contract languages, and data structures, posing challenges for interoperability. Standardized protocols, such as the Interledger Protocol (ILP) and the Symbolic Categorization System (TTF), aim to provide a common language for blockchain entities to communicate and transact seamlessly (Mougayar, 2016).

On the other hand, IoT devices often operate on diverse communication protocols and standards. Each device manufacturer may use proprietary protocols, creating siloed environments that hinder collaboration and data exchange. Standardization efforts, such as the development of the Message Queuing Telemetry Transport (MQTT) and Constrained Application Protocol (CoAP), seek to establish common communication protocols for IoT devices, facilitating interoperability and enabling seamless integration with blockchain networks (Dorri et al., 2017).

The convergence of Blockchain and IoT requires intra-technology standardization as well as interoperability between the two. Blockchain networks should be able to seamlessly integrate with diverse IoT devices, each with its own communication protocols and data formats. Standardization efforts, like the IoTivity framework and the Open Connectivity Foundation (OCF), aim to create common standards that enable blockchain platforms to connect with and retrieve data from IoT devices (Zhang, 2018). The importance of standardization extends to the development of smart contracts. While various blockchain platforms support smart contracts, there is a lack of consistency in the languages and execution environments used. Standardization in smart contract languages, such as the Smart Contracts 1.0 initiative, seeks to establish a common foundation for smart contract development, enabling interoperability across different blockchain networks (Mougayar, 2016; Alamri, 2019).

Thus, addressing scalability issues, navigating regulatory obstacles, and outlining standardized protocols are critical considerations for the future of Blockchain and IoT integration. As businesses and technology ecosystems continue to evolve, collaboration between industry stakeholders, regulatory bodies, and standardization organizations becomes essential. By proactively addressing these challenges, the full potential of Blockchain and IoT integration can be realized, ushering in a new era of efficiency, transparency, and innovation in modern business.

CONCLUSION

In essence, the integration of Blockchain and the Internet of Things (IoT) represents a paradigm shift with extraordinary potential to reshape the landscape of modern business. As organizations embark on this transformative journey, understanding the intricate dynamics and challenges inherent in the integration of these two groundbreaking technologies is paramount. This section aims to provide a comprehensive and insightful analysis, serving as a valuable guide for businesses seeking to embrace and adapt to this new era of innovation. The fundamental rationale behind integrating Blockchain and IoT lies in their complementary resources. Blockchain, with its decentralized, secure, and transparent ledger system, addresses fundamental issues of trust, security, and immutability. Conversely, IoT contributes by enabling a vast network of interconnected devices to generate real-time data, facilitating a new dimension of efficiency and data-driven decision-making. Together, they create a robust synergy, unlocking novel possibilities across various industry sectors. Understanding the fundamentals of Blockchain, including its decentralized and distributed ledger, consensus mechanisms, and smart contracts, lays the foundation for appreciating its unique potential. The technology's key attributes, such as security, immutability, transparency, and reduced fraud, further enhance its applicability and appeal in diverse business environments. Simultaneously, delving into the core concepts of IoT, including interconnected devices, data collection, communication protocols, and edge computing, provides a holistic view of the ecosystem. Real-world applications in smart cities, healthcare, agriculture, and manufacturing highlight the tangible impact of IoT on enhancing efficiency, productivity, and decision-making processes.

The convergence of Blockchain and IoT addresses challenges that each technology faces individually. Blockchain offers solutions to security concerns in IoT, ensuring data integrity and privacy in an interconnected world. It provides a robust framework for the interoperability of various IoT devices, laying the groundwork for standardized communication and collaboration. Examining the advantages of integrating Blockchain with IoT reveals a spectrum of benefits, including enhanced security through cryptographic methods, immutable and transparent data records, efficient and trustless transactions, and decentralized control through consensus mechanisms. These advantages not only bolster the reliability and integrity of data but also pave the way for the development of innovative business models and processes. The applications of Blockchain and IoT in modern business are diverse and significant. From supply chain management and smart contracts in legal and finance to healthcare and patient data management, these technologies offer solutions that streamline processes, enhance transparency, and reduce the risk of fraud. The emergence of decentralized finance (DeFi) applications further illustrates how the integration of Blockchain and smart contracts is transforming traditional financial systems. However, amid the vast potential, it is crucial to identify and address the challenges that arise. Scalability issues in both Blockchain and IoT, regulatory and legal obstacles, and the need for standardization for interoperability are critical considerations that organizations must navigate. Scalability solutions, regulatory frameworks, and standardization efforts are essential for ensuring the seamless integration and widespread adoption of these technologies. Looking forward, future trends indicate evolving business models characterized by tokenization and the rise of decentralized autonomous organizations (DAOs). Tokenization unlocks new revenue streams and democratizes ownership, while DAOs redefine organizational structures, emphasizing transparency and inclusivity. These trends underscore the ongoing evolution and transformative potential inherent in the integration of Blockchain and IoT. In conclusion, the integration of Blockchain and IoT heralds a new era of opportunities for organizations willing to embrace innovation. By understanding the complexities of these technologies, harnessing their synergies, and proactively addressing challenges, organizations can position themselves at the forefront of a rapidly evolving business landscape. As we embark on this journey of transformation, the guidance provided in this section serves as a compass, assisting organizations in navigating the complexities and unlocking the full spectrum of benefits offered by the integration of Blockchain and IoT.

REFERENCES

Al-Rakhami, M. S., & Al-Mashari, M. (2020). Blockchain and internet of things for business process management: Theory, challenges, and key success factors. *International Journal of Advanced Computer Science and Applications*, *11*(10). Advance online publication. doi:10.14569/IJACSA.2020.0111069

Alam, T. (2022). Blockchain-Based Internet of Things: Review, Current Trends, Applications, and Future Challenges. *Computers*, *12*(1), 6. doi:10.3390/computers12010006

Alamri, M., Jhanjhi, N. Z., & Humayun, M. (2019). Blockchain for Internet of Things (IoT) research issues challenges & future directions: A review. *Int. J. Comput. Sci. Netw. Secur*, *19*(1), 244–258.

Alsharari, N. (2021). Integrating blockchain technology with internet of things to efficiency. *International Journal of Technology, Innovation and Management (IJTIM)*, *1*(2), 1-13.

Atlam, H. F., Alenezi, A., Alassafi, M. O., & Wills, G. (2018). Blockchain with internet of things: Benefits, challenges, and future directions. *International Journal of Intelligent Systems and Applications*, *10*(6), 40–48. doi:10.5815/ijisa.2018.06.05

Bayanati, M. (2023). Business Model of Internet of Things and Blockchain Technology in Developing Countries. *International Journal of Innovation in Engineering*, *3*(1), 13–22. doi:10.59615/ijie.3.1.13

Bhushan, B., Sahoo, C., Sinha, P., & Khamparia, A. (2021). Unification of Blockchain and Internet of Things (BIoT): Requirements, working model, challenges and future directions. *Wireless Networks*, *27*(1), 55–90. doi:10.1007/s11276-020-02445-6

Bragadeesh, S. A., & Umamakeswari, A. (2018). Role of blockchain in the Internet-of-Things (IoT). *Int. J. Eng. Technol*, *7*(2), 109–112.

Chilamkurti, N., Poongodi, T., & Balusamy, B. (Eds.). (2021). *Blockchain, Internet of things, and artificial intelligence*. CRC Press. doi:10.1201/9780429352898

Da Xu, L., & Viriyasitavat, W. (2019). Application of blockchain in collaborative internet-of-things services. *IEEE Transactions on Computational Social Systems*, *6*(6), 1295–1305. doi:10.1109/TCSS.2019.2913165

Dai, H. N., Zheng, Z., & Zhang, Y. (2019). Blockchain for Internet of Things: A survey. *IEEE Internet of Things Journal*, *6*(5), 8076–8094. doi:10.1109/JIOT.2019.2920987

de Villiers, C., Kuruppu, S., & Dissanayake, D. (2021). A (new) role for business–Promoting the United Nations' Sustainable Development Goals through the internet-of-things and blockchain technology. *Journal of Business Research*, *131*, 598–609. doi:10.1016/j.jbusres.2020.11.066

Fernández-Caramés, T. M., & Fraga-Lamas, P. (2018). A Review on the Use of Blockchain for the Internet of Things. *IEEE Access : Practical Innovations, Open Solutions*, *6*, 32979–33001. doi:10.1109/ACCESS.2018.2842685

Hassan, M., Chen, J., Iftekhar, A., & Cui, X. (2020). Future of the internet of things emerging with blockchain and smart contracts. *International Journal of Advanced Computer Science and Applications*, *11*(6). Advance online publication. doi:10.14569/IJACSA.2020.0110676

Huckle, S., Bhattacharya, R., White, M., & Beloff, N. (2016). Internet of things, blockchain and shared economy applications. *Procedia Computer Science, 98*, 461–466. doi:10.1016/j.procs.2016.09.074

Hussein, D. M. E. D. M., Taha, M. H. N., & Khalifa, N. E. M. (2018). A blockchain technology evolution between business process management (BPM) and Internet-of-Things (IoT). *International Journal of Advanced Computer Science and Applications, 9*(8). Advance online publication. doi:10.14569/IJACSA.2018.090856

Iftekhar, A., Cui, X., Hassan, M., & Afzal, W. (2020). Application of blockchain and Internet of Things to ensure tamper-proof data availability for food safety. *Journal of Food Quality, 2020*, 1–14. doi:10.1155/2020/5385207

Khrais, L. T. (2020). IoT and blockchain in the development of smart cities. *International Journal of Advanced Computer Science and Applications, 11*(2). Advance online publication. doi:10.14569/IJACSA.2020.0110220

Kumar, R. L., Khan, F., Kadry, S., & Rho, S. (2022). A survey on blockchain for industrial internet of things. *Alexandria Engineering Journal, 61*(8), 6001–6022. doi:10.1016/j.aej.2021.11.023

Mougayar, W. (2016). *The business blockchain: promise, practice, and application of the next Internet technology*. John Wiley & Sons.

Pal, K. (2021). Privacy, security and policies: A review of problems and solutions with blockchain-based internet of things applications in manufacturing industry. *Procedia Computer Science, 191*, 176–183. doi:10.1016/j.procs.2021.07.022

Pal, K., & Yasar, A.-U.-H. (2020). Internet of things and blockchain technology in apparel manufacturing supply chain data management. *Procedia Computer Science, 170*, 450–457. doi:10.1016/j.procs.2020.03.088

Raimi, L., Kah, J. M., & Tariq, M. U. (2022). The Discourse of Blue Economy Definitions, Measurements, and Theories: Implications for Strengthening Academic Research and Industry Practice. In L. Raimi & J. Kah (Eds.), *Implications for Entrepreneurship and Enterprise Development in the Blue Economy* (pp. 1–17). IGI Global. doi:10.4018/978-1-6684-3393-5.ch001

Raimi, L., Tariq, M. U., & Kah, J. M. (2022). Diversity, Equity, and Inclusion as the Future Workplace Ethics: Theoretical Review. In L. Raimi & J. Kah (Eds.), *Mainstreaming Diversity, Equity, and Inclusion as Future Workplace Ethics* (pp. 1–27). IGI Global. doi:10.4018/978-1-6684-3657-8.ch001

Ratta, P., Kaur, A., Sharma, S., Shabaz, M., & Dhiman, G. (2021). Application of blockchain and internet of things in healthcare and medical sector: Applications, challenges, and future perspectives. *Journal of Food Quality, 2021*, 1–20. doi:10.1155/2021/7608296

Rejeb, A., Keogh, J. G., & Treiblmaier, H. (2019). Leveraging the internet of things and blockchain technology in supply chain management. *Future Internet, 11*(7), 161. doi:10.3390/fi11070161

Sharma, D. K., Kaushik, A. K., Goel, A., & Bhargava, S. (2020). Internet of things and blockchain: integration, need, challenges, applications, and future scope. In *Handbook of Research on Blockchain Technology* (pp. 271–294). Academic Press. doi:10.1016/B978-0-12-819816-2.00011-3

Tariq, M. U. (2024). Equity and Inclusion in Learning Ecosystems. In F. Al Husseiny & A. Munna (Eds.), *Preparing Students for the Future Educational Paradigm* (pp. 155–176). IGI Global. doi:10.4018/979-8-3693-1536-1.ch007

Tariq, M. U. (2024). Empowering Educators in the Learning Ecosystem. In F. Al Husseiny & A. Munna (Eds.), *Preparing Students for the Future Educational Paradigm* (pp. 232–255). IGI Global. doi:10.4018/979-8-3693-1536-1.ch010

Tariq, M. U. (2024). Revolutionizing Health Data Management With Blockchain Technology: Enhancing Security and Efficiency in a Digital Era. In M. Garcia & R. de Almeida (Eds.), *Emerging Technologies for Health Literacy and Medical Practice* (pp. 153–175). IGI Global. doi:10.4018/979-8-3693-1214-8.ch008

Tariq, M. U. (2024). Emerging Trends and Innovations in Blockchain-Digital Twin Integration for Green Investments: A Case Study Perspective. In S. Jafar, R. Rodriguez, H. Kannan, S. Akhtar, & P. Plugmann (Eds.), *Harnessing Blockchain-Digital Twin Fusion for Sustainable Investments* (pp. 148–175). IGI Global. doi:10.4018/979-8-3693-1878-2.ch007

Tariq, M. U. (2024). Emotional Intelligence in Understanding and Influencing Consumer Behavior. In T. Musiolik, R. Rodriguez, & H. Kannan (Eds.), *AI Impacts in Digital Consumer Behavior* (pp. 56–81). IGI Global. doi:10.4018/979-8-3693-1918-5.ch003

Tyagi, A. K., Dananjayan, S., Agarwal, D., & Thariq Ahmed, H. F. (2023). Blockchain—Internet of Things Applications: Opportunities and Challenges for Industry 4.0 and Society 5.0. *Sensors (Basel)*, *23*(2), 947. doi:10.3390/s23020947 PMID:36679743

Viriyasitavat, W., Da Xu, L., Bi, Z., & Pungpapong, V. (2019). Blockchain and internet of things for modern business process in digital economy—The state of the art. *IEEE Transactions on Computational Social Systems*, *6*(6), 1420–1432. doi:10.1109/TCSS.2019.2919325

Wu, J., Xiong, F., & Li, C. (2019). Application of Internet of Things and blockchain technologies to improve accounting information quality. *IEEE Access : Practical Innovations, Open Solutions*, *7*, 100090–100098. doi:10.1109/ACCESS.2019.2930637

Yan, C., Zhu, J., Ouyang, Y., & Zeng, X. (2021). Marketing method and system optimization based on the financial blockchain of the internet of things. *Wireless Communications and Mobile Computing*, *2021*, 1–11. doi:10.1155/2021/9354569

Zhang, Y., & Wen, J. (2017). The IoT electric business model: Using blockchain technology for the internet of things. *Peer-to-Peer Networking and Applications*, *10*(4), 983–994. doi:10.1007/s12083-016-0456-1

Chapter 5
Hospitality and Tourism Value Co-Creation in the Light of Artificial Intelligence

Mohammed Majeed
https://orcid.org/0000-0001-9804-5335
Tamale Technical University, Ghana

ABSTRACT

The hotel and tourism industry is undergoing significant changes due to the widespread adoption of digital technologies that enable instant client communication and data gathering. The aim of the chapter was to do a review to understand the AI technologies that influence value co-creation in the hospitality and tourism industry. The author found AI influencing VCC to include natural language processing, chatbot, intelligent agents, voice-activated digital support, personal digital assistants that aid online visitors, ML, etc. The DART model was selected as the primary framework due to its status as a prominent theory and its widespread application in the study of VCC. It was noticed that AI can facilitate dialogue, access, risk, and transparency, leading to customer/guests/visitor engagement. Future research should focus on AI for marketing and promotion. It was concluded that AI technology provides compelling prospects for engaging interactions and virtual gatherings.

INTRODUCTION

In 2020, the hotels and restaurants industry contributed approximately 3.9 billion Ghanaian cedis (GHS) to the country's GDP, equivalent to around 640.9 million US dollars. This was a significant decrease compared to the previous years, likely due to the impact of the COVID-19 pandemic. In 2019, the industry reached a peak of nearly six billion GHS, equivalent to around 985.8 million US dollars, continuing the upward trend observed since 2014. Overall, the total consumer spending on hotels and restaurants in Ghana was projected to reach over 2.43 billion US dollars in 2021, as stated by Sasu (2022).

Businesses in the tourist and hospitality sector have had to adapt to new ways of doing things and interacting with consumers as a result of numerous modifications brought about by the rise of digital

DOI: 10.4018/979-8-3693-2367-0.ch005

technology (Pencarelli, 2020). The idea of value co-creation, in which a company and its customers work together to build and share value, is one example of this shift (Carvalho & Alves, 2022). Technology that allows everybody with an interest, particularly businesses and customers, to participate is crucial for the travel and hospitality industry's value co-creation process [4, 5]. Therefore, technology is an essential tool for facilitating value co-creation. Because it allows customers and businesses to create and trade value, cutting-edge technology can play a pivotal role in co-creation value processes in the tourist and hospitality industry (Samala et al., 2020). How exactly AI will continue to revolutionize businesses is an open subject in light of the current rate of development. There is research that discusses the evolution of AI and its potential effects on the tourism industry (Lv et al., 2022; Mariani et al., 2022; Tussyadiah, 2020). This includes studies on the topic of AI in general. (Kong et al., 2022) These investigations are theoretical, broad in scope, and full of speculation. Few studies describe how AI may affect certain sectors or business functions. Grundner and Neuhofer (2021) and Saydam et al. (2022) explored tourism destinations and hospitality, respectively. In response to the call for further research on AI and its application to the tourism sector made by Samala et al. (2020), this three-part study investigates the possible effects of AI on hotels' marketing functions in order to gain a better understanding of AI's likely effects and its impact on organizations. Among the factors propelling the Fourth Industrial Revolution is artificial intelligence (AI), which is predicted to possess transformational and substitutive capabilities comparable to those of machines or information technology (IT) (Dwivedi et al., 2021). (Schwab, 2017). Along with big data, artificial intelligence is seen as the next generation of general-purpose technology. It has the ability to greatly influence businesses, according to Marinchak et al. (2018) and Magistrati et al. (2019).

AI's superior data processing power, massive storage capacity, and lightning-fast processing speeds allow the hotel industry to better integrate client data and anticipate their demands (Duan et al., 2019). Also, automation allows machines to do programmable and predefined activities while collaborating (Ivanov et al., 2017), such tailoring service offerings to each individual consumer based on their feedback. In fact, AI is so ubiquitous that it can be utilized for heuristic searches, character identification, face recognition systems, processing natural language, and the idea of mobile robots, among other things, and its influence goes well beyond the tourism industry (Samala et al., 2020). There are two types of contacts with clients that use AI-based solutions: direct (where AI does the work of service providers) and indirect (where AI gives information to back up service providers' tasks) (Hollander, 2023). As part of a critical debate on artificial intelligence, experts have questioned the usefulness of these new technologies and whether or not AI is being exaggerated. Here, Ford (2018) introduced the term "AI winter" to draw attention to the gap between the anticipated market breakthrough and the actual advancements made. Although artificial intelligence (AI) has its roots in the early 1980s, it has already made strides in a number of sectors and shows promise for even greater success in the future (Ford 2018). Some examples of industries that have used AI include healthcare (Becker 2019), manufacturing (Lee et al. 2018), service industries, and the tourist industry (Ivanov & Webster 2017; Tussyadiah & Miller 2019).

According to Davenport et al. (2020), Huang and Rust (2021), and Rust (2020), the best AI services are those that seamlessly integrate several technologies. Accordingly, it is critical to learn about AI's role in value co-creation and AI-powered customer experience design (i.e., how to improve customer experience with AI) (Ostrom et al. 2019). Reiterating the inherent benefits of adopting AI and automation to anticipate customer expectations and create unique solutions for clients, Duan et al. (2019) bring attention to the topic once again. Nevertheless, there is a lack of data on the important consumer characteristics that might affect their engagement with the CC process. The apparent immaturity and feasibility of AI and automation as viable VCC mechanisms inspire the current investigation. According to Bolton et al.

(2018), there are still many obstacles to overcome in terms of implementation and customer acceptance before these technologies can be considered viable tools for VCC. This is why, before implementing AI services, it's important to learn about the connections between the two, figure out where they might be useful, and be aware of the elements that will make or break the implementation. Existing literature studies are selective and limited in breadth, despite efforts by scholars like Meurisch and Mühlhäuser (2021) and Li et al. (2021) to gain a better understanding of AI services. They narrow their attention to select service industries (like travel and hospitality) and one perspective on AI services (like data protection). To sum up, these reviews don't take into account different points of view, hence they don't provide enough information to fully grasp the range of AI services. Visitors' actions following adoption, such as value co-creation, have recently been the focus of studies examining the application of artificial intelligence (e.g., robotics) in the travel and hospitality industry. In order to better understand how AI contributes to value creation, a literature study was carried out using the stimulus-organism-response (SOR) paradigm as a guide. Value co-creation (VCC) in the tourist and hospitality sector as it pertains to artificial intelligence (AI) is the focus of this broad evaluation study, which seeks to identify the most important customer-based elements and technologies.

Contributions

Academic discourse and business revolution are both aided by the study's comprehensive review of AI services. Among the little research on AI's impact on the hospitality sector, this study stands out for its examination of how the technology has helped certain establishments gain an edge in the market through value-based customer loyalty programs and VCC. Among the few literature reviews that have attempted to identify the factors that most affect AI performance and VCC in the hospitality industry, this one stands out as a pioneer. Hospitality and tourism organizations can benefit from this research because it provides a better understanding of why guest and visitor participation in value co-creation is important. Organizations in the hospitality and tourist industries can use this structured information to better craft their services and their value propositions.

Objectives of the Chapter

1. To examine the main AI tools used in the VCC process in the hospitality sector
2. To evaluate how AI is used to examine the DART model
3. To formulate hypotheses for future researchers of VCC using AI

LITERATURE

AI

The term "artificial intelligence" (AI) refers to a set of computer programs that mimic human intellect in some way, whether through recognition, analysis, action, learning, or problem-solving (McCartney & McCartney, 2020). Artificial intelligence (AI) is already having an effect on various parts of the tourist industry as it undergoes technological change (Buhalis, 2020; Kong et al., 2022). According to Dwivedi et al. (2023), the possibilities, difficulties, and consequences of AI in every area of life are highlighted by the latest advancements in generative conversational AI. As a result of AI, marketing and operational tasks for tourism locations and organizations are evolving (Hollander, 2023). Technology based on artificial intelligence enables a wide range of applications, including recommendation and personalizing systems, chatbots and voice assistants, forecasting tools, smart travel assistants, language translation apps, smart tourism, and smart destination systems. Artificial intelligence's meteoric rise is mostly attributable to the developments in Industry 4.0 technologies, including IoT, cloud computing, and big data (Abu-Rumman et al., 2021). Machine learning, big data, and natural language processing are all parts of artificial intelligence (Davenport et al. 2020), which is a collection of technologies that mimics human intelligence and allows computers to do tasks normally performed by humans, such as solving problems, making predictions, and optimizing systems. Businesses could see an uptick in the service sector's growth as a result of AI's ability to boost earnings while cutting expenses (Loureiro et al., 2023). When fully implemented, artificial intelligence (AI) might revolutionize the hotel and tourism sectors. To maintain a competitive edge, companies are already making the transition from chatbots and other rule-based automated systems to cognitive agents with the ability to process raw data, interact with humans in a more natural way, and learn and improve over time. More personalized services, better value, and unforgettable guest experiences are now possible thanks to the industry's use of AI in conjunction with cutting-edge analytics tools and property management systems. From marketing campaigns before a guest even books a room to analytics and feedback collected after their stay, AI is reshaping the hotel business at every stage (Abu-Rumman et al., 2021). The application of artificial intelligence in the hospitality industry goes beyond just improving customer service. Revenue management, inventory control, and resource allocation are just a few of the operational areas that it can optimize. Businesses may optimize pricing strategies, allocate resources effectively, and make data-driven decisions with the help of AI-powered analytics. With the use of AI, the hospitality industry can better understand its customers' habits, tastes, and trends. According to Ivanov et al. (2019), companies in the travel and hospitality sector can use consumer data analysis to spot trends, predict what guests might need, and provide tailored recommendations and services. Guest loyalty and repeat bookings are fostered by this level of customization, which also enriches the customer experience via VCC.

Value Co-Creation (VCC)

McCColl-Kennedy et al. (2012) defined VCC a benefit realized from integration of resources through activities and interactions with collaborators in the customer's service network. However, Sanders and Stappers (2008) defined co-creation as "any act of collective creativity initiated by the firm, customer or both" (p. 6). According to Sanders and Stappers (2008), the "collective creativity of the involved actors" is more important than the other definitions, which place an emphasis on the combined action of the actors (p.11). However, according to other research, cocreation is all about working together, interacting, forming partnerships, and combining expertise in order to coinvent (McCall-Kennedy et al., 2012; Vargo & Lusch, 2016; Kornroos & Lusch, 2016). The emphasis has been on employee-customer connection and active participation in service, however there are other ways that value can be co-created (Gronroos & Voima, 2013). Hotel services depend on direct contact with clients, making interactive value co-creation particularly vital in the tourist and hospitality sector (Marques et al., 2017; Morosan & DeFranco, 2016; Oyner & Korelina, 2016). Regardless of how crucial it is, studies investigating the effects of consumer co-creation on travel and lodging companies are scarce. When businesses and their customers work together in a dialogical, interactive service process, the value creation activities of both parties combine to produce the desired result (Gronroos & Gummerus, 2014; Payne et al., 2008). Here, despite the fact that cocreation portrays consumers and employees as collaborating, they really play separate but complementary roles in the many activities in which they engage.

VCC and AI

Ivanov et al. (2019) expect that artificial intelligence will emerge as a game-changer in the coming decade. It has already begun to permeate society. Research by Ramaswamy and Ozcan (2018) and Tussyadiah et al. (2018) shows that recent technological advancements, like AI, can boost productivity, facilitate interactions, and improve experiences, particularly in the service industries. There have been "sprinkles of AI innovation" all over the world, and the events sector is supposedly one of the most promising areas for artificial intelligence to make an impact in the corporate world. Panetta (2017) and Kaartemo and Helkkula (2018) found that hotels can benefit substantially from artificial intelligence (AI) since it automates mundane but necessary activities like booking and cashless check-in, allowing employees more time to focus on clients' individual needs. Chatbots and virtual assistants powered by AI can improve customer service by assisting visitors with reservations booking, query addressing, and suggestion provision (Hollander, 2023). By utilizing sensors and cameras to track the temperature of the space, lighting, and security, AI can enhance cleaning room assignments and upkeep. It can also optimize revenue management and pricing through data analysis and predictive modelling, and smart building systems can improve energy efficiency (Hollander, 2023). In addition to improving the visitor experience through customized suggestions and incidents, AI can increase the overall efficiency of hotel operations through forecasting demand, handling inventory, and logistical optimization.

The Impact AI in H&T Will Have on Society

The impact of Artificial Intelligence (AI) in the Hospitality and Tourism (H&T) industry is profound and multifaceted, influencing various aspects of society in both positive and challenging ways.

Positive Impacts

1. **Enhanced Customer Experience:** AI technologies enable personalized and seamless experiences for travelers, from booking accommodations and recommending destinations to providing tailored recommendations based on individual preferences and past behaviors (Osei & Cheng, 2023). This enhanced customer experience can lead to greater satisfaction and loyalty among travelers.
2. **Efficiency and Automation:** AI-powered systems streamline operations within the H&T industry, automating routine tasks such as customer service inquiries, room bookings, and payment processing (Ponce, 2022). This efficiency not only reduces operational costs for businesses but also frees up human resources to focus on more complex and value-added tasks.
3. **Improved Revenue Management:** AI algorithms analyze vast amounts of data, including historical booking patterns, market demand, and competitor pricing, to optimize pricing strategies in real-time. This dynamic pricing model allows H&T businesses to maximize revenue by adjusting prices based on fluctuating demand and market conditions.
4. **Personalized Marketing and Recommendations:** AI-driven marketing platforms leverage data analytics and machine learning algorithms to deliver targeted advertisements, promotions, and

recommendations to travelers (Osei & Cheng, 2023). By understanding individual preferences and behavior patterns, businesses can create personalized marketing campaigns that resonate with their target audience, leading to higher conversion rates and customer engagement.

5. **Enhanced Safety and Security:** AI technologies, such as facial recognition systems and predictive analytics, enhance safety and security measures within the H&T industry (Ponce, 2022). These systems can identify potential security threats, monitor crowd movements, and detect anomalies in real-time, helping to mitigate risks and ensure the safety of travelers and staff.

Challenges and Considerations

1. **Privacy Concerns:** The widespread adoption of AI in H&T raises concerns about data privacy and security. As AI systems collect and analyze large volumes of personal data, there is a risk of unauthorized access, data breaches, and misuse of sensitive information (Nam et al., 2021). Striking a balance between leveraging data for personalized experiences and safeguarding user privacy is essential.

2. **Displacement of Jobs:** While AI automation improves efficiency and productivity within the H&T industry, it also raises concerns about job displacement and workforce transformation. Routine tasks that were previously performed by humans may become automated, leading to changes in job roles and skill requirements (Nam et al., 2021). Efforts to reskill and upskill workers will be crucial to mitigate the impact of automation on employment.

3. **Bias and Fairness:** AI algorithms are susceptible to bias, reflecting the biases present in the data used to train them. In the context of H&T, biased algorithms could lead to discriminatory outcomes in areas such as pricing, recommendations, and hiring practices (Nozawa et al., 2022). Ensuring the fairness and transparency of AI systems requires ongoing monitoring, evaluation, and mitigation of algorithmic biases.

4. **Digital Divide:** The widespread embracing of AI technologies in H&T may exacerbate existing disparities in access to technology and digital literacy. Travelers from marginalized communities or regions with limited access to technology may face barriers in accessing AI-driven services and experiences (Nozawa et al., 2022). Bridging the digital divide and ensuring equitable access to AI-driven innovations will be essential to avoid further widening socioeconomic disparities.

The impact of AI in the Hospitality and Tourism industry is significant, shaping various aspects of society ranging from customer experiences and operational efficiency to privacy concerns and workforce dynamics. While AI holds immense potential to drive innovation and transformation within the H&T industry, addressing the associated challenges and ethical considerations will be essential to realize its full benefits while minimizing risks to society

AI TOOLS INFLUENCING VCC

NLP

Several businesses in the hotel industry are investigating the potential of artificial intelligence chatbots to streamline customer care at every stage of the client's journey. These businesses range from dealers and intermediates to worldwide brands and individual hotel chains. Among the many types of conversational interfaces, AI chatbots fall under the category of AI-powered messaging platforms. According to Aluri et al. (2018), automated chatbots can help clients with basic questions like finding out when they are going on vacation and then offering transportation and hotel suggestions ahead of time. The chatbot can transfer the dialogue to a human worker for quicker resolution if the question becomes too complex. Conversational chatbots powered by natural language processing and machine learning will be able to assist users through the entire trip process, from planning to researching to making reservations (Ukpabi et al., 2019). Artificial intelligence chatbots can learn a user's likes and dislikes based on their booking history, reviews, and social media activity throughout a conversation in order to provide helpful recommendations for hotels, restaurants, events, and more.

Chatbot

There is already a lot of interest in chatbot capabilities on many platforms, such as an Alexa voice bot for booking and researching trips. Chatbots, which are programs driven by artificial intelligence, allow hotel guests to engage in real-time text message discussions (Ukpabi et al., 2019). According to Calvaresi et al. (2021), their purpose is to provide clients with the necessary information to arrange their desired experience. Chatbots can serve as mobile concierges throughout the encounter, providing customers with pertinent information (Parvez, 2021). According to Parmar et al. (2019), chatbots may comprehend client demands and supply pertinent information by utilizing natural language processing. With just a few voice queries, an AI-powered hotel concierge may search for nearby engaging activities and order the tickets within the platform. The use of artificial intelligence chatbots is revolutionizing the hotel industry, particularly in the areas of booking queries and client conversion. Conversational bots might one day replace hotel front desk agents who handle inquiries about reservations (Ukpabi et al., 2019). Intelligent chatbots can mimic human communication by parsing natural language and generating natural language (text/voice) in a user's native language. This allows for controlled, succinct, and efficient machine-human interactions.

Intelligent Agents

Cognitive agents that are smart can sift through mountains of data, including consumer tastes, actions, and opinions, to provide individualized suggestions and specialized assistance. Guests will have a better experience as a whole since these agents can grasp and answer their questions more naturally (Parvez, 2021). Another advantage that early adopters have is the ability to learn from encounters and gradually enhance their performance.

Voice-Activated Digital Helpers

With the proliferation of user-friendly voice-activated communication (VCC) systems, hotels are able to provide their customers with ever-impressive levels of service (Parvez, 2021). When it comes to in-room technology, guests are expecting the same seamless experience as they have at home with their connected gadgets.

Personal Digital Assistants That Aid Online Visitors

Virtual assistants and Internet-connected voice-activated devices are already being considered as potential advancements by the hospitality industry to enhance the travel experience. For instance, customers staying in rooms outfitted with Amazon's Echo speaker can use the virtual assistant Alexa to operate various room functions. Similarly, guests are able to operate smart room functions by voice command more effectively with virtual assistants like Siri. Consumers and businesses in the travel and hospitality industries are being prompted to reevaluate the traditional notion of a vacation by these virtual assistant platforms. In order for them to succeed, AI-powered curated results are essential (Parvez, 2021).

ML

In order to use AI to generate value for customers, ML, an AI analytical tool, is necessary (Solakis et al., 2022). In their 2020 publication, Mahmoud et al. characterized ML as the "branch of science that enables the machines, i.e. the computers, to learn without being overtly programmed." In artificial intelligence, machine learning typically watches patterns, both changing and staying the same, and the responses given by agents in the past. Then, it starts to generate its own accurate responses, tailored offers, and suggestions that fit in with the travelers' lifestyle choices. Multiple application strategies utilize ML, a potent tool for predictive analytics, which is built on large amounts of data (Calvaresi et al., 2021) and specified models and algorithms (Aluri et al., 2018). Machine learning (ML) can enhance VCC by seeing trends in customer behavior, which allows for more precise segmentation and profile creation. In order to optimize operating costs and decrease service costs, hotels require VCC for the strategic process automation of their internal and customer care services. The use of AI in the hospitality industry is becoming increasingly advantageous for both guests and hotels due to machine learning capabilities.

Improved Price Control With AI

The travel industry has been sluggish to embrace AI in order to move into more dynamic pricing, despite revenue management being one of the first functions to implement advanced analytics. Improving analysis and prediction capabilities based on market demand signals, room availability, and a comprehensive understanding of each customer will soon be possible for hotels because of advancements in machine learning (Parvez, 2021). Also, you can set prices according on features instead of simply room type. One advantage of this trend towards personalized pricing is the ease with which one may provide customers with a selection of well selected products accompanied by their exact price. The value chain as a whole, from well-known hotel chains to fledgling software companies, will benefit from better forecasts made possible by developments in predictive analytics. Pricing techniques can be enhanced to capture more value when demand estimates improve. Businesses can use self-learning algorithms to foretell how prices will go in response to several variables, such as current trends, demand swings, seasonal sales, weather, events, customer tastes, and buying habits.

AI-Powered Self-Service Kiosk

Automating the check-in and check-out processes for customers has led to the widespread use of self-service kiosks in the hospitality industry (Carlisle et al., 2021). Customers can quickly and conveniently check in by entering their details or scanning their ID. Guests can also use AI-powered self-service kiosks during check-in to have their room settings (lighting, temperature, etc.) remembered and customized. Even more crucially, self-service kiosks driven by AI can enable the recording and integration of guest preferences, allowing for a similar experience on subsequent visits (Solakis et al., 2022).

Figure 1. AI enabled technologies and VCC effectiveness (Solakis et al., 2022)

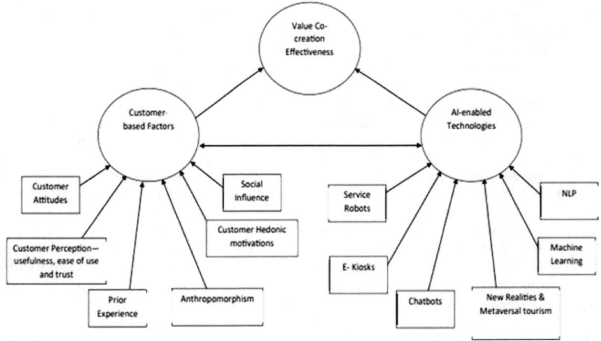

VCC Elements (DART Model)

The DART model was selected as the primary framework due to its status as a prominent theory and its widespread application in the study of VCC. Prahalad and Ramaswamy (2004a) proposed that the DART model can be utilized to develop a customer-organization relationship, which serves as the primary foundation for creating value. The DART model aims to elucidate the fundamental characteristics of VCC (value co-creation) between customers and businesses. Prahalad and Ramaswamy (2004c) suggest that this approach can be implemented in other service sectors, with a specific emphasis on the hotel business. One of the primary features of that industry is the collaborative production of value, which is centered upon the exploration of the client's personal experiences. In the hospitality sector, it is customary to collect information about the needs of clients and to motivate their active involvement in hotel processes. This is because the process of co-creation, which involves both the actions of the hotel and the engaged engagement of customers, plays a crucial role in shaping the client's encounter (González-Mansilla et al., 2019, p. 53).

Dialogue

AI integration in VCC enables discussion by leveraging its extensive database of integrated customer information and advanced computational skills to predict customer expectations and create tailored interactions between the company and its consumers. Furthermore, these traits possess the capability to produce distinct advantages in terms of time and effort conservation (Solakis et al., 2022). Therefore, we propose that the customer's AI utility and VCC process automation will impact their inclination to engage in the process. Dialogue facilitates the exchange of knowledge and encourages active involvement in the process of co-creation. Hotel patrons have the ability to engage and connect with hotel personnel at any given moment, utilizing both conventional (in-person conversation) and unconventional (websites, mobile apps, robotics) means of contact (Buhalis & Leung, 2018; Fan et al., 2019). Prahalad and Ramaswamy (2004b) define conversation as involving active participation, reciprocal interaction, and the inclination to take action by both the company and the consumer. Engaging in communication allows both sides to reconcile opposing interests and collaboratively devise mutually beneficial solutions. The rules of interaction must be unambiguously established when both parties regard each other as equal partners (Solakis et al., 2022). However, the authors emphasize that successful discussion can only occur when customers have equitable access to information and perceive transparency in the information provided by the company. The amalgamation of conversation, availability, and openness empowers customers to evaluate the potential hazards and advantages of actively participating as co-creators. As stated by Solakis et al. (2021), customer interaction functions as a learning process centered upon the customer's experience. Customers' sharing of their consuming experience offers organizations significant insights for re-strategizing their operations and redesigning their offerings (Carlisle et al., 2021). The widespread use of technological advancements has played a significant role in bringing these interactive experiences to life. Technological platforms enable customers to actively participate in the co-creation process, result-ing in the production of experiences that offer economic, functional, and cultural advantages (Cova & Dalli, 2009). In addition, Schiavone, Metallo, and Agrifoglio (2014) provide evidence that technology can play a crucial and supplementary role in the DART model. This is because technology aids in improving the levels of discussion, access to information, trust, and transparency during the co-creation process.

Access

Access pertains to the extent of transparency and level of limitation that the business imposes on the information provided to customers. Access evaluates the nature of the information and the essential tools needed to empower customers in making well-informed decisions regarding the business and its products. Access improves the customer experience by enabling more efficient communication (Albinsson et al., 2016). This phenomenon arises when companies disseminate their expertise and resources to clients, and progress in information and communication technology has enhanced this capability. Access allows hotel guests to actively request and customize their experiences. Hotel clients seek immersive and engaging experiences by actively participating and consuming services, rather than simply buying pre-designed offerings (Buhalis & Leung, 2018). By providing visitors with information and resources, hotels enable them to actively participate in and customize their own experiences according to their preferences and way of living. Access, as a component of DART, is crucial in delivering tailored and favorable experiences within the hotel industry (Neuhofer et al., 2015). Similar to discussion, access has an influence on how clients perceive the quality and price of touristic services. Customer engagement is fostered by factors such as the autonomy to determine service delivery methods, the freedom to choose how to engage with a particular service, the flexibility to select the most suitable time for receiving specific services, and the platform to express customer opinions on how services should be provided. Rather and Sharma (2017) observed that providing customers with relevant, appealing, or personalized information might enhance their attention and foster loyalty.

Risk

The level of risk varies depending on the extent of access. Risk assessment evaluates the degree to which the information provided by the business elucidates the dangers and legal responsibilities linked to the firm and its products (Damali et al., 2020). Access to comprehensive and pertinent information is crucial for customers to construct their perception of a specific hotel. However, there is a distinct category of information known as hazards, as described by Prahalad & Ramaswamy in 2004. Customers should be aware of both the advantages and disadvantages of staying at a specific hotel. Hence, it is imperative to effectively explain any potential hazards, and the hotel staff should provide guidance to clients on utilizing their services to mitigate such issues (Oskam & Boswijk, 2016). Trusting involves acknowledging the inherent danger in a relationship between a consumer and a corporation (Solakis et al., 2021). Consequently, trust can alleviate the perceived danger and uncertainty experienced by customers (Ponnapureddy, Priskin, Ohnmacht, Vinzenz & Wirth, 2017). If the hotel neglects to warn its customers about potential risks, it can lead to a loss of confidence, prompting customers to switch to another hotel provider or even choose another destination. Yang and Peterson (2004) demonstrated that switching costs can function as a limiting factor in this scenario. Nevertheless, the hospitality industry is marked by minimal switching expenses, so a loss of trust can readily dissuade customers and prompt them to opt for an alternative service provider that offers comprehensive information regarding potential drawbacks of its services. Disseminating information about Risks promptly through official communication channels enables consumers to evaluate the standard of services and select a hotel that offers specific information (Damali et al., 2020). If a firm is able to provide a level of quality that aligns with consumers' value judgements, it is probable that they will choose to use the services of that company and have an exceptional guest experience (Ahmad et al., 2019).

Transparency

Transparency is the reciprocal exchange of information between both parties during their interactions (Prahalad & Ramaswamy, 2004c). Additionally, it is a necessary condition for authentic Dialogue between individuals of equal standing (Prahalad & Ramaswamy, 2004b). Sharing managerial information, such as the working conditions of hotel workers, implementation of cleanliness standards, and identities of food suppliers, may be considered irrelevant to disclose to visitors. However, it is crucial for customers to perceive themselves as equal partners and actively participate in VCC (Kornum & Mühlbacher, 2013). Roy et al. (2020) suggests that when patrons perceive fairness in a hotel setting, it increases their trust and encourages them to engage in VCC activities. Transparency is a significant factor in the decision-making process when buying a vacation package (Tanford, Erdem & Baloglu, 2011) and when booking a hotel (Miao & Mattila, 2007). Given the highly distinct nature of services offered by the hotel business, it is unsurprising that transparent pricing can enhance the perception of a certain hotel's offerings. According to Rothenberger's (2015) study, providing customers with more information about pricing leads to a rise in their opinion of fairness regarding the price. Transparency is directly influenced by easy access to information and is therefore reflected in the quality of the product. As a result, this enables customers to not only have a better understanding of product usage, but also to provide suggestions for enhancing the products and services. The concept of transparency aims to mitigate any imbalances in communication and foster more disclosure to customers regarding both the internal and exterior workings of the organization (Kim & Kim, 2016). It is important for firms to recognise that transparency is not always a choice, as customers may already possess certain information due to the widespread availability of information on the internet (Fan et al., 2019). A minimal degree of perceived imbalance may enhance satisfaction with the process and encourage greater consumer participation in co-creation.

Figure 2. Hypothesis and conceptual model

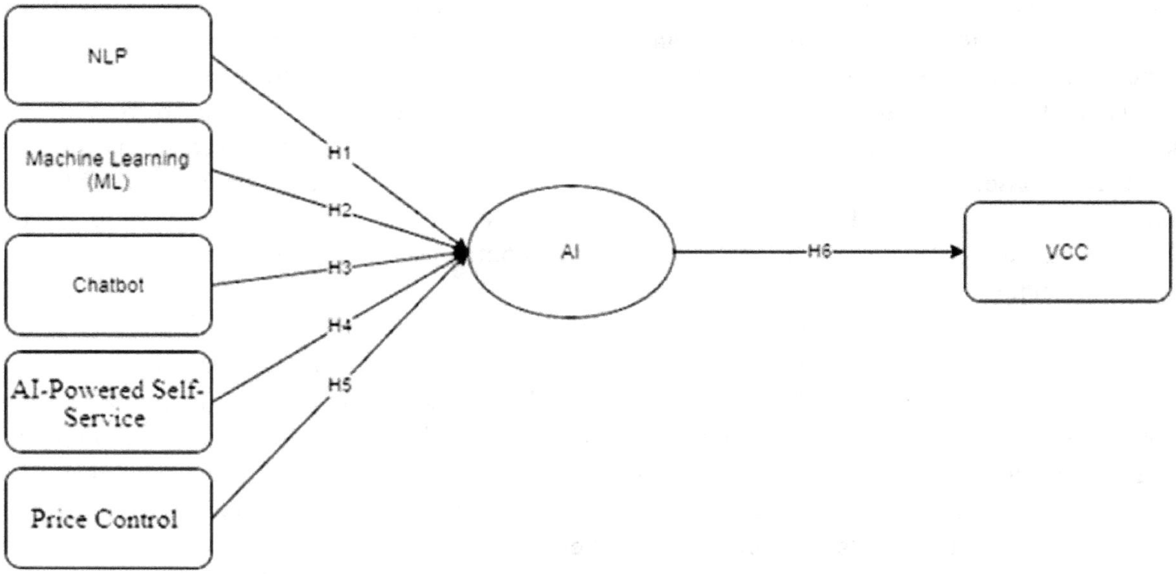

Based on the above model the following hypotheses were formulated

H1: NLP has significant positive impact on AI

H2: ML has significant positive impact on AI

H3: Chatbot has significant positive impact on AI

H4: AI-powered self-service has significant positive impact on AI

H5: Price control has significant positive impact on AI

H6: AI has significant positive impact on VCC

Implications

The goal of this chapter was to look at how AI contributes to VCC in the hospitality and tourism industry. Undoubtedly, AI is already exerting a significant influence on society, and it is imperative for every industry to pay attention. The results of our chapter will assist event planners in making decisions, implementing, and designing the experience of using AI in events, hospitality, and tourism industry. This study assists organizations in accurately forecasting the use of AI by presenting realistic scenarios, therefore mitigating the prevalent mistakes of underestimating or overestimating the extent of change. In order to meet the growing needs and stay ahead of the competition, hospitality and tourism firms like hotels worldwide will need to implement significant technological advancements within limited timeframes. In today's highly interconnected world, hoteliers must embrace the innovative integration of IoT, AI, and consolidated service devices in order to revolutionize their firms and redefine existing service benchmarks. Hotels ought to form partnerships with suitable technology providers to pinpoint deficiencies in their operations, such as customer assistance and concierge reservations, and address them by using Artificial Intelligence and Machine Learning. The key to improving the customer experience, boosting brand identification and loyalty, and achieving substantial revenue benefits. The integration of artificial intelligence in the hospitality industry will undoubtedly lead to a significant transformation of the customer experience through the use of VCC.

It is crucial to comprehend that this situation has two opposing perspectives. Hoteliers that possess the knowledge and skills to effectively utilize AI products will significantly increase their worth and productivity. Individuals and firms that neglect the acquisition of knowledge may encounter a more arduous predicament. Hotel industry experts must comprehend the most recent advancements in artificial intelligence as it might have a substantial influence on our operational procedures and guest service delivery. Artificial intelligence has the capability to mechanism monotonous duties, enabling hotel personnel to concentrate on more strategic endeavors such as cultivating connections with important clients and delivering tailored service to guests. Predictive analytics enables hotel workers to analyze data and predict consumer behavior and market trends, empowering them to make informed decisions and devise more efficient marketing plans. AI-driven personalization and recommendation systems have the capability to offer highly tailored and individualized experiences to guests by analyzing their preferences, prior actions, and demographic information. Artificial intelligence (AI)-driven chatbots and virtual assistants will enable hotel personnel to engage with guests in real-time and offer tailored suggestions and aid. The integration of artificial intelligence with smart room technologies can enhance the comfort and convenience of guests throughout their stay. AI can be utilized to oversee and anticipate maintenance requirements in hotel rooms, optimize pricing and inventory choices, forecast demand and change room availability accordingly, enhance energy efficiency, and minimize the expenses linked to managing and operating the hotel. To maintain competitiveness and enhance guest service, hotel industry personnel can achieve these objectives by comprehending these developments. The key aspect in all cases is that AI, in contrast to prior technologies, provides a comprehensive system that links customer-owned and business-owned technology, enabling customized human experiences tuned to the finest details, thus elevating events to a higher level. The fundamental benefit of AI is its ability to collaboratively create and customize experiences, deliver information, and provide support. This is not limited to a broad audience but extends to the individual level with great detail.

The Future of AI in Hospitality Sector

The integration of AI will significantly influence the character of experiences and the process of value creation during events. AI surpasses the current capabilities of technological advances in communication and information, since it acts as a transformative force by autonomously facilitating a higher level of interaction between humans and non-human entities. AI is a comprehensive non-human entity that will extend its influence across various aspects of life, as it collects and analyses personal data and behavior in everyday situations and utilizes them in specific business transactions when necessary. This implies a shift in existing digital markets, as AI enables interactions that transcend the divisions between different areas of business and living. Consequently, our proposal suggests that we will surpass limited-service ecosystems (Kaartemo and Helkkula 2018) and go towards more interconnected living systems. In the context of hospitality business VCC, this implies that the process through which customers interact with and derive value from the business undergoes a transformation that extends into the various aspects of their lives. By implementing AI, a B2C touchpoint can be established by a push notice far in advance of the event, capturing initial attention and generating interest. Additionally, personalized travel packages, personalized transportation options, and flexible pricing will improve the pre-event experience. With the integration of technology in the event sector, including smartphones, access systems, and applications, artificial intelligence (AI) plays a significant role. According to Kaartemo and Helkkula (2018), AI not only facilitates but also shapes the whole experience by linking various elements into a cohesive system. In the immediate future, AI will primarily bolster the event experience by offering tailored recommendations, aid, and ideas, as well as improving event organization in terms of logistics, crowd control, and access systems.

CONCLUSION

The tourist and hospitality industries are experiencing substantial transformations as a result of the extensive integration of digital technology, which facilitate immediate client communication and data collection. This chapter has focused on examining the existing literature on co-creation experiences in the tourism industry. It has identified theoretical concepts, provided an overview of definitions and topics, and explored the application of AI technologies in enhancing co-creation between customers and tourism companies. The AI tools that have an impact on VCC (Virtual Contact Centre) include natural language processing (NLP), chatbots, intelligent agents, voice-activated digital support, personal digital assistants that assist online visitors, machine learning (ML), improved price control with AI, and AI-powered self-service kiosks. The DART model was chosen as the main framework because of its important reputation as a theory and its extensive use in studying VCC. AI has been observed to enhance dialogue, access, risk management, and transparency, resulting in increased involvement of customers, guests, and visitors. Subsequent investigations should prioritize the exploration of artificial intelligence (AI) in the realm of marketing and promotion. The chapter examines the circumstances surrounding the collaborative process of generating consumer value through the use of artificial intelligence in the hotel and tourism sector. We analyze the primary customer-related factors and various artificial intelligence technologies that impact this process, such as Chatbot, Natural Language Processing (NLP), Machine Learning (ML), and Deep Learning (DL). Travel firms are provided with a substantial volume of data through digital technology. Several travel firms are enhancing their analytical capacity to fully use the value of this data, presenting significant opportunities and possibilities for all travel and hospitality companies. The AI capabilities are rapidly advancing to the point where numerous travel companies can greatly benefit from implementing AI on a large scale in their daily operations. The advancement of computer power, reduction in data storage expenses, and enhanced development in technologies such as machine learning, deep learning, natural language processing, and video recognition will expedite the progress of AI in the hospitality industry. Several hotel companies have initiated the implementation of artificial intelligence (AI) in trial initiatives. The hotel industry undergoes a process of transformation and innovation by integrating AI. Hotels may achieve operational optimization, improve guest experiences, and maintain a competitive edge by utilizing AI-driven solutions. Nevertheless, despite the progress in technology, the human element continues to be and will continue to be essential. AI should function as a potent instrument to enhance the capabilities of hotel personnel and enhance their interactions with clients, rather than supplant them. Hotels will surely reinvent the sector as they embrace the future powered by artificial intelligence. To summarize, this analysis emphasizes the crucial significance of digital technology in facilitating the collaborative generation of consumer value in the tourism and hospitality industries. Emerging AI and technological advancements provide instantaneous communication and customized interactions, hence augmenting client contentment and fostering loyalty. AI technology provides compelling prospects for engaging interactions and virtual gatherings.

Future Research Agenda

The emphasis on utilizing AI for marketing and promotional reasons is very low in this context, despite research suggesting the possible application of AI in marketing. Hence, future study can delve into additional domains where AI can offer enhanced benefits to hotels and their clientele. Furthermore, artificial intelligence (AI) is a sophisticated technological advancement, and there are numerous variables that can impact AI in VCC. Hence, further investigation might be conducted in future research to explore the technological and management elements that contribute to this constraint. To do this, it is necessary to conduct interviews with AI specialists rather than hotel managers. Interviews may not provide a reliable means of determining the extent to which AI impacts hotel performance on a large scale. Hence, future investigations can focus on enhancing the methods and employing longitudinal study. The study's findings indicate that using AI has the capacity to enhance competitive advantage. Investigating the obstacles of employing AI for gaining a competitive edge, such as digital preparedness and corporate culture, appears to be a worthwhile area of study in the future.

REFERENCES

Abu-Rumman, A., Al Shraah, A., Al-Madi, F., & Alfalah, T. (2021). Entrepreneurial networks, entrepreneurial orientation, and performance of small and medium enterprises: Are dynamic capabilities the missing link? *Journal of Innovation and Entrepreneurship*, *10*(29), 1–16. doi:10.1186/s13731-021-00170-8

Ahmad, S. Z., Ahmad, N., & Papastathopoulos, A. (2019). Measuring service quality and customer satisfaction of the small- and medium-sized hotels (SMSHs) industry: Lessons from United Arab Emirates (UAE). *Tourism Review*, *74*(3), 349–370. doi:10.1108/TR-10-2017-0160

Aluri, A., Price, B. S., & Mcintyre, N. H. (2018). Using machine learning to cocreate value through dynamic customer engagement in a brand loyalty program. *Journal of Hospitality & Tourism Research (Washington, D.C.), 43*(1), 78–100. doi:10.1177/1096348017753521

Aman, J., Abbas, J., Mahmood, S., Nurunnabi, M., & Bano, S. (2019). The infuence of Islamic religiosity on the perceived socio-cultural impact of sustainable tourism development in Pakistan: A structural equation modeling approach. *Sustainability (Basel), 11*(11), 3039. doi:10.3390/su11113039

Becker, A. (2019). Artificial intelligence in medicine: What is it doing for us today? *Health Policy and Technology, 8*(2), 198–205. doi:10.1016/j.hlpt.2019.03.004

Bolton, R. N., Mccoll-Kennedy, J. R., Cheung, L., Gallan, A., Orsingher, C., Witell, L., & Zaki, M. (2018). Customer experience challenges: Bringing together digital, physical and social realms. *Journal of Service Management, 29*(5), 776–808. doi:10.1108/JOSM-04-2018-0113

Buhalis, D. (2019). Technology in tourism-from information communication technologies to eTourism and smart tourism towards ambient intelligence tourism: A perspective article. *Tourism Review, 75*(1), 267–272. doi:10.1108/TR-06-2019-0258

Buhalis, D. (2020). Technology in tourism-from information communication technologies to eTourism and smart tourism towards ambient intelligence tourism: A perspective article. *Tourism Review, 75*(1), 267–272. doi:10.1108/TR-06-2019-0258

Buhalis, D., & Leung, R. (2018). Smart hospitality – Interconnectivity and interoperability towards an ecosystem. *International Journal of Hospitality Management, 71*, 41–50. doi:10.1016/j.ijhm.2017.11.011

Buhalis, D., Lin, M. S., & Leung, D. (2022). Metaverse as a driver for customer experience and value co-creation: Implications for hospitality and tourism management and marketing. *International Journal of Contemporary Hospitality Management, 35*(2), 701–716. doi:10.1108/IJCHM-05-2022-0631

Buhalis, D., & Sinarta, Y. (2019). Real-time co-creation and nowness service: Lessons from tourism and hospitality. *Journal of Travel & Tourism Marketing, 36*(5), 563–582. doi:10.1080/10548408.2019.1592059

Calvaresi, D., Ibrahim, A., Calbimonte, J. P., Fragniere, E., Schegg, R. & Schumacher, M.I. (2021). Leveraging inter-tourists interactions via chatbots to bridge academia, tourism industries and future societies. *Journal of Tourism Futures*.

Carlisle, S., Ivanov, S., & Dijkmans, C. (2021). The digital skills divide: evidence from the European tourism industry. *Journal of Tourism Futures*.

Carvalho, P., & Alves, H. (2022). Customer value co-creation in the hospitality and tourism industry: A systematic literature review. *International Journal of Contemporary Hospitality Management, 35*(1), 250–273. doi:10.1108/IJCHM-12-2021-1528

Damali, U., Secchi, E., Tax, S. S., & McCutcheon, D. (2020). Customer participation risk management: Conceptual model and managerial assessment tool. *Journal of Service Management, 32*(1), 27–51. doi:10.1108/JOSM-05-2018-0147

Davenport, T., Guha, A., Grewal, D., & Bressgott, T. (2020). How artificial intelligence will change the future of marketing. *Journal of the Academy of Marketing Science, 48*(1), 24–42. doi:10.1007/s11747-019-00696-0

Duan, Y., Edwards, J. S., & Dwivedi, Y. K. (2019). Artificial intelligence for decision making in the era of Big Data – evolution, challenges and research agenda. *International Journal of Information Management, 48*, 63–71. doi:10.1016/j.ijinfomgt.2019.01.021

Dwivedi, Y. K., Hughes, L., Ismagilova, E., Aarts, G., Coombs, C., Crick, T., Duan, Y., Dwivedi, R., Edwards, J., Eirug, A., Galanos, V., Ilavarasan, P. V., Janssen, M., Jones, P., Kar, A. K., Kizgin, H., Kronemann, B., Lal, B., Lucini, B., ... Williams, M. D. (2021). Artificial Intelligence (AI): Multidisciplinary perspectives on emerging challenges, opportunities, and agenda for research, practice and policy. *International Journal of Information Management, 57*, 101994. doi:10.1016/j.ijinfomgt.2019.08.002

Dwivedi, Y. K., Kshetri, N., Hughes, L., Slade, E. L., Jeyaraj, A., Kar, A. K., Baabdullah, A. M., Koohang, A., Raghavan, V., Ahuja, M., Albanna, H., Albashrawi, M. A., Al-Busaidi, A. S., Balakrishnan, J., Barlette, Y., Basu, S., Bose, I., Brooks, L., Buhalis, D., ... Wright, R. (2023). Opinion Paper: "So what if ChatGPT wrote it?" Multidisciplinary perspectives on opportunities, challenges and implications of generative conversational AI for research, practice and policy. *International Journal of Information Management, 71*, 102642. doi:10.1016/j.ijinfomgt.2023.102642

Fan, D. X. F., Buhalis, D., & Lin, B. (2019). A tourist typology of online and face-to-face social contact: Destination immersion and tourism encapsulation/decapsulation. *Annals of Tourism Research, 78*, 102757. doi:10.1016/j.annals.2019.102757

Ford, M. (2018). *Architects of intelligence: The truth about AI from the people building it.* Packt Publishing.

González-Mansilla, Ó., Berenguer-Contrí, G., & Serra-Cantallops, A. (2019). The impact of value cocreation on hotel brand equity and customer satisfaction. *Tourism Management, 75*, 51–65. doi:10.1016/j.tourman.2019.04.024

Grissemann, U. S., & Stokburger-Sauer, N. E. (2012). Customer co-creation of travel services: The role of company support and customer satisfaction with the co-creation performance. *Tourism Management, 33*(6), 1483–1492. doi:10.1016/j.tourman.2012.02.002

Hollander, J. (2023). *AI in Hospitality: The Impact of Artificial Intelligence on the Hotel Industry.* https://hoteltechreport.com/news/ai-in-hospitality

Huang, M. H., & Rust, R. T. (2021). Engaged to a robot? The role of AI in service. *Journal of Service Research, 24*(1), 30–41. doi:10.1177/1094670520902266

Ivanov, S., Gretzel, U., Berezina, K., Sigala, M., & Webster, C. (2019). Progress on robotics in hospitality and tourism: A review of the literature. *Journal of Hospitality and Tourism Technology,* JHTT-08-2018-0087. doi:10.1108/JHTT-08-2018-0087

Ivanov, S., & Webster, C. (2017). Adoption of robots, artificial intelligence and service automation by travel, tourism and hospitality companies – A cost-benefit analysis. *International scientific conference "contemporary tourism – Traditions and innovations".*

Kaartemo, V., & Helkkula, A. (2018). A systematic review of artificial intelligence and robots in value co-creation: Current status and future research avenues. *Journal of Creating Value, 4*(2), 1–18. doi:10.1177/2394964318805625

Kim, S.-B., & Kim, D.-Y. (2016). The impacts of corporate social responsibility, service quality, and transparency on relationship quality and customer loyalty in the hotel industry. *Asian Journal of Sustainability and Social Responsibility, 1*(1), 39–55. doi:10.1186/s41180-016-0004-1

Kong, H., Wang, K., Qiu, X., Cheung, C., & Bu, N. (2022). 30 years of artificial intelligence (AI) research relating to the hospitality and tourism industry. *International Journal of Contemporary Hospitality Management, 35*. doi:10.1108/IJCHM-03-2022-0354

Lee, J., Davari, H., Singh, J., & Pandhare, V. (2018). Industrial artificial intelligence for industry 4.0-based manufacturing systems. *Manufacturing Letters, 18,* 20–23. https://doi.org/.2018.09.002 doi:10.1016/j.mfglet

Li, M., Yin, D., Qiu, H., & Bai, B. (2021). A systematic review of AI technology-based service encounters: Implications for hospitality and tourism operations. *International Journal of Hospitality Management, 95*, 102930. doi:10.1016/j.ijhm.2021.102930

Loureiro, S. M. C., Bilro, R. G., & Neto, D. (2023). Working with AI: Can stress bring happiness? *Service Business, 17*(1), 233–255. doi:10.1007/s11628-022-00514-8

Lv, H., Shi, S., & Gursoy, D. (2022). A look back and a leap forward: A review and synthesis of big data and artificial intelligence literature in hospitality and tourism. *Journal of Hospitality Marketing & Management, 31*(2), 145–175. doi:10.1080/19368623.2021.1937434

Magistretti, S., Dell'Era, C., & Petruzzelli, A. M. (2019). How intelligent is Watson? Enabling digital transformation through artificial intelligence. *Business Horizons, 62*(6), 819–829. doi:10.1016/j.bushor.2019.08.004

Mahmoud, A. B., Tehseen, S., & Fuxman, L. (2020). *The dark side of artificial intelligence in retail innovation. IN Pantano, E* (R. Futures, Ed.; 1st ed.). Emerald Publishing.

Marques, R., Yamashita, A., & Stefanini, C. (2017). Um encontro da hospitalidade com a cocriação de valor na hotelaria. *Revista Turismo & Desenvolvimento (Aveiro), 27/28*(1), 239–249. doi:10.34624/rtd.v1i27/28.8407

McCartney, G., & McCartney, A. (2020). Rise of the machines: Towards a conceptual service-robot research framework for the hospitality and tourism industry. *International Journal of Contemporary Hospitality Management, 32*(12), 3835–3851. doi:10.1108/IJCHM-05-2020-0450

Meurisch, C., & Mühlhäuser, M. (2021). Data protection in AI services: A survey. *ACM Computing Surveys, 54*(2), 1–38. doi:10.1145/3440754

Morosan, C., & DeFranco, A. (2016). Co-creating value in hotels using mobile devices: A conceptual model with empirical validation. *International Journal of Hospitality Management, 52*(1), 131–142. doi:10.1016/j.ijhm.2015.10.004

Nam, K., Dutt, C. S., Chathoth, P., Daghfous, A., & Khan, M. S. (2021). The adoption of artificial intelligence and robotics in the hotel industry: Prospects and challenges. *Electronic Markets, 31*(3), 553–574. doi:10.1007/s12525-020-00442-3

Nozawa, C., Togawa, T., Velasco, C., & Motoki, K. (2022). Consumer responses to the use of artificial intelligence in luxury and nonluxury restaurants. Food Quality and Preference, 96, 104436. Padma, P., & Ahn, J. (2020). Guest satisfaction & dissatisfaction in luxury hotels: An application of big data. *International Journal of Hospitality Management, 84*, 102318.

Osei, B.A. & Cheng, M. (2023). Preferences and challenges towards the adoption of the fourth industrial revolution technologies by hotels: a multilevel concurrent mixed approach. *European Journal of Innovation Management.* doi:10.1108/EJIM-09-2022-0529

Oskam, J., & Boswijk, A. (2016). Airbnb: The future of networked hospitality businesses. *Journal of Tourism Futures, 2*(1), 22–42. doi:10.1108/JTF-11-2015-0048

Ostrom, A. L., Fotheringham, D., & Bitner, M. J. (2019). Customer acceptance of AI in service encounters: understanding antecedents and consequence. In P. P. Maglio, C. A. Kieliszewski, J. C. Spohrer, K. Lyons, L. Patrício, & Y. Sawatani (Eds.), *Handbook of service science* (Vol. 2, pp. 77–103). Springer.

Oyner, O., & Korelina, A. (2016). The influence of customer engagement in value co-creation on customer satisfaction: Searching for new forms of cocreation in the Russian hotel industry. *Worldwide Hospitality and Tourism Themes, 8*(3), 327–345. doi:10.1108/WHATT-02-2016-0005

Pencarelli, T. (2020). The digital revolution in the travel and tourism industry. *Information Technology & Tourism, 22*(3), 455–476. doi:10.1007/s40558-019-00160-3

Pham, L. H., Woyo, E., Pham, T. H., & Dao, T. X. T. (2022). Value co-creation and destination brand equity: Understanding the role of social commerce information sharing. *J Hosp Tour Insights, 2*(3), 22–42.

Ponce, D. C. (2022). *Perceptions of artificial intelligence service-chatbots and brand affection in the hotel industry in Australia* (Doctoral dissertation, RMIT University).

Ponnapureddy, S., Priskin, J., Ohnmacht, T., Vinzenz, F., & Wirth, W. (2017). The influence of trust perceptions on German tourists' intention to book a sustainable hotel: A new approach to analysing marketing information. *Journal of Sustainable Tourism, 25*(7), 970–988. doi:10.1080/09669582.2016.1270953

Prahalad, C. K., & Ramaswamy, V. (2004a). Co-creation experiences: The next practice in value creation. *Journal of Interactive Marketing, 18*(3), 5–14. doi:10.1002/dir.20015

Prahalad, C. K., & Ramaswamy, V. (2004b). *The Future of Competition: Co-creating Unique Value with Customers.* Harvard Business Review Press.

Prahalad, C. K., & Ramaswamy, V. (2004c). Co-creation experiences: The next practice in value creation. *Journal of Interactive Marketing, 18*(3), 5–14. doi:10.1002/dir.20015

Ramaswamy, V., & Ozcan, K. (2018). What is co-creation? An interactional creation framework and its implications for value creation. *Journal of Business Research, 84*, 196–205. doi:10.1016/j.jbusres.2017.11.027

Rather, R. A., & Sharma, J. (2017). Customer engagement for evaluating customer relationships in hotel industry. *European Journal of Tourism. Hospitality and Recreation, 8*(1), 1–13. doi:10.1515/ejthr-2017-0001

Rust, R. T. (2020). The future of marketing. *International Journal of Research in Marketing, 37*(1), 15–26. doi:10.1016/j.ijresmar.2019.08.002

Schwab, K. (2017). *The fourth industrial revolution.* Crown Business.

Solakis, K., Pena-Vinces, J., & Lopez-Bonilla, J. M. (2022). Value co-creation and perceived value: A customer perspective in the hospitality context. *European Research on Management and Business Economics, 28*(1), 100175. doi:10.1016/j.iedeen.2021.100175

Solakis, K., Pena-Vinces, J., Lopez-Bonilla, J. M., & Aguado, L. F. (2021). From value Co-creation to positive experiences and customer satisfaction. A customer perspective in the hotel industry. *Technological and Economic Development of Economy, 27*(4), 948–969. doi:10.3846/tede.2021.14995

Stylos, N., Fotiadis, A. K., Shin, D., & Huan, T. C. (2021). Beyond smart systems adoption: Enabling diffusion and assimilation of smartness in hospitality. *International Journal of Hospitality Management, 98*, 103042. doi:10.1016/j.ijhm.2021.103042

Stylos, N., Zwiegelaar, J., & Buhalis, D. (2021). Big data empowered agility for dynamic, volatile, and time-sensitive service industries: The case of tourism sector. *International Journal of Contemporary Hospitality Management, 33*(3), 1015–1036. doi:10.1108/IJCHM-07-2020-0644

Troisi, O., Grimaldi, M., & Monda, A. (2019). Managing smart service ecosystems through technology: How ICTs enable value cocreation. *Tourism Analysis, 24*(3), 377–393. doi:10.3727/108354219X15511865533103

Tussyadiah, I., & Miller, G. (2019). Perceived impacts of artificial intelligence and responses to positive behaviour change intervention. In J. Pesonen & J. Neidhardt (Eds.), *Information and communication Technologies in Tourism 2019* (pp. 359–370). Springer. doi:10.1007/978-3-030-05940-8_28

Tussyadiah, I. P., Jung, T. H., & tom Dieck, M. C. (2018). Embodied of wearable augmented reality technology in tourism experiences. *Journal of Travel Research, 57*(5), 597–611. doi:10.1177/0047287517709090

Chapter 6
Demystifying Artificial Intelligence and Customer Engagement:
A Bibliometric Review Using TCCM Framework

Arabinda Bhandari
ⓘ https://orcid.org/0000-0001-6444-9147
Sarala Birla University, Ranchi, India

Mudita Sinha
ⓘ https://orcid.org/0000-0002-6003-4013
Christ University, Bangalore, India

ABSTRACT

Artificial intelligence (AI) has grabbed the attention of the extent of literature and customer engagement of many business organizations in the past decade, especially with the advancement of machine learning and deep learning. However, despite the great potential of AI to solve customer problems and engage customers, there are still many issues related to practical uses and lack of knowledge to create value through customer engagement. In this context, the present study aims to full fill the gap by providing a critical literature review based on 53 A* and A categories of Australian Business Deans Council (ABDC) journals (2011-2023) by highlighting the benefits, challenges, framework, and future research directions in theory, context, characteristic and methodology (TCCM) areas. These findings contribute to both theoretical and managerial perspectives for developing a future novel theory and new forms of management practices.

DOI: 10.4018/979-8-3693-2367-0.ch006

1. INTRODUCTION

In this digital era, the business world has less response time and given more attention to competitive advantage. Against this backdrop, many organizations are using the latest technology to enhance business performance. Among the many technologies, artificial intelligence (AI) has been used prominently by many organizations to attract customers and to develop different business models (Borges, Laurindo, Spịnola, Rodrigo, & Claudia, 2021). Artificial Intelligence refers to computational agents that act, respond, or behave intelligently in humanoid and non-humanoid forms, can perform human-instructed tasks, solve problems, analysis and interpret data for a decision (Prentice, Weaven, & Wong, 2020).

Customer engagement is a process of reaching out to customers and engaging them in cognitive, emotional, behavioral, sensorial, and social response perspectives. It is a state of mind and a psychological process that leads to customer loyalty. The outcomes of customer engagement are many like organization performance, customer repeat purchase, as well as to increase the share holders' value (Prentice & Nguyen, 2020).

McCarthy in 1956 coined the term "Artificial intelligence", as a science and engineering to make an intelligent machine. Though there was some slowdown of people's interest in the initial stage of this remarkable innovation but the data generated by the recent past and enhancement of computation processing capacities has made Artificial Intelligence a necessity to expand the scope in marketing, new product development, and service industry.

Considering the advantages of artificial intelligence in swift decision-making with a high-volume customer database enables organizations to make the right decision among many options of strategic planning. However, the literature evidence is not sufficient enough to support the role of AI in the strategic planning of customer engagement process. Since there is less theoretical and empirical evidence of how AI could be used to enhance customer engagement and value creation for any organization, this article attempts to address the above research gap by examining the intersection of the extent of literature about artificial intelligence and customer engagement strategy through a systematic literature review.

Last 10 years there are 53 articles have been published by 33 top category journals (A* and A Category ABDC Journals) across the globe, out of which there are only 3 review articles (Table 2) published by 11 researchers related to AI and Organization strategy, customer analytics, and social media. While going through the intext analysis, out of 53 selected articles based on predetermined inclusion and exclusion criteria published to date are related to digital assistance, E-Commerce, e-WOM, food security, gamification, health, luxury brand, online brand communities (OBC), retail, social media, value co-creation and so on. It has been observed that out of 53 selected articles, near about 36 percent (35.84%) gas given thrust to customer engagement. However, none of the authors has analyzed artificial intelligence and customer engagement from a theory, context, characteristic, and methodology (TCCM) perspective to date.

Given the identified gaps, this article highlights the concept of artificial intelligence and customer engagement, the top ten most contributing authors, potential journals, most productive countries, different themes, and sub-themes. Apart from this, a content analysis based on recently published articles in 2021, 2022, and 2023, has helped to identify the recent research trends and proposed a future research direction in artificial intelligence and customer engagement research.

In the subsequent research, a discussion on artificial intelligence and customer engagement concepts based on the identified article helped to conceptualize the idea. Justification of research, research methodology, descriptive research, future research, TCCM framework, limitation, and conclusion have been discussed.

1.1 Artificial Intelligence and Customer Engagement: The Concept

Though the concept of Artificial Intelligence and customer engagement concept was developed years back, it is essential to know the concept and definition of AI and customer engagement from the identified literature.

Table 1. Different definitions and domains of AI and customer engagement

Sl No	Authors	Title	Journal Name	DOI	Definition	Domain	Author Keywords
1	Marbach et al(2016)	Who are you and what do you value? Investigating the Role of personality traits and customer-perceived Value in online customer engagement	Journal of Marketing Management	10.1080/0267257X.2015.1128472	Technology that helps online customer engagement (OCE) and value creation	Online customer engagement	Customer engagement; customer-perceived value; online brand communities; personality traits; social media
2	Grewal et al(2017)	The Future of Retailing	Journal of Retailing	10.1016/j.jretai.2016.12.008	Helps to identify the cognitive, affective, emotional, social, and physical responses of the customer in a retail set-up.	Retail	Futuristic view; Retailing; Strategy
3	Buhalis & Sinarta(2019)	Real-time co-creation and nowness service: lessons from tourism and hospitality	Journal of Travel and Tourism Marketing	10.1080/10548408.2019.1592059	Technology that helps to engage the customer in social media platform	Brand	Hospitality; instant gratification; interactive; marketing; nowness; Real-time; smart; social media; strategy; tourism
4	Kumar et al(2019)	Understanding the role of artificial intelligence in personalized engagement marketing	California Management Review	10.1177/0008125619859317	Artificial intelligence (AI) is an engagement marketing tool to create, communicate, and deliver personalized offerings to customers	Marketing	Artificial intelligence; CRM technology; Customer relationship management; Customization; Marketing; Personalization
5	Prentice & Nguyen(2020)	Engaging and retaining customers with AI and employee service	Journal of Retailing and Consumer Services	10.1016/j.jretconser.2020.102186	Artificial intelligence (AI) is a tool that permeates to enhance operational efficiency and improve customer experience in a service industry	Service	Artificial intelligence; Customer engagement; Customer loyalty; Emotional intelligence; Service experience
6	Schuetzler et al(2020)	The impact of chatbot conversational skill on engagement and perceived humanness	Journal of Management Information Systems	10.1080/07421222.2020.1790204	Technology that leverages natural language processing to engage in conversations with human users	Conversational agents (CAs)	Anthropomorphism; chatbots; Conversational agents; social presence; system humanness; user engagement
7	Prentice et al(2020)	Linking AI quality performance and customer engagement: The moderating effect of AI preference	International Journal of Hospitality Management	10.1016/j.ijhm.2020.102629	Artificial intelligence (AI) as a commercial service in examining its influence on customer engagement	Service	AI preference; AI satisfaction; Artificial intelligence; Customer engagement; Service quality

Continued on following page

Table 1. Continued

Sl No	Authors	Title	Journal Name	DOI	Definition	Domain	Author Keywords
8	Gupta et al(2020)	Digital Analytics: Modeling for Insights and New Methods	Journal of Interactive Marketing	10.1016/j.intmar.2020.04.003	Technology that generates consumer insights based on data-driven decision-making.	Customer engagement	Artificial intelligence; Blockchain; Digital analytics; Drones; Firm capabilities; Internet of things
9	Huang & Rust(2021)	Engaged to a Robot? The Role of AI in Service	Journal of Service Research	10.1177/1094670520902266	Technology that helps customer engagement in the service industry	Service	Artificial intelligence; augmentation; automation; engagement; feeling AI; human intelligence; mechanical AI; personalization; renationalization; replacement; robots; service process; service strategy; standardization; thinking AI
10	Borges et al(2021)	The strategic use of artificial intelligence in the digital era: Systematic literature review and future research directions	International Journal of Information Management	10.1016/j.ijinfomgt.2020.102225	Artificial Intelligence is a tool (machine learning techniques) to solve problems strategically and to create business value.	Business Value Creation	Artificial intelligence; Business strategy; Deep learning; Information technology; Literature review; Machine learning
11	Moriuchi et al(2021)	Engagement with chatbots versus augmented reality interactive technology in e-commerce	Journal of Strategic Marketing	10.1080/0965254X.2020.1740766	Artificial intelligence is a means of differentiation. E-commerce organization	E-Commerce	Augmented reality interactive technology; chatbots; consumers; e-commerce; retail; technology engagement
12	Perez-Vega et al(2021)	Reshaping the contexts of online customer engagement behavior via artificial intelligence: A conceptual framework	Journal of Business Research	10.1016/j.jbusres.2020.11.002	It is a technology that can improve automated service interactions between the firm and its customers	Service	Artificial intelligence; Information processing systems; Online customer engagement behaviors; Stimulus-organism-response
13	Singh et al(2021)	One-Voice Strategy for Customer Engagement	Journal of Service Research	10.1177/1094670520910267	It is a service interface	Service	Artificial intelligence; automated coordination; automated learning; collective intelligence; customer engagement; local intelligence; one-voice strategy; service interaction space; service interface
14	Grimes et al(2021)	Mental models and expectation violations in conversational AI interactions	Decision Support Systems	10.1016/j.dss.2021.113515	AI is the form of conversational agents (CAs) such as Siri, Alexa, and chatbots used for customer service on websites and other information systems.	Conversational agents (CAs)	Chatbots; Conversational agents; Conversational AI; Engagement

Continued on following page

Table 1. Continued

Sl No	Authors	Title	Journal Name	DOI	Definition	Domain	Author Keywords
15	Utami et al(2021)	A social justice logic?: how digital commerce enables value co-creation at the bottom of the pyramid	Journal of Marketing Management	10.1080/0267257X.2021.1908399	AI is a technology that innovates in value co-creation (VCC) at the bottom of the pyramid (BOP) and markets.	Value co-creation	agri-food digital retailing; competitive solutions; marketing at the bottom of the pyramid; social justice; Value co-creation
16	Mostafa & Kasamani(2022)	Antecedents and consequences of chatbot initial trust	European Journal of Marketing	10.1108/EJM-02-2020-0084	Technology that shifting the nature of online services by revolutionizing the interactions of service providers with consumers	Conversational agents (CAs)	Artificial intelligence; Chatbot initial trust; Chatbot trust; Chatbot usage intention; Customer engagement
17	Chandra et al(2022)	To Be or Not to Be? Human? Theorizing the Role of Human-Like Competencies in Conversational Artificial Intelligence Agents	Journal of Management Information Systems	10.1080/07421222.2022.2127441	Artificial intelligence (AI)-based interactional technologies, such as conversational AI agents and chatbots, that obviate the need for having human service agents for the provision of customer service	Customer service	AI; Artificial Intelligence; chatbot; conversational agents; human-like competencies; human-like trust; media naturalness theory; mixed methods; user engagement
18	Wei & Prentice(2022)	Addressing service profit chain with artificial and emotional intelligence	Journal of Hospitality Marketing and Management	10.1080/19368623.2022.2058671	Artificial intelligence (AI) is a powered application in service organizations,	Service	Artificial intelligence; consumer behaviors; emotional intelligence; service profit chain
19	Rahman et al(2023)	The new wave of AI-powered luxury brands online shopping experience: The role of digital multisensory cues and customers? engagement	Journal of Retailing and Consumer Services	10.1016/j.jretconser.2023.103273	Artificial intelligence (AI)-powered digital assistance and digital multisensory cues on real-life customers' luxury brand online shopping experience	Luxury Brand	AI-powered digital assistance; Customer engagement; Digital multisensory cue; Online platform; Online shopping experience
20	Xie et al(2023)	Friend, mentor, lover: does chatbot engagement lead to psychological dependence?	Journal of Service Management	10.1108/JOSM-02-2022-0072	artificial intelligence (AI) helps in service technology engagement and it is a relationship development drivers	Service	Attachment; Psychological dependence; Relationship development; Social chatbot

Continued on following page

Table 1. Continued

Sl No	Authors	Title	Journal Name	DOI	Definition	Domain	Author Keywords
21	Bapat & Hollebeek(2023)	Customer value, customer engagement, and customer-based brand equity in the context of a digital payment app	Marketing Intelligence and Planning	10.1108/MIP-09-2022-0417	AI technology helps to enhance quality value, hedonic value, social value, price value, customer engagement and customer-based brand equity	Customer Engagement	Customer engagement; Customer perceived value; Customer-based brand equity; Perceived customer value theory; Stimulus-organism-response theory
22	Oteh et al(2023)	Marketing Capabilities, Market Orientation, and Food Security of Biofortified Cassava Producers in Nigeria	Journal of Macromarketing	10.1177/02761467231187307	Technology that helps to enhance knowledge of intelligence and competitive strategy, aspects of market capability	Food security	Base of Pyramid (BoP) producers; biofortification; cassava production; food security; G14; J54; L66; market orientation; marketing capabilities

Source: Authors

Out of 22 definitions given by different authors related to Artificial Intelligence (AI) and customer engagement, AI helps to enhance customer engagement which leads to value creation through different interfaces and platforms of business models.

From Table 1 it can be concluded that Artificial Intelligence is a data-driven customer engagement technology that helps to create and enhance quality value, hedonic value, social value, and price value in a customer engagement process to enhance competitiveness based on the market capabilities.

1.2 Justification of Research

Considering the significance of AI & customer engagement above, the present research article wants to examine the past research pattern and potential future research direction in AI & customer engagement research. The uniqueness of this article is that to date there are 3 various review articles (table 2) related to AI & customer engagement research published by many authors, but none of the authors has published any single literature review article based on TCCM (Theory, Context, Characteristic, and Methodology) framework. There would be many reasons why this topic has not been considered with the TCCM framework for review to date, as it is a very vast and deep topic with a plethora of theoretical applications, difficulties in managing vast databases of existing literature, etc

Table 2. Details of previously published review articles

Authors	Article Title	Journal Name	DOI	Arguments	Method Used	Future Research Directions	Whether Used TCCM Framework
Li et al(2023)	Social media in marketing research: Theoretical bases, methodological aspects, and thematic focus	Psychology and Marketing	10.1002/mar.21746	Social media is an intelligent strategic marketing tool to create value through CRM	SLR based on 418 articles (2009-2021).	Future studies should specifically shed light on how new machine learning algorithms and techniques can capture visual data, as well as how these data can be used for customer value creation	No
Hossain et al(2022)	Operationalizing Artificial Intelligence-Enabled Customer Analytics Capability in Retailing	Journal of Global Information Management	10.4018/JGIM.298992	New-generation AI technology can create a competitive advantage	SLR and Thematic Analysis based on 65 selected articles	Customer centricity, customer linking, customer equity, and the benefit of society.	No
Borges et al(2021)	The strategic use of artificial intelligence in the digital era: Systematic literature review and future research directions	International Journal of Information Management	10.1016/j.ijinfomgt.2020.102225	Retail practitioners will engage and enhance customer delight through AI	SLR based on 41 articles (2009-2020).	Human and AI, Customer and employee engagement, automation, new products & services.	No

Source: Authors

Based on the above discussion, it is clear that there is a big void in literature review research on AI and Customer engagement research. Moreover, out of these 3 articles mentioned above, no authors have used systemic literature review (SLR), bibliometric analysis, and TCCM framework directly to explore this area till now. In this way, this present research article is unique and a source of inspiration.

Based on the identified research gap above, the objective of this research study is to find out the below-mentioned research questions-

RQ1. What are the year-wise publication and citation trends, top most 10 authors based on citation numbers, most contributing country and journal in AI & customer engagement research (descriptive analysis)?

RQ2. How the research on AI & customer engagement research is diversified or clustered.

RQ3. What are the different theories that have been applied to this subject?

Rana et al (2023) in their recent literature review article related to POWER (Planning, Operationalizing, Writing, Embedding, Reflecting) framework stated that there are many frameworks for writing systematic literature review articles like ADO (antecedents, decisions, and outcomes), TCCM (Theory, context, characteristics, and methodology) by Paul and Rosado-Serrano (2019), PRISMA (Preferred reporting items for systematic reviews and meta-analysis) and 6W (who, when, where, what, why and how). PRISMA framework is one of the most preferred frameworks for systematic literature articles. This framework primarily focuses on the reporting of reviews evaluating the effects of interventions with objectives other than evaluating interventions (Rana, Singh, & Kathuria, 2023).

Based on the above logical discussion, this research followed the PRISMA (Moher, Tetzlaff, & Altman, 2009) framework. To write this review research paper, articles are collected from Scopus data. Then articles are shortened as per the relevancy of the topic by reading the topic, abstract, and in-text details. In the next step, all the selected articles are critically analyzed for synthesis. Next, bibliometric analysis helps to find out the most contributing journals citation-wise, country contributions, and different clusters. To identify the trends of current research and to find out future research directions, content analysis has been carried out.

This study critically analyses the different research articles on AI & customer engagement research presenting an overall structure of intellectual analysis. The important outcome of this research work will benefit academicians and practicing managers in understanding the research status, structure, and evolution of AI & customer engagement research. The future research direction of this research will give a direction about the future research to the new researchers in this area. To the best of my understanding, this is the first research study in AI & customer engagement research that has applied systematic literature review (SLR), bibliometric analysis, and TCCM framework at a time to get a result that will answer the pre-identified research questions.

The contribution of this research work to the AI & customer engagement research can be mentioned in three ways. No previous research work has considered the SLR and bibliometric analysis to find out the insight like most-cited authors, journal name with publication details, and country-wise contribution in this area. Secondly, the previous researcher has not given the focus on the TCCM framework.

2. RESEARCH METHODOLOGY

There are many ways to perform a literature review systematic literature review, meta-analysis, bibliometric analysis, and content analysis (Duque-Uribe, Sarache, & Gutierrez, 2019). This study follows the established five-step process to conduct the systematic literature review described by (Denyer & Tranfield, 2009). illustrated in the below Figure 1.

Figure 1. Systematic review process
Source: Based on (Denyer & Tranfield, 2009).

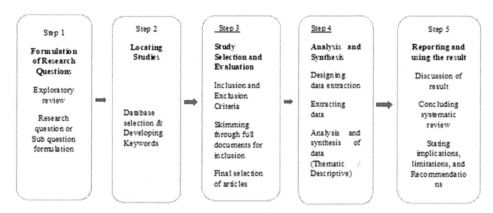

In the first steps, as per the guideline of Denyer & Tranfield (2009) on CIMO (Context, Interventions, Mechanism, and Outcomes) guideline, a set of 3 questions has been developed to get the answer from this review article.

In the second step, articles are extracted from the Scopus database with the help of selected keywords like "Customer*" AND "Engagement*" OR "Customer*" AND "Intelligence*" OR "Customer*" AND "Digital age*" AND "Artificial Intelligence*", Customer Insight, etc

When it is been searched with the same keywords for published articles in Business, Management, Accounting, and Social Science Journals in the English language, the number of articles is 2568. The same type of article extraction process has been used by Bazhair et al (2022) in their recently published article in a sustainability journal (Bazhair, Khatib, & AI Amosh, 2022). In the third recommended step, all the articles are examined based on keywords, titles, abstract, and in-text reading and presented in a synthesized manner based on the PRISMA (Fig 2) framework and inclusion-exclusion criteria (Table 3). After reviewing the title of the articles, abstract, and in-text study, a total of 2513 articles were removed from the study. In this stage, out of 55 articles, 2 articles have been removed as those 2 articles do not have sufficient information regarding the articles. The earlier researcher that used the PRISMA framework includes patient satisfaction (Batbaatar, Dorjdagva, Luvsannyam, & Savino, 2017), the application of Punctuated Equilibrium Theory(PET) in policy change (Kuhlmann & van der Heijden, 2018), to measure the quality the life framework (Monsalve, Morán, Alcedo, & Lombardi, 2020) and Digital libraries research (Maryati, Purwandari, Budi Santoso, & Budi, 2020). The reason for the Scopus database selection as it provides 20% more exposure compared to the WoS database (Falagas, 2008), and Google Scholar provides poor data for the analysis (Battisti & Salini, 2013).

Table 3. Criteria for inclusion and exclusion of articles

Inclusion Criteria	Exclusion Criteria
Articles related to only AI & customer engagement	Conference papers
Only peer-reviewed Scopus Indexed articles with ABDC A* & A.	Book Chapter, book review
Articles published in the English language during 2011-2023	Articles in press

Source: Authors

Figure 2. PRISMA framework (Adopted from Moher, Tetzlaff, & Altman, 2009)

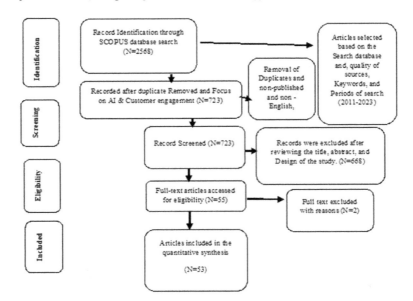

In the fourth stage, all 53 articles that are highly focused on AI and customer engagement have been exported to CSV files for bibliometric analysis.

To perform the bibliometric analysis, VOSviewer software has been used to calculate the local citations, country-wise contributions, co-citation analysis, co-occurrence of keywords, and the bibliometric coupling for cluster analysis. On the other hand, Microsoft spreadsheet has been used to calculate year-wise publication trends, global citations, journal contributions, etc (Paul & Criado, 2020). Each software is simple to use and gives a superior visual impact, as well as the ability to handle various data display formats (Mulet-Forteza, Martorell-Cunill, Merigo, & Mauleon-Mendez, 2018). To get an insight into organizational success research, a content analysis of the past four years' published articles has been analyzed to give the future research direction systematically. The same procedures have been used by many authors in their review research articles related to cause-related marketing (Rajan, Dhir, & Sushil, 2020).

3. DESCRIPTIVE ANALYSIS (RQ 1)

3.1 Publication Trends

Figure 3. Year-wise publications and citations trend

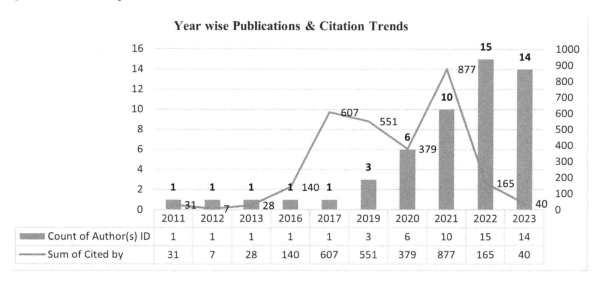

The publication trends in customer engagement through AI have gained momentum since 2020. After 2021 more numbers of authors have given high attention to published articles with an average of 360 global citations per year. The number of articles in 2023 is less (only 14) because the academic year is yet to complete.

Table 4. Top 10 contributing authors based on the number of citations

Sl No	Authors	Title	Source Title	Cited Numbers	DOI	Main Arguments	Domain
1	Grewal et al (2017)	The Future of Retailing	Journal of Retailing	607	10.1016/j.jretai.2016.12.008	AI can help in decision-making, visual display, and merchandise and can enhance the profitability of an organization	Retail
2	Buhalis & Sinarta (2019)	Real-time co-creation and nowness service: lessons from tourism and hospitality	Journal of Travel and Tourism Marketing	322	10.1080/10548408.2019.1592059	Foster organic consumer engagement and connect consumer	Tourism and hospitality
3	Huang & Rust (2021)	Engaged to a Robot? The Role of AI in Service	Journal of Service Research	293	10.1177/1094670520902266	Artificial intelligence (AI) to engage customers for different service benefits	Service
4	Borges et al(2021)	The strategic use of artificial intelligence in the digital era: Systematic literature review and future research directions	International Journal of Information Management	203	10.1016/j.ijinfomgt.2020.102225	AI has great potential to solve different customer problems	Business Value Creation
5	Kumar et al(2019)	Understanding the role of artificial intelligence in personalized engagement marketing	California Management Review	190	10.1177/0008125619859317	Artificial intelligence (AI) can enhance personalized customer engagement.	Marketing
6	Marbach et al(2016)	Who are you and what do you value? Investigating the Role of personality traits and customer-perceived Value in online customer engagement	Journal of Marketing Management	140	10.1080/0267257X.2015.1128472	AI can enhance online customer engagement (OCE).	Social Media
7	Prentice & Nguyen (2020)	Engaging and retaining customers with AI and employee service	Journal of Retailing and Consumer Services	112	10.1016/j.jretconser.2020.102186	AI will enhance operational efficiency and improve customer experience.	Service
8	Hamilton et al(2021)	Traveling with Companions: The Social Customer Journey	Journal of Marketing	100	10.1177/0022242920908227	Helps to improve the decision-making process	Tourism and hospitality
9	Schuetzler et al (2020)	The impact of chatbot conversational skill on engagement and perceived humanness	Journal of Management Information Systems	92	10.1080/07421222.2020.1790204	AI can engage in conversations with human users.	Conversational agents (CAs)
10	Prentice et al (2020)	Linking AI quality performance and customer engagement: The moderating effect of AI preference	International Journal of Hospitality Management	84	10.1016/j.ijhm.2020.102629	AI can influence customer engagement	Service

Source: Authors

The top 10 authors based on global citation numbers with article details are given in the table. All the articles are based on customer-centric discussion and the majority of the authors have emphasized service, tourism hospitality, and retail domain.

The top most cited article in this research is- The Future of Retailing, which has highlighted the AI application in the areas of (1) decision making, (2) visual display and merchandise offer decisions, (3) consumption and engagement, (4) big data collection and usage, and (5) analytics and profitability.

Table 5. Top contributing journal details

Journal Name	2011	2012	2013	2016	2017	2019	2020	2021	2022	2023	Grand Total	Percentage Contribution
Journal of Business Research							1		2	3	6	11.32%
Journal of Retailing and Consumer Services							1		1	1	3	5.66%
Journal of Service Management									2	1	3	5.66%
Journal of Services Marketing							1		2		3	5.66%
European Journal of Marketing	1								1		2	3.77%
Information Systems Frontiers									1	1	2	3.77%
Journal of Business and Industrial Marketing								1		1	2	3.77%
Journal of Management Information Systems								1		1	2	3.77%
Journal of Marketing Management				1				1			2	3.77%
Journal of Service Research								2			2	3.77%
Journal of Strategic Marketing			1					1			2	3.77%
Marketing Intelligence and Planning		1							1		2	3.77%
Psychology and Marketing									2		2	3.77%
Australian Journal of Management									1		1	1.89%
California Management Review						1					1	1.89%
Decision Support Systems								1			1	1.89%
Information Systems Journal									1		1	1.89%
Information Technology and People						1					1	1.89%
International Journal of Hospitality Management						1					1	1.89%
International Journal of Information Management								1			1	1.89%
International Journal of Medical Informatics									1		1	1.89%
Journal of Brand Management									1		1	1.89%
Journal of Global Information Management									1		1	1.89%
Journal of Hospitality Marketing and Management									1		1	1.89%
Journal of Interactive Marketing						1					1	1.89%
Journal of International Management									1		1	1.89%
Journal of Macro-marketing									1		1	1.89%
Journal of Marketing								1			1	1.89%
Journal of Retailing					1						1	1.89%
Journal of Travel and Tourism Marketing						1					1	1.89%
Production and Operations Management									1		1	1.89%
Technological Forecasting and Social Change									1		1	1.89%
Tourism Management									1		1	1.89%
Grand Total	**1**	**1**	**1**	**1**	**1**	**3**	**6**	**10**	**15**	**14**	**53**	**100.00%**

Source: Authors

Above are the 33 journals with year-wise articles published details. Out of 53 articles, to date, the Journal of Business Research has published 6 articles (11.32%) on AI in customer engagement research. It has been observed that while the majority of the journals are inconsistent in this research area, but Journal of Business Research has given a consistent approach to enhance the number of article publications year after year.

Table 6. Most productive countries

Country Name	Articles Published	Total Global Citations Numbers	Percentage of Articles Published by the Country (N=53)
United States	15	1449	28.30%
United Kingdom	12	635	22.64%
Australia	8	266	15.09%
India	8	94	15.09%
China	5	145	9.43%
Finland	5	112	9.43%
Italy	4	47	7.55%

Source: Authors

The United States is the number one country in this research with 15 articles publications and 28.30% research publication contributions. The United Kingdom is the second country with 12 articles and 22.64% research contribution. Followed by Australia and India with 8 publications and 15.09% publication contribution each.

Table 7. Analysis of co-occurrence of keywords

Keywords	Occurrences	Total Link Strength
Artificial Intelligence	19	113
Customer Engagement	19	101
Social Media	7	53
Chatbots	4	19
Engagement	3	27
Marketing	3	25
Conversational agents	3	16
Emotional intelligence	3	11
Personalization	2	19
Social media marketing	2	18
Digital Marketing	2	16
Market Orientation	2	15
User Engagement	2	13
AI	2	12
Strategy	2	11

Source: Authors

4. ANALYSIS OF CLUSTER FORMATION (RQ 2)

Figure 4. Keyword co-occurrence of themes network

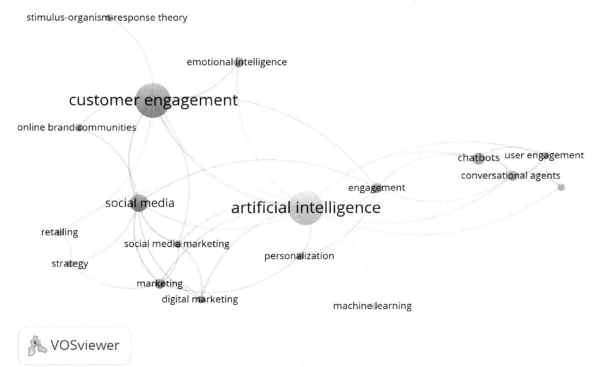

4.1 Application of Artificial Intelligence in Marketing Domain

Artificial intelligence (AI) is breaking new ground in delivering value to users (Kumar, Rajan, Venkatesan, & Lecinski, 2019). In the case of a developed economy, AI will aid in personalization by creating superior brand experiences for customers.

In the long run, firms will be better prepared to offer AI-driven solutions that are comprehensive solutions impacting the entire customer lifecycle, rather than the focused, tactical solutions in the short run. There are three critical areas of customer relationship management—acquisition (brand value), retention (human-machine interface), and growth (customer knowledge value)—that have long-term relevance to firms and that can serve as the cornerstones of their marketing strategy with the help of AI (Kumar, Rajan, Venkatesan, & Lecinski, 2019).

4.2 AI and Conversational Agent

Conversational Agents (CA) often called chatbots, are computer systems that leverage language processing to engage customers by providing technical support, customer services, and digital personal assistance. Many organizations are deploying chatbots to provide customer service, provide technical support, conduct medical interviews, provide student counseling services, etc. (Schuetzler, Grimes, & Scott Giboney, 2020).

4.3 AI and Customer Engagement

AI in the service industry can enhance customer engagement and enhance operational effectiveness and customer experience. Study shows that overall experience with both employees and AI significantly influences customer engagement and loyalty. When regressing all sub-dimensions of employee and AI service, none of the AI dimensions are significantly related to customer engagement. Nevertheless, employee responsiveness, empathy, and assurance exert significant effects on the outcome variable (Prentice & Nguyen, 2020). Studies have also stated that AI power services not only enhance operational efficiency but also help to enhance customer engagement and attract loyal customers (Prentice & Nguyen, 2020).

4.4 AI and Machine Learning

Many organizations are using customer analytics and information systems to know about its customers who are using the products or services (Jansen, Jung, & Salminen, 2023). Recent past, AI and Machine learning have been integrated to analyze this data to identify the trends and help to segment within large populations. Many organizations use this persona analytic system to engage customers (Jansen, Jung, & Salminen, 2023).

4.5 AI and Personalization

Analytical AI is designed to explore customer diversity to identify meaningful patterns (i.e., data mining, text mining). The more advanced intuitive AI is designed for maximizing decision-making accuracy (i.e., solving problems, and maximizing the accuracy of answering questions in data science language). Thus, thinking AI is ideal for service personalization for optimal service productivity (Rust and Huang 2012). As AI capabilities are cumulative, intuitive AI also may process all of the capabilities of analytical AI. Thinking AI is ideal for service personalization, especially when there is abundant customer data available and when the problems are well-defined, for example, predicting which new services will be appealing to which customers. In this situation, there are ample existing customer preference data that can be used to suggest different new services to different customers. The analytical subtype of thinking AI is good for uncovering or discovering meaningful patterns in data as the basis of personalization (Huang & Rust, 2021).

4.6 AI and Retail Strategy

Retailer has embraced many technologies to engage their customers which helps to enhance the decision-making process and merchandise offers. Retailers that can draw effective insights from big data can make better predictions about consumer behavior, design more appealing offers, better target their customers, and can develop tools that encourage consumers to make purchase decisions. Thus, big data can initiate beneficial, cyclical processes of consumer consumption and engagement that in turn lead to enhanced profitability (Grewal, Roggeveen, & Nordf, 2017).

5. THE THEORY-CONTEXT-CHARACTERISTICS-METHODS (TCCM) FRAMEWORK (RQ 3)

This section of the article deals with the identification of the research gap in the present literature and provides some new possibilities for future studies in the neuromarketing context. To ensure this objective of the research, a TCCM framework has been used (Paul & Rosado-Serrano, 2019). Many earlier authors in different academic research also used the same TCCM framework in different areas like marketing (Rajan, Dhir, & Sushil, 2020), culture, and international business (Srivastava, Singh, & Dhir, 2020) to develop the framework.

5.1 Theory

Current literature in the AI and customer engagement area comprises the expansion and conceptualization of the topic as a whole to understand customer engagement with the assistance of diverse AI tools. Earlier research works that cemented the way for increasing thoughtfulness for AI & customer engagement research concentrated on numerous theoretical approaches such as Generational Theory (Buhalis & Sinarta, 2019), Theory of Planned Behaviour (Huang & Rust, 2021), Social Influence theory, Social Impact Theory (Hamilton, Ferraro, Haws, & Mukhopadhyay, 2021), Social Presence Theory (Schuetzler, Grimes, & Scott Giboney, 2020) and so on. There are twenty prominently used theories and models that have been used in AI and customer engagement research. Details of the same have been presented in the above table (Table no 8).

Although significant development has been made over the last many years in AI and customer engagement research there are some inadequacies in terms of growth and presentation of different theories related to this area.

Table 8. Theory used in artificial intelligence and customer engagement research

Theory Used	Brief concept	Author Details	Title	Journal Name	DOI
Generational Theory	This theory has been proposed by Karl Mannheim in 1928. According to this theory, people are significantly influenced by the socio-historical environment.	Buhalis & Sinarta(2019)	Real-time co-creation and nowness service: lessons from tourism and hospitality	Journal of Travel and Tourism Marketing	10.1080/10548408.2019.1592059
Theory of Planned Behavior	Icek Ajzen (1985) proposed the theory of planned behavior. The theory states that three core components, namely, attitude, subjective norms, and perceived behavioral control, together shape an individual's behavioral intentions.	Huang & Rust(2021)	Engaged to a Robot? The Role of AI in Service	Journal of Service Research	10.1177/1094670520902266
Social Influence Theory, Socal Impact Theory	Social influence comprises how individuals adjust their behavior to meet the demands of a social environment. It takes many forms and can be seen in conformity, socialization, peer pressure, obedience, leadership, persuasion, sales, and marketing	Hamilton et al(2021)	Traveling with Companions: The Social Customer Journey	Journal of Marketing	10.1177/0022242920908227
Social Presence Theory	Social presence theory explores how the "sense of being with another" is influenced by digital interfaces in human-computer interactions	Schuetzler et al(2020)	The impact of chatbot conversational skill on engagement and perceived humanness	Journal of Management Information Systems	10.1080/07421222.2020.1790204
The theory of conversation (ToC)	conversation theory is a cybernetic approach to the study of conversation, cognition, and learning that may occur between two participants who are engaged in conversation with each other	Moriuchi et al(2021)	Engagement with chatbots versus augmented reality interactive technology in e-commerce	Journal of Strategic Marketing	10.1080/0965254X.2020.1740766
Organization learning theory, Organization capabilities theory, and Dynamic capabilities theory.	Organizational learning is the process of creating, retaining, and transferring knowledge within an organization	Gupta et al(2020)	Digital Analytics: Modeling for Insights and New Methods	Journal of Interactive Marketing	10.1016/j.intmar.2020.04.003

Continued on following page

Table 8. Continued

Theory Used	Brief concept	Author Details	Title	Journal Name	DOI
Social Response Theory	According to the **Social Responsibility Theory**, before making a decision or completing a task, one must ensure the decision or act is ethically sound.	Kull et al(2021)	How may I help you? Driving brand engagement through the warmth of an initial chatbot message	Journal of Business Research	10.1016/j.jbusres.2021.03.005
Social Capital Theory	Social capital is "the networks of relationships among people who live and work in a particular society, enabling that society to function effectively"	Meek et al(2019)	A multidimensional scale for measuring online brand community social capital (OBCSC)	Journal of Business Research	10.1016/j.jbusres.2019.03.036
Configurational theory	Configurational theorizing is premised on the assumption that configurations (or combinations) of causally relevant conditions should be linked to the outcome of interest.	Singh et al(2021)	One-Voice Strategy for Customer Engagement	Journal of Service Research	10.1177/1094670520910267
Expectation Violation Theory	Expectancy violation theory (EVT) is a theory of communication that analyzes how individuals respond to unanticipated violations of social norms and expectations	Grimes et al(2021)	Mental models and expectation violations in conversational AI interactions	Decision Support Systems	10.1016/j.dss.2021.113515
Organization theory.	Organizational theory refers to a series of interrelated concepts that involve the sociological study of the structures and operations of formal social organizations	Aspara et al(2011)	Exploration and exploitation across three resource classes: Market/customer intelligence, brands/bonds, and technologies/processes	European Journal of Marketing	10.1108/03090561111111352
Social Intelligence Theory	Social intelligence is the ability to understand one's own and others' actions. Social intelligence is learned and developed from experience with people and learning from successes and failures in social settings	Stone & Woodcock(2013)	Social intelligence in customer engagement	Journal of Strategic Marketing	10.1080/0965254X.2013.801613
Commitment-Trust Theory (Morgan and Hunt 1994)	The commitment-trust theory of relationship marketing says that two fundamental factors, trust and commitment, must exist for a relationship to be successful	Pangarkar et al(2022)	Exploring phygital omnichannel luxury retailing for immersive customer experience: The role of rapport and social engagement	Journal of Retailing and Consumer Services	10.1016/j.jretconser.2022.103001

Continued on following page

Table 8. Continued

Theory Used	Brief concept	Author Details	Title	Journal Name	DOI
Assemblage theory of Deleuze and Guattari(1983),	Assemblage (from, "a collection of things which have been gathered together or assembled") is a philosophical approach to studying the ontological diversity of agency, which means redistributing the capacity to act from an individual to a socio-material network of people, things, and narratives.	Kozinets(2022)	Algorithmic branding through platform assemblages: core conceptions and research directions for a new era of marketing and service management	Journal of Service Management	10.1108/JOSM-07-2021-0263
Stimulus-organism-response theory, Consumer empowerment theory	The stimulus–response model is a characterization of a statistical unit (such as a neuron). The model allows the prediction of a quantitative response to a quantitative stimulus	Shaikh et al(2023)	Mobile money as a driver of digital financial inclusion	Technological Forecasting and Social Change	10.1016/j.techfore.2022.122158
Value co-creation Theory(VCC)	value co-creation is defined as the interactive process whereby multiple actors cooperate to generate new value through their voluntary contribution	Utami et al(2021)	?A social justice logic?: how digital commerce enables value co-creation at the bottom of the pyramid	Journal of Marketing Management	10.1080/0267257X.2021.1908399
The relationship marketing theory (RMT)	Relationship marketing theory proposes that as a company delivers value to the customer, the strength of its relationship with the customer will improve and increase customer retention.	Ghouri et al(2022)	The micro-foundations of social media use: Artificial intelligence integrated routine model	Journal of Business Research	10.1016/j.jbusres.2022.01.084
Uncanny Valley Theory (UVT), proposed by Mori (1970)	The uncanny valley is a theory in aesthetics that explains why humanoid objects or robots that look almost but not exactly like humans can evoke eeriness or revulsion.	Sharma et al(2022)	Impact of Digital Assistant Attributes on Millennials? Purchasing Intentions: A Multi-Group Analysis using PLS-SEM, Artificial Neural Network and fsQCA	Information Systems Frontiers	10.1007/s10796-022-10339-5
Relational cohesion theory	relational cohesion theory explains how and when people who are exchanging things of value develop stable, cohesive relations	Hern ndez-Ortega et al(2022)	Relational cohesion between users and smart voice assistants	Journal of Services Marketing	10.1108/JSM-07-2020-0286

Continued on following page

Table 8. Continued

Theory Used	Brief concept	Author Details	Title	Journal Name	DOI
Hexad model	This model presents the first typology to classify users of gamified systems, enabling clustering them based on intrinsic and extrinsic motivational factors	Elmashhara et al(2023)	How gratifying AI shapes customer motivation, engagement, and purchase behavior	Psychology and Marketing	10.1002/mar.21912

Source: Authors

5.2 Characteristics

Over the years, a limited number of scholars tried to expose the antecedents or enablers of AI and customer engagement research. Hossain et al (2022) in a research study stated that AI-enabled customer analytics can be ensured through six distinct dimensions via the themes of value creation (Offering capability, personalization capability), value delivery (Distribution capabilities, communication capabilities), and value management (data Management capability, data protection capability). Catherine et al (2020) stated that AI power tools as service indicators that specifically cater to customers to create opportunities for customer actions and behaviors.

5.3 Context

The development of AI and customer research has innovated our knowledge through different key factors like the significance of different methods and their advantage and disadvantages. While reviewing the research articles (N=53, where context is explained), it has been observed that the majority of the customer engagement study is focused on the retail perspective. Some of the other areas where studies have been done to date are chatbots, online brands, business intelligence, and supply chain management (Table 9).

Table 9. Different context used in artificial intelligence and customer engagement research

Authors	Title	Journal Name	DOI	Context
Buhalis & Sinarta (2019)	Real-time co-creation and nowness service: lessons from tourism and hospitality	Journal of Travel and Tourism Marketing	10.1080/10548408.2019.1592059	Retail
Prentice & Nguyen(2020)	Engaging and retaining customers with AI and employee service	Journal of Retailing and Consumer Services	10.1016/j.jretconser.2020.102186	Retail
Schuetzler et al(2020)	The impact of chatbot conversational skill on engagement and perceived humanness	Journal of Management Information Systems	10.1080/07421222.2020.1790204	Chatbot
Prentice et al(2020)	Linking AI quality performance and customer engagement: The moderating effect of AI preference	International Journal of Hospitality Management	10.1016/j.ijhm.2020.102629	AI
Moriuchi et al(2021)	Engagement with chatbots versus augmented reality interactive technology in e-commerce	Journal of Strategic Marketing	10.1080/0965254X.2020.1740766	Chatbot and AI in Retail
Gupta et al(2020)	Digital Analytics: Modeling for Insights and New Methods	Journal of Interactive Marketing	10.1016/j.intmar.2020.04.003	Digital Analytics
Kull et al(2021)	How may I help you? Driving brand engagement through the warmth of an initial chatbot message	Journal of Business Research	10.1016/j.jbusres.2021.03.005	Chatbot
Meek et al(2019)	A multidimensional scale for measuring online brand community social capital (OBCSC)	Journal of Business Research	10.1016/j.jbusres.2019.03.036	Online brand Communities
Singh et al(2021)	One-Voice Strategy for Customer Engagement	Journal of Service Research	10.1177/1094670520910267	Customer Engagement
Aspara et al(2011)	Exploration and exploitation across three resource classes: Market/ customer intelligence, brands/bonds, and technologies/processes	European Journal of Marketing	10.1108/03090561111111352	Exploration & Exploitation Opportunities in Innovation
Stone & Woodcock(2013)	Social intelligence in customer engagement	Journal of Strategic Marketing	10.1080/0965254X.2013.801613	Customer Engagement
Lee et al(2020)	Analyzing online reviews to investigate customer behavior in the sharing economy: The case of Airbnb	Information Technology and People	10.1108/ITP-10-2018-0475	Business Intelligence
Pangarkar et al(2022)	Exploring phygital omnichannel luxury retailing for immersive customer experience: The role of rapport and social engagement	Journal of Retailing and Consumer Services	10.1016/j.jretconser.2022.103001	Customer Experience in Retailing
Battisti & Brem(2021)	Digital entrepreneurs in technology-based spinoffs: an analysis of hybrid value creation in retail public & private partnerships to tackle showrooming	Journal of Business and Industrial Marketing	10.1108/JBIM-01-2020-0051	Retail
Kozinets(2022)	Algorithmic branding through platform assemblages: core conceptions and research directions for a new era of marketing and service management	Journal of Service Management	10.1108/JOSM-07-2021-0263	Algorithmic Branding
Utami et al(2021)	A social justice logic: how digital commerce enables value co-creation at the bottom of the pyramid	Journal of Marketing Management	10.1080/0267257X.2021.1908399	Supply Chain

Source: Authors

5.4 Method Used

In the area of AI and Customer engagement research, it has been observed some of the statistical methods that have been prominently used are exploratory research, CFA, SEM, POMDP, ANOVA, Content analysis, T-Test, thematic analysis, Longitudinal qualitative study, etc (Table No 10). Further, it will be worthwhile for future research if they give more importance to the meta-analysis review and various econometric tools for augmenting the methodological rigor in the AI & customer engagement research arena.

Table 10. Methods used in AI and customer engagement research

Authors	Article	Journal Name	DOI	Method Used
Buhalis & Sinarta(2019)	Real-time co-creation and nowness service: lessons from tourism and hospitality	Journal of Travel and Tourism Marketing	10.1080/10548408.2019.1592059	Exploratory research
Prentice & Nguyen(2020)	Engaging and retaining customers with AI and employee service	Journal of Retailing and Consumer Services	10.1016/j.jretconser.2020.102186	confirmatory factor analysis (CFA)
Schuetzler et al(2020)	The impact of chatbot conversational skill on engagement and perceived humanness	Journal of Management Information Systems	10.1080/07421222.2020.1790204	SEM
Prentice et al(2020)	Linking AI quality performance and customer engagement: The moderating effect of AI preference	International Journal of Hospitality Management	10.1016/j.ijhm.2020.102629	Factor Analysis
Moriuchi et al(2021)	Engagement with chatbots versus augmented reality interactive technology in e-commerce	Journal of Strategic Marketing	10.1080/0965254X.2020.1740766	Partially observable Markov decision process(POMDP)
Kull et al(2021)	How may I help you? Driving brand engagement through the warmth of an initial chatbot message	Journal of Business Research	10.1016/j.jbusres.2021.03.005	ANOVA
Meek et al(2019)	A multidimensional scale for measuring online brand community social capital (OBCSC)	Journal of Business Research	10.1016/j.jbusres.2019.03.036	CFA
Grimes et al(2021)	Mental models and expectation violations in conversational AI interactions	Decision Support Systems	10.1016/j.dss.2021.113515	T - Test
Lee(2020)	Analyzing online reviews to investigate customer behavior in the sharing economy: The case of Airbnb	Information Technology and People	10.1108/ITP-10-2018-0475	longitudinal analysis and the seasonal analysis
Pangarkar(2022)	Exploring phygital omnichannel luxury retailing for immersive customer experience: The role of rapport and social engagement	Journal of Retailing and Consumer Services	10.1016/j.jretconser.2022.103001	Content analysis
Battisti & Brem(2021)	Digital entrepreneurs in technology-based spinoffs: an analysis of hybrid value creation in retail public?private partnerships to tackle showrooming	Journal of Business and Industrial Marketing	10.1108/JBIM-01-2020-0051	Longitudinal qualitative study
Utami et al(2021)	?A social justice logic?: how digital commerce enables value co-creation at the bottom of the pyramid	Journal of Marketing Management	10.1080/0267257X.2021.1908399	Thematic analysis
Sharma et al(2022)	Impact of Digital Assistant Attributes on Millennials? Purchasing Intentions: A Multi-Group Analysis using PLS-SEM, Artificial Neural Network and fsQCA	Information Systems Frontiers	10.1007/s10796-022-10339-5	fsQCA

Continued on following page

Table 10. Continued

Authors	Article	Journal Name	DOI	Method Used
Hern ndez-Ortega (2022)	Relational cohesion between users and smart voice assistants	Journal of Services Marketing	10.1108/JSM-07-2020-0286	CFA
Elmashhara(2023)	How gratifying AI shapes customer motivation, engagement, and purchase behavior	Psychology and Marketing	10.1002/mar.21912	ANOVA

Source: Authors

6. DISCUSSION AND CONCLUSION

After identifying the 53 articles from the Scopus database based on the PRISMA framework and pre-identified research questions, a comprehensive literature review based on SLR, bibliometric and TCCM framework analysis has been done. The publication trends in customer engagement through AI have gained momentum since 2020. After 2021 more numbers of authors have given high attention to published articles with an average of 360 global citations per year The top most cited article in this research is- The Future of Retailing, which has highlighted the AI application in the areas of (1) decision making, (2) visual display and merchandise offer decisions, (3) consumption and engagement, (4) big data collection and usage, and (5) analytics and profitability. Out of 53 articles, to date, the Journal of Business Research has published 6 articles (11.32%) in AI in customer engagement research. It has been observed that while the majority of the journals are inconsistent in this research area, but Journal of Business Research has given a consistent approach to enhance the number of article publications year after year. The United States is the number one country in this research with 15 articles publications and 28.30% research publication contributions. The United Kingdom is the second country with 12 articles and 22.64% research contribution. Followed by Australia and India with 8 publications and 15.09% publication contribution each. A VOSviewer data analysis shows that there are six prominent clusters in this research with different themes and sub-themes. An examination of the extent of literature on AI & customer engagement research has proven that there is still room for theory development in the area of Uncanny Valley Theory. In this connection, future researchers should also pay attention to multiple case study methods and use additional analytical methods such as meta-analysis, hybrid review methods, and tools related to econometric analysis to improve methodological rigor in AI & customer engagement research.

Until now, in the study of AI & customer engagement, many systematic research methods have been used. However, there is a gap in the area of mixed methodologies, multiple case studies, meta-analyses, hybrid review methods, and the use of econometric tools. It is seen that earlier research on AI & customer engagement is mostly focused on organizations belonging to the United States and the United Kingdom This provides opportunities for various organizations which belong to developing countries. Moreover, a researcher should try to explore this opportunity in some of the organization that belongs to emerging markets like Brazil, Russia China. A cross-cultural study will be more helpful in this direction. The widely used methodologies in AI & customer engagement research are co-relation, structural equation modeling, factor analysis, Systematic literature review, T-Test Etc. This research also recommends the researcher use some advanced methods like semantic network analysis, data mining, total interpretive structural modeling, and comparative case studies to understand the various factors and their outcomes in AI & customer engagement research. This research article, like other research articles, has some limitations. The keywords used in the research article are not exhaustive; different words may produce different results, resulting in different cluster formations. Working with other software that uses different algorithms and frameworks may yield different results. Because of the time constraints of the data extraction process, some of the articles from 2023 were not available during the extraction of research article details from the Scopus database.

These articles also encourage the academician and scholar to add more value by proposing a framework in AI & customer engagement research. Researchers and academicians may also review identified research gaps, in theory, context, content, and methods to further explore AI & customer engagement research with more review articles.

REFERENCES

Batbaatar, E., Dorjdagva, J., Luvsannyam, A., Savino, M. M., & Amenta, P. (2017). Determinants of patient satisfaction: A systematic review. *Perspectives in Public Health*, *137*(2), 89–101. doi:10.1177/1757913916634136 PMID:27004489

Battisti, D. F., & Salini, S. (2013). Robust analysis of bibliometric data. *Statistical Methods and Applications, 22*(October), 269-283.

Bazhair, A., Khatib, S., & Amosh, A. I. (2022). Taking stock of carbon disclosure research while looking to the future: A systematic literature review. *Sustainability (Basel)*, *14*(20), 13475. doi:10.3390/su142013475

Borges, A., Laurindo, F., Spínola, M. M., Gonçalves, R. F., & Mattos, C. A. (2021, April). Spjnola, M., Rodrigo, F., & Claudia, A. (2021). The strategic use of artificial intelligence in the digital era: Systematic literature review and future research directions. *International Journal of Information Management*, *57*, 102225. Advance online publication. doi:10.1016/j.ijinfomgt.2020.102225

Boz, H., Arslan, A., & Koc, E. (2017). Neuromarketing aspect of tourism pricing psychology. *Tourism Management Perspectives*, *23*(1), 119–128. doi:10.1016/j.tmp.2017.06.002

Buhalis, D., & Sinarta, Y. (2019). Real-time co-creation and nowness service: Lessons from tourism and hospitality. *Journal of Travel & Tourism Marketing*, *36*(5), 563–582. doi:10.1080/10548408.2019.1592059

Denyer, D., & Tranfield, D. (2009). Producing a Systematic Review. In D. Buchanan & A. Bryman (Eds.), *The Sage Handbook of Organizational Research Methods* (pp. 671–689). Sage.

Dimoka, A., Pavlou, P., & Davis, F. (2011). NeuroIS: The potential of cognitive neuroscience for information systems research. *Information Systems Research*, *22*(4), 687–702. doi:10.1287/isre.1100.0284

Duque-Uribe, V., Sarache, W., & Gutierrez, E. (2019). Sustainable supply chain management practice and sustainable performance in hospitals: A systematic review and integrative framework. *Sustainability (Basel)*, *11*(21), 5949. doi:10.3390/su11215949

Falagas, M. P., Pitsouni, E. I., Malietzis, G. A., & Pappas, G. (2008). Comparison of PubMed, Scopus, Web of Science, and Google Scholar: Strengths and weaknesses. *The FASEB Journal*, *22*(2), 338–342. doi:10.1096/fj.07-9492LSF PMID:17884971

Grewal, D., Roggeveen, A., & Nordfält, J. (2017). The Future of Retailing. *Journal of Retailing*, *93*(1), 1–6. doi:10.1016/j.jretai.2016.12.008

Hamilton, R., Ferraro, R., Haws, K., & Mukhopadhyay, A. (2021). Traveling with Companions: The Social Customer Journey. *Journal of Marketing*, *85*(1), 68–92. doi:10.1177/0022242920908227

Hsu, L., & Chen, Y.-J. (2020). Neuromarketing, subliminal advertising, and hotel selection: An EEG study. *Australasian Marketing Journal*, *28*(4), 200–208. doi:10.1016/j.ausmj.2020.04.009

Hsu, M.-T., & Cheng, J.-S. (2018). fMRI neuromarketing and consumer learning theory: Word-of-mouth effectiveness after product harm crisis. *European Journal of Marketing*, *52*(1), 199–223. doi:10.1108/EJM-12-2016-0866

Huang, M., & Rust, R. (2021). Engaged to a Robot? The Role of AI in Service. *Journal of Service Research*, *24*(1), 30–41. doi:10.1177/1094670520902266

Huang, M.-H., & Rust, R. (2021). Engaged to a Robot? The Role of AI in Service. *Journal of Service Research*, *30*(41), 30–41. doi:10.1177/1094670520902266

Hubert, M. (2010). Does neuroeconomics give new impetus to economic and consumer research? *Journal of Economic Psychology*, *31*(5), 812–817. doi:10.1016/j.joep.2010.03.009

Jansen, B., Jung, S., & Salminen, J. (2023). Finetuning Analytics Information Systems for a Better Understanding of Users: Evidence of Personification Bias on Multiple Digital Channels. *Information Systems Frontiers*. Advance online publication. doi:10.1007/s10796-023-10395-5

Jones, W., Childers, T., & Jiang, Y. (2012). The shopping brain: Math anxiety modulates brain responses to buying decisions. *Biological Psychology*, *89*(1), 201–213. doi:10.1016/j.biopsycho.2011.10.011 PMID:22027087

Kuhlmann, J., & van der Heijden, J. (2018). What Is Known about Punctuated Equilibrium Theory? And What Does That Tell Us about the Construction, Validation, and Replication of Knowledge in the Policy Sciences? *The Review of Policy Research*, *35*(2), 326–347. doi:10.1111/ropr.12283

Kumar, V., Rajan, B., Venkatesan, R., & Lecinski, J. (2019). Understanding the role of artificial intelligence in personalized engagement marketing. *California Management Review*, *61*(4), 135–155. doi:10.1177/0008125619859317

Lai, C.-H., & Fu, J. (2021). Humanitarian Relief and Development Organizations' Stakeholder Targeting Communication on Social Media and Beyond. *Voluntas*, *32*(1), 120–135. doi:10.1007/s11266-020-00209-6

Lim, W. (2018). Demystifying neuromarketing. *Journal of Business Research*, *90*(1), 205–220. doi:10.1016/j.jbusres.2018.05.036

Maryati, I., Purwandari, B., Budi Santoso, H., & Budi, I. (2020). Implementation Strategies for Adopting Digital Library Research Support Services in Academic Libraries in Indonesia. *Proceedings - 2nd International Conference on Informatics, Multimedia, Cyber, and Information Systems, ICIMCIS 2020* (pp. pp 188-194). South Jakarta: Institute of Electrical and Electronics Engineers Inc. 10.1109/ICIMCIS51567.2020.9354327

Moher, D., Tetzlaff, A., & Altman, D. (2009). Preferred reporting items for systematic reviews and meta-analysis: The PRISMA statement. *PLoS Medicine, 6*(7), e1000097. doi:10.1371/journal.pmed.1000097 PMID:19621072

Monsalve, A., Morán, M., Alcedo, M., & Lombardi, M. (2020). Measurable indicators of credit for people with intellectual and developmental disabilities within the quality of life framework. *International Journal of Environmental Research and Public Health, 17*(14), 1–25. doi:10.3390/ijerph17145123

Montazeribarforoushi, S., Keshavarzsaleh, A., & Ramsøy, T. (2017). On the hierarchy of choice: An applied neuroscience perspective on the AIDA model. *Cogent Psychology, 4*(1), 1363343. Advance online publication. doi:10.1080/23311908.2017.1363343

Mulet-forteza, C., Martorell-cunill, O., Merigo, J., & Mauleon-mendez, E. (2018). Twenty-five years of the Journal of travel and Tourism Marketing: a bibliometric ranking. *Journal of Travel and Tourism Management, 35*, 263-296.

Paul, J., & Criado, A. (2020). The art of writing literature review: What do we know and what do we need to know? *International Business Review, 29*(4), 1–7. doi:10.1016/j.ibusrev.2020.101717

Paul, J., & Rosado-Serrano, A. (2019). Gradual internationalization vs. born-global/international new venture models: A review and research agenda. *International Marketing Review, 36*(6), 830–858. doi:10.1108/IMR-10-2018-0280

Prentice, C., & Nguyen, M. (2020). Engaging and retaining customers with AI and employee service. *Journal of Retailing and Consumer Services, 56*, 102186. Advance online publication. doi:10.1016/j.jretconser.2020.102186

Prentice, C., Weaven, S., & Wong, I. (2020). Linking AI quality performance and customer engagement: The moderating effect of AI preference. *International Journal of Hospitality Management, 90*, 102629. Advance online publication. doi:10.1016/j.ijhm.2020.102629

Rajan, R., Dhir, S., & Sushil. (2020). Alliance Termination Research: A bibliometric review and research agenda. *Journal of Strategy and Management, 13*(3), 351–375. doi:10.1108/JSMA-10-2019-0184

Rana, S., Singh, J., & Kathuria, S. (2023). Parameters and Decision Elements on Writing Effective Literature Review Papers: Empirical Evidence from Multiple Stakeholders of POWER Framework. In *Advancing Methodologies of Conducting Literature Review in Management Domain (Review of Management Literature)* (Vol. 2, pp. 1–25). Emerald Publishing Limited. doi:10.1108/S2754-586520230000002001

Rawnaque, F., Rahman, K., Anwar, S., Vaidyanathan, R., Chau, T., Sarker, F., & Mamun, K. (2020). Technological advancements and opportunities in Neuromarketing: A systematic review. *Brain Informatics, 7*(1), 10. Advance online publication. doi:10.1186/s40708-020-00109-x PMID:32955675

Riedl, R., Hubert, M., & Kenning, P. (2010). Are there neural gender differences in online trust? An empathizing-systemizing-theory-based fMRI study on the perceived trustworthiness of eBay offers. *Management Information Systems Quarterly, 34*(2), 397–428. doi:10.2307/20721434

Schuetzler, R., Grimes, G., & Scott Giboney, J. (2020). The impact of chatbot conversational skill on engagement and perceived humanness. *Journal of Management Information Systems, 37*(3), 875–900. doi:10.1080/07421222.2020.1790204

Senior, C., & Lee, N. (2013). The state of the art in organizational cognitive neuroscience: The therapeutic gap and possible implications for clinical practice. *Frontiers in Human Neuroscience, 7*(Dec). doi:10.3389/fnhum.2013.00808

Srivastava, S., Singh, S., & Dhir, S. (2020). Culture and International business research: A review and research agenda. *International Business Review, 29*(9), 101709. doi:10.1016/j.ibusrev.2020.101709

Strong, E. (2022). *The psychology of selling and advertising.* Retrieved from The Psychology of selling and Advertising, by Edward K. Strong: https://babel.hathitrust.org/cgi/pt?id=mdp.39015021085074&view=1up&seq=18

Yang, D.-J. (2018). Exploratory Neural Reactions to Framed Advertisement Messages of Smoking Cessation. *Social Marketing Quarterly, 24*(3), 216–232. doi:10.1177/1524500418788306

Chapter 7
AI Chatbots as a Catalyst for Customer Loyalty Investigating Digital Experience Preferences Across Age Groups

Yamijala Suryanarayana Murthy
https://orcid.org/0000-0002-9561-5395
Vardhaman College Engineering, India

Ravi Chandra B. S.
https://orcid.org/0000-0002-6416-5010
Vardhaman College of Engineering, India

ABSTRACT

This study examines the growing role of AI chatbots in customer loyalty by examining digital experience preferences across age groups. The study examines AI chatbot features like availability, simplicity of use, accuracy, responsiveness, assurance, and empathy, which are thought to affect digital experience and loyalty. The research uses hybrid methodologies to capture a variety of user interactions and viewpoints. Quantitative data is collected by administering structured surveys to a demographically diverse sample to examine chatbot attributes' effects on behavioral and attitudinal customer loyalty. The expected results may show a complex relationship between AI chatbots and customer loyalty. Younger generations value simplicity and quickness, whereas older people value accuracy and confidence. The scholarly discussion on digital customer engagement benefits from this study. This study helps organizations optimize their AI chatbot strategy to serve a wide range of clients. It emphasizes the need to understand generational preferences in the digital ecosystem.

DOI: 10.4018/979-8-3693-2367-0.ch007

INTRODUCTION

In the contemporary business landscape, where digital interaction is paramount, artificial intelligence (AI) chatbots represent a significant breakthrough. These advanced digital tools are not only reshaping how businesses interact with their customers but are also redefining the pathways to customer loyalty. The emergence of AI chatbots as a key player in the customer service domain has sparked a new paradigm in customer engagement strategies. This study, aims to explore the pivotal role of AI chatbots in influencing customer loyalty, with a particular focus on understanding how these preferences and experiences vary across different age demographics.

Context and Significance

The digital revolution has led to an unprecedented shift in consumer behavior and expectations. In this era of instant gratification, customers demand not only immediate responses but also personalized and empathetic interactions. AI chatbots, equipped with capabilities such as natural language processing and machine learning, offer a promising solution to these evolving customer demands. They have the potential to enhance customer experience, streamline service delivery, and foster deeper customer relationships. However, the effectiveness of AI chatbots in achieving these goals may vary across different age groups, making it crucial to understand the diverse digital preferences and expectations of various generational cohorts.

Theoretical Framework

The theoretical foundation of this research is anchored in the convergence of customer relationship management (CRM) and user experience (UX) design principles. CRM theories emphasize the significance of tailored interactions in building strong, enduring customer relationships. UX design principles, on the other hand, focus on creating user interfaces that are intuitive, engaging, and satisfying. This study seeks to marry these principles to dissect how AI chatbots can be optimally designed and utilized to meet the varying needs of different customer segments.

AI Chatbot Attributes: Central to this study are several critical attributes of AI chatbots, believed to be influential in shaping customer loyalty. These include:

1. **Availability:** The round-the-clock accessibility of chatbots, catering to the modern customer's expectation of constant availability.
2. **Ease of Use:** The user-friendliness and intuitiveness of the chatbot interface, which are crucial in determining user adoption and satisfaction.
3. **Accuracy:** The precision and correctness of the information provided by chatbots, essential for building trust and dependability.
4. **Responsiveness:** The promptness of chatbots in responding to customer queries, reflecting their efficiency and impact on the customer experience.
5. **Assurance:** The security and privacy aspects of chatbot interactions, vital for customer confidence in digital platforms.
6. **Empathy:** The ability of chatbots to deliver responses that are perceived as understanding and considerate of the user's needs.

Generational Differences in Digital Preferences

A key aspect of this study is the exploration of generational differences in digital preferences and expectations. It acknowledges that age is a significant factor influencing how individuals interact with and perceive AI chatbots. Different generations, from Baby Boomers to Millennials and Gen Z, have varied levels of digital literacy, comfort, and expectations, which can significantly affect their experiences with AI chatbots. This research aims to unearth these generational nuances, providing insights into how chatbots can be tailored to enhance the digital customer experience across age groups.

Customer Loyalty Dimensions: The study examines two primary dimensions of customer loyalty as influenced by interactions with AI chatbots:

1. **Behavioural Loyalty:** Reflected in customer actions such as repeat purchases, continued usage, and other forms of brand patronage.
2. **Attitudinal Loyalty:** Represented by the customer's emotional connection, preference, and advocacy for the brand.

In summary, this research seeks to offer a comprehensive understanding of how AI chatbots can be leveraged as a catalyst for customer loyalty. By investigating digital experience preferences across various age groups and analyzing the impact of key chatbot attributes on customer loyalty dimensions, the study aims to provide valuable insights for businesses looking to enhance their digital customer engagement strategies in an increasingly AI-driven world.

Problem Background: The rapid advancement of AI technology has led to the proliferation of AI chatbots in various customer interaction contexts. These chatbots have been increasingly adopted due to their potential to offer round-the-clock service, handle a large volume of queries simultaneously, and provide quick responses. However, while there is considerable enthusiasm about their capabilities, there is also uncertainty regarding how these digital assistants impact customer loyalty, particularly across different age groups. The digital experience preferences of customers can vary widely based on generational differences, with each group having unique expectations and comfort levels with technology. The challenge lies in understanding these varied preferences and effectively leveraging AI chatbots to enhance customer loyalty across all demographics.

Research Gap: Existing research predominantly focuses on the technical development and efficiency of AI chatbots, with less emphasis on understanding the nuanced customer experience they offer, especially in relation to customer loyalty. Furthermore, there is a lack of comprehensive studies examining how different age groups perceive and interact with AI chatbots, and how these perceptions influence their loyalty to a brand. This gap is significant because generational differences can substantially impact the effectiveness of chatbots in customer engagement strategies. Therefore, a detailed study is required to explore the relationship between AI chatbot attributes and customer loyalty, taking into account the variations in digital experience preferences across different age demographics.

Research Questions

- How do the attributes of AI chatbots (availability, ease of use, accuracy, responsiveness, assurance, empathy) influence digital Experience
- How digital Experience will lead to customer loyalty across different age groups?

Research Purpose: The primary purpose of this research is to investigate the role of AI chatbots as a tool for enhancing customer loyalty, with a focus on understanding how digital experience preferences vary across different age groups. The study aims to identify key AI chatbot attributes that are most influential in fostering customer loyalty and to determine whether these attributes have varying levels of impact on different age demographics. By exploring these aspects, the research seeks to provide insights into how businesses can strategically employ AI chatbots in their customer engagement and loyalty programs, ensuring that they cater effectively to the diverse needs and expectations of their customer base. The ultimate goal is to contribute to the body of knowledge on AI chatbots and customer loyalty, offering practical guidelines for businesses to optimize their digital customer engagement strategies in an increasingly AI-driven market landscape.

Research Objectives

1. To investigate the relationship between availability of AI chatbots and digital experience.
2. To examine the relationship between the ease of use of AI chatbots and digital experience.
3. To assess the relationship between accuracy of response of AI chatbots and digital experience.
4. To evaluate the relationship between responsiveness of AI chatbots and digital experience.
5. To analyze the relationship between assurance provided by AI chatbots and digital experience.
6. To explore the relationship between empathy expressed by AI chatbots and digital experience.
7. To investigate the relationship between digital experience and customer loyalty.

Research Design: The study adopts a mixed-methods research design, which combines both quantitative and qualitative research methodologies. This design is chosen to provide a comprehensive understanding of the impact of AI chatbots on customer loyalty and to explore the nuances of digital experience preferences across different age groups.

Survey Methodology: A structured survey will be conducted to collect data from a diverse set of participants representing various age groups. The survey will include questions designed to measure the impact of key AI chatbot attributes (such as availability, ease of use, accuracy, responsiveness, assurance, empathy) on customer loyalty dimensions (behavioural loyalty and attitudinal loyalty).

Sampling: The sampling will be stratified to ensure representation across different age demographics, including Baby Boomers, Generation X, Millennials, and Generation Z. A sufficient sample size will be determined to ensure statistical significance.

Data Analysis: Statistical analysis tools will be used to analyze the survey data. Techniques such as SEM, regression analysis, ANOVA, and correlation analysis will be employed to examine the relationships between AI chatbot attributes and customer loyalty, as well as to identify any significant differences in digital experience preferences across age groups.

Research Approach

a) **Exploratory:** The study begins with an exploratory approach, particularly in the qualitative phase, where open-ended questions in interviews and focus groups aim to explore new insights and understandings about user interactions with AI chatbots and their impact on customer loyalty.

b) **Explanatory:** In the quantitative phase, the research takes on a more explanatory approach. The objective is to test hypotheses derived from the literature review and theoretical framework, and to explain the relationships between AI chatbot attributes and customer loyalty across different age groups.

Sample Size: 279

LITERATURE REVIEW

Availability and Digital Experience: Availability in the context of digital experience refers to the extent to which digital services, websites, or applications are accessible and functioning as expected. Ensuring high availability is critical for providing users with a seamless and satisfactory digital experience.

1. **Digital Experience and User Satisfaction:** Researchers have explored the relationship between digital experience and user satisfaction. Studies by Hassenzahl and Tractinsky (2006) and Hassenzahl et al. (2003) discuss the importance of user experience in digital environments.
2. **Website Availability and Performance:** Authors like Almeida et al. (2011) and Shaikh et al. (2008) have investigated the impact of website availability and performance on user experience and business outcomes. They often discuss the significance of low latency and fast loading times.
3. **E-commerce and Digital Experience:** Literature on e-commerce, such as papers by Li et al. (2011) and Kim and Moon (1998), often examine how availability, usability, and functionality influence user satisfaction and digital purchase behavior.
4. **Mobile Apps and Availability:** In the context of mobile applications, research by Li and Karahanna (2015) and Lin et al. (2017) has explored the role of app availability and performance in shaping user satisfaction and retention.
5. **Network Reliability and Digital Services:** The availability of digital services often depends on network reliability. Authors like Vaquero et al. (2011) have discussed the importance of cloud service availability and its impact on user experience.
6. **Quality of Service (QoS) Metrics:** Various studies have proposed and evaluated QoS metrics to measure availability and digital experience. Look into work by Alqahtani and Nelson (2011) for insights into QoS measurement.
7. **User-Centric Monitoring and Management:** Recent research has also focused on user-centric monitoring and management of digital services. Authors like Vasic et al. (2019) have discussed the importance of real-time monitoring and adaptation to ensure availability and a positive user experience.

H_1: There is a significant relationship between Availability of AI Chatbot and Digital Experience

Ease of Use and Digital Experience: Ease of use, often referred to as usability, is a fundamental component of digital experience. It encompasses the user-friendliness of digital interfaces, applications, and websites. A positive digital experience is strongly linked to how easily users can interact with and navigate through digital platforms.

1. **Usability and User Experience:** Nielsen (1993) emphasizes the importance of usability engineering, highlighting that usability is a fundamental component of the user experience. Usability, defined as the effectiveness, efficiency, and satisfaction with which users can achieve their goals, is a cornerstone of designing digital interfaces. Bevan (1995) extends the usability perspective by introducing the idea

of measuring usability as quality of use. This concept implies that the quality of the user's experience directly impacts their perception of a system's usability. In other words, a system's ease of use significantly contributes to the overall digital experience.

2. **User-Centered Design:** Cooper, Reimann, and Cronin (2007) assert that user-centered design is key to creating digital interfaces that are easy to use and provide a positive user experience. This approach involves actively involving users throughout the design and development process, ensuring that their needs and preferences are taken into account. Rubin and Chisnell (2008) provide a practical guide to usability testing, emphasizing its role in validating ease of use. Usability testing helps identify usability issues early in the design process, leading to improved digital experiences.

3. **Heuristic Evaluation:** Nielsen and Molich (1990) introduce heuristic evaluation as a method for assessing usability. This approach involves experts evaluating a system based on a set of usability principles (heuristics). It serves as a valuable tool for identifying usability problems and improving the overall user experience.

4. **User Experience Design Principles:** Garrett (2010) outlines the elements of user experience, emphasizing the significance of user-centered design, information architecture, interaction design, visual design, and usability. These principles collectively contribute to creating digital interfaces that are both easy to use and provide a positive digital experience. Norman (2002) underscores the importance of intuitive and user-friendly design. He argues that well-designed digital interfaces should afford users a natural and intuitive interaction, reducing the cognitive load required to navigate and use the system.

5. **Accessibility and Inclusivity:** Henry and Gordon (2003) advocate for accessibility, inclusivity, and usability. They emphasize that digital products and services should be designed to accommodate users with disabilities, ensuring that ease of use extends to all users. Lazar, Goldstein, and Taylor (2015) discuss the importance of ensuring digital accessibility through policies and processes. Their work highlights the ethical dimension of ease of use, emphasizing the need for digital experiences that are inclusive and barrier-free.

6. **Cognitive Load and Emotional Design:** Sweller (1988) explores cognitive load theory, which suggests that minimizing cognitive load enhances the ease of use and overall user experience. Designing digital interfaces with cognitive load in mind can lead to smoother interactions. Plass and Kaplan (2015) delve into emotional design, demonstrating that visual elements, such as shape and colour, can influence users' emotional responses and, consequently, their digital experiences.

H_2: There is a significant relationship between the Ease of Use of AI chatbots and Digital Experience.

Accuracy of Response and Digital Experience: The accuracy of response in digital interactions refers to the correctness and relevance of the information or actions provided by digital systems, such as AI chatbots or search engines. It is a crucial component of digital experiences, as users rely on accurate responses to achieve their goals and tasks.

1. **The Importance of Accurate Responses:** One of the fundamental aspects of a positive digital experience is the system's ability to provide accurate and relevant responses to user interactions. Nielsen (1993) emphasizes that the effectiveness of digital systems is closely tied to their ability to meet users' goals accurately.

2. **User-Centered Design and Accuracy:** User-centered design principles, as outlined by Cooper, Reimann, and Cronin (2007), emphasize the importance of understanding user needs and expectations. Accurate responses are a direct result of a user-centric approach, where designers actively involve users to ensure that systems align with user goals and expectations.

3. **Feedback and Error Handling:** Providing accurate feedback and effective error handling mechanisms is crucial for maintaining a positive digital experience. Rubin and Chisnell (2008) emphasize the role of usability testing in identifying issues related to feedback and error messages. Systems that offer clear and accurate feedback enhance user confidence and trust.

4. **Accurate Data Presentation:** In digital environments, the accuracy of data presentation plays a significant role in user decision-making. Garrett (2010) highlights the importance of information architecture and interaction design in ensuring that data is presented accurately and comprehensibly. Misrepresenting data can lead to user confusion and frustration.

5. **Data Accuracy and Trust:** Users' trust in digital systems is closely linked to the accuracy of the information provided. Norman (2002) discusses the concept of trust in design and underscores that users must trust the system's responses for a positive digital experience. When users trust that a system provides accurate information, they are more likely to have a favourable experience.

6. **Accurate Content and Accessibility:** Henry and Gordon (2003) argue that accuracy in digital content is essential, particularly for users with disabilities who rely on digital content for information. Ensuring the accuracy and accessibility of content is not only a matter of usability but also a matter of inclusivity.

H$_3$: There is a significant relationship between Accuracy of Response of AI chatbots and Digital Experience.

Responsiveness and Digital Experience: Responsiveness in the context of digital experience refers to the speed and efficiency with which digital systems, websites, or applications respond to user actions or requests. It is a critical factor in providing users with a seamless and satisfactory digital experience.

1. **The Significance of Responsiveness:** Responsiveness is a critical aspect of user satisfaction in digital interactions. Users often equate a responsive system with efficiency and reliability. A slow or unresponsive system can lead to frustration and a poor digital experience (Hassenzahl et al., 2003).

2. **User-Centered Design and Responsiveness:** A user-centered design approach, as advocated by Cooper, Reimann, and Cronin (2007), emphasizes the importance of responsiveness in meeting user needs. User testing and feedback play a crucial role in optimizing the responsiveness of digital interfaces to align with user expectations.

3. **Performance Optimization:** Performance optimization is central to achieving responsiveness in digital systems. Nielsen (1993) emphasizes that performance directly impacts the overall user experience. Ensuring fast loading times, low latency, and efficient processing of user requests is essential for a positive digital experience.

4. **Mobile Responsiveness:** In an era of mobile computing, ensuring responsiveness on various devices is crucial. Li and Karahanna (2015) discuss the importance of mobile app responsiveness in retaining users and providing a seamless experience across different platforms.

5. **Responsive Web Design:** Responsive web design principles, as outlined by Garrett (2010), focus on creating interfaces that adapt to various screen sizes and resolutions. This adaptability contributes

to a positive digital experience, as users can access content easily regardless of the device they are using.

6. **Feedback and User Perception:** Rubin and Chisnell (2008) highlight the significance of feedback mechanisms in responsiveness. Providing timely feedback to users about the status of their interactions enhances their perception of a system's responsiveness. Users are more likely to have a favourable experience when they feel in control and informed.

H_4: There is a significant relationship between Responsiveness of AI chatbots and Digital Experience.

Assurance and Digital Experience: Assurance in the context of digital experience refers to the trustworthiness and reliability of digital systems, services, or products. It encompasses aspects such as security, privacy, and compliance, which are essential for providing users with a safe and trustworthy digital experience.

1. **The Importance of Assurance:** Assurance is a fundamental component of user trust in digital interactions. Users expect that the systems they interact with are reliable, secure, and capable of safeguarding their data and privacy. A lack of assurance can lead to anxiety and hesitation in using digital services (Dwivedi et al., 2019).

2. **User-Centered Assurance:** User-centered assurance approaches, as advocated by Cooper, Reimann, and Cronin (2007), emphasize that trust and assurance should be central considerations in the design and implementation of digital systems. These authors argue that users must perceive a system as trustworthy for a positive digital experience to occur.

3. **Security and Assurance:** Security is a key aspect of assurance. Ensuring the security of user data and transactions is essential for building user trust (Whitman & Mattord, 2018). A secure system not only protects user information but also enhances the overall digital experience.

4. **Privacy and Data Protection:** In the digital age, privacy and data protection are integral components of assurance. Users expect their personal information to be handled with care and in compliance with relevant regulations (Solove, 2006). Digital systems that prioritize privacy contribute to a more positive user experience.

5. **Transparency and Communication:** Assurance also involves transparency and effective communication. Users should have a clear understanding of how their data is used and protected (Dinev & Hart, 2006). Transparent practices contribute to user confidence and a more favourable digital experience.

6. **Compliance and Assurance:** Meeting regulatory and compliance requirements is essential for digital assurance. Organizations must adhere to legal and industry standards to ensure the trustworthiness of their digital services (Dwivedi et al., 2019).

H_5: There is a significant relationship between Assurance of AI chatbots and Digital Experience.

Empathy and Digital Experience: Empathy in the context of digital experience refers to the ability of digital interfaces, applications, or systems to understand and respond to the emotions, needs, and feelings of users. It plays a crucial role in creating meaningful and user-centered digital interactions.

1. **Empathy in Digital Design:** Empathy in digital design refers to the practice of understanding and considering the emotions, needs, and perspectives of users during the design and development

process. It involves creating digital experiences that resonate with users on an emotional level (Cooper, Reimann, & Cronin, 2007).

2. **User-Centered Design and Empathy:** User-centered design, as advocated by Cooper, Reimann, and Cronin (2007), emphasizes empathy as a core principle. Designers are encouraged to put themselves in the shoes of the users, understanding their goals, frustrations, and desires. Empathy-driven design leads to products and interfaces that are more user-friendly and emotionally engaging.

3. **Empathetic User Interfaces:** Empathetic user interfaces aim to mirror human interaction and emotions. They utilize cues such as animations, language tone, and visual elements to convey empathy (Mayer & Schulte-Mecklenbeck, 2019). Empathetic design can reduce user frustration and create a more enjoyable digital experience.

4. **Chatbots and Virtual Assistants:** Chatbots and virtual assistants are increasingly incorporating empathetic responses to user queries and concerns. These systems use natural language processing and sentiment analysis to detect user emotions and respond empathetically (Luger, Sellen, & Brostoff, 2006). Empathetic chatbots can enhance user satisfaction in customer support and interactions.

5. **Emotional Design:** Emotional design, as discussed by Norman (2002), focuses on creating digital experiences that evoke positive emotions. Interfaces that elicit joy, trust, or curiosity through design elements can contribute to a more memorable and enjoyable digital experience.

6. **The Role of AI and Machine Learning:** Artificial intelligence and machine learning technologies enable digital systems to become more empathetic over time. They can learn user preferences and adapt interactions accordingly (Bickmore et al., 2005). This personalization enhances the digital experience by catering to individual needs and emotional states.

H_6: There is a significant relationship between Empathy of AI chatbots and Digital Experience.

Digital Experience and Customer Loyalty: Digital experience encompasses all aspects of user interaction with digital platforms, including websites, mobile apps, and online services. Customer loyalty, on the other hand, refers to the degree of commitment and repeat business a customer exhibits towards a brand or organization. Understanding how digital experiences influence customer loyalty is critical in today's digital age.

1. **Digital Experience and Customer Satisfaction:** The digital experience encompasses a user's interactions with a brand through digital channels, such as websites, mobile apps, and social media. Hassenzahl et al. (2010) highlight that a positive digital experience is closely linked to customer satisfaction. When customers have a smooth, enjoyable experience with a brand's digital offerings, they are more likely to be satisfied.

2. **User-Centered Design and Loyalty:** User-centered design principles, as advocated by Cooper, Reimann, and Cronin (2007), emphasize the importance of understanding and meeting user needs. A user-centric approach to digital design can lead to interfaces and experiences that resonate with users, enhancing their loyalty to a brand.

3. **Personalization and Customer Engagement:** Personalization of digital experiences can significantly impact customer loyalty. Tailoring content, recommendations, and interactions to individual preferences and behaviours can make customers feel valued and engaged (Li & Karahanna, 2015). Personalization can strengthen the emotional connection between customers and a brand.

4. **Ease of Use and Loyalty:** A seamless and user-friendly digital experience can contribute to customer loyalty. Users are more likely to return to a website or app that is easy to navigate, resulting

in repeat business (Nielsen, 1993). Ensuring that customers can achieve their goals effortlessly is crucial for building loyalty.

5.   **Trust and Digital Security:** Trust is a critical component of customer loyalty, and digital security plays a significant role. Whitman and Mattord (2018) emphasize that customers need to trust that their personal information is secure when interacting with a brand's digital platforms. A breach of trust can lead to a loss of loyalty.

6.   **Emotional Connection and Loyalty:** Creating an emotional connection with customers through digital experiences is essential for building loyalty. Emotional design principles, as discussed by Norman (2002), focus on evoking positive emotions in users. Interfaces that foster joy, trust, or excitement can create a stronger bond between customers and a brand.

H$_7$: There is a significant relationship between Digital Experience and Customer Loyalty.

Figure 1. Conceptual model

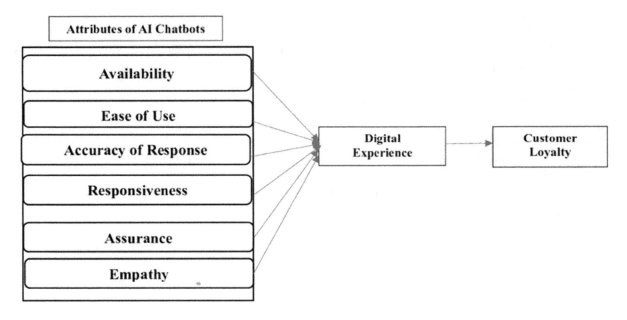

RESULTS AND DISCUSSIONS

Table 1. Reliability

Variables	Number of Items	Cronbach Alpha
Digital Experience	5	0.911
Customer Loyalty	5	0.900
Availability	5	0.904
Ease of Use	5	0.903
Accuracy	5	0.911
Responsiveness	5	0.941
Assurance	5	0.931
Empathy	5	0.935

Cronbach Alpha values for all variables are high (all above 0.900), indicating a high level of internal consistency among the items on each scale. This implies that the items within each variable effectively measure the same underlying idea.

Digital Experience and Accuracy: The Cronbach Alpha for both is 0.911, which is among the highest in the collection. This implies that the items used to assess digital experience and correctness are measured in a consistent manner.

Customer Loyalty, Availability, and Ease of Use: These variables have Cronbach Alpha values that are slightly lower but still strong (range from 0.900 to 0.904), indicating good internal consistency.

Responsiveness, Assurance, and Empathy: These variables exhibit the greatest Cronbach Alpha values, which span from 0.931 to 0.941. This indicates scales with a high degree of dependability, as it suggests that these variables are measured with exceptional internal consistency.

Table 2. Fit indices model of confirmatory factor analysis

Fit Indices	Recommended	Observed
CMIN	>5 Terrible, >3 Acceptable, >1 Excellent	2.188
CFI	<0.90 Terrible, <0.95 Acceptable, >0.95 Excellent	0.919
TLI	> 0.9	0.906
PNFI	> 0.5	0.748
RMSEA	>0.08 Terrible, >0.06 Acceptable, >0.05 Excellent	0.065

The observed value of CMIN (Chi-Square/df Ratio), which is 2.188, is within the "Acceptable" range (>3 Acceptable, >1 Excellent). This shows that the model and the data have an appropriate fit. The observed value of 0.919 for the Comparative Fit Index (CFI) places it in the "Acceptable" category (<0.95 Acceptable, >0.95 Excellent). This indicates that there is potential for improvement even though the model matches the data very well. Tucker-Lewis Index (TLI) the observed value is 0.906, somewhat higher than the suggested cutoff point of 0.9. This suggests a decent fit, but since it is close to the acceptable range's lower bound, more investigation might be necessary. Parsimonious Normed Fit Index (PNFI) shows a strong balance between model complexity and fit, with a value of 0.748, much above the suggested threshold of 0.5. The measured value of 0.065 falls into the "acceptable" range (>0.08 Terrible, >0.06 Acceptable, >0.05 Excellent) for RMSEA (Root Mean Square Error of Approximation).

Figure 2. Confirmatory factor analysis (CFA)

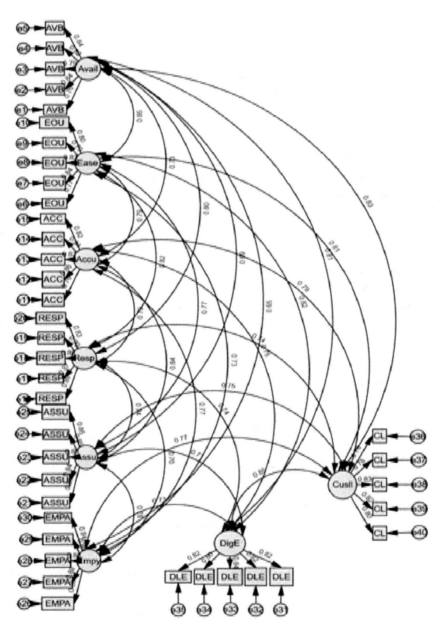

In summary, the model provides a good fit across several indices while balancing complexity and accuracy. The model's strengths include its parsimony and overall fit, as evidenced by PNFI and CFI. However, there is room for improvement in the model's performance, notably as measured by CMIN and RMSEA. Future efforts could concentrate on fine-tuning the model parameters or reconsidering some of the underlying assumptions in order to improve the model's fit from acceptable to great.

Table 3. Structural equation modelling

Fit Indices	Recommended	Observed
CMIN	>5 Terrible, >3 Acceptable, >1 Excellent	4.317
CFI	<0.90 Terrible, <0.95 Acceptable, >0.95 Excellent	0.965
TLI	> 0.9	0.938
PNFI	> 0.5	0.643
RMSEA	>0.08 Terrible, >0.06 Acceptable, >0.05 Excellent	0.06

The observed result of 4.317 is within the "Acceptable" range for CMIN (Chi-Square/df Ratio). This means that the model has a good fit to the data. CFI (Comparative Fit Index) The CFI value of 0.965 is significantly higher than the excellence threshold (>0.95 Excellent), indicating that the model has an excellent fit in terms of predictive accuracy. TLI (Tucker-Lewis Index) with an observed value of 0.938, the TLI is significantly higher than the recommended threshold of 0.9, indicating a very strong model fit. The PNFI score of 0.643 exceeds the recommended threshold of 0.5, indicating that the model strikes a solid balance between complexity and fit to the data. RMSEA (Root Mean Square Error of Approximation) value of 0.060 is near to the "Excellent" range and at the top limit of the "Acceptable" range. This indicates that the model has a reasonable level of approximation error.

Figure 3. Structure equation modelling

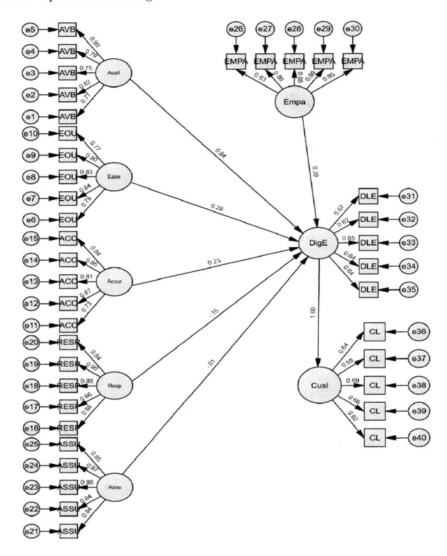

Overall, the model exhibits a solid fit across all fit indices, excelling in CFI and TLI in particular, showing excellent predictive accuracy and good model fit. While the RMSEA value is adequate, it might be improved further to reach a great match. Although the CMIN number is respectable, it also suggests that there is space for small changes to obtain a greater level of fit efficiency. The high PNFI value indicates that the model strikes an effective balance between simplicity and explanatory power.

Table 4. Hypothesis testing

Hypothesis	P-Value	Result
H$_1$: Availability→ Digital Experience	0.00	Significant
H$_2$: Ease of Use → Digital Experience	0.00	Significant
H$_3$: Accuracy → Digital Experience	0.00	Significant
H$_4$: Responsiveness → Digital Experience	0.00	Significant
H$_5$: Assurance → Digital Experience	0.631	Not Significant
H$_6$: Empathy→ Digital Experience	0.00	Significant
H$_7$: Digital Experience → Customer Loyalty	0.00	Significant

INTERPRETATIONS

Hypotheses H$_1$, H$_2$, H$_3$, H$_4$, and H$_6$ (related to the influence of Availability, Ease of Use, Accuracy, Responsiveness, and Empathy on Digital Experience) are significant (P-Value = 0.00). This suggests that these elements have a good impact on Digital Experience. Improvements in these areas are expected to improve the digital experience of users. Hypothesis H$_5$ (Assurance → Digital Experience) is not statistically significant, as indicated by a P-Value of 0.631. Within the scope of this investigation, it is indicated that Assurance does not exert a substantial influence on augmenting Digital Experience. The significance of Hypothesis H7, which suggests that Digital Experience has an impact on Customer Loyalty, is confirmed (P-Value = 0.00). This highlights the significance of Digital Experience in cultivating consumer loyalty.

DISCUSSION

The results reaffirm how important some elements are in creating a great digital experience: availability, ease of use, accuracy, responsiveness, and empathy. Businesses that concentrate on these areas might anticipate improved digital connections with their customers. The non-significant result for Assurance may suggest that usability or responsiveness are more important in the context of Digital Experience than criteria like security or reliability, which are frequently related to Assurance. Depending on the sector, client requirements, or digital platform, this might change. The strategic significance of investing in digital platforms is highlighted by the noteworthy correlation found between Customer Loyalty and Digital Experience. Improving the user experience has a direct impact on increasing client loyalty.

Limitations

The research is specifically centered on AI chatbots, which may restrict the applicability of the findings to other digital technologies or scenarios. The dynamics of engagement and user expectations for AI chatbots may vary from those of other digital tools or platforms. Using self-reported measures to evaluate digital experience and customer loyalty in research can introduce biases, such as social desirability or recall bias, which can compromise the accuracy of the data. AI chatbots are swiftly advancing technology. The findings of this research may rapidly become obsolete as further progress in AI and machine learning continues to revolutionize the capabilities and functionalities of chatbots. Assessing intangible aspects such as empathy and assurance offered by AI chatbots can pose difficulties. The ratings can exhibit substantial variations depending on the subjective views and personal experiences of each user. Demographic characteristics, including age, technological proficiency, and cultural background, can impact user experiences with AI chatbots. The research may not adequately consider this variability, thereby restricting the comprehensiveness of the conclusions. Customer loyalty is impacted by various elements that extend beyond the realm of digital experience. It can be difficult to separate the effects of digital experience from other elements that influence it, and this may not provide us a comprehensive understanding. Technical constraints or faults can impact the performance and capabilities of AI chatbots, including their availability, accuracy, and reactivity. These factors can influence the accuracy of evaluating the correlation between chatbot attributes and digital experience. The concept of digital experience involves a wide array of interactions and extends beyond the sole usage of chatbots. This study specifically targets a certain facet of the digital experience, perhaps overlooking the complete range of user interactions and experiences inside the digital domain.

Future Scope for Research

Future studies could extend beyond AI chatbots and into other future digital technologies. This could lead to a more comprehensive knowledge of digital experiences across several platforms and their impact on customer loyalty. Future research might look into how AI chatbots interact with and supplement other digital channels (such as social media, email, or mobile apps), as well as how this integrated approach affects overall consumer experience and loyalty. Examining the influence of emotional intelligence and natural language processing developments within AI chatbots might provide insights into how these technology advancements affect user experience. Extending the research to several corporate sectors might assist understand how the success of AI chatbots and user expectations differ across businesses such as retail, healthcare, finance, and education. Future research could look into how AI chatbot interactions influence user behavior and engagement, considering measures like session duration, frequency of use, and user satisfaction. Investigating the ethical implications of AI chatbots, as well as how they affect user trust and perceived confidence, could be an important subject of future research, particularly in contexts where privacy and data protection are critical. Conducting research in various geographical places could reveal how cultural differences affect the adoption and usefulness of AI chatbots in improving digital experience and consumer loyalty.

REFERENCES

Almeida, J. M., Almeida, V. A., & Falcone, T. P. (2011). On the predictability of large transfer TCP throughput. *Computer Communication Review, 41*(4), 179–190.

Alqahtani, S., & Nelson, S. (2011). A review of network QoS measurement and management tools. In *International Conference on Computer and Communication Engineering (ICCCE)* (pp. 256-260). IEEE.

Bevan, N. (1995). Measuring usability as quality of use. *Software Quality Journal, 4*(2), 115–130. doi:10.1007/BF00402715

Cooper, A., Reimann, R., & Cronin, D. (2007). *About Face 3: The Essentials of Interaction Design*. Wiley.

Garrett, J. J. (2010). *The Elements of User Experience: User-Centered Design for the Web and Beyond.* New Riders.

Hassenzahl, M., Diefenbach, S., & Göritz, A. (2010). Needs, affect, and interactive products – Facets of user experience. *Interacting with Computers*, *22*(5), 353–362. doi:10.1016/j.intcom.2010.04.002

Hassenzahl, M., & Tractinsky, N. (2006). User experience – a research agenda. *Behaviour & Information Technology*, *25*(2), 91–97. doi:10.1080/01449290500330331

Henry, S. L., & Gordon, C. (2003). Accessibility, usability, and inclusion. *Interaction*, *10*(6), 19–24.

Kim, S. S. S., & Moon, J. Y. (1998). Designing towards emotional usability in customer interfaces: Trustworthiness of Cyber-banking system interfaces. *Interacting with Computers*, *10*(1), 1–29. doi:10.1016/S0953-5438(97)00037-4

Li, X., Hess, T. J., Valacich, J. S., & Enns, H. G. (2011). The effect of decision aids and choice set size on e-commerce sales. *Management Information Systems Quarterly*, *35*(3), 625–642.

Li, X., & Karahanna, E. (2015). Online service providers' differentiation strategy for mobile app adoption: Cross-industry evidence. *Management Information Systems Quarterly*, *39*(3), 669–692.

Luger, E., Sellen, A., & Brostoff, S. (2006). Towards a multimodal user interface for an intelligent cognitive assistant. In *Proceedings of the SIGCHI Conference on Human Factors in Computing Systems* (pp. 1073-1082). ACM.

Mayer, R. C., & Schulte-Mecklenbeck, M. (2019). Cognitive empathy in virtual reality. *Psychology of Aesthetics, Creativity, and the Arts*, *13*(1), 26–35.

Nielsen, J. (1993). *Usability Engineering.* Academic Press. doi:10.1016/B978-0-08-052029-2.50007-3

Norman, D. A. (2002). *The Design of Everyday Things.* Basic Books.

Plass, J. L., & Kaplan, U. (2015). Emotional design in multimedia learning: Effects of shape and color on affect and learning. *Learning and Instruction*, *39*, 10–20.

Rubin, J., & Chisnell, D. (2008). *Handbook of Usability Testing: How to Plan, Design, and Conduct Effective Tests.* Wiley.

Shaikh, A., Schulzrinne, H., & Jenkins, M. (2008). The impact of DDoS attacks on VoIP systems. In *International Workshop on Quality of Service* (pp. 41-56). Springer.

Solove, D. J. (2006). A taxonomy of privacy. *University of Pennsylvania Law Review*, *154*(3), 477–560. doi:10.2307/40041279

Sweller, J. (1988). Cognitive load during problem solving: Effects on learning. *Cognitive Science*, *12*(2), 257–285. doi:10.1207/s15516709cog1202_4

Vaquero, L. M., Rodero-Merino, L., Caceres, J., & Lindner, M. (2011). A break in the clouds: Towards a cloud definition. *Computer Communication Review*, *39*(1), 50–55. doi:10.1145/1496091.1496100

Vasic, B., Qazi, Z. A., & Yeom, I. (2019). User-centric real-time performance management for cloud applications. *Future Generation Computer Systems*, *100*, 151–166.

Whitman, M. E., & Mattord, H. J. (2018). *Principles of Information Security*. Cengage Learning.

Chapter 8
Service Industry Alchemy:
A Symphony of Digital Innovations in Customer Engagement

Shikha Bhagat
https://orcid.org/0000-0001-8745-5558
Christ University, India

Rashmi Rai
https://orcid.org/0000-0001-8347-9982
Christ University, India

K. Lakshmypriya
https://orcid.org/0000-0002-4117-7000
Christ University, India

Sunita Kumar
https://orcid.org/0000-0002-0628-1873
Christ University, India

ABSTRACT

The emergence of digitization, automation, and artificial intelligence has transformed service delivery, allowing businesses to increase productivity, tailor client experiences, and provide cutting-edge solutions. The delivery, use, and accessibility of services are changing in various service sectors due to innovations. Among them, healthcare, education, and finance have received considerable attention in recent years. To synthesize prior research on innovations in the service industry, the chapter attempts a thematic, sentiment, and bibliometric analysis of the research domain. For the analysis, data was extracted from the Scopus database and was filtered by application of inclusion-exclusion, with the use of NVivo and Bibliometric software VOS viewer. Most productive and influential articles, authors, journals, and affiliations were recognized. Thematic mapping and trend analysis revealed past and present research subdomains that were used for the prediction of future research agendas.

DOI: 10.4018/979-8-3693-2367-0.ch008

1. INTRODUCTION

The digital era has appeared in a transformative wave of technological advancements, reshaping how we live, work, and interact. By fostering an innovative culture, leveraging digital capabilities, and staying attuned to market trends, organizations can position themselves as industry leaders and seize the opportunities presented by the digital era. In the modern era of cutthroat competition and global cooperation, achieving flexibility and adaptability has become imperative for business survival. Amid the digital revolution, companies must navigate between two distinct strategies: a closed approach that relies on internal capabilities and a more open system that leverages external resources to meet evolving market demands. This delicate balance is essential for successful digital innovation (DX) in today's rapidly changing environment. To understand deeply, we can opt for a 2 × 2 typology, classifying firms into four types based on their collaboration scope and innovation approach. The operational innovator (Type 1) focuses on internal efficiency and productivity, employing defensive innovation strategies. The technological innovator (Type 2) collaborates widely while embracing technologies like IoT and AI. The competitive innovators (Type 3) prioritize customer value creation and delivery through aggressive innovation, while the transformative innovators (Type 4) build open digital networks for business model innovation (Park & Hong, 2022). The rapid progress of digital technology has opened up new possibilities for enhancing transparency in the value chain. Visual management, a fundamental Kaizen technology in the IoT era, is crucial in navigating abundant information. By visualizing data and embracing digital tools such as IoT, AR, VR, and more, businesses can expand their understanding of processes, detect abnormalities, and implement effective countermeasures (Hodapp & Hanelt,2022).

Moreover, as visual management evolves, integrating other senses like hearing, touch, smell, and taste becomes essential to develop a holistic approach to problem-solving and decision-making. By honing all five senses, businesses can achieve safe, high-quality, and efficient operations, ensuring sustainable growth and resilience in an ever-changing landscape of the digital era (Murata, 2019). Integrating digital technologies provides unprecedented insights into human behavior, enabling targeted influence through microtargeting and nudge tech. This empowers businesses to tailor value propositions and communication strategies and launch innovative products and services (Pochenchuk et al., 2018).

Rapid innovation has defined this era, with breakthroughs in computing power, connectivity, and data analytics leading to a wide array of novel applications and solutions (Zhang et al., 2022). Several vital technological enablers have fuelled the pace of innovation in the digital era. These include artificial intelligence (AI) and machine learning advancements, which have unlocked new possibilities in data analysis, natural language processing, and predictive modeling. The proliferation of the Internet of Things (IoT) enabled billions of devices to connect and share information, creating intelligent environments that optimize efficiency and enhance user experiences.

Fintech startups have revolutionized payment systems, lending, and personal finance management in the financial sector, while blockchain technology has opened up possibilities for secure and transparent transactions (Cai,2018). Healthcare has witnessed significant advancements through telemedicine, personalized medicine, and wearable health devices, improving patient care and outcomes. In the education sector, online learning platforms have expanded access to knowledge and skills, making education more inclusive and flexible as shown in Figure 1.

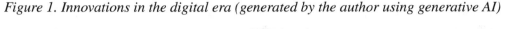

Figure 1. Innovations in the digital era (generated by the author using generative AI)

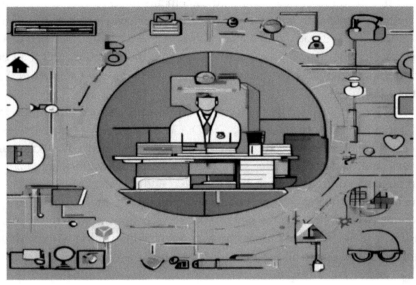

The digital era has democratized creativity and innovation, and amidst the promising developments of the digital age, specific challenges and concerns have emerged. Cybersecurity threats have escalated, requiring constant vigilance to safeguard sensitive data and infrastructure. Privacy concerns have also been amplified as personal information becomes increasingly accessible. Issues related to the digital divide and unequal access to technology persist, exacerbating existing social and economic disparities (Schang et al., 2010).

Moreover, ethical considerations surrounding AI, automation, and autonomous systems need careful attention to ensure responsible innovation. Access to online platforms and digital tools has enabled individuals to showcase their talents, whether in art, music, writing, or entrepreneurship (Dery et al., 2017). Crowdsourcing platforms have harnessed the collective intelligence of communities, leading to collaborative problem-solving and innovative projects. Startups and small businesses have thrived in the digital ecosystem, disrupting established industries and challenging traditional norms.

Embracing the possibilities while addressing the challenges will be vital to harnessing the full potential of technology to improve the human experience in the decades to come. Service Industries, too, have been fuelled by service innovation through technological advancements in dynamic environments (Van, 2002). In today's rapidly evolving business landscape, the digital era has ushered in a paradigm shift in how organizations conceptualize, deliver, and improve their services. In the digital age, service innovation refers to various tactics for utilizing technology to enhance customer experiences, data analytics is a popular strategy to acquire insights into customer behavior and preferences. With this knowledge, businesses may customize services to meet specific demands, increasing consumer satisfaction, loyalty and organizational effectiveness (Den et al., 2010).

Additionally, the introduction of AI and automation has transformed the provision of services. Virtual assistants and chatbots offer 24/7 customer service and immediate assistance. This increases client satisfaction and employees can focus on more challenging jobs that are critical to increasing productivity. Besides adding value to the company that creates it, an innovation also alters the market, inspiring other businesses to follow suit and mimic it, creating a new market (Schumpeter, 1934). Despite the rigorous nature of this definition of new, recent advancements in service, much research has indicated that service innovation is frequently understood as "a new service" (Witell et al. 2016). This suggests that service innovation, when aligned with current market trends, multiple sectors, or various offers, is more crucial than novelty and that service improvements are more incremental than dramatic. This is challenging since it implies that new services can be viewed as innovations, regardless of how minor it is (Gustafsson et al., 2020).

For businesses looking to succeed in a cutthroat environment, service innovation in the digital age is more than just a trendy buzzword (Den et al., 2007). Creating improved experiences, business models, and customer-centric strategies becomes possible when combined with technical improvements and customer-centric approaches (Garzella et al., 2020). Service innovations are generally exceedingly participatory, although more gradual, with less Research and Development, and less structured than manufacturing innovation (Rubalcaba et al. 2012), with significant interactions between management, employees, and clients. To fully exploit the potential of service innovation in the digital era, firms must master these hurdles, which are present along the way. Service innovation will continue as technology develops, allowing organizations to add value and stand out in the digital era.

2. THEORETICAL BACKGROUND

In today's digital competitive world, the ability to innovate has become a critical aspect in establishing a competitive edge. Companies typically find a solution to this increased pressure for innovation by utilizing their workers' intrinsic ability to develop unique ideas. These concepts are the cornerstone for developing better goods, services, and operational procedures (Curzi et al., 2019). As a result, individual invention develops as a critical ability demanded of workers, with repercussions on the managerial approach to guiding employee contributions towards organizational objectives and assessing their success. If the organization spends money on streamlining its operational and deployment flaws through digital transformation (in this example, automating manual procedures), It will be able to bring mobile capabilities to market more quickly with continual incremental value. Additionally, it encourages clients to use their products more quickly and effectively, which saves time and money. (Laster, 2021). Businesses always look for methods to improve and enhance their innovation strategies because innovation is one of the primary forces behind economic growth and wealth creation as well as a source of long-term competitive advantage. Activities that promote innovation are used to put innovations into practice. A few examples of internal innovation activities are internal planning and design, internal research and development, internal surveys, in-house feasibility analysis and testing. The external aspects involve consultancy services, Research, and development through collaboration, and external know-how exchange and investment in machinery and equipment for innovation. Through collaboration, ideas can be put into practice. Collaboration on innovation involves taking an active role in activities with businesses or other governmental entities, universities, government research institutions other public organizations and citizens can all be potential partners for collaboration as users, suppliers, or clients, as well as other public or private companies or organizations (Normann, 2002). At every level of the innovation process, cooperation is critical (Bloch, C. 2011; Cankar, S.S.& Petkovšek, V,2013). One of these aspects has been identified as a crucial component of effective innovation: the application of outside information.

2.1 Service Innovation

The domain of service innovation poses a significant challenge due to its complexity. Despite the best efforts of new service development (NSD) and service design theories, these frameworks fall short of accurately reflecting and explaining organizational and empirical practice.

The worth of innovations has historically been determined by their economic impact on the developing firm, while more recent definitions have changed this. (Witell et al., 2016). An understanding of how different types of innovation in the service, manufacturing, and digital domains interact for value creation and address new market's needs (Ostrom et al., 2015). Any innovation from a firm's perspective should have a commercial value but in the case of service innovation, this may not be the case as profit may not be an indicator of a service innovation's success in all cases (Snyder et al., 2020). "The service innovation concept becomes all-encompassing, [and] identifying the exact loci of service innovation research becomes more difficult" (Kowalkowski et al., 2014). In a study on methods to group and categorize service innovation (Coombs and Miles, 2000) comprehension, demarcation, and synthesis are three criteria to group service innovation. According to (Toivonen & Tuominen,2009), service innovation is a newly developed service or revisions made to the existing ones that provides economic benefit to an organization which developed it through value addition to customers. Furthermore, the novelty in service and value addition should be in the perspective of the markets it is intended for or the societal context at large.

2.2 Service Innovation in Various Sectors

The body of knowledge on service innovation is growing, encompassing perspectives from the fields of management, organizational science, marketing, and economics. There is a correlation between the development of the innovation process and the extent of development of outward innovation activities, according to empirical data from service companies serving the retail, health, and education sectors. These sectorial focuses are more on the value chain in the network and the majority of service innovation processes are oriented towards customers and suppliers and barely on the entire value chain (Mello, 2020). Innovation managers might strengthen their capability for internal innovation to correctly balance internal and external operations but, In the service industry of healthcare, it is difficult to meet the requirements of patients and their families. The healthcare industry has a highly challenging task as service providers to meet the requirements of patients and bystanders while focusing on the complexity, cost, and the need to incorporate empathetic content of the service, as well as technical advancements to meet industry competitiveness. (Randhawa, K., & Scerri, M., 2015). A system of continuous innovation culture is being successfully established by futuristic healthcare institutions, and these institutions are implementing tactical and strategic service components that are advantageous to them and their stakeholders (Berry, 2019). They value institutional confidence and commitment to continuous innovation as a non-negotiable objective and include patients and families on the innovation team. A few forward-thinking oncology centers are exemplifying what is possible to enhance the patient and family service experience in the face of a critical demand for service innovation in the cancer care industry. Robots have always piqued our interest, and their usage in healthcare is growing. The literature on healthcare robotics emphasizes how the social and technological aspects of robots interact, redefine, and impact one another over time (Berry,2019). We advocate placing more attention on the sociological aspects of robot use, taking into account how social and professional relationships are altered by changes in practice. Furthermore, we suggest the value of a "service logic" in shedding light on the potential impact of robots on healthcare innovation. Improvements in care quality and effectiveness, cost-cutting measures, and the need to adapt to changing patient and provider needs are the main forces behind service innovation in the healthcare industry (Hund et al.,2021). The primary obstacles to the development of new healthcare services are a lack of resources, the lack of coordination between stakeholders, and the resistance to change (Massaro, G,2017). The need for service innovation to permeate every aspect of how healthcare organizations operate is now critical. Service innovation is causing a paradigm shift in the education sector. Researchers have looked at how technology, particularly adaptive learning systems and online learning platforms, is changing how education is delivered (Christensen et al.,2013). The literature places a strong emphasis on the value of educational innovation in meeting the changing requirements of students in the digital age. It also emphasizes the difficulties in adopting service innovations in education, such as access inequities and the requirement for teacher preparation (Edvardsson, B. & Olsson, J., 2016). However, Scholars have looked into typical obstacles that prevent the adoption of service improvements in both healthcare and education. Among these hindrances include resource shortages, legislative complexity, and stakeholder resistance to change (Gremyr et al.,2014).

Information and communication technology (ICT) "plays a significant role in service innovation and provides transformative opportunities to the services industries. Big data, and Machine Learning are all heavily emphasized in the publications that support innovation in healthcare (Bhattacharya et al,2017). It is crucial to emphasize that using technology involves co-creating value rather than that value being provided by the technology on its own (Guarcello, & de Vargas,2020). Collaboration and co-creation thus play a crucial part in the innovation and implementation process.

2.3 Relevance of Cross-Industry Innovation and Open Innovation in Service Innovation

Too many companies still operate with a silo mentality and neglect to seek outside of their industry for solutions and ideas. "In cross-industry innovation, already existing solutions from other industries are creatively imitated and retranslated to meet the needs of the company's current market or products. Such solutions can be technologies, patents, specific knowledge, capabilities, business processes, general principles, or whole business models" (Enkel and Gassmann, 2010).

Cross-industry innovation is becoming more prevalent, and it's not so much a trend as it is a way for firms to develop and a way to improve what they already do. It is a method for acquiring the knowledge you need, overcoming significant obstacles, and finally, picking someone else's brain who can provide a different perspective (Nasiri, 2023). Cross-industry innovation is a planned process whereby retranslation of the existing pool of knowledge or transfer of existing technology or business models in one domain is used to solve problems innovate and provide solutions in other industries thereby deriving new synergies. Internal and external organizational procedures, as well as the makeup of teams working on new product development, are organizational structures and mechanisms that support (Carmona et al.,2013). To combat employee niche specialization, interdisciplinary teams inside the organization are essential. These teams should include people from various functional areas as well as those with various academic and professional backgrounds, experiences, and personal interests (Kalogerakis et al., 2010). Apart from establishing heterogeneous teams, organization practices should be aligned to establishing a creative culture of interdisciplinary innovation with policies on setting standards and fostering a culture of information sharing; promoting frequent employee movement between teams or projects, revision of incentives and employee engagement systems to reinforce the effective use of analogies, and providing instruction in analytical thinking (Lyytinen, 2021). These strategies include informal face-to-face interactions among diverse groups to enable the transmission of tacit knowledge, and knowledge transfer mediators who are generalists with experience in various domains to connect specialists to solve problems (Behne et al., 2021). Further harnessing external organizational capacities would include a systematic search in knowledge domains which are unfamiliar to the team, this will improve new insights on building innovative solutions. This can be accomplished by 1) bringing in fresh talent with the expertise that the organization lacks, 2) fostering connections with or access to other information sources (such as those found in other areas or industries), 3) utilizing knowledge management systems and exposing the problem to professionals from various sectors and technological fields (Behne et al., 2021).

3. RESEARCH DESIGN AND METHODS

Step 1: Identification and Selection of Database

The Scopus database was used to retrieve the bibliographic information used in this investigation. A wide variety of papers and articles on the topic of business and management were covered by Scopus, the biggest multidisciplinary peer-reviewed database in social science research (Donthu et al., 2021).

Step 2: Identification of Search Terms

The prerequisite for doing a bibliometric analysis is keywords or search terms. This analysis expressed the author's perspective on the selected keywords. The search box of Scopus had the terms "Innovations" AND "Service Industry," which produced results for publications between 1995 and 2023 on 10th August 2023.

Step 3: Data Filtering

Inclusion-exclusion criteria method was used for the refinement of the acquired data set. The only "Articles" published in "Journal" on the topics of "Business, Management, Economics," and "Education," were referred for this document selection. Additionally, only English-language publications were thought to have higher reader engagement. The total output from the aforementioned process was 1922 papers. Following this, 496 documents were determined by content analysis as irrelevant to the research field and excluded. 1426 documents were ultimately retained for bibliometric analysis.

Step 4: Selection of Bibliometric, Thematic, and Sentiment Analysis

The study employed NVivo software for thematic and sentiment analysis and a VOS viewer for bibliometric analysis. Certain network mapping tasks were carried out using VOS Viewer, an open-source software for constructing and visualizing bibliometric networks (Van Eck and Waltman, 2017). The search protocol is presented in Figure 2

Figure 2. Methodology

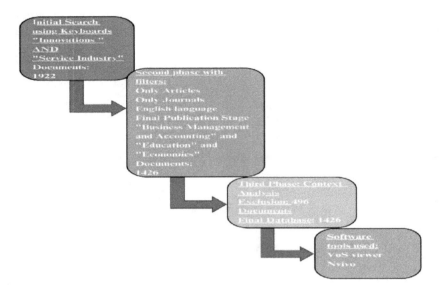

3.1 Descriptive STATISTICS

Table 1 provides general information on the research domain. 1426 research articles (documents) were published in 924 journals in approximately 28 years (from 1995 to 2023) receiving a total of 11017 citations and receiving 7.725 citations on average.

Table 1. General information about the scholarly contribution

Description	Results
Period of Analysis	1995-2023
Sources	924
Total Documents	1426
Single Authored documents	332
Multi Authored	1094
Author's keywords	6912
Total number of authors	4384
Authors per document	3.074
Authors per document	2

Out of 1426 documents, only 332 are single-authored documents (23.92%) while 1094 (76.7%) documents are multi-authored which shows growing collaboration among authors.

3.2 Year-Wise Articles Production

Figure 3 depicts year-wise publication for the topic of "Innovations in the Service Industry." Except a few intervening years, there is a rising trend in papers published, notably after 2016. A possible explanation for this increase in publications is that service providers were forced to adapt and develop fresh, creative solutions due to the rapid advancement of technology and shifting consumer behavior. The highest number of articles was published in the year 2022.

Figure 3. Year-wise annual production of articles

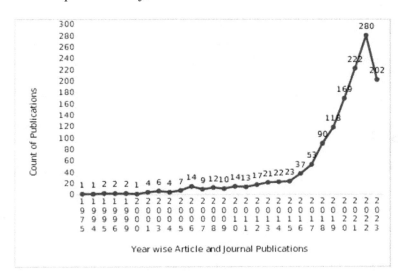

3.3 Most Prolific Authors

The most prolific authors in terms of both article production and impact are shown in Table 2. The output of an author is measured by the quantity of papers they write and by the average number of citations they receive for each article. With a total of 25 citations, SNOWBALL J., TARENTAAL D., and SAPSED J. have the most publications (12) to their name. According to Scopus data, his first article, "Innovation and digital culture" (Snowball, Tarentaal, & Sapsed (2022), appeared in the journal Arts, Entrepreneurship, and Innovation in 2022.

Table 2. Most prolific authors

Sno	Author	Articles	Citations	Average Citations per Document	Year
1	JAVAID M.; HALEEM A.; PRATAP SINGH R.; SUMAN R.	2	74	37	2021
2	SEALY W.U.	5	69	13.8	2003
3	MAGADÁN-DÍAZ M.; RIVAS-GARCÍA J.I.	4	28	7	2018
4	HUGHES K.H.	4	27	6.75	2005
5	SNOWBALL J.; TARENTAAL D.; SAPSED J.	12	25	2.08	2022
6	PELLEGRINI T.	2	21	10.5	2012
7	MH BRUN, C LANNG	4	16	4	2006
8	ROY JP	3	12	4	2019
9	SINGH M.; JIAO J.; KLOBASA M.; FRIETSCH R.	8	10	1.25	2022
10	INDRIASARI E.; PRABOWO H.; GAOL F.L.; PURWANDARI B.	4	7	1.75	2022

3.4 Thematic Analysis

The NVivo 12 software enabled automated topic modeling and theme recognition from text-based datasets. The important keywords that were extracted from the topic of "Innovations in Service Industry" by the study using NVivo software are listed below (displayed in Figure 4 below). The thematic analysis identified the highest area of study in digital (2566), innovation (1703), technology (1803) concerning service sector (1796) shown in table 3. Digital innovations have become a transformative force in the service sector as a result of the constantly changing landscape of business and technology. The way services are conceptualized, provided, and experienced has undergone a fundamental upheaval as a result of the widespread adoption of digital transformation. The service sector has adopted digital advances to improve efficiency, customize experiences, and satisfy customer expectations which includes individualized customer interactions and efficient processes. For example, it is crucial to convert the conventional campus-based education system to the Massive Online Open Courses (MOOC) system. Even while MOOCs are initially thought of as an addition to the current higher education system based on campuses, they may eventually entirely replace it. Higher education emphasizes expanding knowledge, abilities, experience, and confidence, which may be provided equally effectively on the internet using wireless video channels and by adopting digital technologies (Aithal, P. S., & Aithal.S, 2019).

Table 3. Themes identified

Sno	Themes Identified	1: Files\\scopus (6)
1	business	612
2	development	644
3	digital	2566
4	innovation	1703
5	model	599
6	process	545
7	research	584
8	sector	1180
9	services	1796
10	technology	1803

Figure 4. Thematic analysis of the Scopus database

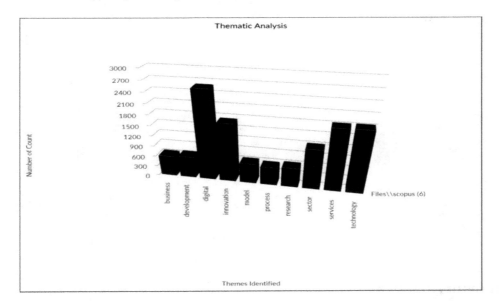

3.5 Hierarchy Map of Most Frequently Occurred Keywords

Keywords are the essence of any research work. It can be used by readers to find the manuscripts relevant to their research topic, increasing article viewing and ultimately leading to more citations. Additionally, they represent the evolving trends in a specific scientific field. The ten author keywords that appeared the most often in the Hierarchy map are shown in (Figure 5). With 2566 and 1803 mentions, "Digital" and "Technology" are the top two keywords which are followed by Innovation, services and sector etc.

The hierarchy map revealed that some of the key research features of the study domain include phrases like digital technology and digital innovation in various service sectors.

For instance, digital marketing is the activity of advertising products or services online or through other digital media, such as mobile devices, display ads, and other digital media. The term "digital marketing technology" refers to the delivery of advertisements using online and digital channels, such as search engines, websites, social media, email, and mobile apps. As a result of the use of general-purpose technology and ICCT (Information Communication and Computation Technology), digital business and marketing have become an essential future business and marketing activities of all companies to compete in the competitive world (Bala & Verma, 2018).

Figure 5. Hierarchy chart

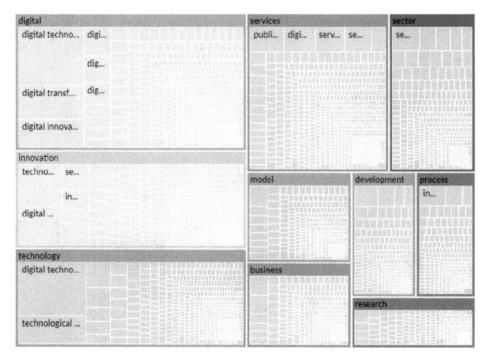

3.6 Sentiment Analysis

The sentimental Analysis in this exploratory study using NVivo software of the Scopus database produced high positivity for innovations in the service industry with 94.7% as explained in figure 6 below. The service industry has undergone substantial innovations in recent years, driven by technological improvements, shifting client preferences, and the demand for greater efficiency. Many service businesses are undergoing digital transformations to improve client experiences, streamline operations and processes. This includes adopting digital tools for online reservations, customer communication, and payment processing (Zaki,2019). Many companies are using a variety of quantitative analytical techniques and mathematical models to analyze huge business data with the help of big data and business analytics to study patterns and provide descriptive, predictive, and prescriptive information to help decision-makers solve business problems. For efficient decision-making, predictive analytics are becoming increasingly important in a variety of functional areas such as marketing, retail (customer analytics/supply chain analytics), sports and healthcare analytics etc. Furthermore, It also optimizes judgments for various portfolios or complicated business predictions, sales force and retail judgments etc. which will have a futuristic impact on making right business decisions (Hoyos, Aguilar & Toro,2023).

Figure 6. Sentiment analysis

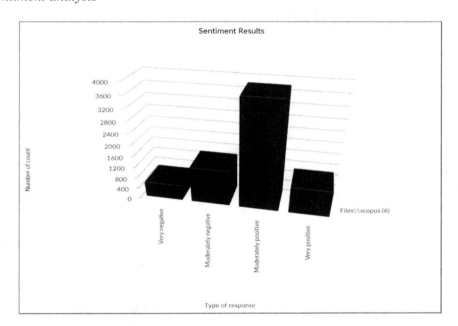

3.7 Word Cloud Analysis

It is clear from the word cloud analysis (shown in Figure 7) that technological advancements are not just improvements, but rather catalysts for a completely new method of conceiving and providing services. As we move through this landscape, we'll see how human imagination and technology capability collide, paving the way for a day when the service sector combines ease, personalization, and efficiency in astonishing new ways. The service sector, which includes a variety of industries like education, hospitality, finance, healthcare, retail, transportation, and more, has seen a transformation due to digital advancements (Wu, 2023). These advancements have ushered in a new era of possibilities in each of these industries, changing conventional paradigms and stimulating innovative methods for solving both customer's wants and operational difficulties (Xia, Baghaie, & Sajadi,2023).

Figure 7. Word cloud analysis

3.8 Authors Keywords Co-Occurrence

A threshold of 10 was applied for these 1426 highly cited articles, which resulted in many keywords. The bubble size pertains to the overall count of extensively referenced articles, whereas the thickness of the lines and the colors are indicative of the strength of connections and the formation of clusters, respectively. The top author keywords indicated the research area focus and interests of various researchers and academicians in the field of innovation in the service industry. According to these keywords, the top five highly referenced total occurrences were Innovation (146), digital transformation (114), digitalization (70), fintech (55), and artificial intelligence (47) shown in Table 4.

Table 4. Co-occurrence of author's keyword

Sno	Keyword	Occurrences	Total Link Strength
1	Innovation	146	86
2	Digital transformation	114	42
3	Digitalization	70	45
4	Fintech	55	27
5	Artificial intelligence	47	35
6	Covid-19	42	22
7	Blockchain	37	23
8	Digital economy	36	25
9	Technology	36	23
10	Digital technologies	31	22

Innovation exhibited the highest link strength or cooccurrence among all author keywords and is highly connected to digital transformation which is also represented in (Figure 8). The strength of the network between innovation and digital transformation indicated a strong and direct relationship between these two keywords. There is still high interest among many researchers regarding innovations in the service sector. For example, the worldwide pandemic (COVID-19) has opened up new possibilities for numerous service robot applications since it raised awareness of the importance of maintaining a minimum distance between service employees and service clients to prevent contact. Moreover, demand for professional cleaning robots also increased by 92% in terms of units sold and 51% in terms of turnover (Financial Times, 2020).

Figure 8. Co-occurrence network of the most frequently used author keyword

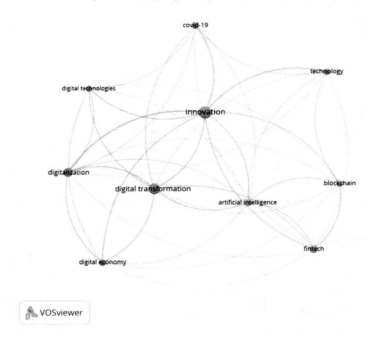

4. DISCUSSION

The insights have several practical implications for managers and practitioners in the business and service sectors: The thematic analysis revealed that digital innovation, technology, and sector-specific innovations like fintech, artificial intelligence and Blockchain are significant themes in the service industry. The service industry is undergoing significant changes, mainly enhanced by the broad adoption of modern technology like fintech, AI, and Blockchain (Bhatt et al., 2022). These technological innovations pave the way for novel service delivery methods, improving operational efficiency and fostering an environment ripe for innovation. Fintech, an umbrella term encompassing the application of technology to financial services, spans various offerings, including online banking, mobile payment solutions, and robot-advisory services (Castro et al., 2020). Its disruptive impact on traditional financial institutions is unmistakable, as it brings forth more convenient, efficient, and cost-effective services for consumers, characterized by machines' ability to learn and perform tasks that typically necessitate human intelligence, is making its mark in the service industry by automating processes, enhancing customer service interactions, and making predictive analyses (Arslanian & Fischer, 2019). For instance, AI plays a pivotal role in fraud detection, tailoring personalized marketing strategies, and suggesting products and services to consumers.

Large data sets are frequently used by fintech and AI systems, which raises privacy and data protection issues. It is crucial to make sure that consumer data is managed safely and morally (Raajpoot & Sharma, 2021). AI and blockchain technologies' ability to automate processes could result in employment losses in the service sector. Making sure displaced workers receive retraining and opportunities for other employment is one of the ethical considerations and building trust in the use of these technologies requires accountability and openness.

Blockchain technology is renowned for its secure and transparent transaction record-keeping. Blockchain finds applications in tracking the ownership of digital assets, notably cryptocurrencies (Andersen & Bogusz, 2019). It possesses transformative potential within the service sector, simplifying data tracking and management, curbing fraudulent activities, and elevating transparency. The convergence of fintech, AI, and Blockchain is at the heart of a burgeoning wave of innovation within the service industry. These technologies collectively drive the creation of fresh products and services, streamline existing processes for greater efficiency, and give rise to innovative business models.

Integrating fintech, AI, and Blockchain into the service industry is still nascent. However, it holds tremendous promise, reshaping how individuals engage with businesses. These technologies empower service providers to offer more accessible, efficient, and secure services, ultimately enhancing the consumer experience (Giudici, 2018). Managers can use this information to understand where the industry is headed and where to focus their efforts for competitive advantage and create strategies that prioritize individualized experiences, fulfilling customer expectations, and optimizing service delivery procedures.

Imagine a bustling, lively urban landscape adorned with recognizable structures emblematic of distinct service sectors (such as a hotel, a restaurant, a retail store, a bank, etc.). Digital screens that show a variety of cutting-edge customer interaction strategies, like customized offers, virtual assistants, augmented reality experiences, and interactive touchpoints, are lit up in every building. A busy street with a diverse crowd employing various digital technologies is seen in the foreground. There are people utilizing chatbots on smartphones, others trying on virtual clothes using AR glasses, dining in virtual reality with a group, and so on. A digital cloud floats over the metropolis, signifying the digital infrastructure driving these breakthroughs. The cloud is made up of symbols that stand for cloud computing, artificial intelligence, data analytics, and other digital technologies that are revolutionizing customer involvement. Overall, the graphic presents a dynamic and futuristic landscape in which digital advances provide a seamless and immersive experience for clients by orchestrating a symphony of customer involvement across diverse service industries as shown in Figure 9.

Figure 9. Innovations in the digital era (generated by the author using generative AI)

Managers should foster an environment that encourages employees to think creatively, experiment with new ideas to improve, and continuously improve their services. The increase in multi-authored articles reflects a growing trend of collaboration among authors. Managers can take inspiration from this and encourage cross-functional teamwork and collaboration within their organizations to drive innovation and research-backed improvements. Collaboration within and outside partners is vital to new services' success. With the aid of technology, businesses must quickly combine various information and abilities to create successful global services. Coordination of the distinctive qualities of external resources is advantageous while achieving this. It is both prudent and profitable. Collaboration with other parties shields service providers from the adverse effects of potentially disruptive technologies. As a result, service managers will be better off if they actively seek out and work with outside partners. Finding information, skills, and technologies exclusive to the external organizations and areas in which they lack experience and can profit from external partners should be the initial step in the search for external partners (De Luca & Atuahene-Gima, 2007).

Keeping track records of the authors and their contributions can help managers to be updated and informed on the latest development happenings in the service industry. This can guide strategic decision-making and innovative initiatives. The shift towards digital innovations has educational implications and can be implanted for better teaching and learning. Managers can incorporate this information for ongoing and future research for strategic decision-making in the current domain. Keywords such as innovation, services and technological upgradation etc. highlighted in the hierarchy map can offer insights into the language researchers and practitioners use. These keywords can be used for better marketing communication and a more targeted audience. Managers can allocate resources to research and development to stay ahead of the curve and create new, cutting-edge service offerings. By doing so, organizations can position themselves to thrive in a rapidly changing environment and deliver exceptional value to their customers.

Though intellectual discourses on innovations in the service sector have been on the rise. A huge population is still ignorant of the notions of digitization and DigiTech tools - blockchain technology for example; this has made the implementation of blockchain technology widely unfeasible and caused a detachment from reality. A profound knowledge of financial services and payment systems, as well as a thorough understanding of big data and data analytics, are among the specific skills required to master this technology (Sharma, 2018). Many of these early adopters are exploring Blockchain potential as it provides greater efficiency of products and services, but these developments are still in the early stages, which highlights the significant obstacles that must be overcome before blockchain technology is widely adopted. The stakeholder's ignorance and lack of understanding, as well as the nature and pace of development, are some of the major obstacles. The technological advancement of blockchain and the difficulties in integrating operations and cultures among various stakeholder groups and organizations is still a challenge. As they understand and implement associated technological solutions, securities market participants may want to take into account the unique challenges that AI-based applications bring. When adopting AI-based applications, market participants should specifically consider the following elements, if applicable: supervisory control systems, model risk management, data governance, and consumer privacy. Workforce, books and records, cybersecurity, outsourcing, and vendor management are additional variables that may be considered.

5. FUTURE RESEARCH DIRECTIONS

Based on the co-occurrence analysis of author keywords in highly cited articles within the field of innovation in the service industry, several promising avenues for future research can be identified. These research directions are informed by the significance of specific keywords and their interconnections, reflecting the current trends and interests in the field Like:

- Enhancing Service Innovation Through Digitalization
- The Influence of Fintech and Artificial Intelligence on Services
- Post-Pandemic Service Innovations
- Digital Economy and Blockchain Applications
- Technological Advancements in Service Delivery
- Cross-Sector Collaboration
- Global Perspectives on Service Innovation

In summary, the phenomenon analysis of author keywords in highly cited articles points to exciting research opportunities in the service industry. Future studies can explore the intricate relationship between innovation and digitalization, the transformative potential of fintech and AI, and the ongoing impact of external events like the COVID-19 pandemic. Moreover, examining service innovation's ethical and cross-sector dimensions alongside a global outlook can contribute to a holistic understanding of this dynamic field.

6. CONCLUSION

The current study provides a thorough overview of the existing trends, collaboration dynamics, and thematic focus within the "Innovations in the Service Industry. "The study further emphasizes the importance of digital innovation technology and industry-specific advancements in shaping the service industry landscape. The increasing trend of collaboration among authors signifies a collective endeavor to explore and contribute to the growth of this field. The research explains how digital advancements have revolutionized the service industry, establishing new definitions for the conception, delivery, and experience of services. The widespread adoption of digital technologies has improved efficiency, personalized customer experiences, and new service delivery models. This evolution aligns with shifts in consumer behavior and advancements in technology. The application of bibliometric analysis, exploration of thematic areas, and identification of influential authors by the research all contribute to a comprehensive comprehension of the current state of this domain. This knowledge can be an insight for the researchers, practitioners, and managers to align their work in this area of innovation in the service sector. Leveraging these insights for informed strategic planning and decision-making as the service sector changes is important for maintaining an organization's competitiveness and capacity to meet changing customer and market needs. The research has provided a comprehensive overview of the trends, collaboration patterns, and thematic focus within the domain of "Innovations in the Service Industry". The findings highlight the growing importance of digital innovations, technology, and sector-specific advancements in shaping the service sector landscape. This information can guide researchers, practitioners, and managers in aligning their efforts with ongoing trends to identify potential areas for innovation and apply these informed solutions as the service business industry evolves to capture the dynamic market.

REFERENCES

Aithal, P. S., & Aithal, S. (2019). Management of ICCT underlying technologies used for digital service innovation. *International Journal of Management, Technology, and Social Sciences*, *4*(2), 110–136. doi:10.47992/IJMTS.2581.6012.0077

Andersen, J. V., & Bogusz, C. I. (2019). Self-organizing in blockchain infrastructures: Generativity through shifting objectives and forking. *Journal of the Association for Information Systems*, *20*, 1242–1273. doi:10.17705/1jais.00566

Arslanian, H., & Fischer, F. (2019). *The future of finance the impact of fintech, AI, and crypto on Financial Services*. Springer International Publishing., doi:10.1007/978-3-030-14533-0

Bala, M., & Verma, D. (2018). A Critical Review of Digital Marketing. *International Journal of Management, IT & Engineering*, *8*(10), 321–339. https://ssrn.com/abstract=3545505

Behne, A., Beinke, J. H., & Teuteberg, F. (2021). A framework for cross-industry innovation: Transferring technologies between industries. Int. J. Innovation. *International Journal on Management of Innovation & Technology*, *18*(3), 1–27. doi:10.1142/S0219877021500115

Berry, L. L. (2019, May 24). Service innovation is urgent in healthcare. AMS Review; Springer Science, Business Media. doi:10.1007/s13162-019-00135-x

Bhatt, A., Joshipura, M., & Joshipura, N. (2022). Decoding the Trinity of Fintech, Digitalization and financial services: An Integrated Bibliometric Analysis and thematic literature review approach. Cogent Economics &amp. *Cogent Economics & Finance*, *10*(1), 2114160. Advance online publication. doi:10.1080/23322039.2022.2114160

Bhattacharya, S., Wainwright, D., & Whalley, J. (2017). Internet of Things (IoT) enabled assistive care services: Designing for value and trust. *Procedia Computer Science, 113*, 659–664. doi:10.1016/j.procs.2017.08.333

Bloch, C. (2011). Measuring Public Innovation in the Nordic Countries (MEPIN). Danish Centre for Studies in Research and Research Policy. urn:nbn:se:norden:org:diva-2822

Cai, C. W. (2018). Disruption of financial intermediation by FinTech: A review on crowdfunding and blockchain. *Accounting and Finance, 58*(4), 965–992. doi:10.1111/acfi.12405

Cankar, S. S., & Petkovšek, V. (2013, November/December). Private And Public Sector Innovation And The Importance Of Cross-Sector Collaboration. *Journal of Applied Business Research, 29*(6), 1597. Advance online publication. doi:10.19030/jabr.v29i6.8197

Carmona-Lavado, A., Cuevas-Rodríguez, G., & Cabello, C. (2013). Service Innovativeness and Innovation Success in Technology-based Knowledge-Intensive Business Services: An Intellectual Capital Approach. *Industry and Innovation, 20*(2), 133–156. Advance online publication. doi:10.1080/13662716.2013.771482

Castro, P., Rodrigues, J. P., & Teixeira, J. G. (2020). Understanding FinTech ecosystem evolution through service innovation and Socio-Technical System Perspective. Exploring Service Science, 187–201. doi:10.1007/978-3-030-38724-2_14

Christensen, C. M., Horn, M. B., & Staker, H. (2013). Is K-12 blended learning disruptive? An introduction to the theory of hybrids. Clayton Christensen Institute for Disruptive Innovation. https://www.christenseninstitute.org/publications/hybrids/ DOI:https://eric.ed.gov/?id=ed566878

Coombs, Rod & Miles, I. (2000). Innovation, Measurement and Services: The New Problematique. . doi:10.1007/978-1-4615-4425-8_5

Curzi, Y., Fabbri, T., Scapolan, A. C., & Boscolo, S. (2019, July 17). Performance Appraisal and Innovative Behavior in the Digital Era. *Frontiers in Psychology, 10*, 1659. Advance online publication. doi:10.3389/fpsyg.2019.01659 PMID:31379682

De Luca, L. M., & Atuahene-Gima, K. (2007). Market knowledge dimensions and cross-functional collaboration: Examining the different routes to product innovation performance. *Journal of Marketing, 71*(1), 95–112. doi:10.1509/jmkg.71.1.095

Den Hertog, P., & de Jong, G. (2007). Randstad's business model of innovation: Results from an exploratory study in the temporary staffing industry. *Innovation (North Sydney, N.S.W.), 9*(3-4), 351–364. doi:10.5172/impp.2007.9.3-4.351

Den Hertog, P., van der Aa, W., & de Jong, G. (2010). Capabilities for managing service innovation: Towards a conceptual framework. *Journal of Service Management, 21*(4), 490–514. doi:10.1108/09564231011066123

Dery, K., Sebastian, I. M., & van der Meulen, N. (2017). The digital workplace is key to digital innovation. MIS Quarterly Executive, 16(2). https://aisel.aisnet.org/misqe/vol16/iss2/4

Donthu, N., Kumar, S., Mukherjee, D., Pandey, N., & Lim, W. M. (2021). How to conduct a bibliometric analysis: An overview and guidelines. *Journal of Business Research, 133*, 285–296. doi:10.1016/j.jbusres.2021.04.070

Edvardsson, B., & Olsson, J. (2016). Key concepts for new service development in healthcare. *Journal of Service Management, 27*(1), 4–33. doi:10.1016/j.jbusres.2021.04.070

Enkel, E., Gassmann, O., & Chesbrough, H. (2009). Open R&D and open innovation: Exploring the phenomenon. *R & D Management, 39*(4), 311–316. doi:10.1111/j.1467-9310.2009.00570.x

Garzella, S., Fiorentino, R., Caputo, A., & Lardo, A. (2020). Business model innovation in SMEs: The role of boundaries in the digital era. *Technology Analysis and Strategic Management, 33*(1), 31–43. doi:10.1080/09537325.2020.1787374

Giudici, P. (2018). Fintech Risk Management: A research challenge for artificial intelligence in finance. *Frontiers in Artificial Intelligence, 1*, 1. Advance online publication. doi:10.3389/frai.2018.00001 PMID:33733089

Gremyr, I., Witell, L., Löfberg, N., Edvardsson, B., & Fundin, A. (2014). Understanding new service development and service innovation through innovation modes. *Journal of Business and Industrial Marketing, 29*(2), 123–131. doi:10.1108/JBIM-04-2012-0074

Guarcello, C., & de Vargas, E. R. (2020). Service Innovation in Healthcare: A Systematic Literature Review. *Latin American Business Review, 21*(4), 353–369. doi:10.1080/10978526.2020.1802286

Gustafsson, A., Snyder, H., & Witell, L. (2020). Service Innovation: A New Conceptualization and Path Forward. *Journal of Service Research, 23*(2), 111–115. doi:10.1177/1094670520908929

Herstatt, C., & Kalogerakis, K. (2005). How to use analogies for breakthrough innovations. *International Journal on Management of Innovation & Technology, 2*(3), 331–347. doi:10.1142/S0219877005000538

Hodapp, D., & Hanelt, A. (2022). Interoperability in the era of digital innovation: An information systems research agenda. *Journal of Information Technology, 37*(4), 407–427. doi:10.1177/02683962211064304

Hoyos, W., Aguilar, J., & Toro, M. (2023). PRV-FCM: An extension of fuzzy cognitive maps for prescriptive modeling. *Expert Systems with Applications, 120729*, 120729. Advance online publication. doi:10.1016/j.eswa.2023.120729

Hund, A., Wagner, H., Beimborn, D., & Weitzel, T. (2021). Digital innovation: Review and novel perspective. *The Journal of Strategic Information Systems, 30*(4), 101695. doi:10.1016/j.jsis.2021.101695

Kalogerakis, K., Lu, C., & Herstatt, C. (2010). Developing innovations based on analogies: Experience from design and engineering consultants. *Journal of Product Innovation Management, 27*(3), 418–436. doi:10.1111/j.1540-5885.2010.00725.x

Kowalkowski, C., Carlborg, P., & Kindström, D. (2014). The Evolution of Service Innovation Research: A Critical Review and Synthesis. *Service Industries Journal, 34*(5), 373–398. doi:10.1080/02642069.2013.780044

Lars, W., Hannah, S., Anders, G., Paul, F., & Per, K. (2016). Defining Service Innovation: A Review and Synthesis. *Journal of Business Research*, *69*(8), 2863–2872. doi:10.1016/j.jbusres.2015.12.055

Laster, D. (2021). Council Post: Why The Era of Digital Transformation Is Important For Companies Of All Sizes. Forbes. https://www.forbes.com/sites/forbesbusinesscouncil/2021/09/23/why-the-era-of-digital-transformation-is-important-for-companies-of-all-sizes/

Lyytinen, K. (2021). Innovation logics in the digital era: A systemic review of the emerging digital innovation regime. *Innovation (North Sydney, N.S.W.)*, *24*(1), 13–34. doi:10.1080/14479338.2021.1938579

Massaro, G., Sicotte, C., & Denis, J.-L. (2017). Service innovation in healthcare: A systematic literature review. *Health Care Management Review*, *42*(2), 173–186.

MelloS. L. D. M.LudolfN. V. E.QuelhasO. L. G.MeiriñoM. J. (2020). Innovation in the digital era: New labor market and educational changes. Ensaio: Avaliação e Políticas Públicas Em Educação, 28(106), 66-87. https://doi.org/ doi:10.1590/S0104-40362019002702511

Murata, K. (2019). On the role of visual management in the era of Digital Innovation. *Procedia Manufacturing*, *39*, 117–122. doi:10.1016/j.promfg.2020.01.246

Nasiri, M., Saunila, M., Ukko, J., Rantala, T., & Rantanen, H. (2023). Shaping Digital Innovation Via Digital-related Capabilities. *Information Systems Frontiers*, *25*(3), 1063–1080. doi:10.1007/s10796-020-10089-2

Normann, R. (2002). Service Management; Strategy and Leadership in Service Business (3rd ed.). Wiley. Retrieved from: https://www.wiley.com/en-ie/Service+Management+:+Strategy+and+Leadership+in+Service+Business,+3rd+Edition-p-9780471494393 DOI: https://cir.nii.ac.jp/crid/1130282272095638784

Ostrom, A. L., Parasuraman, A., Bowen, D. E., Patrício, L., & Voss, C. A. (2015). Service Research Priorities in a Rapidly Changing Context. *Journal of Service Research*, *18*(2), 127–159. doi:10.1177/1094670515576315

Park, Y. W., & Hong, P. (2022). A Research Framework for Sustainable Digital Innovation: Case Studies of Japanese Firms. *Sustainability (Basel)*, *14*(15), 15. Advance online publication. doi:10.3390/su14159218

Pochenchuk, G., Babuch, I., & Baraniuk, D. (2018). Innovations of the digital era and economic choice. The USV Annals of Economics and Public Administration, 18. http://www.annals.seap.usv.ro/index.php/annals/article/viewArticle/1053

Raajpoot, N., & Sharma, A. (2021). The function of innovation culture in the success of New Services. *Journal of Global Scholars of Marketing Science*, *31*(3), 392–414. doi:10.1080/21639159.2021.1924818

Randhawa, K., & Scerri, M. (2015). Service Innovation: A Review of the Literature. Springer eBooks. doi:10.1007/978-1-4471-6590-3_2

Rubalcaba, L., Michel, S., Sundbo, J., Brown, S. W., & Reynoso, J. (2012). Shaping, organizing, and rethinking service innovation: A multidimensional framework. *Journal of Service Management*, *23*(5), 696–715. doi:10.1108/09564231211269847

Schang, S. S. C., Wu, S. H., & Yao, C. Y. (2010). A dynamic innovation model for managing capabilities for continuous innovation. International Journal of Technology Management, 51(2/3/4), 300-318. doi:10.1504/IJTM.2010.033807

Schumpeter, J. A. (1934). *The Theory of Economic Development*. Harvard University Press.

Snowball, J., Tarentaal, D., & Sapsed, J. (2022). Innovation and diversity in the digital cultural and creative industries. In Arts, Entrepreneurship, and Innovation (pp. 187-215). Cham: Springer Nature Switzerland. doi:10.1007/978-3-031-18195-5_8

Snyder, H., Witell, L., & Gustafsson, A. (2020). Service Innovation: A New Conceptualization and Path Forward. *Journal of Service Research*, *23*(2), 111–115. doi:10.1177/1094670520908929

Toivonen, M., & Tuominen, T. (2009). Emergence of innovations in services. *Service Industries Journal*, *29*(7), 887–902. doi:10.1080/02642060902749492

Van der Aa, W., & Elfring, T. (2002). Realizing innovation in services. *Scandinavian Journal of Management*, *18*(2), 155–171. doi:10.1016/S0956-5221(00)00040-3

Van Eck, N. J., & Waltman, L. (2017). Citation-based clustering of publications using CitNetExplorer and VOSviewer. *Scientometrics*, *111*(2), 1053–1070. doi:10.1007/s11192-017-2300-7 PMID:28490825

Wu, T. (2023). Analysis of the Digital Transformation of Big Data Era. Highlights in Business. *Economics and Management*, *16*, 288–293. doi:10.54097/hbem.v16i.10572

Xia, L., Baghaie, S., & Sajadi, S. M. (2023). The digital economy: Challenges and opportunities in the new era of technology and electronic communications. *Ain Shams Engineering Journal*, *102411*. Advance online publication. doi:10.1016/j.asej.2023.102411

Zaki, M. (2019). Digital transformation: Harnessing digital technologies for the next generation of services. *Journal of Services Marketing*, *33*(4), 429–435. doi:10.1108/JSM-01-2019-0034

Zhang, K., Feng, L., Wang, J., Qin, G., & Li, H. (2022). Start-Up's road to disruptive innovation in the digital era: The interplay between dynamic capabilities and business model innovation. *Frontiers in Psychology*, *13*, 925277. Advance online publication. doi:10.3389/fpsyg.2022.925277 PMID:35800925

Chapter 9
ARise to the Occasion:
Elevating Customer Engagement

Anagha Sathiabalan Nair
Christ University, India

Dinesh Kumar R.
(iD) https://orcid.org/0000-0002-3794-8255
Christ University, India

ABSTRACT

Augmented reality (AR) is being used to transform the landscape of online retail by enhancing customer engagement and experience. This chapter delves into how AR's unique capabilities, such as virtual try-on and interactive product visualisation, can overcome the limitations of traditional online shopping and create deeper connections between brands and consumers. It explains how AR personalises the customer journey by providing customised product recommendations and immersive virtual experiences that drive purchase decisions. By analysing past implementations and future trends, this chapter demonstrates how ARM can usher in a new era of customer engagement and personalised experiences in online retail.

INTRODUCTION

Information Technology development has changed many business practices. Marketers are driven to experiment with novel techniques that catch attention and establish a more significant and profound relationship with their intended audience. Retailers have started adopting omnichannel approaches to connect with their customers and provide what they prefer (*What Is Omnichannel Marketing?*, 2022). With the emergence of social networking sites, push-based, traditional communication has given way to network-based communication, where information is pulled based on the requirements and interests of the audience (Popovici et al., 2018). Over the past two decades, as digital platforms expanded, corporations' marketing tactics led to investments focused at creating distinctive brand experiences through immersive multimedia environments (Paruthi & Kaur, n.d.). E-commerce sites and mobile applications are among them, which have become critical channels for online retailers to reach customers to make them purchase

DOI: 10.4018/979-8-3693-2367-0.ch009

products online and make payments (Kim et al. 2013). The adoption of digital technologies in marketing aids in drawing in more viewers, converting them into clients, and keeping them loyal (Gauri, 2022).

According to Grant Thornton 2021, the eCommerce market size in India is expected to be worth US$ 188 billion by 2025, with a turnover of US$ 50 billion in 2020. In addition, the Deloitte India Report 2023 states that India is moving towards becoming the third-largest consumer market after China and the US, with an online shopper base of 150 million in FY21 and is expected to reach US$ 325 billion by 2030 due to the increase in smartphone penetration.

Witnessing the rise in the eCommerce market, online retailers face challenges for new and creative methods to engage their customers and establish deep connections with brands (Reinartz et al. 2019). Customer engagement is also seen as creating customer interaction and participation. It involves both transactions (including purchase) and non-transactions (i.e., going beyond purchase) and relates to customers' behavioural manifestations towards the brand or firms (Vivek et al. 2014). Online retailers portray customer engagement as an approach to creating, building and enhancing customer relationships (Brodie et al. 2013).

As customers become more aware of using online retail websites and mobile application platforms, they are actively engaging in technology-facilitated service interactions such as buying flight or movie tickets online, getting online consultations, buying daily use items and playing online games (Islam & Rahman, 2017). They desire excellent products, affordable costs, and a good shopping experience (Neslin, 2022). As a result of this change in how customers interact, it has become essential for marketers to engage with them to build brand relationships and improve profitability (Gligor et al., 2019).

According to Sorenson & Adkins, 2022, Gallup's research reveals noteworthy insights that "fully engaged" customers across various industries exhibited significantly higher patronage and spending compared to "actively disengaged" customers. Specifically, banking customers who were fully engaged generated a 37% greater annual revenue increase for their banks compared to their disengaged counterparts. Similarly, fully engaged consumer electronics shoppers made 44% more annual visits to their preferred online retailers, and fully engaged hotel guests spent 46% more annually than their actively disengaged counterparts. A few studies explored customer engagement in an online context (Mollen & Wilson, 2010); (Hollebeek et al., 2014); (Calder et al., 2009); (Brodie et al., 2013); (Pagani & Mirabello, 2011) and website as a focal object (Demangeot & Broderick, 2016). However, the question of why and how retail mobile applications can engage customers during their customer journey or during the search for a particular product which fits their need remains unanswered.

According to statistic, by 2024, the surge in mobile subscribers will have crossed over one billion, and mobile internet penetration is ever-growing. Users increasingly spend time on mobile applications like social media networks like Facebook and Instagram and entertainment applications like YouTube, Spotify, Gaana, and Wynk Music. Apart from these, mobile shopping apps and payments grew, leading shopping applications to spend huge advertising budgets.

For marketers to succeed in the cutthroat business world and attain commercial excellence, they must engage consumers and manage connections with them (Mazurek-Łopacińska & Sobocińska, 2021). Therefore, engaging customers during their online shopping, whether in mobile applications or website visits, is the biggest challenge in this competitive environment. In a world of such promising technologies, this book chapter aims to study how AR is being a tool for creating new concepts of online retail stores among customers and how it impacts customer engagement throughout their customer journey.

Augmented Reality for Customer Engagement

It is difficult for modern marketers to satisfy consumers' demands for individualised knowledge and prompt resolutions when they shop (Rasool et al. 2020). In order to overcome this obstacle, marketers are implementing digital technology to create a highly customised experience that provides real-time engaging data transfer between the customer and the brand, such as location-based, virtual reality and augmented mobile applications. With these technological improvements, businesses may now provide clients with platforms or methods to interact with their brands, such as web pages, social networking sites, and mobile applications (McLean and Wilson 2019). The modern consumer is in charge, has access to a wide range of reliable information sources, and completes the "buying process" at their speed (Mehta & Kaushik, 2015). The process of purchasing anything online is becoming an experience that is integrated into numerous other activities. In simple terms, the proper experience will have consumers so engaged and curious that they do not even realise they are purchasing.

While many businesses consider customer engagement an important factor, different people interpret it differently (Bolton 2011). Brodie et al. 2013 describe customer engagement as a multifaceted notion that includes cognitive, mental, and behavioural components. It entails forging a meaningful bond between customers and brands, cultivating attachment, and encouraging customer involvement. Alexander and Jaakkola (2014) defined customer engagement as "behaviours in which customers make resource commitments voluntarily that have a brand or organisation focus but go further what constitutes the core to the transaction". According to Brodie et al. (2011), customer engagement is a psychological condition resulting from interactive, cocreative encounters with a primary agent/object, such as a brand, in service relationships.

Engagement is an individual-specific, motivating, and context-dependent characteristic that emerges from interactions that are bilateral involving significant engagement subject(s) and object(s) (Alvarez-Milán et al., 2018). Harms and Rindone (2022) state that it is an entirely different set of interactions and experiences than in the early years of online retail and e-commerce. While many customers value efficient, consuming experiences delivered by standardised products and services, such offers frequently fail to engage customers in active, innovative, and pleasing activities. Even if customers do not buy during their time in your store, their greater engagement means they have formed a connection with the company and its brand and product, as well as generated a memory, resulting in them being more likely to remember the brand in their later years (Lu and Smith 2008). On the other hand, Alvarez-Milán et al. (2018) stated that customer engagement practitioners emphasised that customer engagement must contribute to purchases and be measurable by means of sales numbers, retweets, likes, or tags. Pinto and Loureiro (2020) pointed out that customer engagement depends on customer interaction, dialogue, and sharing of comments with firms, other customers, and network actors. There is another perception that customer engagement can also be measured by customer engagement behaviours like positive or bad Word-of-Mouth, recommendations and reviews which can have a global influence due to the usage of technology and multimedia. The element of interactiveness is also parameter for customer engagement as this benefits both consumers and businesses by increasing customer value, which leads to higher sales (Urdea & Constantin, 2021).

Firms use multiple projects, activities, or initiatives to affect customer engagement directly and, by offering an enjoyable experience for consumers, cover the weaknesses of functional initiatives and influence customers' emotional involvement with firms (Barari et al. 2021). Technological advancements, particularly the usage of interactive tools, have fundamentally altered consumers' shopping experiences and consumer engagement settings (Rajagopal 2022).

The use of Augmented Reality (AR) is one such example. When somebody has to think about buying a product online and experience it before buying it, Augmented Reality Marketing (ARM) comes like a genie. ARM enables a distinct form of product or service visualisation by effortlessly), conveying virtual content (e.g., a virtual sofa) into the customer's view of the physical environment (e.g., their living room), reducing intangibility, increasing inspiration, and promising to enable innovative thinking in customers' purchase decisions (Jessen et al. 2020).

According to the Eclipse Report on "The Impact of Augmented Reality on Retail", 55% of the AR users said that using AR to shop makes the entire process more engaging and thrilling. Additionally, studies indicate that AR may customise marketing efforts by providing bespoke content based on user preferences and behaviour, resulting in a more appealing and focused marketing strategy. One can witness the presence of AR not only in the retail sector but also in the health care, defence, navigation, gaming, art, education, construction, and tourism sectors.

The Concept of Augmented Reality in Marketing

The ability of retailers to be available everywhere and at any time is yielding notable results in boosting profits. Augmented Reality (AR) is a game-changing technology recognised as an influential factor in this effort. Augmented Reality is created by overlaying computer-generated pictures on real-world photos. Augmented reality (AR) and virtual reality (VR) have emerged as rapidly developing technologies used in both physical and online retailing to enhance the selling environment and shopping experience (Bonetti et al. 2018). Augmented reality (AR) is a variant of Virtual Reality (VR) in which digital devices superimpose supplemental sensory information on the real-world environment, improving appearance, utility, and enjoyment and providing a more immersive interactive experience (Wedel et al. 2020).

People use the terms 'Virtual Reality' and 'Augmented Reality' interchangeably, even though they are different. Although it is commonly stated that augmented and virtual reality are closely related, there are some significant distinctions between them. Virtual reality is seventy-five per cent virtual and twenty-five per cent real. On the other hand, augmented reality is seventy-five per cent real and only twenty-five per cent virtual. Virtual reality often substitutes the real environment with a simulation, engaging users in a simulated or another reality. Augmented reality augments the current world, developing a mixed reality rather than replacing it (Rauschnabel et al. 2022). Augmented Reality aims to improve the user's perception of and interaction with the real environment. Users are completely enveloped in a digital world without being able to view the actual one, termed "virtual reality" or "virtual environment". AR usually only requires a smartphone and, occasionally, AR glasses. To truly enjoy the experience, the user does not need to clear the space because he or she will be completely aware of his or her surroundings.

AR is one of the promising technologies expected to create a new concept of retail stores where traditional and digital stores cooperate. AR technology is not a stand-alone notion; it is impacted and shaped by numerous industry actors (Liao 2015). Companies, organisations, and individuals involved in creating, manufacturing, and distributing AR technology are examples of such industry actors. With most customers interested in purchasing through AR and expecting it to change the way they shop—especially since most have devices capable of enabling these experiences—augmented reality has the potential to transform the shopping experience completely. By learning about consumers' preferences, usage patterns, and purchasing habits, trying new things, and embracing technology, brands may use augmented reality (AR) to improve customer engagement. The mixing of advertising with technology like augmented reality (AR) is sure to develop and retain interest among a younger target demographic, who are now the primary users of AR, according to a Global Web Index survey of 4,000 internet users. Therefore, from industrial fringes to mainstream technology, augmented reality is evolving in various ways and has entered various industrial sectors.

Augmented Reality Marketing (ARM) has been described as a strategic notion that integrates digital data or objects into the participant's perspective of the actual world, often in association with additional media, to disclose, articulate, or illustrate consumer value to achieve organisational goals (Rauschnabel et al. 2022). Strategic refers to an extensive, properly planned, resource-intensive, long-term set of activities. Rauschnabel et al. (n.d.) state that although the definition of an ARM campaign will alter over time, general aims, technology resources, skills, and long-term coordination with other strategies are all expected to be crucial to success. Customers may gain insight into products in augmented reality (AR) by connecting generic facts in real-time.

According to Tan et al. (2021), ARM can be implemented to accomplish a range of marketing and, ultimately, organisational goals in addition to producing sales. Blasco-Arcas et al. (2016) state that personalised suggestions, interactive product demonstrations, and other elements that improve the enjoyment and engagement of online shopping can be included in AR. The use of AR apps also impacts the brand attitude. When users are happy with an app, they are more likely to use it again and more often. Therefore, AR allows the user to create data about the real world and present them with previously gathered information (Farshid et al., 2018). Rauschnabel et al. (2019b) found that a high degree of inspiration, which arises from the high-quality and blending of virtual material into the consumer's understanding of the actual world, propels shifts in brand attitude. The hedonic advantages that the user receives from implementing the AR software act as a source of fuel for inspiration. However, utilitarian advantages play a significant role in determining how customers view augmented reality software.

Rauschnabel et al. (2019b) add that customers' opinions on an AR app that they find "boring" or "inefficiently designed" might have a detrimental impact on the brand's attitude in general. On the other hand, if users find an AR app to be "helpful", "entertaining", "engaging", and "designed effectively", these favourable reviews may create new associations and enhance the general perception of the business. Initiatives involving augmented reality should focus more on the user experience than technology (Scholz & Smith, 2016). At times, the activity determines how effective augmented reality is, and users will frequently evaluate it against their current shopping habits (Raska & Richter, 2017). Customer insights on distinctive, engaging, and worthwhile experiences made available by AR technologies should direct marketers' efforts.

Alkhamisi and Monowar (2013) describe in detail the AR system's four functions: scene extraction, scene identification to select the exact details to be boosted, scene processing, and augmented scene visual representation. There are two types of scene extraction technologies used in augmented reality: See-through devices, like head-mounted displays, acquire reality and layer augmented information, and video-through devices, which record reality in a different way than other kinds of gadgets like cameras and smartphones (López et al., 2010). There are two sorts of strategies for scene identification in reality augmentation: marker-based and non-marker-based (Grasset et al., 2012). Scene identification is a crucial action. A marker-based method locates virtual models in three dimensions by using visible tags in the actual world. The non-marker-based approach helps users locate digital material in the real world using tools like tagged AR browsers. The next scene processing is a technical procedure for locating the virtual model corresponding to a given marker's location in real space to be superimposed in an augmented reality app. The last function of Augmented Reality is augmented scene visual representation. The technology can create an image that blends actual space with a projected 3D object. After that, this image is projected into the scene, combining virtual and real-world aspects to create a visual depiction. McLean Wilson (2019) states that augmented reality attributes or characteristics significantly impact consumers' brand engagement and purchasing intent.

Characteristics of Augmented Reality

While augmented reality's characteristics produce various customer experiences like flow, sense of presence, and interactivity, these experiences through AR also lead to several advantages and disadvantages, which ultimately support decision-making and shape consumers' perceptions of the technology and brand (Barhorst et al., 2021). Because of its distinctive characteristics, augmented reality (AR) has become a game-changing tool that dissolves the old boundaries separating the real and virtual worlds and dramatically increases customer engagement.

i) Augmentation

Augmented reality (AR) offers immersive experiences that parallel or exceed traditional retail store and online purchasing experiences by bringing engaging product representations to customers wherever they are. According to Javornik (2016), augmentation is regarded as one of the essential distinguishing elements of AR, as AR can overlay real-world environments with the virtual world, producing immersion and seamless experiences like fun and enjoyment for users and eventually altering the cognitive and emotional states of customers.

Watson et al. (2018) emphasise that experiences with augmentation elicit a more pleasant emotional reaction than experiences without augmentation. The whole purchasing experience is improved by this visual component, which results in more knowledgeable and contented customers. The augmentation quality creates stimulation, resulting in a noticeable shift in brand attitude after implementing an AR app (in contrast to before). It is also an important aspect of the acceptance of AR apps. AR-driven platform augmentation offers a less expensive option to existing product trial services (such as free return regulations and sampling). It lets users get a feel for products online (Rosa et al., 2006). This benefit is particularly pertinent to consumer interactions with experiential items, including clothing, furniture, and cosmetics, primarily judged by fit and feel qualities.

ii) Interactivity

The consumer's confusion during a purchase increases the likelihood that a negotiation will be undefined by a lack of knowledge, little information, or the incapacity to know how to choose an item in particular, which increases the risk of tearing down the consumers' confidence (Gallardo et al., 2018). These issues within an organisation create a disconnect waiting for innovative strategies to reach the customer, creating curiosity and satisfaction for any particular product. AR has been described by Van Esch et al. (2019) as a technology with interactive features that allow marketers to digitally enhance vision, providing customers with entertainment and information. Interactivity is one such attribute of AR which influences retailers to adopt it and consumers to use it to gain as much information about the product as possible.

Steuer (1992) defines interactivity as "the degree to which users can participate in real-time modification of the form and subject matter of a mediated environment." AR technology can be used in fashion retail to provide customers with a virtual try-on that allows them to visualise the way a product of clothing might appear on them through a digital projection. Compared to non-AR eCommerce scenarios, AR eCommerce interactions are 200% more engaging (*23 Augmented Reality Statistics You Should Know in 2023*, n.d.). And the more time customers spend personalising and immersing themselves in the goods, the more inclined they are to purchase. For instance, buyers may try on various cosmetic looks before purchasing them using Sephora's Virtual Artist app. This allows users to be creative using various looks and determine which one best suits them. The ability for customers to actively engage, personalise how they communicate, and receive immediate access to information enhances the relevance and engagement of the marketing content.

A study of US and international customers by Deloitte Digital and Snap Inc. predicts that the number of worldwide users who frequently use augmented reality (AR) will increase from 1.5 billion to around 4.3 billion by 2025. Furthermore, the study shows that 76% of respondents anticipate using augmented reality (AR) as a useful tool in their daily lives, despite the fact that 65% of consumers said they use it for fun—the primary reason for AR use now.

iii) Sense of Presence

The sense of presence is thought to be a fundamental underlying component that explains how virtual encounters can be experienced as real. The "feeling of being spatially positioned in a different place and perceiving possibilities for action" is referred to as spatial presence (Wirth et al., 2007). AR allows customers to interact with products in real time, creating a sense of presence that may influence their purchasing decisions (Daassi & Debbabi, 2021). Smartphones and other mobile devices that can be used in a range of places that are both private as well as public are frequently employed to access augmented reality (Courtois et al., 2011).

Ahn et al. (2016) explain that the number of senses engaged by the entire experience and the amount of control one has over the experience determines the customer's level of presence. On the other hand, a non-AR app delivers a more indirect experience with the product (e.g., an image or clip of the product) with fewer possibilities for user involvement and sensory interaction. Previous research also found that when in contrast to other product display formats, AR resulted in an increased sense of spatial presence (or similar notions)(Smink et al., 2020). Consumers start to believe that the location of service experience is real and begin to feel as though they are trying on items in a real service interaction, for example, when customers try out sunglasses using AR. Scholz and Duffy (2018) point out that prominent companies such as Wayfair, Sephora, and IKEA have all released mobile augmented reality shopping apps that let users "try out" things virtually on physical bodies or even in their personal spaces.

iv) Vividness

The term "vividness" is used to describe "the capability of a technology to generate a sensorially rich mediated environment" (Steuer, 1992). According to research, increasing engagement and vividness of the interaction might increase enjoyment while purchasing online (Yim & Park, 2019). Vividness has an impact on customer engagement, thereby having an effect on the brand perception of the customers and one's purchase intention (Nikhashemi et al., 2021).

From the standpoint of technology (Yim et al., 2017), vividness is believed to be strengthened by increasing depth, which refers to the perceived quality of the represented information by media consumers, and breadth, which refers to the number of auditory dimensions a communication medium may give. AR can deliver more information and specifics about goods or services using a visually pleasing and easy-to-digest style. This informs clients and improves their overall experience, increasing their likelihood of engaging with the brand.

v) Personalisation

By offering highly personalised service, a very vivid experience, and related digital material, augmented reality (AR) enables customers to engage with both online and offline services via smart devices (Beck & Crié, 2018). Individualisation or personalisation fosters a closer, more customised relationship between the consumer and the brand. Customers' entire relationship with the company is strengthened, and their psychological connection is increased when they believe that the augmented reality experience is tailored just for them. Through personalisation, augmented reality experiences can be tailored according to user profiles, inclinations, and previous exchanges. Delivering information that corresponds with certain interests increases the likelihood that customers will find the experience interesting and relevant. For example, customers can also use customised options for augmented reality beauty applications to customise styles and makeup to their liking and discover related items, allowing them to create entertaining and joyful experiences (Hsu et al., 2021). Put another way, personalised augmented reality apps enhance customers' experiences consistently. When customers believe that the material connects directly to their preferences, they are more inclined to participate, which results in a more relevant and personalised customer journey.

vi) Media Quality

A well-designed augmented reality (AR) experience that includes realistic visual elements, dynamic animations, and images with excellent resolution increases user satisfaction. When the media quality makes the encounter smooth and engaging, users are more inclined to stay engaged for longer. Superior AR has the potential to set you out in a congested market. Companies that invest in high-quality media distinguish themselves from rivals by showcasing their dedication to innovation and excellence. Lower-quality AR content might be difficult to stand out in a crowded market. The quality of the presentation thus has an impact on the purchase decisions made by a customer (Flavin et al., 2017). As a result, vibrant product displays are more likely to affect customers' thinking processes since they are more engaging and encourage a more in-depth assessment of the information linked to the products than would be the case with pallid displays. Customers' opinions of how simple it is to use the technology are likely to be influenced by such precision, attention to detail, and well-defined presentation, which produce an appealing display of the real and virtual worlds (McLean & Wilson, 2019). Customers frequently perceive an enhanced information quality that influences their opinions of the technology's usefulness because of the augmented reality's clear and detailed nature and the ability to communicate with it by moving products around on the screen. At the same time, they are superimposed over real-world environments (Beck & Crié, 2018).

Augmented Reality throughout the Customer Journey

Visitors want a unique experience that fits their specific requirements and interests. Even small businesses can use technology to record individual buyers' preferences and tastes in order to create a more personalised buying experience. Brands that effectively utilise AR technology can develop unforgettable and compelling marketing campaigns that are well-received by their intended customer base. AR also plays a role in influencing how individuals feel about their decisions to buy a particular product. Mobile augmented reality (AR) apps in shopping malls are expected to significantly boost customers' confidence in buying and the joy they experience throughout the process. At the same time, AR provides them with greater ease while making online purchases. Hilken et al. (2017) point out that customers can use augmented reality to see how things fit them individually or in their surroundings while still enjoying the comfort of online purchases. AR not only guides customers but also improves their overall shopping experience, making them more likely to engage with the brand. A customer's journey begins with the need awareness and continues through the stages of initial assessment, persistent evaluation, purchase, and post-purchase (Kietzmann et al., 2018). Throughout the pre-purchase, purchase, and post-purchase stages, consumers are subjected to various experiences that influence their customer engagement (Romano et al., 2020).

i) Pre-Purchase Stage of Customer Journey

Hauser (2014) has reported that consumers' initial considerations for every purchase are determined by their impressions of and familiarity with the product category. At this pre-purchase, when AR is implemented, the scenario gets altered. For example, AR virtual try-on broadens the range of designs and styles customers consider. Consumers are more open to trying new things and looking when shopping in the comfort of their homes. Customers can alter their image and try out different looks with AR, keeping them engaged throughout the process (Romano et al., 2020b). They do not feel pressured by others' opinions and judgements when they are in the comfort of their own homes and are more willing to test new designs with augmented reality.

Through AR, consumers can extend their comfort zone and broaden their scope of contemplation by doing away with social standards and judgement. This attitude makes the customers more willing to test out unusual brands where they want to evaluate the product and collect as much new information as possible sitting in their comfort zone. Consumers are more interested in style than brand when employing augmented reality (AR) for virtual try-ons. Therefore, reputable brands may need to update their style and appearance (Pantano et al., 2017).

ii) Purchase Point of Customer Journey

By decreasing the overload of options and confusion, enhancing choice confidence, and giving consumers a sense of certainty about their product selection, augmented reality can benefit consumers. Because augmented reality (AR) lets customers see various things without having to try them on physically, it lessens the work involved in the purchasing experience. One of the main advantages of utilising augmented reality (AR) at the stage of purchase is playfulness, which increases customer satisfaction and engagement. AR offers an enjoyable and captivating experience that helps break up the monotony of online purchasing. But AR's initial effect might fade eventually, striking the right balance between the perceived fun and utility. According to Kang et al. (2020) findings, because augmented reality was new, users were open to trying it. Still, any immediate improvement in customer experience might not have intrinsic value over the span of time. Once the initial attraction and playfulness wear off, the extent to which AR Technology is changing, and the customer experience is probably going to diminish. However, the impact of augmented reality during the customer journey does not stop as soon as the purchase has been made.

iii) Post-Purchase Stage of Customer Journey

Customers tend to be satisfied with both the product and the brand when the product they have purchased lives up to their expectations based on perceived quality in marketing. They also tend to share eWOM about their experiences with the products, including opinions regarding how they like them and usage parameters ("How Digital Technologies Reshape and Transform Marketing: The Participation of Augmented Reality in Brand Loyalty Building," 2022d). Positive word-of-mouth and subsequent purchase intents are expected to increase online conversion rates, stop virtual abandonment of shopping carts (Janakiraman et al., 2016), and prevent web rooming (i.e., the practice of buyers researching about the products online before making in-person purchases). AR can be employed to create interactive product demonstrations and manuals for users. Customers can use augmented reality (AR) to get detailed instructions instead of reading a standard handbook, making it much simpler to set it up and use the product efficiently. Customers may display their recent purchases engagingly and dynamically by sharing AR experiences on social media. These user-generated materials may act as effective brand ambassadors.

Marketers Using Augmented Reality Across the World

AR has simplified the digital signage process and demonstrated its efficacy in drawing in customers and boosting revenue. Every day, a new corporation declares its desire to invest in augmented reality. Scholz and Smith (2016) state that marketing designers can create augmented reality material that gives viewers enough time and room to immerse themselves in the story of the encounter. One way to do this is to have AR material from the user's perspective.

IKEA Place is an AR (augmented reality) app unveiled in September 2017 by the company. It allows users to explore, experiment, and share how well-designed spaces, such as homes, offices, schools, or studios, can be transformed (*Launch of New IKEA Place App – IKEA Global*, n.d.). Every item at IKEA Place, from coffee tables to couches and armchairs, is 3D printed and accurate in size, ensuring that every selection is the ideal combination of form, function, and size. Being one of the first house furnishings companies in the world to provide this technology to consumers, IKEA is changing how we buy furniture going forward. With a promising accuracy rate of 98%, the app adjusts products based on the room's measurements. It would relieve not only the difficulty of buying furniture but also the trouble of returning pieces that do not fit. IKEA establishes a service-centred dimension with this free app by indicating that it recognises the difficulties associated with furniture purchasing and provides assistance (Öztürkcan, 2020). Customers can choose which furniture to purchase with the help of the IKEA Place App, which protects them from undesirable outcomes. In order to achieve this, furniture buyers can use the app to digitally fill their spaces with about 2,000 items and accessories from the IKEA catalogue. The well-organised and lucid IKEA website has been commended for offering easy access to a wealth of product information. According to a study by Stumpp et al. (2019), most test subjects expressed amazement at how lifelike the virtual items in the environment appeared. "How fast and easy it is to learn the application and plan the room before buying" delighted the test subjects.

Flipkart is also developing new ideas to improve the mobile shopping experience. Integrating technology such as augmented reality (AR) and visual browsing allows consumers to virtually test things before making a purchase, which helps them make better-educated selections (Balaji, et al.,2023). This will enable the customers to differentiate it from its competitors.

Manufacturers and automobile industry suppliers are also constantly looking for fresh approaches to give customers a more engaging and pleasant driving experience (Rao et al., 2014). Omni-commerce is already starting to influence car buying (Panel, 2020). These days, buyers can peruse automobiles, complete a transaction, and obtain financing without ever setting foot in a showroom. For example, Volkswagen's designers always search for new ways to set their cars apart from the competition and enhance the driving experience (*Lessons Learned: Volkswagen Shares Best Practices in Augmented Reality*, 2023). Volkswagen consumers enjoy more and more feature-rich driving comforts as their cars become more technologically advanced. Interactive brochures and virtual test drives are available from Volkswagen. Consumers can explore Volkswagen automobiles and discover their characteristics more engagingly by using augmented reality (AR) applications. Similarly, with the introduction of the BMW X5 xDrive45e M, BMW Malaysia has launched a comprehensive augmented reality (AR) experience that lets users explore the car whenever and wherever they want (*BMW et al. on AR Experience for Consumers to Explore New Car*, 2020). BMW debuted its first virtual showroom in 2017. Through an augmented reality smartphone app, prospective customers could examine up-close 3D representations of BMW vehicles and engage in a special interactive experience. The list does not end here. Porsche released the "Mission E Augmented Reality" app in 2018. iOS and Android cellphones can download and make use of it for free. Businesses market their electric sports cars using this augmented reality application (Morozova & Morozova, 2019). Users of the AR app can consider the car's design and learn more about it with 3D visualisation in the "Explore" mode. Additionally, users can experience an exhilarating, immersive augmented reality test drive in the "Drive" mode. Hyundai's Virtual Guide app teaches car owners how to do routine servicing using augmented reality (Tan et al., 2021).

Augmented Reality has also been used in the cosmetic industry. One such example is that of L'Oreal. By means of its Makeup Genius app, L'Oreal has been employing augmented reality to enhance the makeup-buying experience for its customers (*L'Oreal Improving Customer Experience With Augmented Reality*, 2023). With the use of real-time facial scans and the app, users may virtually test on foundation and lipstick hues. Nowadays, consumers don't even need to leave their houses to access a wide range of products. Additionally, the business has developed a Virtual Try-On Experience tool that combines picture processing and face recognition software to enable clients to match their appearance with a range of products precisely. Clients only need to snap a selfie or upload an image, and the system will determine which hue and product would look best on them. Belonging to the same industry using Google Search technology, the upscale clothing company Burberry unveiled a new augmented reality shopping tool. Customers may now search for specific Burberry products with Google Search on their cellphones to experience augmented reality.

When we move on to the apparel industry, one can think of Nike and its implementation of Augmented Reality for marketing campaigns. With Nike augmented reality experience, users can quickly change the colour of a real white shoe. This new technological advancement results from a collaboration between SmartPixels, a French business specialising in augmented retail programmes, and Nike's online NikeID customisation service.

Future of Augmented Reality Marketing

The future of online retail marketing using augmented reality (AR) is assured. With augmented reality (AR) technology, marketers can produce interactive experiences that blur the lines between the real and virtual worlds, offering a distinctive, captivating and engaging method for promoting goods and services. Real-time visual encounters and interactive methods are created by integrating AR with traditional and cultural content in various dialects (Nanda, 2023). In order to thrive in the realm of augmented reality e-commerce, entrepreneurs must have a creative mindset when it comes to customer engagement. After all, the success and engagement of the final user experience are largely determined by integrating AR technologies into one's website. The originality of augmented reality generates eagerness in its application (*Augmented Reality Advertising*, n.d.). With AR, each of the ads one creates can directly converse with customers. AR ads improve the percentage of people who click through to purchase by 33 per cent, increase engagement rates by 20 per cent, and hold viewers' attention for more than 85 seconds.

As augmented reality continues to evolve, its role in determining the foreseeable future of customer interactions will become increasingly important. More factual and experimental research and case studies are required to evaluate the theoretical framework and analyse the Practical implications of deploying AR in various industry scenarios. Furthermore, other technologies utilised for augmented reality, such as the interface for users, storage, power for processing, and memory card space, need to be upgraded to a higher degree for a generation highly tech-savvy in order for augmented reality to be fully adaptive (Ng & Ramasamy, 2018).

As given by Sifted (2022), augmented reality may be used in almost any industry, it is anticipated that by 2024, there will be 1.73 billion mobile AR users, increasing the yearly growth rate of augmented reality to 76% in India. Alkhamisi and Monowar (2013b) have pointed out that even while augmented reality (AR) is widely employed in the consumer sector—for instance, in social engagement, amusement, and marketing—new applications for it are being developed on a daily basis. Similar to other marketing tools, augmented reality provides precise, quantifiable data. This helps the retailers keep a check on who visited their websites or product sites and how long they stayed engaged through the process.

Accordingly, the retailers can implement changes or personalise the whole system according to the needs of the hour. A business card with a QR code can be scanned by the customer's smartphone to take them to a website that offers a WebAR experience. This can make the business card an interactive, lively, three-dimensional marketing tool for your company. Additionally, augmented reality business cards could provide connections to one's company website and a product demonstration (*Augmented Reality Business Cards Demo: Use AR for Brand Promotion & Advertising*, 2023). Collaborative purchasing experiences, in which users engage with the same augmented reality piece simultaneously from multiple places, could be made easier by AR. For communal decision-making or online purchasing parties, this could be especially helpful. Companies can create augmented reality shopping apps that use the camera on the device to superimpose promotions, prices, and product details onto real goods. This real-time information empowers Customers with instant details, which helps them make better-informed purchase decisions.

Like any other tool, even augmented reality has its limitations and challenges. Even if ARM can give an organisation a meaningful view on customer preferences because of the personally identifiable data obtained, it can be invasive and harmful, with no rules yet in place to ensure that people's privacy is not compromised (Dwivedi et al., 2021). ARM seems to be more effective for younger consumers, while the elderly have more established consuming habits (Rauschnabel, 2021). However, age can be a barrier to implementing AR technology on products or in commerce. On the other hand, individuals with higher levels of technological anxiety tend to hesitate in trying out augmented reality in an uncertainty of safety of personal information involved (Meuter et al., 2003).

CONCLUSION

The main goal of using Augmented Reality Marketing (ARM) is to make the consumer journey more engaging across all channels, while businesses are developing strategies to drive conversions through the internet and mobile channels. By providing immersive and engaging experiences at several touch-points, augmented reality (AR) has the potential to improve customer engagement across every step of the customer journey. Augmented reality is a game-changing technology that combines the real and digital worlds, opening new avenues for client connection. Heller et al. (2019) state that augmented reality makes customers more at ease when making online purchases. The distinct qualities of augmented reality (AR) have completely changed the way that companies interact with their target consumers, from the early phases of recognition and thought to the key stages of purchase and beyond. It is recommended that users invest in applications that use AR to bring about a shift in the way customers think about the given product because AR particularly leads to benefits throughout the online buying experience (rather than simply providing a photo of the consumers' faces) (Xu et al., 2024).

If a brand manager realises that customers are more cognitively engaged, he or she can devise strategies to boost emotional involvement so that consumers seem more driven and enthusiastic about the brand. Understanding the roles of different actors in the engagement process allows marketers to tailor engagement techniques to specific actors in the network (Pinto & Loureiro, 2020). Marketers may create a more individualised and engaging experience when a client makes a purchase by adopting augmented reality (AR). This will increase customer satisfaction and increase the possibility of repeat business and favourable word-of-mouth recommendations. As a commonplace advertising strategy, brands will continue to use augmented reality, enabling customers to actively participate in commercials that they find enjoyable, captivating, and eye-catching. Ultimately, this will raise consumer awareness of the brand, encourage a higher product conversion rate, boost revenues, and help enhance customer-retailer relationships.

Therefore, integrating the digital and physical spheres throughout the customer journey creates a synergistic alliance that propels businesses into a new era where customer involvement is a dynamic storyline constantly evolving, augmented to engage and capture each individual.

REFERENCES

Ahn, S. J., Bostick, J., Ogle, E., Nowak, K. L., McGillicuddy, K. T., & Bailenson, J. N. (2016). Experiencing nature: Embodying animals in immersive virtual environments increases inclusion of nature in self and involvement with nature. *Journal of Computer-Mediated Communication*, *21*(6), 399–419. doi:10.1111/jcc4.12173

Alkhamisi, A. O., & Monowar, M. M. (2013). Rise of augmented Reality: Current and future application areas. *International Journal of Internet and Distributed System*, *01*(04), 25–34. doi:10.4236/ijids.2013.14005

Alvarez-Milán, A., Felix, R., Rauschnabel, P. A., & Hinsch, C. (2018). Strategic customer engagement marketing: A decision making framework. *Journal of Business Research*, *92*, 61–70. doi:10.1016/j.jbusres.2018.07.017

Augmented Reality advertising. (n.d.). https://www.flippar.com/ar-advertising.html

Augmented Reality Business Cards demo: Use AR for brand promotion & advertising. (2023, November 6). MobiDev. https://mobidev.biz/blog/augmented-reality-business-card-development

Augmented Reality in Ecommerce: How Does it Work? (n.d.). BigCommerce. https://www.bigcommerce.com/articles/ecommerce/ecommerce-augmented-reality/

Augmented Reality statistics you should know in 2023. (n.d.). https://www.threekit.com/23-augmented-reality-statistics-you-should-know-in-2023

Balaji, K., & Rao, P. S. (2023). Unravelling success: A case study on Flipkart's e-commerce journey. *Commerce, Economics & Management*, 43.

Barari, M., Ross, M., Thaichon, P., & Surachartkumtonkun, J. (2020). A meta-analysis of customer engagement behaviour. *International Journal of Consumer Studies*, *45*(4), 457–477. doi:10.1111/ijcs.12609

Barhorst, J. B., McLean, G., Shah, E. D., & Mack, R. W. (2021). Blending the real world and the virtual world: Exploring the role of flow in augmented reality experiences. *Journal of Business Research*, *122*, 423–436. doi:10.1016/j.jbusres.2020.08.041

Beck, M., & Crié, D. (2018). I virtually try it . . . I want it! Virtual Fitting Room: A tool to increase on-line and off-line exploratory behavior, patronage and purchase intentions. *Journal of Retailing and Consumer Services*, *40*, 279–286. doi:10.1016/j.jretconser.2016.08.006

Blasco-Arcas, L., Ortega, B. H., & Martínez, J. J. (2016). Engagement platforms. *Journal of Service Theory and Practice*, *26*(5), 559–589. doi:10.1108/JSTP-12-2014-0286

BMW MY starts ignition on AR experience for consumers to explore new car. (2020, July 22). Marketing-Interactive. https://www.marketing-interactive.com/bmw-my-starts-ignition-on-ar-experience-for-consumers-to-explore-new-car

Bolton, R. N., McColl-Kennedy, J. R., Cheung, L., Gallan, A., Orsingher, C., Witell, L., & Zaki, M. (2018). Customer experience challenges: Bringing together digital, physical and social realms. *Journal of Service Management*, *29*(5), 776–808. doi:10.1108/JOSM-04-2018-0113

Bonetti, F., Warnaby, G., & Quinn, L. (2018). *Augmented Reality and Virtual Reality in Physical and Online Retailing: A Review, Synthesis and Research Agenda*. doi:10.1007/978-3-319-64027-3_9

Brodie, R. J., Hollebeek, L. D., Jurić, B., & Ilić, A. (2011). Customer engagement. *Journal of Service Research*, *14*(3), 252–271. doi:10.1177/1094670511411703

Brodie, R. J., Ilić, A., Jurić, B., & Hollebeek, L. D. (2013). Consumer engagement in a virtual brand community: An exploratory analysis. *Journal of Business Research*, *66*(1), 105–114. doi:10.1016/j.jbusres.2011.07.029

Courtois, C., Mechant, P., Paulussen, S., & De Marez, L. (2011). The triple articulation of media technologies in teenage media consumption. *New Media & Society*, *14*(3), 401–420. doi:10.1177/1461444811415046

Daassi, M., & Debbabi, S. (2021). Intention to reuse AR-based apps: The combined role of the sense of immersion, product presence and perceived realism. *Information & Management*, *58*(4), 103453. doi:10.1016/j.im.2021.103453

Deloitte. (n.d.-a). *Augmented reality in retail transforms consumer experience*. Deloitte United States. https://www2.deloitte.com/us/en/pages/technology/articles/augmented-reality-retail-vcommerce.html

Deloitte. (n.d.-b). *Snap Consumer AR Global Report 2021*. deloitte.com. Retrieved March 19, 2021, from https://www2.deloitte.com/content/dam/Deloitte/xe/Documents/About-Deloitte/Snap%20Consumer%20AR_Global%20Report_2021.pdf

Dwivedi, Y. K., Ismagilova, E., Hughes, D. L., Carlson, J., Filieri, R., Jacobson, J., Jain, V., Karjaluoto, H., Kéfi, H., Krishen, A. S., Kumar, V., Rahman, M. M., Raman, R., Rauschnabel, P. A., Rowley, J., Salo, J., Tran, G. A., & Wang, Y. (2021). Setting the future of digital and social media marketing research: Perspectives and research propositions. *International Journal of Information Management*, *59*, 102168. doi:10.1016/j.ijinfomgt.2020.102168

E-commerce in India: industry overview, market size & growth. (n.d.-a). India Brand Equity Foundation. https://www.ibef.org/industry/ecommerce

Farshid, M., Paschen, J., Eriksson, T., & Keitzmann, J. H. (2018). Go boldly! *Business Horizons*, *61*(5), 657–663. doi:10.1016/j.bushor.2018.05.009

Flavin, C., Gurrea, R., & Ors, C. (2017). The influence of online product presentation videos on persuasion and purchase channel preference: The role of imagery fluency and need for touch. *Telematics and Informatics*, *34*(8), 1544–1556. doi:10.1016/j.tele.2017.07.002

Gallardo, C., Rodríguez, S. P., Chango, I. E., Quevedo, W. X., Santana, J., Acosta, A. G., Tapia, J. C., & Andaluz, V. H. (2018). Augmented reality as a new marketing strategy. In Lecture Notes in Computer Science (pp. 351–362). doi:10.1007/978-3-319-95270-3_29

Gauri. (2022). Digital Marketing vs. Traditional Marketing- A Comparative view. *International Journal of Research in Engineering and Science, 10*(5), 2320–9364. https://www.semanticscholar.org/paper/Digital-Marketing-Vs.-Traditional-Marketing-A-View-Prof.Gauri-Kalmegh/bcccc88f1d223eaaee2ed-8928beaffb5f7a51594

Grasset, R., Langlotz, T., Kalkofen, D., Tatzgern, M., & Schmalstieg, D. (2012). Image-driven view management for augmented reality browsers. *IEEE International Symposium on Mixed and Augmented Reality (ISMAR)*. 10.1109/ISMAR.2012.6402555

Harms, T., & Rindone, S. (2022, April 1). *When experience defines how consumers buy, what will retailers sell?* https://www.ey.com/en_in/consumer-products-retail/the-retail-space-of-the-future

Hauser, J. R. (2014). Consideration-set heuristics. *Journal of Business Research, 67*(8), 1688–1699. doi:10.1016/j.jbusres.2014.02.015

Heller, J., Chylinski, M., De Ruyter, K., Mahr, D., & Keeling, D. I. (2019). Touching the Untouchable: Exploring Multi-Sensory Augmented Reality in the context of online Retailing. *Journal of Retailing, 95*(4), 219–234. doi:10.1016/j.jretai.2019.10.008

Hilken, T., De Ruyter, K., Chylinski, M., Mahr, D., & Keeling, D. I. (2017). Augmenting the eye of the beholder: Exploring the strategic potential of augmented reality to enhance online service experiences. *Journal of the Academy of Marketing Science, 45*(6), 884–905. doi:10.1007/s11747-017-0541-x

How Digital technologies reshape and transform marketing: The participation of Augmented Reality in brand loyalty building. (2022d). *Academic Journal of Business & Management, 4*(9). doi:10.25236/AJBM.2022.040904

Hsu, S. H., Tsou, H., & Chen, J. (2021). "Yes, we do. Why not use augmented reality?" customer responses to experiential presentations of AR-based applications. *Journal of Retailing and Consumer Services, 62*, 102649. doi:10.1016/j.jretconser.2021.102649

Jaakkola, E., & Alexander, M. (2014). The role of customer engagement Behavior in Value Co-Creation. *Journal of Service Research, 17*(3), 247–261. doi:10.1177/1094670514529187

Janakiraman, N., Syrdal, H. A., & Freling, R. (2016). The Effect of return policy leniency on consumer purchase and return decisions: A meta-analytic review. *Journal of Retailing, 92*(2), 226–235. doi:10.1016/j.jretai.2015.11.002

Javornik, A. (2016). Augmented reality: Research agenda for studying the impact of its media characteristics on consumer behaviour. *Journal of Retailing and Consumer Services, 30*, 252–261. doi:10.1016/j.jretconser.2016.02.004

Jessen, A., Hilken, T., Chylinski, M., Mahr, D., Heller, J., Keeling, D. I., & De Ruyter, K. (2020). The playground effect: How augmented reality drives creative customer engagement. *Journal of Business Research, 116*, 85–98. doi:10.1016/j.jbusres.2020.05.002

Kang, H. J., Shin, J., & Ponto, K. (2020). How 3D virtual reality stores can shape consumer purchase decisions: The roles of informativeness and playfulness. *Journal of Interactive Marketing, 49*(1), 70–85. doi:10.1016/j.intmar.2019.07.002

Kietzmann, J., Paschen, J., & Treen, E. (2018). Artificial intelligence in advertising. *Journal of Advertising Research, 58*(3), 263–267. doi:10.2501/JAR-2018-035

L'Oreal improving customer experience with augmented reality. (2023, October 12). Intuji. https://intuji.com/loreal-customer-experience-augmented-reality/

Launch of new IKEA Place app – IKEA Global. (n.d.). IKEA. https://www.ikea.com/global/en/newsroom/innovation/ikea-launches-ikea-place-a-new-app-that-allows-people-to-virtually-place-furniture-in-their-home-170912/

Lee, Y. J., Yang, S., & Johnson, Z. (2017). Need for touch and two-way communication in e-commerce. *Journal of Research in Interactive Marketing, 11*(4), 341–360. doi:10.1108/JRIM-04-2016-0035

Lessons learned: Volkswagen shares best practices in augmented reality. (2023, September 11). PTC. https://www.ptc.com/en/blogs/corporate/volkswagen-best-practices-in-augmented-reality

Liao, T. (2014). Augmented or admented reality? The influence of marketing on augmented reality technologies. *Information Communication and Society*, *18*(3), 310–326. doi:10.1080/1369118X.2014.989252

López, H. A., Navarro, A., & Relaño, J. (2010). An Analysis of Augmented Reality Systems. *Fifth International Multi-Conference on Computing in the Global Information Technology (ICCGI 2010)*. doi:10.1109/ICCGI.2010.24

Mazurek-Łopacińska, K., & Sobocińska, M. (2021). Social media in marketing activities of enterprises in the light of the analysis of empirical research results. *European Research Studies*, *XXIV*(4B), 647–658. doi:10.35808/ersj/2695

McLean, G., & Wilson, A. (2019). Shopping in the digital world: Examining customer engagement through augmented reality mobile applications. *Computers in Human Behavior*, *101*, 210–224. doi:10.1016/j.chb.2019.07.002

Mehta, R., & Kaushik, N. (2015). A Study of Emerging Trends in Brand Engagement through Digital Marketing. *Journal of Marketing & Communication, 11*(2). doi:10.1177/1094670511414582

Meuter, M. L., Ostrom, A. L., Bitner, M. J., & Roundtree, R. I. (2003). The influence of technology anxiety on consumer use and experiences with self-service technologies. *Journal of Business Research*, *56*(11), 899–906. doi:10.1016/S0148-2963(01)00276-4

Morozova, A., & Morozova, A. (2019, January 24). *How augmented reality will change driving and car manufacturing.* https://jasoren.com/ar-in-automotive/#:~:text=In%202017%2C%20BMW%20launched%20its,experience%20of%20interacting%20with%20them

Nanda, K. (2023, July 2). *Impact of Augmented reality on marketing Experience.* https://india.gaee.org/2023/07/02/impact-of-augmented-reality-on-marketing-experience/

Neslin, S. A. (2022). The omnichannel continuum: Integrating online and offline channels along the customer journey. *Journal of Retailing*, *98*(1), 111–132. doi:10.1016/j.jretai.2022.02.003

New Epsilon research indicates 80% of consumers are more likely to make a purchase when brands offer personalized experiences. (n.d.). https://www.epsilon.com/us/about-us/pressroom/new-epsilon-research-indicates-80-of-consumers-are-more-likely-to-make-a-purchase-when-brands-offer-personalized-experiences

Ng, C. C., & Ramasamy, C. (2018). Augmented reality marketing in Malaysia—Future scenarios. *Social Sciences (Basel, Switzerland)*, *7*(11), 224. doi:10.3390/socsci7110224

Nikhashemi, S. R., Knight, H. H., Nusair, K., & Liat, C. B. (2021). Augmented reality in smart retailing: A (n) (A) Symmetric Approach to continuous intention to use retail brands' mobile AR apps. *Journal of Retailing and Consumer Services*, *60*, 102464. doi:10.1016/j.jretconser.2021.102464

Panel, E. (2020, September 4). 10 Industries likely to benefit from AR/VR Marketing. *Forbes*. https://www.forbes.com/sites/forbesagencycouncil/2020/09/04/10-industries-likely-to-benefit-from-arvr-marketing/?sh=30c66ffe2ed2

Pantano, E., Rese, A., & Baier, D. (2017). Enhancing the online decision-making process by using augmented reality: A two country comparison of youth markets. *Journal of Retailing and Consumer Services*, *38*, 81–95. doi:10.1016/j.jretconser.2017.05.011

Paruthi, M., & Kaur, H. (2017, April 3). Scale Development and Validation for Measuring Online Engagement. *Journal of Internet Commerce*, *16*(2), 127–147. doi:10.1080/15332861.2017.1299497

Pinto, F. R., & Loureiro, S. M. C. (2020). The growing complexity of customer engagement: A systematic review. *EuroMed Journal of Business*, *15*(2), 167–203. doi:10.1108/EMJB-10-2019-0126

Popovici, V., Silvia, M., & Lavinia, P. A. (2018). Traditional versus Online Marketing for B2B Organizations: Where the Line Blurs. *DOAJ (DOAJ: Directory of Open Access Journals)*. https://doaj.org/article/652a6b475e004407a7e1ec47655d60e1

Rajagopal, R. (2022). Impact of retailing technology during business shutdown. *Marketing Intelligence & Planning*, *40*(4), 441–459. doi:10.1108/MIP-08-2021-0255

Rao, Q., Tropper, T., Grünler, C., Hammori, M., & Chakraborty, S. (2014). AR-IVI — Implementation of In-Vehicle Augmented Reality. *IEEE International Symposium on Mixed and Augmented Reality 2014 Science and Technology Proceedings*. https://doi.org/10.1109/ISMAR.2014.6948402

Raska, K., & Richter, T. (2017). Influence of Augmented Reality on Purchase Intention : The IKEA Case [Major in Business Administration]. *Jönköping University*. Retrieved May 22, 2017, from http://hj.diva-portal.org/smash/record.jsf?pid=diva2:1115470

Rasool, A., Shah, F. A., & Islam, J. U. (2020). Customer engagement in the digital age: A review and research agenda. *Current Opinion in Psychology*, *36*, 96–100. doi:10.1016/j.copsyc.2020.05.003 PMID:32599394

Rauschnabel, P. A. (2021). Augmented reality is eating the real-world! The substitution of physical products by holograms. *International Journal of Information Management*, *57*, 102279. doi:10.1016/j.ijinfomgt.2020.102279

Rauschnabel, P. A., Babin, B. J., Dieck, M. C. T., Krey, N., & Jung, T. (2022, March). What is augmented reality marketing? Its definition, complexity, and future. *Journal of Business Research*, *142*, 1140–1150. doi:10.1016/j.jbusres.2021.12.084

Rauschnabel, P. A., Felix, R., & Hinsch, C. (2019). Augmented reality marketing: How mobile AR-apps can improve brands through inspiration. *Journal of Retailing and Consumer Services*, *49*, 43–53. doi:10.1016/j.jretconser.2019.03.004

Romano, B., Sands, S., & Pallant, J. (2020). Augmented reality and the customer journey: An exploratory study. *Australasian Marketing Journal*, *29*(4), 354–363. doi:10.1016/j.ausmj.2020.06.010

Rosa, J. A., Garbarino, E., & Malter, A. J. (2006). Keeping the body in mind: The influence of body esteem and body boundary aberration on consumer beliefs and purchase intentions. *Journal of Consumer Psychology*, *16*(1), 79–91. doi:10.1207/s15327663jcp1601_10

Scholz, J., & Duffy, K. (2018). We ARe at home: How augmented reality reshapes mobile marketing and consumer-brand relationships. *Journal of Retailing and Consumer Services, 44*, 11–23. doi:10.1016/j.jretconser.2018.05.004

Scholz, J., & Smith, A. (2016). Augmented reality: Designing immersive experiences that maximize consumer engagement. *Business Horizons, 59*(2), 149–161. doi:10.1016/j.bushor.2015.10.003

Shotwell, L. (2023, December 20). *7 Retail Technology Innovations Reviving the stores in 2024*. MobiDev. https://mobidev.biz/blog/7-technology-trends-to-change-retail-industry

Sifted. (2022, October 7). *The future of augmented reality in four charts | Sifted*. Sifted. https://sifted.eu/articles/future-augmented-reality-data-brnd

Smink, A. R., Van Reijmersdal, E. A., Van Noort, G., & Neijens, P. (2020). Shopping in augmented reality: The effects of spatial presence, personalization and intrusiveness on app and brand responses. *Journal of Business Research, 118*, 474–485. doi:10.1016/j.jbusres.2020.07.018

Steuer, J. (1992). Defining virtual reality: Dimensions determining telepresence. *Journal of Communication, 42*(4), 73–93. doi:10.1111/j.1460-2466.1992.tb00812.x

Stumpp, S., Knopf, T., & Michelis, D. (2019, September). User experience design with augmented reality (AR). In *Proceedings of the ECIE 2019 14th European conference on innovation and entrepreneurship* (pp. 1032-1040). Academic Press.

Tan, Y. C., Chandukala, S. R., & Reddy, S. K. (2021). Augmented reality in retail and its impact on sales. *Journal of Marketing, 86*(1), 48–66. doi:10.1177/0022242921995449

The impact of augmented Reality on retail | Retail Perceptions. (n.d.). http://www.retailperceptions.com/2016/10/the-impact-of-augmented-reality-on-retail/

Urdea, A., & Constantin, C. (2021). Experts' perspective on the development of Experiential Marketing Strategy: Implementation steps, benefits, and challenges. *Journal of Risk and Financial Management, 14*(10), 502. doi:10.3390/jrfm14100502

Van Esch, P., Arli, D., Gheshlaghi, M. H., Andonopoulos, V., Von Der Heidt, T., & Northey, G. (2019). Anthropomorphism and augmented reality in the retail environment. *Journal of Retailing and Consumer Services, 49*, 35–42. doi:10.1016/j.jretconser.2019.03.002

Watson, A., Alexander, B., & Salavati, L. (2018). The impact of experiential augmented reality applications on fashion purchase intention. *International Journal of Retail & Distribution Management, 48*(5), 433–451. doi:10.1108/IJRDM-06-2017-0117

Wedel, M., Bigné, E., & Zhang, J. (2020). Virtual and augmented reality: Advancing research in consumer marketing. *International Journal of Research in Marketing, 37*(3), 443–465. doi:10.1016/j.ijresmar.2020.04.004

What is omnichannel marketing? (2022, August 17). McKinsey & Company. https://www.mckinsey.com/featured-insights/mckinsey-explainers/what-is-omnichannel-marketing

Wirth, W., Hartmann, T., Böcking, S., Vorderer, P., Klimmt, C., Schramm, H., Saari, T., Laarni, J., Ravaja, N., Gouveia, F. R., Biocca, F., Sacau, A., Jäncke, L., Baumgärtner, T., & Jäncke, P. (2007). A process model of the formation of spatial presence experiences. *Media Psychology*, *9*(3), 493–525. doi:10.1080/15213260701283079

Xu, X., Jia, Q., & Tayyab, S. M. U. (2024). Exploring the stimulating role of augmented reality features in E-commerce: A three-staged hybrid approach. *Journal of Retailing and Consumer Services*, *77*, 103682. doi:10.1016/j.jretconser.2023.103682

Yim, M. Y., Chu, S., & Sauer, P. (2017). Is augmented reality technology an effective tool for e-commerce? An interactivity and vividness perspective. *Journal of Interactive Marketing*, *39*, 89–103. doi:10.1016/j.intmar.2017.04.001

Yim, M. Y., & Park, S. (2019). I am not satisfied with my body, so I like augmented reality (AR). *Journal of Business Research*, *100*, 581–589. doi:10.1016/j.jbusres.2018.10.041

Chapter 10
Webrooming:
Bridging the Digital Divide in Customer Engagement

Sahil Kohli

https://orcid.org/0000-0002-3792-988X
Chandigarh University, India

Rishi Prakash Shukla
Chandigarh University, India

Piyush Samant
MiRXES Lab, Singapore

ABSTRACT

This chapter explores the evolving phenomenon of webrooming in the retail landscape. It delves into how technological advancements and changing consumer behaviors are reshaping the way customers engage with both online and offline retail environments. It highlights the importance of a seamless omnichannel strategy, addressing the synergy between digital browsing and physical purchasing. The chapter also emphasizes the role of personalization, customer experience, and sustainable practices in appealing to webroomers. Through a comprehensive analysis, it offers insights into how retailers can effectively harness webrooming to enhance customer engagement and drive sales, navigating the complexities of modern retail.

INTRODUCTION

The evolution of customer engagement has witnessed a transformative journey, particularly catalysed by the rapid advancements in technology and the dynamic shifts in consumer behaviours. Amidst these changes, one phenomenon has steadily risen to prominence, capturing significant attention in the realms of retail and consumer research: webrooming.

DOI: 10.4018/979-8-3693-2367-0.ch010

To comprehend the importance of webrooming in contemporary markets, it is essential to examine the wider spectrum of customer engagement strategies. Traditionally, engaging with customers was predominantly a physical interaction, confined to the spatial and temporal boundaries of brick-and-mortar establishments. However, the emergence and proliferation of the internet and digital technologies signalled a paradigm shift. Consumers were suddenly liberated from the constraints of store hours and locations; the digital marketplace ushered in an era of unparalleled convenience and choice.

This digital revolution not only altered the locales of shopping; it fundamentally transformed the shopping process itself. The mid-1990s marked this turning point with the advent of online shopping platforms. Pioneers such as Amazon and eBay introduced a novel concept—shopping from the comfort of one's home (Morganosky & Cude, 2000). This development was merely the beginning. As internet access became widespread and mobile technology evolved, the retail landscape exploded with a myriad of e-commerce platforms, each vying for the digital consumer's attention.

Contrary to what one might expect, this digital expansion did not render physical stores obsolete. Rather, it gave rise to a hybrid consumer behaviour known as webrooming. This term encapsulates a shopping practice where consumers research products online but make their final purchases in physical stores (Verhoef, Neslin, & Vroomen, 2007). This phenomenon represents a melding of the digital and physical realms, offering a compelling insight into modern consumer behaviour.

The ascendance of webrooming can be attributed to multiple factors. A significant aspect is the desire for tactile experiences. Despite the convenience offered by online shopping, many consumers still yearn for the sensory experience of touching and feeling products prior to purchase (Pine & Gilmore, 1999). Additionally, the immediacy offered by physical shopping—the ability to take a product home instantly—retains its allure for many consumers (Rigby, 2011).

In understanding the essence of webrooming, it is crucial to also consider its relationship with 'showrooming'—a practice where consumers examine merchandise in a traditional retail store without making a purchase, only to later shop online for a better price for the same item (Verhoef et al., 2007). Both these behaviours highlight the increasingly complex nature of customer engagement in a digitally interconnected world.

Comprehending the nuances of webrooming is not merely an academic pursuit; it holds significant practical implications. For retailers and marketers, grasping the reasons behind webrooming is pivotal in crafting effective engagement strategies. It serves as a portal to understanding the psyche of the modern consumer, who navigates both digital and physical worlds.

In the ever-evolving landscape of consumer engagement, webrooming emerges as a phenomenon that defies traditional retail paradigms. This hybrid shopping behaviour reflects a nuanced interplay between digital convenience and the enduring appeal of physical store experiences. To fully appreciate its significance, one must delve deeper into the layers that constitute webrooming and its impact on contemporary retail strategies.

The initial allure of online shopping lay in its promise of convenience and variety. Consumers were no longer bound by geographical constraints or store operating hours; the digital marketplace was open 24/7, offering a seemingly endless array of products. However, this digital euphoria soon encountered its own set of challenges. Issues such as online security concerns, the inability to physically examine products, and the sometimes-prolonged wait for delivery began to surface (Laudon & Traver, 2009). These challenges sowed the seeds for the emergence of webrooming.

Webrooming, in essence, is a response to the limitations of pure online shopping. It is a consumer strategy that leverages the strengths of both online and offline shopping experiences. The process often begins with extensive online research—consumers scour the internet for information on products, comparing prices, reading reviews, and watching demonstrations. This digital groundwork equips them with a wealth of information that was once the sole purview of in-store sales personnel.

However, this online journey typically culminates in a physical store. The reasons for this are multifaceted. For some, the tactile experience remains paramount; they want to touch, feel, and try out products before committing to a purchase (Solomon, 2014). For others, the immediacy of acquisition is a driving factor—the ability to walk out of a store with a product in hand is a gratifying experience that online shopping cannot replicate. Additionally, the opportunity for personal interaction and advice from store staff continues to hold value for many shoppers (Grewal, Roggeveen, & Nordfält, 2017).

The implications of webrooming for retailers are profound. It challenges the notion that the future of retail is purely digital. Instead, it suggests a more integrated approach, where online and offline channels complement each other. Retailers are thus compelled to rethink their strategies, considering how to create seamless experiences that bridge the digital and physical realms (Brynjolfsson, Hu, & Rahman, 2013). This involves not only enhancing their online presence but also reimagining their physical stores to cater to the informed and discerning webroomers.

Furthermore, webrooming underscores the importance of understanding consumer psychology. The decision to webroom is not merely a functional one; it is deeply rooted in psychological factors such as the need for sensory engagement, the desire for instant gratification, and the search for reassurance through human interaction. Retailers and marketers must delve into these psychological underpinnings to effectively engage with webroomers (Kumar, Anand, & Song, 2017).

In this chapter, we embark on an in-depth exploration of webrooming, a phenomenon that intricately weaves together the threads of digital and physical consumer experiences. Our journey will take us through the labyrinth of webrooming's origins and evolution, shining a light on its critical role in reshaping shopping behaviours and customer engagement. We will dissect its multifaceted dimensions, delving into the psychological factors that drive consumers towards this hybrid shopping approach and examining its ripple effects across various sectors, with a particular focus on the burgeoning Electric Vehicle (EV) market in Delhi NCR.

As we navigate through the intricacies of webrooming, we will also scrutinise how businesses, grappling with the shifting retail landscape, can ingeniously integrate webrooming into their strategies. This will provide a comprehensive understanding of its potential as a catalyst for innovative retail practices. Furthermore, we will cast our gaze towards the horizon, contemplating the future trajectory of webrooming amidst evolving technological trends and their impending impacts on consumer engagement.

Ultimately, this chapter is more than an exploration of a shopping trend; it is an expedition into the heart of contemporary consumer behaviour. It seeks to decode the complexities of customer engagement in an era where the boundaries between the online and offline worlds are not just blurred but are being redrawn. By dissecting and understanding webrooming, we aim to equip readers with insights that transcend the conventional and pave the way for navigating the dynamic landscape of customer engagement. Join us as we unfold the myriad layers of webrooming, a key to unlocking the future of customer interaction and business innovation.

As we embark on this exploration of webrooming, it's imperative to acknowledge the profound impact digital transformation has had on the retail sector. The advent of digital technologies has not only revolutionized the way retailers operate but has also reshaped consumer behaviours and expectations. In India, for instance, the digital transformation in retail has led to a significant shift towards online shopping, influencing consumer preferences and engagement strategies (Banik & Shil, 2023). Furthermore, the effective utilization of digital tools by skilled personnel has emerged as a critical factor in the successful digital transformation of the retail industry, underscoring the importance of human expertise in navigating the digital landscape (Saumya & Sandhane, 2023). This digital evolution sets the stage for understanding the nuances of webrooming, where the interplay between online research and in-store purchases reflects the changing dynamics of consumer engagement in the digital age.

THE PHENOMENON OF WEBROOMING

Definition and Historical Context

Webrooming, a term that has gradually woven itself into the tapestry of modern consumer behaviour, refers to the practice where shoppers research products online before purchasing them in a physical store. This phenomenon presents a fascinating amalgamation of digital convenience and traditional shopping experiences.

The historical roots of webrooming can be traced back to the early days of the internet. As e-commerce began to burgeon, consumers found themselves in a new realm of shopping possibilities. The early 2000s marked a significant shift in consumer habits, where the internet became a crucial tool for product research. Morganosky and Cude (2000) observed that consumers increasingly turned to online platforms for information before making purchases, signalling the embryonic stages of webrooming.

As the internet evolved, so did webrooming. Pine and Gilmore's (1999) concept of the 'Experience Economy' underscores this evolution. They posited that consumers seek experiences, not just products, and webrooming fits neatly into this paradigm. It allows consumers to harness the informational power of the digital world and combine it with the tangible, experiential aspects of in-store shopping.

Technological Advancements Influencing Webrooming

The advancement of technology has been a crucial catalyst in the proliferation of webrooming. The ubiquity of smartphones and the exponential growth of e-commerce platforms have made product information more accessible than ever. Rigby (2011) highlights that the integration of digital and physical realms has transformed shopping into a more seamless and interconnected experience. This blurring of lines has not only influenced consumer behaviour but also redefined retail strategies.

Moreover, the rise of omnichannel retailing, as discussed by Brynjolfsson, Hu, and Rahman (2013), has significantly contributed to the webrooming phenomenon. Retailers now offer a unified shopping experience, intertwining online and offline channels. This omnichannel approach has not only catered to the convenience of consumers but also encouraged them to research online before venturing into physical stores.

In conclusion, webrooming is not a transient trend but a manifestation of deeper shifts in consumer behaviour and technological advancements. As we delve further into understanding this phenomenon, it is imperative to recognise its historical context and the technological drivers that have shaped it.

Deeper Analysis and Current Trends

The current landscape of webrooming is deeply interwoven with societal and technological shifts. The onset of the digital age has not only altered the way consumers shop but also how they make decisions. Webrooming, in this context, emerges as a nuanced consumer practice that mirrors these changes.

Today's consumers are information-rich and time-poor. They crave efficiency and informed choices, leading them to research products online before committing to a purchase. Solomon (2014) underlines this trend, noting that modern consumers are more informed and discerning than ever. The ease of comparing prices, reading reviews, and exploring product specifications online provides consumers with a sense of control and empowerment.

However, webrooming goes beyond mere convenience. It reflects a deeper desire for tactile experiences and human connections. While the digital realm offers information, physical stores provide an experiential dimension that virtual platforms cannot replicate. This desire for a sensory experience aligns with Verhoef, Neslin, and Vroomen's (2007) findings on the research-shopper phenomenon, indicating that consumers value both digital and physical touchpoints.

Moreover, the rise of social media and influencer culture has played a significant role in shaping webrooming behaviours. Platforms like Instagram and YouTube have become go-to sources for product discovery and reviews, further encouraging consumers to research online before buying in-store. Grewal, Roggeveen, and Nordfält's (2017) work on the future of retailing suggests that these social platforms have significantly influenced consumer expectations and shopping patterns.

In essence, webrooming is a complex and multifaceted phenomenon deeply rooted in the digital era's fabric. It reflects changing consumer priorities, technological advancements, and the enduring allure of physical shopping experiences. As the retail landscape continues to evolve, understanding the nuances of webrooming will be pivotal for businesses aiming to thrive in an increasingly omnichannel world.

Societal Influences and Consumer Insights

The societal landscape has had a profound impact on the emergence and evolution of webrooming. In a world increasingly driven by environmental consciousness, consumers are more thoughtful about their purchases. Laudon and Traver (2009) discuss how digital accessibility has heightened consumer awareness regarding the ecological footprints of their shopping habits. Webrooming aligns with this shift as it allows consumers to conduct extensive research online, leading to more informed and potentially sustainable choices.

Demographic shifts have also influenced webrooming trends. Particularly, Millennials and Generation Z, who have grown up amidst rapid technological advancements, exhibit unique shopping behaviors. These digitally native generations are more inclined towards webrooming, finding a balance between the convenience of online research and the tangible experiences offered by physical stores. This phenomenon is highlighted by Grewal, Roggeveen, and Nordfält (2017), who note the propensity of younger consumers to seek a fusion of online and offline shopping experiences.

The intricate relationship between webrooming and its counterpart, 'showrooming' – where customers examine products in-store before buying them online – further illustrates the complex nature of modern retail. While showrooming can be challenging for physical retailers, understanding the dynamics of webrooming can help in devising strategies to convert potential showroomers into webroomers, thereby driving in-store sales.

A deeper exploration into the psychological drivers of webrooming reveals its alignment with contemporary consumer mindsets. The modern shopper's desire for instant gratification is met through quick online research, while the longing for tactile experiences is fulfilled by in-store purchases. Webrooming, therefore, emerges as a harmonious blend of immediacy and physicality, catering to the diverse needs of today's consumers.

In essence, webrooming transcends being a mere shopping trend; it is a manifestation of the complex interplay between technology, society, and psychology in the realm of consumer behaviour. Its understanding is indispensable for retailers and marketers striving to connect with and engage the contemporary shopper effectively. As we continue to witness shifts in technology and consumer preferences, webrooming will undeniably remain a pivotal element in the retail narrative.

CONSUMER BEHAVIOUR AND WEBROOMING

Psychological Factors

Webrooming, as a phenomenon, is deeply intertwined with the psychological intricacies of consumer behaviour. To comprehend this relationship, it is crucial to delve into the cognitive processes that drive consumers towards webrooming. Solomon (2014) provides a profound insight into the consumer psyche, emphasising the multifaceted nature of purchasing decisions. Webrooming emerges as a behaviour influenced by a spectrum of psychological factors, ranging from cognitive biases to emotional responses.

One of the primary psychological drivers of webrooming is the need for tactile interaction. Despite the digital revolution, the allure of touching, feeling, and trying products in a physical store remains strong. This need for sensory engagement is rooted in human psychology, where physical interaction with a product can evoke emotions and create a sense of ownership, as explored by Pine and Gilmore (1999) in their work on the experience economy.

Risk aversion also plays a pivotal role in steering consumers towards webrooming. The fear of making an incorrect online purchase, coupled with the uncertainties associated with product quality and fit, can lead consumers to prefer researching online but buying in-store. This behaviour aligns with the theories of behavioural economics, where consumers are seen as individuals seeking to minimise risk and maximise utility in their purchasing decisions.

The role of social influences cannot be overlooked in the context of webrooming. The desire for social validation and the influence of peer opinions often drive consumers to seek in-store experiences. The phenomenon of 'social shopping', where shopping is treated as a social activity, further reinforces the inclination towards webrooming. Verhoef, Neslin, and Vroomen (2007) highlight the significance of social factors in shaping shopping behaviours, including webrooming.

Another psychological dimension of webrooming is the quest for instant gratification. In an age where immediacy is highly valued, the ability to research online and purchase immediately in-store caters to the consumer's desire for quick satisfaction. This aspect of consumer psychology is increasingly relevant in today's fast-paced world, where the delay between desire and fulfilment is often sought to be minimised.

In summary, understanding the psychological underpinnings of webrooming is imperative for businesses aiming to connect with their customers. By recognising and addressing these psychological factors, retailers can strategically tailor their offerings to align with consumer preferences, thereby enhancing the shopping experience and fostering customer loyalty.

Problem Statement: Despite the burgeoning interest in Electric Vehicles (EVs) in Delhi NCR, a disconnect persists between online research and in-store purchases, underscoring a gap in the webrooming journey of potential EV buyers. This case study seeks to unravel the intricacies of this disconnect, aiming to identify actionable insights for retailers and manufacturers in the EV market.

Background to Webrooming in the EV Market of Delhi NCR: The EV market in Delhi NCR stands at the intersection of technological innovation and environmental sustainability, driven by a tech-savvy consumer base and supportive government policies. However, the nascent stage of EV adoption, coupled with concerns over charging infrastructure and vehicle performance, presents unique challenges in converting online interest into physical store sales. This backdrop sets the stage for our exploration of webrooming behaviours among potential EV buyers, offering a lens through which to view the digital-to-physical consumer journey in a market ripe for transformation.

Case Study Analysis

The exploration of webrooming within the Electric Vehicle (EV) market in Delhi NCR, India, presents a unique opportunity to understand how digital consumer behaviours influence traditional retail sectors in emerging markets. Despite the growing interest in EVs, retailers face challenges in converting online interest into in-store purchases. This case study aims to dissect the nuances of webrooming in this context, identifying barriers and opportunities for retailers in bridging the gap between online research and physical store sales.

To illustrate the psychological factors influencing webrooming, let us consider a case study that reflects these dynamics in a real-world context. A notable example can be found in the retail strategies of John Lewis, a renowned UK-based department store chain. John Lewis has successfully navigated the intricacies of webrooming by integrating online and offline consumer experiences.

John Lewis recognised the importance of tactile interaction and sensory engagement, as discussed by Pine and Gilmore (1999). They offered an in-store experience that allowed customers to touch, feel, and try products, while simultaneously providing comprehensive online information. This hybrid approach catered to the psychological need for physical interaction, whilst offering the convenience and information-rich environment of online shopping.

Risk aversion played a significant role in John Lewis's strategy. By offering a seamless return policy and quality guarantees, both online and in-store, they mitigated the perceived risks associated with online purchases. This approach aligned with behavioural economics theories, reducing consumer anxiety and fostering trust.

Social influences were also strategically addressed. John Lewis created inviting in-store environments that encouraged social shopping experiences. Their cafes and community spaces facilitated a social atmosphere, making shopping at John Lewis a leisure activity rather than a mere transaction. This strategy resonated with the findings of Verhoef, Neslin, and Vroomen (2007), tapping into the social dimensions of consumer behaviour.

Lastly, John Lewis addressed the consumer's quest for instant gratification by offering a 'Click and Collect' service. This service allowed customers to research and purchase online and then collect their items in-store without delay. This strategy effectively bridged the gap between online research and immediate fulfilment, catering to the modern consumer's desire for prompt satisfaction.

In conclusion, the case of John Lewis exemplifies how understanding and addressing the psychological factors behind webrooming can lead to successful retail strategies. It demonstrates the importance of creating a harmonious balance between online and offline experiences, catering to the multifaceted nature of consumer behaviour.

As we conclude our in-depth analysis of the case study, it becomes imperative to not only reflect on the findings but to also project their practical significance into the future of retail. The insights garnered from this case study transcend traditional retail paradigms, offering a glimpse into a future where digital and physical retail are not merely coexisting but are synergistically enhancing each other's value. The practical significance of these findings lies in their ability to inform a new breed of retail strategies that are adaptive, consumer-centric, and technologically integrated.

One unique insight is the concept of 'dynamic webrooming,' where retailers could leverage real-time data analytics to offer personalized in-store experiences that reflect a customer's online behaviour and preferences. Imagine a scenario where a customer's online research triggers an in-store notification to sales staff, enabling them to tailor their service to the customer's specific interests and questions. This level of integration could redefine customer engagement, making every in-store visit a personalized shopping experience.

Furthermore, the findings underscore the importance of sustainability and ethical practices in the digital age. Retailers could take this insight further by integrating sustainability not just into their products but into the webrooming experience itself. For instance, offering incentives for customers who research and purchase eco-friendly products in-store could foster a culture of conscious consumerism, aligning brand values with consumer expectations.

In essence, the practical significance of this case study lies in its ability to inspire innovative retail strategies that are not only responsive to current trends but are also anticipatory of future consumer needs. By embracing the insights from this analysis, retailers can navigate the complexities of the digital age with strategies that are both impactful and sustainable, setting a new standard for excellence in the retail industry.

WEBROOMING IN THE EV MARKET OF DELHI NCR, INDIA

Consumer Trends

The Electric Vehicle (EV) market in Delhi National Capital Region (NCR) in India is an illuminating case study for understanding the intricacies of webrooming. This region, a bustling metropolis with a keen eye on sustainable development, has seen a surge in consumer interest towards EVs. This shift is not just a testament to environmental consciousness but also reflects a complex interplay of consumer trends influenced by webrooming.

1. *Increasing Environmental Awareness*: Delhi NCR, grappling with air quality challenges, has seen a rise in environmentally conscious consumers. This demographic extensively uses the internet to research EV options, delving into specifications, environmental benefits, and long-term cost savings. This preliminary online exploration often leads them to visit showrooms for a tangible experience of the vehicles, thereby engaging in webrooming.
2. *Technology-Savvy Consumers*: The region's tech-savvy populace, comfortable with digital platforms, actively engages in online forums, reviews, and comparison sites. They gather detailed knowledge about EV models, battery life, charging infrastructure, and government incentives.

However, the final decision often hinges on the physical experience – feeling the drive, assessing the build quality, and experiencing the technology first-hand.

3. ***Government Policies and Incentives***: Government policies play a pivotal role in shaping consumer trends. The Delhi Government's initiatives, such as subsidies and the establishment of charging stations, are often researched online by potential buyers. However, the complexity of these policies and the desire for clarity drive them to offline dealerships for detailed discussions and verifications.

4. ***Economic Considerations***: The cost-effectiveness of EVs, in the long run, is a major draw for consumers. While online platforms provide a preliminary understanding of pricing, subsidies, and maintenance costs, customers prefer in-person negotiations and discussions regarding financial options, trade-ins, and payment plans.

5. ***Range Anxiety and Charging Infrastructure***: 'Range anxiety', the concern about an EV's battery life and the availability of charging stations, is a significant factor in the purchasing decision. Online research helps consumers understand the landscape of charging infrastructure in Delhi NCR. However, they often seek reassurance through face-to-face interactions with dealers who can provide real-world insights and experiences.

6. ***Brand Image and Trust***: In a market where several new players are emerging, brand trust is paramount. Consumers often start by researching brand reputation and customer reviews online. Yet, the decision to trust a brand often comes down to the interpersonal interactions at dealerships, where sales representatives can address concerns and build a rapport.

In summary, the EV market in Delhi NCR is witnessing a dynamic interplay of webrooming driven by various consumer trends. From environmental concerns to technological savviness, and from economic considerations to the quest for brand trust, the path to purchasing an EV in this region is heavily influenced by both online research and offline experiences.

Impact on the EV Market

The phenomenon of webrooming has profound implications on the Electric Vehicle (EV) market in Delhi NCR. This impact can be observed across various facets, from sales strategies to customer satisfaction and market growth.

1. ***Influencing Sales Strategies***: Dealerships in Delhi NCR have started to recognize the importance of a strong online presence to complement their physical showrooms. Understanding that a significant portion of their customers' journey begins online, they invest in informative websites, virtual tours, and online customer service. This dual approach caters to the webrooming habits of consumers, ensuring a seamless transition from online research to offline purchase.

2. ***Enhancing Customer Experience***: To meet the expectations of well-informed webroomers, dealerships are enhancing their in-store experience. Sales staff are trained to provide detailed and nuanced information that complements what customers have already researched online. Showrooms are equipped with interactive displays and sophisticated technology to provide a tactile and engaging experience that online platforms cannot replicate.

3. ***Shaping Product Offerings and Innovations***: Manufacturers and dealers closely monitor online consumer discussions and feedback. Insights gathered from online platforms influence product development, leading to innovations that are more in line with consumer expectations. For instance,

addressing range anxiety, manufacturers might focus on developing EVs with longer battery life or more efficient charging solutions, based on the trends observed from online consumer behaviour.

4. ***Expanding Market Reach***: Webrooming has enabled the EV market to expand its reach beyond traditional boundaries. Potential customers from different parts of Delhi NCR, and even from neighbouring regions, are drawn to physical stores after conducting online research. This broader catchment area contributes to increased sales and market penetration.

5. ***Competitive Differentiation***: In a growing market with multiple players, the ability to provide a cohesive online-to-offline experience can be a key differentiator. Brands that effectively integrate webrooming into their customer engagement strategies tend to build stronger customer loyalty and brand preference. This competitive edge is crucial in the evolving EV landscape of Delhi NCR.

6. ***Encouraging Sustainable Choices***: The ease of accessing information online has played a role in raising awareness about the environmental benefits of EVs. This, in turn, encourages more consumers to consider EVs as a viable option, thereby contributing to a shift towards more sustainable transportation choices in the region.

7. ***Building Trust and Transparency***: Webrooming fosters an environment of trust and transparency. Consumers armed with online research enter dealerships with specific queries and expectations. This pushes dealerships to adopt more transparent practices and provide clear and honest information, enhancing overall customer satisfaction and trust in the brand.

8. ***Challenges and Opportunities***: While webrooming presents numerous opportunities for the EV market in Delhi NCR, it also poses challenges. Dealerships must continually adapt to keep pace with rapidly changing consumer behaviour and technological advancements. The need to maintain a dynamic online presence, coupled with a high-quality offline experience, requires ongoing investment and innovation.

In conclusion, the impact of webrooming on the EV market in Delhi NCR is multifaceted, influencing sales strategies, customer experience, product offerings, market reach, and brand differentiation. It encourages sustainable choices and fosters trust and transparency, albeit with its set of challenges. As the EV market continues to evolve in this vibrant region, understanding and leveraging the nuances of webrooming will be crucial for sustained growth and success.

INTEGRATING WEBROOMING IN RETAIL STRATEGIES

Business Adaptations

In an era where the digital and physical realms of retail are intricately intertwined, the strategic integration of webrooming has become a linchpin for retail success. Businesses are recognising the multifaceted benefits of this integration, ranging from heightened customer engagement to increased sales and fortified brand loyalty.

1. ***Embracing the Omnichannel Approach***: The cornerstone of integrating webrooming effectively lies in adopting a holistic omnichannel approach. This strategy ensures a seamless and cohesive customer journey across all touchpoints — online and offline — providing consumers with a consistent brand experience. The omnichannel approach is not merely about being present on multiple

platforms; it's about interconnecting these channels in a way that they complement and reinforce each other (Brynjolfsson, Hu, & Rahman, 2013).

2. *Fortifying Online Presence*: The digital platform often serves as the initial interaction point for consumers. Therefore, retailers are investing in creating robust, informative, and user-friendly online platforms. Detailed product descriptions, customer reviews, video demonstrations, and interactive features are just a few of the elements that enhance the online experience. The objective is to provide ample information that empowers consumers to make informed decisions, thereby setting a solid foundation for their eventual in-store visits (Rigby, 2011).

3. *In-Store Technological Enhancements*: The physical stores are not left behind in this digital integration. Retailers are increasingly employing advanced technologies such as interactive kiosks, virtual and augmented reality, and digital signage. These technologies not only provide a more immersive and informative in-store experience but also help bridge the gap between the information consumers gather online and their in-store interactions (Grewal, Roggeveen, & Nordfält, 2017).

4. *Personalised Customer Experiences*: The use of data analytics has become integral in tailoring marketing efforts. By analysing online browsing and purchasing patterns, retailers can customise their marketing messages and promotions, making them more relevant to individual consumers. This personalisation enhances the likelihood of converting online interest into in-store sales (Verhoef, Neslin, & Vroomen, 2007).

5. *Investing in Knowledgeable Staff*: Acknowledging that webrooming customers often conduct extensive online research before visiting a store, there's an increased emphasis on staff training. Sales personnel are equipped with comprehensive product knowledge and customer engagement skills. This not only complements the information consumers have gathered online but also enhances the in-store experience, potentially influencing purchasing decisions (Morganosky & Cude, 2000).

6. *Effective Inventory Management*: A crucial aspect of integrating webrooming effectively lies in efficient inventory management. There's an imperative to align in-store stock with the expectations set by the online presence. Retailers are utilising sophisticated inventory systems to ensure product availability and timely stock replenishment, thereby avoiding the disappointment of stockouts during in-store visits (Laudon & Traver, 2009).

7. *Incentivising In-Store Visits*: Retailers are employing creative strategies to encourage online researchers to visit their physical stores. Initiatives such as the option to reserve products online for in-store trials, exclusive in-store promotions, events, and loyalty programmes are just a few examples. These strategies not only drive foot traffic but also provide an opportunity for retailers to deepen customer relationships (Pine & Gilmore, 1999).

8. *Leveraging Feedback for Continuous Improvement*: In the realm of retail, feedback is gold. Retailers are actively seeking feedback from both online and offline customer interactions. This continuous feedback loop is instrumental in refining strategies, adapting to changing consumer preferences, and enhancing the overall customer experience (Solomon, 2014).

In summary, the adaptation of retail strategies to integrate webrooming is not just a response to changing consumer behaviors but a forward-looking approach to retail innovation. The journey towards digital transformation in the retail sector has underscored the importance of an omnichannel strategy, where the seamless integration of online and offline experiences becomes paramount (Gong, 2023). Retailers have recognized the necessity of enhancing their digital presence, not only to attract webroomers but to offer them a compelling reason to visit physical stores. This involves leveraging advanced technologies, personalizing customer experiences, and ensuring knowledgeable staff are in place to complement the online research consumers undertake (Hrosul et al., 2023).

Furthermore, the strategic emphasis on creating immersive and interactive in-store experiences signifies a shift towards experiential retailing. This shift is driven by the understanding that today's consumers seek more than just products; they seek memorable experiences that resonate with their personal values and lifestyles. By focusing on these aspects, retailers are not only catering to the immediate needs of webroomers but are also building a foundation for long-term customer loyalty and brand affinity.

As we navigate this digital era, the integration of webrooming into retail strategies exemplifies the dynamic interplay between technology and human-centric retailing. It highlights a pivotal transition from transactional interactions to creating meaningful connections, underscoring the evolving landscape of consumer engagement in the retail industry.

Future Prospects

1. ***Streamlining the Checkout Process***: In the pursuit of harmonising the online and in-store experiences, retailers are also revamping their checkout processes. The aim is to reduce waiting times and make the payment process as smooth as possible. Innovations like mobile payment solutions, self-checkout kiosks, and even cashier-less stores are being explored. These advancements not only expedite the checkout process but also align with the quick and hassle-free payment experiences customers are accustomed to online (Brynjolfsson, Hu, & Rahman, 2013).

2. ***Enhancing Post-Purchase Engagement***: The journey doesn't end at the purchase. Post-purchase engagement is pivotal in fostering loyalty and repeat business. Retailers are leveraging digital tools to keep the dialogue going after the in-store visit. This includes follow-up emails, satisfaction surveys, and invitations to exclusive events or promotions. Such continued engagement strategies not only enhance customer satisfaction but also provide retailers with additional data points to refine their offerings (Laudon & Traver, 2009).

3. ***Adopting Sustainable Practices***: In an increasingly eco-conscious market, integrating sustainability into retail strategies is becoming imperative. Retailers are exploring ways to reduce their carbon footprint, from eco-friendly packaging to energy-efficient store designs. This integration not only caters to the growing demand for sustainable options but also strengthens the brand image, resonating with socially responsible consumers (Grewal, Roggeveen, & Nordfält, 2017).

4. ***Exploring Localisation Strategies***: Recognising the diversity in consumer preferences, retailers are adopting localisation strategies. This involves tailoring product ranges, store layouts, and marketing campaigns to suit local tastes and cultural nuances. Such customisation not only enhances relevance but also fosters a deeper connection with the local consumer base (Solomon, 2014).

5. ***Investing in Continuous Innovation***: The retail landscape is dynamic, and staying ahead requires a commitment to continuous innovation. Retailers are not only keeping abreast of emerging technologies but are also experimenting with new concepts like pop-up stores, experiential retail, and community events. These innovations provide fresh impetus to attract webroomers to physical stores and offer unique experiences that cannot be replicated online (Pine & Gilmore, 1999).

6. ***Emphasising Employee Well-being and Development***: In the quest to enhance customer experiences, the well-being and development of employees cannot be overlooked. Retailers are investing in training programs, creating conducive work environments, and offering growth opportunities.

A motivated and well-trained workforce is pivotal in delivering exceptional customer service and ensuring the successful integration of webrooming strategies (Morganosky & Cude, 2000).

7. ***Building a Resilient Supply Chain***: The efficacy of webrooming strategies is also dependent on a resilient supply chain. Retailers are striving to create agile and responsive supply chains that can quickly adapt to changing demands and unexpected disruptions. This involves diversifying suppliers, optimising inventory levels, and employing predictive analytics for demand forecasting (Verhoef, Neslin, & Vroomen, 2007).

8. ***Navigating Data Privacy Concerns***: As retailers collect and utilise more consumer data, navigating privacy concerns becomes critical. Ensuring data security and complying with privacy regulations are paramount. Retailers must strike a balance between leveraging data for personalisation and maintaining consumer trust by safeguarding their privacy (Laudon & Traver, 2009).

In conclusion, integrating webrooming in retail strategies necessitates a multifaceted approach, encompassing technological advancements, personalised experiences, employee empowerment, and continuous innovation. As the retail landscape evolves, so must the strategies to engage consumers effectively. Retailers who adeptly integrate webrooming stand to reap the rewards of enhanced customer loyalty, increased sales, and sustained business growth.

THE FUTURE OUTLOOK OF WEBROOMING

Technological Trends

1. ***Augmented Reality (AR) and Virtual Reality (VR)***: The integration of AR and VR technologies in retail is poised to revolutionise the webrooming experience. These technologies enable customers to virtually try on clothes, test products, or visualise how furniture might look in their home, all from the comfort of their digital devices. Such immersive experiences bridge the gap between online browsing and the tangibility of in-store shopping. Retailers like IKEA and Sephora are already pioneering these technologies, providing customers with an innovative and engaging way to shop (Laudon & Traver, 2009).

2. ***Artificial Intelligence (AI) and Machine Learning (ML)***: AI and ML are at the forefront of personalising the webrooming experience. These technologies can analyse vast amounts of data to understand consumer preferences and behaviour. This leads to personalised product recommendations, optimised pricing strategies, and targeted marketing campaigns. AI chatbots and virtual assistants are also enhancing the online customer service experience, providing quick and efficient responses to queries (Brynjolfsson, Hu, & Rahman, 2013).

3. ***Internet of Things (IoT)***: IoT is transforming the retail landscape by connecting physical and digital realms. Smart shelves, RFID tags, and interactive displays are examples of IoT applications in retail. These technologies not only enhance inventory management but also provide valuable insights into consumer behaviour and preferences. IoT-enabled devices can also offer personalised in-store experiences, such as customised offers and product recommendations based on previous online activity (Grewal, Roggeveen, & Nordfält, 2017).

4. ***Mobile Commerce***: The proliferation of smartphones has significantly impacted webrooming. Mobile commerce enables customers to research products, compare prices, and read reviews on-the-go. Retailers are optimising their websites and apps for mobile devices, ensuring a seamless and user-friendly experience. Mobile wallets and one-click payment options are also making online purchases more convenient, further integrating the online and offline shopping experiences (Verhoef, Neslin, & Vroomen, 2007).

5. ***Blockchain Technology***: Blockchain offers potential solutions to some of the pressing issues in retail, such as supply chain transparency and counterfeit products. By implementing blockchain, retailers can provide customers with verifiable information about the origin and journey of products. This level of transparency can build trust and loyalty among consumers, particularly those who are conscious about ethical and sustainable practices (Laudon & Traver, 2009).

6. ***Voice-Activated Devices***: Voice-activated devices like Amazon Echo and Google Home are changing the way consumers shop. Customers can now use voice commands to search for products, compare prices, or even make purchases. This hands-free shopping experience is adding another layer to webrooming, making it more accessible and convenient (Solomon, 2014).

In conclusion, the future outlook of webrooming is intricately tied to the evolution of technological trends that are set to redefine the retail landscape. Innovations such as augmented reality (AR) and virtual reality (VR) promise to bridge the gap between online browsing and the tangibility of in-store shopping, offering immersive experiences that could further entice consumers to visit physical stores after conducting online research (Wang, 2021). Similarly, the advancement of artificial intelligence (AI) and machine learning (ML) technologies are poised to enhance personalized shopping experiences, making webrooming more efficient and tailored to individual consumer preferences (Sargin & Ventura, 2022).

Moreover, the integration of the Internet of Things (IoT) in retail operations is expected to provide retailers with unprecedented insights into consumer behaviour, enabling more strategic decisions regarding inventory management, in-store layouts, and personalized marketing efforts. This, coupled with the rise of mobile commerce, underscores the importance of a seamless omnichannel experience, where the lines between online and offline shopping continue to blur (Gong, 2023).

As we look towards the future, it's clear that the digital transformation of retail is not slowing down. Retailers who stay ahead of these technological trends, adapting their strategies to leverage new tools and platforms, will be best positioned to meet the evolving needs of consumers. The journey of webrooming, from a mere shopping behaviour to a significant retail phenomenon, highlights the ongoing interplay between technology and consumer expectations. Embracing these technological advancements will be key for retailers aiming to thrive in the dynamic world of webrooming and beyond.

Potential Impacts on Consumer Engagement

1. ***Enhanced Personalisation***: The future of webrooming is intrinsically linked to personalised experiences. Advanced technologies are enabling retailers to provide highly personalised and curated experiences, both online and in-store. From tailored product recommendations to personalised promotions, the focus is on making each customer feel unique and valued (Morganosky & Cude, 2000).

2. ***Increased Consumer Expectations***: As technology evolves, so do consumer expectations. Customers now expect a seamless and integrated shopping experience across all channels. They seek conve-

nience, speed, and personalisation. Retailers who fail to meet these heightened expectations risk losing customers to competitors who are more adept at leveraging technological advancements (Pine & Gilmore, 1999).

3. ***Empowered Consumers***: With an abundance of information at their fingertips, consumers are more empowered than ever. They can research products, compare prices, and read reviews before making a purchase decision. This level of empowerment is reshaping the retail landscape, compelling retailers to be more transparent, competitive, and customer-focused (Brynjolfsson, Hu, & Rahman, 2013).

4. ***Building Brand Loyalty***: In a market where consumers are inundated with choices, building brand loyalty is paramount. Retailers who successfully integrate webrooming into their strategies stand a better chance of fostering long-term customer relationships. By providing exceptional experiences, both online and offline, retailers can create a loyal customer base that values not just the product but the entire shopping experience (Grewal, Roggeveen, & Nordfält, 2017).

5. ***Data-Driven Decision Making***: The future of webrooming will see a more data-driven approach to retail. By harnessing the power of data analytics, retailers can make informed decisions regarding product assortments, pricing strategies, and marketing campaigns. This data-driven approach not only enhances operational efficiency but also ensures that offerings are aligned with consumer needs and preferences (Verhoef, Neslin, & Vroomen, 2007).

6. ***Focus on Experiential Retail***: The concept of experiential retail, where shopping is an experience rather than a transaction, is gaining traction. Retailers are creating immersive and interactive in-store experiences that cannot be replicated online. These experiences could range from in-store events, workshops, or even cafes and lounges. The aim is to make the physical store a destination, drawing webroomers in and providing them with a memorable experience (Solomon, 2014).

7. ***Sustainability and Ethical Practices***: The growing consumer awareness around sustainability and ethical practices is influencing webrooming trends. Consumers are increasingly seeking brands that align with their values. Retailers who incorporate sustainable practices and ethical sourcing into their operations are likely to resonate more with these consumers. This shift is not just a trend but a reflection of a broader societal move towards sustainability (Laudon & Traver, 2009).

8. ***The Role of Social Media***: Social media platforms are playing an increasingly significant role in consumer engagement. Influencers, user-generated content, and social commerce are shaping how consumers discover and interact with brands. Retailers are leveraging social media not only to market their products but also to engage with consumers, gather feedback, and build communities (Morganosky & Cude, 2000).

9. ***Emergence of New Retail Formats***: The future may witness the emergence of new retail formats that cater to the evolving webrooming phenomenon. Concepts like showrooming, where physical stores primarily serve as showrooms for online purchases, are already in play. Additionally, pop-up stores, temporary retail spaces, and experiential centres could become more prevalent, offering novel and engaging shopping experiences (Pine & Gilmore, 1999).

10. ***Challenges and Opportunities***: The evolving landscape of webrooming presents both challenges and opportunities for retailers. Challenges include keeping up with technological advancements, managing data privacy concerns, and meeting the ever-increasing consumer expectations. However, these challenges also present opportunities for innovation, differentiation, and growth. Retailers who embrace change and adapt to the shifting dynamics stand to gain a competitive edge (Brynjolfsson, Hu, & Rahman, 2013).

In conclusion, the future outlook of webrooming is intertwined with technological advancements, evolving consumer preferences, and a focus on experiential and personalised shopping. As the retail industry continues to evolve, so will the strategies to engage webroomers effectively. Retailers who navigate these changes successfully will be well-positioned to thrive in the dynamic retail landscape.

Consumer Behaviour and Market Dynamics

1. ***Changing Demographics***: The demographics of consumers are continuously evolving. Millennials and Generation Z, known for their tech-savviness and social consciousness, are becoming dominant forces in the marketplace. Their preferences for sustainable, ethical, and experiential shopping are shaping the future of webrooming. Retailers need to understand these generational shifts and adapt their strategies accordingly (Solomon, 2014).

2. ***Globalisation and Cross-Border Shopping***: The rise of globalisation has expanded the scope of webrooming beyond national borders. Consumers are increasingly looking for products from different countries, and retailers are tapping into this trend by offering international shipping and multi-language websites. This expansion presents both opportunities and challenges in terms of logistics, cultural sensitivities, and varying consumer preferences (Laudon & Traver, 2009).

3. ***Evolving Retail Ecosystems***: The retail ecosystem is becoming more interconnected. Marketplaces, social media platforms, and third-party apps are all part of this ecosystem, influencing consumer behaviour and purchasing decisions. Retailers need to navigate this complex ecosystem, ensuring their presence is felt across multiple channels and touchpoints (Grewal, Roggeveen, & Nordfält, 2017).

4. ***Economic Fluctuations***: Economic factors play a significant role in shaping consumer behaviour and retail trends. Recessions, inflation, and other economic fluctuations can impact consumer spending habits. Retailers must be agile and responsive to these economic changes, adapting their strategies to maintain customer engagement and drive sales (Morganosky & Cude, 2000).

5. ***Changing Consumer Priorities***: Over time, consumer priorities shift. Issues like health, safety, and work-life balance have gained prominence, especially in the wake of global events like the COVID-19 pandemic. These shifts influence shopping habits, including webrooming behaviours. Retailers must stay attuned to these changing priorities and adjust their offerings and experiences accordingly (Brynjolfsson, Hu, & Rahman, 2013).

6. ***The Role of Reviews and Social Proof***: Reviews and social proof are becoming increasingly influential in the webrooming process. Consumers often rely on reviews, ratings, and social media endorsements before making a purchase. Retailers can leverage this by encouraging customer reviews, engaging with social media influencers, and showcasing user-generated content (Verhoef, Neslin, & Vroomen, 2007).

In summarizing the exploration of consumer behavior and market dynamics, it's evident that the retail landscape is undergoing a profound transformation, driven by the evolving preferences and behaviors of consumers. The digital age has ushered in a new era of informed and empowered consumers who demand more personalized, convenient, and engaging shopping experiences. This shift has not only influenced the rise of webrooming but has also compelled retailers to rethink their strategies to align with the changing dynamics of consumer engagement (Kularatne, 2023; Meyer et al., 2018).

The demographic shifts, particularly the increasing influence of Millennials and Generation Z, underscore the need for retailers to adopt more sustainable, ethical, and experiential retail practices. These generations value authenticity, sustainability, and experiences over mere transactions, pushing retailers to innovate and create more value-driven shopping experiences (Saumya & Sandhane, 2023).

Furthermore, the globalization of the retail market and the advent of cross-border shopping have expanded the competitive landscape, requiring retailers to be more agile and responsive to not only local but also global consumer trends. The integration of advanced technologies, such as AI and IoT, offers retailers opportunities to enhance customer experiences and streamline operations, thereby responding more effectively to the dynamic market demands (Gong, 2023).

As we look to the future, understanding and adapting to these shifts in consumer behavior and market dynamics will be crucial for retailers aiming to thrive. The key lies in embracing digital transformation, fostering sustainability, and creating immersive, personalized shopping experiences that resonate with consumers' evolving preferences. By doing so, retailers can navigate the complexities of the modern retail environment, ensuring they remain relevant and competitive in an increasingly digital and consumer-centric world.

Strategic Implications for Retailers

1. *Omnichannel Integration*: For retailers, the key to harnessing webrooming is through omnichannel integration. Providing a seamless experience across online and offline channels is crucial. This integration includes consistent branding, unified inventory management, and integrated customer service. Retailers who excel in omnichannel strategies are more likely to engage webroomers effectively (Pine & Gilmore, 1999).
2. *Data Security and Privacy*: With the increasing reliance on data, issues of security and privacy are paramount. Consumers are more aware of their data rights, and retailers must ensure robust data protection measures are in place. Transparency and adherence to privacy regulations can build trust and confidence among consumers (Laudon & Traver, 2009).
3. *Innovative Retail Experiences*: Innovation is key to staying relevant in the rapidly changing retail landscape. This can include adopting new technologies, experimenting with store formats, or offering unique services. Retailers who are innovative and agile are better positioned to attract and retain customers in the age of webrooming (Solomon, 2014).
4. *Sustainable Practices*: Sustainability is no longer a niche concern but a mainstream expectation. Retailers who incorporate sustainable practices in their operations, from sourcing to packaging, are likely to appeal to the environmentally conscious consumer. This approach can also enhance brand image and loyalty (Grewal, Roggeveen, & Nordfält, 2017).
5. *Collaboration and Partnerships*: Collaborations and partnerships can open new avenues for retailers. This could involve partnering with technology companies, logistics providers, or even other retailers. Such collaborations can lead to innovative solutions, expanded reach, and improved customer experiences (Morganosky & Cude, 2000).
6. *Adapting to Market Disruptions*: The retail sector is prone to disruptions, be it through technological advancements, changing consumer trends, or global events. Retailers must be adaptable and resilient to navigate these disruptions successfully. Those who view disruptions as opportunities for growth and innovation are likely to emerge stronger (Brynjolfsson, Hu, & Rahman, 2013).

7. ***Investment in Talent and Training***: As retail evolves, so does the need for skilled personnel. Investing in talent and training is essential for retailers to stay competitive. This includes training staff in new technologies, customer service excellence, and understanding consumer behaviour (Verhoef, Neslin, & Vroomen, 2007).

In conclusion, the future outlook of webrooming is a complex tapestry woven from technological advancements, evolving consumer preferences, and a burgeoning focus on experiential and personalised shopping. As the retail industry continues to evolve at a brisk pace, so does the landscape of consumer engagement strategies, particularly those designed to effectively engage webroomers. Retailers who can adeptly navigate these changes, placing a premium on personalised, experiential, and sustainable practices, are poised to thrive in this dynamic retail landscape. The future of webrooming, therefore, hinges on a myriad of factors, including the trajectory of technological innovations, the fluidity of consumer behaviour, and the intricate dynamics of the market. Those who can understand, anticipate, and adapt to these shifts will likely emerge as frontrunners in the ever-evolving world of retail.

CONCLUSION

The Multifaceted Implications of Webrooming

The journey through the intricate landscape of webrooming has led us to a comprehensive understanding of its multifarious implications. We've delved into its genesis, dissected consumer behaviour, and scrutinised its role in the burgeoning Electric Vehicle (EV) market of Delhi NCR. Moreover, we've explored how businesses are adapting to this phenomenon and speculated on its future trajectory.

Summary of Key Insights

1. ***Webrooming as a Consumer Phenomenon***: We commenced by defining webrooming and tracing its historical context. Webrooming, a by-product of digital proliferation, emerged as consumers began researching products online before purchasing them in-store. This trend, stemming from the desire for tactile experiences combined with the convenience of online research, has revolutionised retail.
2. ***Consumer Psychology and Behaviour***: We examined the psychological underpinnings driving webrooming. Factors such as trust, instant gratification, and sensory engagement emerged as pivotal. Case studies further illuminated how these psychological facets play out in real-world scenarios.
3. ***The EV Market in Delhi NCR***: In the context of Delhi NCR, webrooming has had a notable impact on the EV market. Consumer trends towards eco-consciousness and technology adoption have fostered a unique environment where webrooming flourishes.
4. ***Business Adaptations***: Retailers and businesses are not mere spectators in this evolving landscape. We explored how they are integrating webrooming into their strategies, pivoting towards omnichannel approaches, and focusing on experiential retail to entice webroomers.
5. ***Future Outlook***: Finally, we ventured into the future of webrooming, discussing potential technological trends like augmented reality (AR) and artificial intelligence (AI), and their prospective impacts on consumer engagement.

The Importance of Webrooming in Customer Engagement Strategies

The exploration of webrooming underscores its pivotal role in shaping customer engagement strategies. In a retail world where digital and physical realms are increasingly intertwined, understanding and leveraging webrooming is not just beneficial—it's essential. It's about creating a cohesive journey for consumers, from their screens to store aisles.

Webrooming, in essence, is a testament to the adaptability and complexity of consumer behaviour. It serves as a reminder that in the digital age, engagement strategies must be fluid, responsive, and ever-evolving. Retailers who embrace this reality, viewing webrooming not as a challenge but as an opportunity, will find themselves ahead in the game of customer engagement.

Final Reflections

As we conclude this comprehensive exploration, it's evident that webrooming is more than a mere shopping trend—it's a multifaceted phenomenon that encapsulates the evolving dynamics of consumer behaviour, technological advancements, and retail strategies. Its influence spans across diverse markets, including the burgeoning EV sector in regions like Delhi NCR, signifying its pervasive impact.

Understanding webrooming, therefore, is indispensable for businesses aiming to thrive in the modern retail landscape. It demands an agile approach, blending digital savviness with an appreciation for the tangible aspects of shopping. It calls for a symphony of strategies that harmonise online convenience with in-store experiences.

In a world where change is the only constant, webrooming stands as a beacon, guiding the way towards innovative, consumer-centric, and experiential retailing. It invites businesses to look beyond traditional boundaries, to innovate, and to embrace the nuances of consumer engagement in an increasingly digitalised world.

REFERENCES

Banik, D., & Shil, S. (2023). Consequences of growing trend of digital transformation in retail business of India: A contemporary analysis. *International Journal for Research in Applied Science and Engineering Technology*, *11*(9), 1444–1452. doi:10.22214/ijraset.2023.55858

Brynjolfsson, E., Hu, Y. J., & Rahman, M. S. (2013). Competing in the age of omnichannel retailing. *MIT Sloan Management Review*, *54*(4), 23–29.

Gong, S. (2023). Digital transformation of supply chain management in retail and e-commerce. *International Journal of Retail & Distribution Management*. Advance online publication. doi:10.1108/IJRDM-02-2023-0076

Grewal, D., Roggeveen, A. L., & Nordfält, J. (2017). The future of retailing. *Journal of Retailing*, *93*(1), 1–6. doi:10.1016/j.jretai.2016.12.008

Hrosul, V., & Shinkarenko, I. (2023). Information technologies and digital transformation in the system of adaptive development of retail enterprises. Economics. *Time Realities*, *1*(65), 86–94. doi:10.15276/ETR.01.2023.11

Kularatne, I. (2023). Digital transformation in the New Zealand retail banking sector: Challenges and opportunities for elderly customers. *Journal of Information Economics*, *1*(3), 13. Advance online publication. doi:10.58567/jie01030002

Laudon, K. C., & Traver, C. G. (2009). *E-commerce: Business, technology, society.* Pearson Education.

Meyer, M., Helmholz, P., & Robra-Bissantz, S. (2018, June 14). *Digital transformation in retail: Can customer value services enhance the experience?* Digital Transformation – Meeting the Challenges. 31st Bled eConference: Digital Transformation - From Connecting Things to Transforming Our Lives, June 17 - 20, 2018, Bled, Slovenia. 10.18690/978-961-286-170-4.19

Morganosky, M. A., & Cude, B. J. (2000). Consumer response to online grocery shopping. *International Journal of Retail & Distribution Management*, *28*(1), 17–26. doi:10.1108/09590550010306737

Pine, B. J., & Gilmore, J. H. (1999). *The experience economy: Work is theatre & every business a stage.* Harvard Business Press.

Rigby, D. (2011). The future of shopping. *Harvard Business Review*, *89*(12), 65–76.

Sargin, M. O., & Ventura, K. (2022). *Digital transformation in retail industry: The case of Watsons.* Pressacademia., doi:10.17261/Pressacademia.2022.1578

Saumya, & Sandhane, R. (2023). Digital transformation in retail industry: Impact of skilled and trained personnel for effective utilization of digital tools for successful digital transformation. AIP Conference Proceedings. 11th Annual International Conference (AIC) 2021: On Sciences and Engineering, Banda Aceh, Indonesia. doi:10.1063/5.0110617

Solomon, M. (2014). *Consumer behavior: Buying, having, and being.* Pearson.

Verhoef, P. C., Neslin, S. A., & Vroomen, B. (2007). Multichannel customer management: Understanding the research-shopper phenomenon. *International Journal of Research in Marketing*, *24*(2), 129–148. doi:10.1016/j.ijresmar.2006.11.002

Wang, H. (2021). Realizing digital transformation in retail businesses with a digital technology platform and solutions: A case study of NEXTTAO. In Business Innovation with New ICT in the Asia-Pacific: Case Studies (pp. 133–151). Springer Nature Singapore. doi:10.1007/978-981-15-7658-4_7

Chapter 11
Shifting Consumer Behaviors Towards Sustainability Through Eco-Packaging:
An Examination of Literature and a Guiding Framework

Uttam Kaur
Chandigarh University, India

Prashant Kumar Siddhey
 https://orcid.org/0000-0002-4236-0966
Chandigarh University, India

ABSTRACT

The present study highlights the critical role that marketing plays in promoting sustainable consumption through eco-packaging. It does this by reviewing academic research in the fields of behavioral science and marketing that looks at the best practices for changing consumer behavior towards sustainability through eco-packaging. During the review process, the writers create a thorough framework for imagining and promoting long-term changes in customer behavior. The framework, which goes by the abbreviation SHIFT, suggests that when a message or context makes use of the psychological elements of social influence, habit formation, individual self, feelings and cognition, and tangibility, customers are more likely to act in ways that support the environment. In addition, the researchers list five major obstacles to promoting sustainable behavior, and they utilize them to formulate original theoretical ideas and suggest future lines of inquiry. Lastly, the authors describe how this paradigm might be applied by practitioners who want to promote ecological behaviour among consumers.

DOI: 10.4018/979-8-3693-2367-0.ch011

INTRODUCTION

Our personal shopping choices are affecting the environment in ways never seen before. A new approach to conducting business is indicated by the convergence of factors that society and business must deal with, which is partly caused by our consumption patterns. These factors include poverty and social inequality, pollution and destruction of the environment, and climate change (Rutitis et al., 2022). The present investigation offers an overview of the literature on how consumers may switch from conventional to eco-packaging sustainably. It also presents a thorough psychological framework that can help practitioners and researchers promote sustainable behavior (Korhonen et al., 2020). In recent years, there has been a profound evolution in consumer attitudes, marked by a growing awareness of environmental issues and a heightened commitment to sustainable living. Central to this transformative shift is the discernible demand for eco-friendly packaging solutions, a reflection of consumers' increasing scrutiny of the environmental impact of their purchasing decisions. As concerns over climate change, plastic pollution, and resource depletion intensify, individuals are actively seeking products packaged with eco-conscious materials and methods. Governments worldwide are responding with regulatory measures to address environmental degradation, emphasizing the imperative of sustainable packaging (Lan et al., 2023). Simultaneously, businesses are recognizing the strategic importance of integrating eco-packaging into their practices, not only as a response to regulatory pressures but also as a means to align with consumer values and fulfill corporate social responsibility (CSR) objectives. This evolving landscape underscores the pivotal role that eco-packaging plays in shaping contemporary consumer behaviors towards a more sustainable and environmentally responsible future.

Several compelling case studies exemplify the tangible impact of eco-packaging on shifting consumer behaviors towards sustainability. One such instance is the success story of a global beverage company that transitioned from traditional plastic bottles to plant-based, fully recyclable packaging. This initiative not only reduced their carbon footprint but also resonated with environmentally conscious consumers, leading to a significant increase in market share. In the fashion industry, a leading apparel brand's shift to using recycled and biodegradable packaging materials not only enhanced their brand image but also attracted a new segment of eco-conscious consumers. Additionally, a regional grocery chain's switch to reusable and compostable bags prompted a notable reduction in single-use plastic waste, aligning with both consumer expectations and governmental regulations. These case studies collectively underscore the transformative power of eco-packaging in driving consumer preferences and fostering a sustainable market paradigm (Jestratijevic & Vrabic-Brodnjak, 2022)

Marketing and Sustainable Consumer Behavior Towards Eco-Packaging

Marketers should be interested in understanding the drivers of sustainable customer behaviour for a variety of reasons. Marketers need to understand that one of the main causes of the detrimental effects on the environment is the consuming attitude that traditional packaging promotes. Companies that can adjust to the ever-changing needs of the world, such as the pressing need for sustainability, will have a higher chance of long-term success and strategic advantages. Finding new goods and markets, using emerging technology, fostering creativity, increasing organisational efficiency, and inspiring and keeping staff are just a few benefits of having a sustainable company focus (Oliver et al., 2023). Furthermore, studies indicate that adopting socially and ecologically conscious practices may boost a company's profitability and foster more favourable customer opinions of the enterprise. Businesses that can think of innovative business models that promote and enable sustainable consumption in addition to operating more sustainably may be able to generate higher long-term earnings. The burgeoning "sharing economy" serves as one illustration of the significant economic and environmental benefits that may be achieved by reorienting consumer behavior sustainably, in this case from product ownership to product and service access. Scholars currently demand research on the predictors of sustainable consumption through eco-packaging, even though the issue of how marketing relates to ecological consumption has historically been addressed through the identification of the "green consumer" group (Lan et al., 2023). For the long-term joint benefit of the company and the environment, marketers can broaden their market rather than only focusing on the green customer category. Therefore, companies that operate and package their goods and services more sustainably may also hope that customers will identify, accept, and reward them for their environmentally friendly actions and values in ways that encourage environmentally friendly consumption and optimize the company's sustainability and strategic business advantages. The necessity for a thorough analysis and framework about the primary forces behind long-term changes in customer behavior is what spurred the current effort. We expand upon prior research that succinctly describes the actions that marketers may take to recognize, encourage, and assess sustainable behavior about eco-packaging (Popovic et al., 2019). While the current body of work describes the notion of social marketing and provides examples, it falls short of offering a thorough psychological framework for persuading consumers to switch from conventional packaging to eco-packaging. Current research frequently focuses on a narrower range of variables that encourage sustainable behavior in the direction of environmentally friendly packaging. Therefore, the primary goal of this study is to provide a thorough framework that will assist academics and practitioners in promoting ecological customer behavior in the direction of environmentally friendly packaging. Practitioners will be able to create the most successful treatments if they have access to a more comprehensive framework that incorporates all of the key elements from the literature (Wang & Wang, 2021). Second, our framework's distinct, process-driven focus (as opposed to earlier research's intervention focus) guarantees that practitioners may quickly adapt our framework to new circumstances as technology and societies evolve. Our ability to provide a wide range of tools that businesses may utilize to achieve their sustainability and strategic business objectives is therefore a major contribution. Third, by doing a more thorough study, we were able to identify a wider range of obstacles to long-term changes in consumer behavior that can help practitioners and researchers alike. In the theoretical contribution part, we address four issues: the self-other trade-off, the long time horizon, the need for communal action, the abstractness problem, and the necessity of substituting controlled processes for automated ones. Lastly, we employ these obstacles to environmentally friendly buyer behavior to present a series of original theoretical ideas that will direct conceptual development moving forward and inform future studies (Van Birgelen et al., 2009).

Economic and Logistics Challenges

For organizations, the transition to environmentally friendly packaging and ecological consumer behaviors poses logistical and financial obstacles. Financially speaking, the initial expenses of implementing eco-friendly packaging may be greater because of the efforts made in R&D and the use of sustainable materials. Changing supply chains and production methods to accept eco-packaging may also result in higher operating costs (Mahajan et al., 2023). Financial planning is necessary to carefully weigh these expenses against any possible long-term rewards. To guarantee a smooth transition, supply chain modifications can be required, which might necessitate working with new suppliers or creating other distribution routes. A systematic strategy is necessary to navigate these logistical and economic obstacles as businesses look to integrate environmentally friendly packaging initiatives with cost-effective measures to meet their environmental objectives (Asim et al., 2022).

Shifting Consumers to Behave Sustainably

From an initial observation, it may seem that the objectives and presumptions of sustainability and marketing are mutually exclusive. Conventional marketing tends to perceive resources as perpetually available, stimulates expansion, and supports an unending pursuit of requirements and desires satisfaction. On the other hand, a sustainability approach acknowledges that resources and the environment have limited capacity and proposes that exhausted resources may be replenished by imitating the natural cycles of resource flow. We contend that this seeming paradox is the reason why marketing and sustainability are closely related (Capiene et al., 2022). Moreover, we have an optimistic stance, believing that behavioral science and marketing might provide valuable insights on how to encourage more sustainable consumption. We examine the research and provide strategies for motivating customers to adopt more environmentally friendly practices. The acronym SHIFT emerged from our literature study and emphasizes the significance of taking into account how Social influence, Habit formation, Individual self, Feelings and cognition, and Tangibility may be used to promote more sustainable consumer behaviors. In sustainable contexts, a common observation is the "attitude–behavior gap," which may be addressed with the use of the SHIFT framework. While consumers express positive sentiments towards pro-environmental behaviors, they frequently fail to behave sustainably after reporting favorable attitudes (Sharma & Painuly, 2023). The largest obstacle facing marketers, businesses, public policymakers, and charitable organizations that want to encourage sustainable purchasing is undoubtedly the disparity between what customers say and do. Therefore, even if there is evidence that consumers are becoming more and more demanding when it comes to sustainable options—for example, they are ready to pay more for them—there is still the opportunity to promote and support sustainable consumer behaviour. Responsible consumer behaviour is defined as behaviours that, throughout a product, behaviour, or service's lifespan, reduce both the negative effects on the environment and the use of natural resources. While concentrating on sustainability in the environment, we also point out that enhancing environmental sustainability may lead to social and economic advancements, which is compatible with a holistic approach to sustainability. We look at the consuming process in a way that promotes more sustainable results, including information search, decision-making, acceptance of a product or behaviour, product usage, and disposal (De Bauw et al., 2022). Numerous businesses have adopted environmental sustainability by using creative environmentally friendly packaging techniques, which has a favourable impact on customer behaviour. Unilever, for instance, has pledged that by 2025, all of its plastic packaging will be recyclable, reusable, or compostable, promoting eco-friendly options among its customers. All Birds, an environmentally friendly footwear business, reduces waste and raises awareness of environmental issues by using shoeboxes made of 90% recycled cardboard and removing needless printing. Another example is Loop, a business that is partnering with well-known companies to produce reusable packaging that enables customers to return empty containers for refills. These real-world examples demonstrate how businesses are actively promoting eco-packaging projects, providing customers with tangible alternatives, and encouraging a change in customer behaviour towards environmentally friendly purchase habits. Therefore, selecting items with ecologically sound sources, manufacturing, and characteristics; safeguarding energy, water, and materials while using them; and adopting more environmentally friendly methods of disposing of products are examples of environmentally friendly consumer behaviors. Sustainable consumer decisions take into account longer-term advantages to other people and the environment, as opposed to usual consumer decision-making, which traditionally concentrates on maximizing immediate benefits for the self. In this field, more general marketing approaches can be helpful, but to encourage sustainability, marketers also require a certain set of tools. We want to provide the main forces behind sustainable consumption within a single, all-encompassing framework (Xu & Ward, 2023).

THE SHIFT FRAMEWORK

Social Influence

Social influence is the first step in changing customer behavior towards environmentally friendly packaging. The expectations, actions, and presence of others frequently affect customers. When it comes to influencing consumers to switch from conventional to environmentally friendly packaging, social reasons are among the most powerful. We look at how social norms, social identities, and social desirability—three distinct aspects of social influence—can sway consumers towards more sustainability (Lan et al., 2023).

Social Norms

Environmentally friendly consumer behaviors can be significantly impacted by social norms, which are views on what is considered acceptable and socially acceptable in a certain setting. Social norms influence decisions about things like not littering, recycling and composting, energy conservation, buying food that is sourced sustainably, choosing eco-friendly travel, booking green accommodations, and installing solar panels. According to the Theory of Planned behavior, attitudes, and perceived behavioral control, in addition to subjective standards, influence intentions, which in turn predict conduct (Siddiqui et al., 2022).

Social Identities

Social influence has an effect based on people's "social identities," or feeling of self that comes from belonging to a group. For instance, when individuals in their group participate in sustainable behaviour, customers are more inclined to follow suit. Furthermore, a major factor influencing pro-environmental decisions and behaviours is the perception of oneself as a member of a pro-environmental in-group. People's desire to regard their in-groups favourably and to avoid having their in-group outperformed by other groups is another aspect of social identities. People in the focus group boosted their positive behaviours towards environmentally friendly packaging when they discovered that a dissociated reference group had outperformed them in a positive, environmentally friendly behaviour towards eco-packaging. Since the communal self is most significant in public contexts, these effects were amplified there. Knowledge of environmentally friendly behaviors can be more readily accepted when it emphasizes a superordinate shared identity inside the group, particularly among high in-group identification individuals (Getersleben et al., 2019).

Social Desirability

"Social desirability" is another way that social influence may affect sustainable behaviours towards eco-packaging. Customers like high-involvement sustainable alternatives to communicate social status to others and choose sustainable solutions to leave a good impression on others. However, some customers avoid doing pro-environmental measures because they see sustainable behaviours adversely. In one case, men tried to avoid being seen as "eco-friendly" since it was seen as a sign of femininity. Making environmentally friendly packaged goods or attitudes towards eco-packaging socially acceptable is one way to address any possible unfavourable views associated with sustainable consumption. Furthermore, when customers are acting in public and have others around to see and judge them, they are more inclined to behave in a socially desirable way. Furthermore, promoting public pledges to adopt environmentally friendly packaging practices might boost these kinds of initiatives (Roozen & Pelsmacker, 1998).

Habit Formation

While many sustainable behaviours just call for a single action, many others necessitate the development of new habits through repeated activities. Behaviours that endure because they have mostly become automatic over time due to frequent exposure to environmental signals are referred to as habits. A key element of behaviour towards sustainable packaging transformation is habit modification, as many popular practices are unsustainable. Numerous actions that have an impact on sustainability, such purchasing, product disposal, energy and resource usage, transportation choice, and food intake, are highly ingrained habits. Bad habits can be broken by interventions that prevent repetition, such discontinuities and sanctions. Positive habits may be reinforced by repeated acts that promote recurrence, such as simplifying sustainable behaviours and using prompts, rewards, and feedback (White et al., 2019).

Discontinuity to Change Bad Habits

According to the habit discontinuity theory, it becomes more difficult to engage in regular behaviors when the environment in which they develop shifts. Stated differently, the optimum conditions for habit modification might be created by a disturbance to the stable context that gives birth to habitual behaviors. People are more inclined to switch from traditional packaging to eco-packaging practices when their lives change. Therefore, promoting behaviors towards eco-packaging may be accomplished in part by fusing habit formation strategies with context modifications (Kurz et al., 2015).

Penalties

In essence, penalties are forms of discipline that lessen a person's propensity to participate in undesired behaviour about environmentally friendly packaging. A tax, fee, or tariff on unsustainable behaviour are some examples of penalties. Taxes and tariffs can be successful in domains that include strong habits, while fines can induce change in domains that can be monitored, such as garbage disposal. Penalties have the potential to discourage unsustainable behaviour in some situations, but they can also have unintended consequences and cause defensive and negative reactions if they appear irrational. Furthermore, it might be challenging to monitor and execute fines. As a result, using positive behaviour modification techniques—which we address next—is frequently preferable (Ding et al., 2023).

Implementation Intentions

Asking people to reflect on their implementation intentions—their plans for how they intend to act out the action—is one way to help them go from an old habit to a new one. Purchase habits for eco-friendly packaged goods and recycling can both benefit from such objectives. Positive habit formation approaches include making the new behavior easy, providing prompts, feedback, and rewards, as well as repetition, which may then be used to reinforce it (Boz et al., 2020).

Making It Easy

Sustainable behaviors may be hindered by the perception that they require a lot of work, are time-consuming, or are challenging to implement. Making the activity easy to do is therefore one tactic to promote the creation of durable habits. Environmentally friendly packaging practices are encouraged by contextual modifications that make sustainable behavior easier to adopt. Examples of these contextual adjustments include having recycling bins close by, needing less complicated recycling sorting, and providing showerheads with "low-flow" options (Ketelsen et al., 2020).

Prompts

The use of prompts—messages delivered before an action to remind the customer of the intended behaviour regarding sustainable packaging—is another strategy for promoting the development of sustainable habits. Incentives have a favourable impact on a variety of behaviours related to environmentally friendly packaging, such as recycling, energy use, and garbage disposal. The most effective way to encourage people to engage in sustainable behaviours is to place them close to the behaviour's intended location. Prompts are a simple and affordable way to encourage people to start changing their behaviour, but they work best when combined with other strategies (Minton & Rose, 1997).

Incentives

Extrinsic incentives, such as discounts, gifts, and rewards, can reinforce beneficial habit development and desired behaviours related to environmentally friendly packaging. People can be encouraged to adopt and maintain sustainable behaviours towards environmentally friendly packaging by offering monetary rewards such as cash, tiered pricing, and rebates. Rewards have been demonstrated to affect environmentally friendly practices related to packaging, including energy use, transportation decisions, and garbage disposal and cleanup. Incentives have the potential to be detrimental, even if they can promote the adoption and upkeep of sustainable behaviours related to eco-packaging. Smaller financial incentives, such as gifts, lottery tickets, or social recognition, are frequently more compelling than larger monetary ones. Second, rewards for adopting sustainable behaviours may result in transient behaviours. Rewards initially elicit a good response from customers, but when the incentive is removed, environmentally friendly behaviour frequently vanishes. Therefore, it is simpler to use incentives to promote one-time sustainable behaviours than it is to stimulate longer-term improvements. Additionally, because incentives lessen the intrinsic motivation to perform the activity, they may unintentionally have the effect of reducing the desired behaviour (Stern, 1999).

Feedback

Using feedback is another way to promote the development of durable habits. Giving customers precise information on how well they performed a job or behaved is part of this. Feedback on behaviors such as water and energy use can be offered, and it can be based on the customer's historical packaging behaviors or compared to other people's performances. According to research, feedback works best when it is given, in real-time, and over a lengthy period. Giving collective feedback to families and coworkers may also be a productive way to implement environmentally friendly packaging reform (Nemat et al., 2019).

The Individual Self

Personal factors can have a significant impact on how consumers behave when it comes to eco-packaging. Positive self-concept, self-interest, self-consistency, self-efficacy, and different people are among the ideas covered in this section (Zaman et al., 2023).

The Self-Concept

People like to think well of themselves, and using eco-packaging may help them reiterate how good they think of themselves. People frequently respond defensively to information about how their actions affect the environment and disparage those who behave in more sustainable ways because they want to see themselves as good people. People also shy away from adopting certain sustainable practices when it comes to packaging change because they perceive it as a threat to their identity. Consumer behaviors regarding eco-packaging are also influenced by one's self-concept, as personal belongings can serve as extensions of one's personality (Sharma et al., 2020).

Self-Consistency

People want to perceive themselves as consistent, in addition to being excellent role models. According to self-consistency research, when a consumer engages in a sustainable behaviour towards eco-packaging at one point in time, such as reaffirming that they are environmentally conscious, or when they engage in behaviour towards eco-packaging, they are likely to continue in that direction in the future. Furthermore, the same context might give rise to both consistency and inconsistency. Following their purchase, shoppers who carried reusable bags to the store spent more money on eco-friendly products. Additionally, for customers who are not very concerned about the environment, making a sustainable decision reduces their following environmentally friendly behaviours towards eco-packaging, while for those who are, it boosts these behaviours (Cheah & Phau, 2011).

Self-Interest

When self-relevant incentives are satisfied, customers are more influenced by sustainable features. Emphasizing self-benefits that can overcome obstacles to environmentally friendly behavior is another way to appeal to customer self-interest. Self-interest isn't always the best course of action. Furthermore, self-interests have the potential to overshadow environmental concerns, particularly when arguments for sustainable behavior combine personal and environmental goals (Corbett, 2005).

Feelings and Cognition

Since customers often follow one of two paths to action—one that is more motivated by cognition and one that is more motivated by affect—we present the notions of feelings and cognition together. This claim is in line with theories that contend that decision-making processes can be dominated by either an emotive, intuitive pathway or a cognitive, deliberate one. We see that this differentiation is probably going to be quite important when it comes to responding to information concerning environmental concerns. This study first outlines how pro-environmental behaviors related to sustainable packaging may be influenced by both good and negative emotions. After that, talk about how knowledge and learning, eco-labeling, and framing all play a part in how cognition determines actions that are environmentally friendly (Koenig-Lewis et al., 2014).

Negative Emotions

Customers frequently think about the detrimental emotional effects of adopting sustainable behaviors— whether they involve eco-packaging or not. In general, it's best to refrain from inducing really strong negative emotions. But once the feeling subsided, there was no longer any difference in the eco-friendly behaviors of the individuals who had received the message of grief as opposed to the non-affective one. As a result, when customers are feeling certain emotions, like melancholy, they have greater influence (Taufique, 2022).

Positive Emotions

When a consumer has a hedonic pleasure or pleasant effect from an action, they are more likely to participate in pro-environmental behavior. Reducing negative emotions and enhancing pleasant ones can be achieved through sustainable behaviors related to sustainable packaging. It has been demonstrated that positive feelings like pride and happiness affect consumers' intentions to use fewer plastic water bottles, and optimism can encourage people to stick with sustainable practices over time, including using eco-packaging. Positive feelings, on the other hand, have the power to sway sustainable consumer behavior in favor of environmentally friendly packaging. Lastly, encouraging environmental deeds may inspire optimism, which in turn can spur climate advocacy and encourage customers to adopt environmentally friendly packaging practices (Koenig-Lewis et al., 2014).

Information, Learning, and Knowledge

Providing information on desirable (and unwanted) behaviors towards eco-packaging and their effects is a fundamental strategy for influencing customers to do eco-friendly activities through eco-packaging. Some have bemoaned the lack of awareness and knowledge among people, which they attribute to information overload, misunderstanding, and lack of exposure to information. This, they claim, might lead to consumers adopting sustainable behaviours less frequently, including using environmentally friendly packaging. Furthermore, there is a correlation between higher IQ, education, and knowledge and increased receptivity to environmental cues and adoption of environmentally beneficial practices (Taufique et al., 2016). Knowledge is applicable to all of our SHIFT elements in various ways. The customer has to grasp information on self-values, self-benefits, self-efficacy, and other similar topics. They also need to be aware of and cognizant of the prompt or feedback. Giving customers the basic information they need to make decisions about environmentally friendly packaging may be accomplished by making appeals that emphasise why the desired behaviour or product is ecological (Adrita & Mohiuddin, 2020).

Eco-Labeling

One way to notify consumers about a product's environmentally friendly packaging features is through eco-labeling. Buyers may make more educated judgments about buying eco-friendly packaged goods if labels are eye-catching, simple to read, and consistent across categories. If eco-labeling is approved by an independent body that verifies its environmental claims, it may appear more impartial and transparent. It's crucial to remember, though, that some research indicates eco-labels may not be very effective in forecasting consumer behaviour in relation to eco-packaging (Jozwik-Pruska et al., 2022).

Cost-Benefit Analysis

A cost-benefit analysis of using eco-packaging to influence consumer behaviour towards sustainability entails assessing the possible benefits and financial fallout from using eco-friendly packaging techniques. Regarding expenses, businesses must take into account the one-time expenditure needed to switch to environmentally friendly production methods, materials, and package designs (Mahajan et al., 2023). The long-term advantages are complex, though. Using eco-friendly packaging may improve a business's reputation and draw in customers who care about the environment. Businesses may also gain from improved public relations, a rise in consumer loyalty, and a competitive advantage in a market where sustainability is becoming more and more important. Because of this, companies may use the cost-benefit analysis as a strategic tool to balance the initial costs of adopting sustainable packaging methods with the long-term benefits to the economy, the environment, and society (Granato et al., 2022).

Supply Chain Adjustments

A major transformation of the whole supply chain is required to nudge consumer behaviour towards sustainability through eco-packaging. To be in line with ecologically friendly methods, businesses must rethink and maybe even restructure every step of the process, from acquiring raw materials to production and distribution. Selecting and incorporating environmentally friendly materials into packaging is part of this, as is working with vendors that follow green guidelines (Purcarea et al., 2022). To guarantee that eco-friendly packaging materials and products are transported efficiently, distribution networks and logistics may also need to be adjusted. For a smooth shift to sustainable practices, businesses may also need to work in tandem and educate their manufacturers, distributors, and suppliers. In addition to helping firms adapt to changing customer tastes, such supply chain modifications also help to create a more robust and ecologically conscious supply chain ecosystem (Sharma & Mahlawat, 2021).

Consumer Price Sensitivity

In the context of changing consumer behaviours towards sustainability through eco-packaging, price sensitivity among consumers is critical. Customers' willingness to pay more for eco-friendly products and packaging is becoming increasingly important as they place a higher priority on environmental issues. Businesses that follow sustainable practices have to walk a tightrope between providing affordable packaging and being ecologically conscious (Dinh et al., 2022). In order to meet customer expectations, firms must carefully evaluate the appropriate pricing range, taking into account variables like income levels, demographic trends, and geographical variances. Finding the ideal balance between cost and value may have a big influence on how well sustainable packaging projects work, affecting consumer adoption rates and keeping environmentally friendly options available to more people (Granato et al., 2022).

Geographical and Cultural Contexts

The transition towards ecological customer behaviour through environmentally friendly packaging is contingent upon both geographical and cultural circumstances. Significant regional and cultural differences exist in consumer attitudes, tastes, and understanding of sustainability. For businesses looking to adopt sustainable packaging techniques, it is crucial to comprehend the various cultural viewpoints on environmental responsibility, recycling habits, and knowledge of eco-friendly substitutes (Nguyen et al., 2021). Geographical differences in legislative frameworks and infrastructure capacities can also affect the availability and adoption of eco-friendly goods and activities. To effectively manoeuvre through these environments, companies must customise their sustainability programmes, communications, and packaging options to connect with regional values and inclinations, guaranteeing that the transition to environmentally sustainable methods is consistent with the varied cultural environments in which they function (Branca et al., 2023).

THEORETICAL IMPLICATIONS AND DIRECTIONS FOR FUTURE RESEARCH

This investigation outlined particular behaviour change techniques for each of the five approaches to sustainable behaviour towards eco-packaging transformation in our literature assessment. The review section of this article has focused on identifying the primary factors, as determined by current research, that influence consumer behaviour towards eco-packaging. We will elaborate on a few theoretical claims on the relative relevance of each of the SHIFT factors—that is, the pathways to ecological behaviour change towards environmentally friendly packaging—in the following part. To achieve this, outline several significant obstacles that set the usage of eco-packaged products apart from conventional customer behaviors. These obstacles include the need to substitute automated procedures with controlled ones, the long time horizon, the self-other trade-off, the need for collective action, and the problem of abstractness. Using our SHIFT framework as a lens, we analyze each of these obstacles to customer behavior shift towards environmentally friendly packaging and provide important theoretical ideas and future research objectives.

The Self-Other Trade-Off

One of the primary obstacles to ecological buyer behavior is the perception held among customers that certain acts, such as choosing environmentally friendly packaging, come at a personal cost in terms of time, expense, or quality. In addition, sustainable consumption practices have beneficial external effects on the environment and society. Thus, opinions regarding customer behavior towards environmentally friendly packaging often imply setting aside desires that are associated with the self and prioritizing and valuing entities that are outside of the self, despite the conventional viewpoint of customer behavior towards environmentally friendly packaging holding that customers will select and utilize goods and services in ways that meet their desires and requirements. The self-other trade-off affects how social influence could function when promoting environmentally friendly packaging practices among consumers. While it is true that environmentally friendly consumption frequently has a cost to the self, we propose that identity signaling can have a beneficial, self-relevant effect that can offset the costs of taking sustainable action. Research demonstrates that when the setting is public or when status incentives are aroused, customers are more likely to choose sustainable solutions, which supports this argument. Building on this study, a fresh premise suggests that when a product is positioned on sustainable rather than traditional features, its symbolism may have a greater influence on customer attitudes and decisions. When we talk about items being "symbolic," we mean that they have a greater ability to communicate to others significant aspects of who they are. Since there may not be as many direct benefits to oneself from an environmentally friendly action, the marketer may choose to focus on either symbolic advantages (i.e., sharing pertinent information about oneself with others) or the functional features (i.e., knowledge about meeting practical desires) associated with a product.

P1: Customers may show more positive attitudes and behaviors if a choice is presented in terms of being environmentally friendly packaged instead of a conventional packaged item when a given behavior or item is presented based on its symbolic characteristics of environmentally friendly packaging (vs. operational characteristics).

Examining the unique self is another strategy for resolving the self-other trade-off. In particular, ecological customer behaviors towards eco-packaging may be predicted by the individual's perception of their self-concept. Investigation might also look at ways to activate even more expansive, transcendent conceptions of the self, ones that include not just the self and personal relationships, but also other species and the planet. Promoting such transcendental self-views might well promote environmentally conscious behavior.

P2: More environmentally friendly packaging-related behaviors will result from promoting the idea that one is either transcendent or interdependent from one's self.

Simultaneously, a particular emphasis on the self may be motivatingly connected to behaviour that is environmentally friendly in a way that surmounts uncertainty. People who are given a feeling of agency—that is, who can believe that they are the ones who cause behavioural outcomes—feel empowered and have the capacity to truly affect change. Because the results of environmentally friendly behaviours towards environmentally friendly packaging are frequently ambiguous and abstract, agency priming may be a useful motivational technique in the area of environmentally friendly behaviour shift from traditional packaging to environmentally friendly packaging. This could be accomplished by using agency priming to encourage people to attain a specific sustainable goal.

P3: Agent primes that exist will cause a greater propensity to use environmentally friendly packaging to promote ecological behaviors.

Investigation of the person's self in prosocial settings also emphasizes how moral identity may play a role in helping people overcome the trade-off between their own and other selves. A mental schema centered on moral qualities, objectives, and ideals is referred to as a moral identity. As far as we are aware, no previous research has looked at whether people see moral duties to engage in environmentally friendly packaging practices as being determined by moral identity.

P4: Personal variations in moral identity, as well as moral identity primes, will drive more environmentally conscious customers to act related to packaging.

The self-other trade-off is associated with customers' perceptions of the advantages and disadvantages of packaging sustainable goods. There isn't enough research in the literature to look at how consumers associate environmentally friendly packaging with good things. Few studies specifically look at the beneficial links, despite the abundance of research on customers' unfavorable perceptions of environmentally friendly packaging. Moreover, probably, fresh, local food, the outdoors, and the environment are all positively correlated with sustainability.

P5: Contrasted with typical packaging solutions, environmentally friendly choices, and behaviors may offer certain advantages, such as being more inventive, healthier, and connected to the outside and the environment.

An increased focus on the significance of "negative self-related" emotions, such as dread and guilt, is highlighted by the self-other trade-off. Subsequent research endeavors may delve deeper into the impact of "affirmative affective states associated with external entities" on customer behavior, to propel environmentally friendly packaging usage. But as far as we are aware, no research has examined how awe affects environmentally friendly customer attitudes towards environmentally friendly packaging. Prospects for further study include investigating emotions such as astonishment, compassion, and ethical elevation.

P6: Environmentally friendly customer behaviors towards eco-packaging will be predicted by outwardly oriented positive emotions including astonishment, compassion, and ethical elevation.

A related option to comparing oneself to others is to look at how aspirational social influence affects environmentally friendly customer behaviour in the direction of packaging change. Is it feasible to associate a sustainable choice or behaviour with inspirational role models like sports and celebrities, making it socially acceptable to the self? This might be achieved by marketers creating a relationship between aspirational individuals and sustainable acts in a way that makes environmentally friendly packaged goods and behaviours seem desirable, opulent, and valuable.

P7: By creating a sense of luxury and inspiration by associating sustainably packaged goods and behaviors with inspirational role models, customers may be more inclined to adopt environmentally friendly packaging practices.

It has been observed that customers find payoffs less appealing the further they are in the future. Most conventional customer behaviours have more immediate repercussions than ecological customer behaviours when it comes to environmentally friendly packaging. While it would seem that the literature on self-control has a lot to say about changing behaviour sustainably, there hasn't been much research that specifically examines how self-regulation affects the choice of environmentally friendly behaviours. Perhaps even more self-control is needed for sustainable behaviours than for other self-control behaviours. This might be investigated and strategies for improving self-control in the environmental field could be considered.

P8: Customers who engage in environmentally friendly behaviors towards environmentally friendly packaging are more inclined to slip in those whose regulatory resources are somewhat constrained.

Individuals typically have to incur hedonic costs to themselves in the present to maximize some beneficial ecological consequence in the future, which is why sustainable behavior towards eco-packaging has a lengthy time horizon. Customers' sustainable behaviors may rise if attention is paid to how eco-packaging practices may have a beneficial impact now.

P9: Longer-term perspectives of the long-term horizon will be lessened and the chance of environmentally friendly choices will rise with environmentally friendly behaviors that produce more warm glow sensations or pleasant effects in the short term as opposed to the long run.

Additionally connected to tangibility is the extended time horizon. Even if most people don't give a damn about what will happen in the future, everyone cares differently about it. Higher "discount rate" individuals are less concerned with the future. Similarly, those who give less thought to the effects of their actions down the road also tend to have less environmental goals.

P10: People who have greater rates of discounting and pay less attention to future effects may be more susceptible to making ecological results more tangible.

Furthermore, there is a connection between the self-other trade-off and the long-term perspective in terms of how tangibility may influence environmentally friendly buyer behavior. Generations that follow are more likely to be the ones to notice environmental effects in the future. Therefore, interventions that make the consequences of behaving (or not behaving) responsibly more tangible for future generations may catalyze more sustainable behavior.

P11: When people consider future generations from a situational or dispositional standpoint, they will be more inclined to engage in ecological customer behaviors related to environmentally friendly packaging.

The lengthy time horizon has one last consequence that is connected to each and every SHIFT component. It would be financially advantageous for future studies to investigate the long-term impacts of various interventions on customers' sustainable packaging behaviours. Furthermore, the framework draws attention to a contradiction between the various behaviour modification techniques' short- and long-term foci. While certain constructions are influenced by the current situation and result in rapid behavioural changes, other constructs have a longer-lasting effect on behaviour. This option might be tested by future study.

P12: Utilising several techniques for immediate and long-term change can be the most effective way to encourage ecological customer behaviours towards environmentally friendly packaging.

The Difficulty of Group Action Collective activity is frequently more necessary for sustainable behaviours than solo action. For the advantages to be completely realised, a sizable population must adopt environmentally friendly behaviours towards environmentally friendly packaging. This is not like typical customer behaviour when the person acts alone to get the desired result. In light of this research, make the case for communal effectiveness as a strong inducement for sustainable consumer behaviour. Collective action may be more motivating in the context of the sustainability domain than other positive behaviour domains since sustainable results need very large-scale acts. There is still room for more study to look into this.

P13: Information conveying the effectiveness of collective action as well as other people's behaviors will heighten the propensity to take environmentally friendly actions.

Taking emotions into account may have an impact on how to get beyond the obstacle of group action. While some study has examined the importance of collective emotions—that is, sentiments that members of a group share widely—when group objectives are pursued or obstructed, the emotions examined in this area have only included feelings of pride or remorse from previous group acts. In the meanwhile, other kinds of group emotions may work better to promote environmentally friendly behaviors.

P14: Emotions that are focused on the future, like optimism and fury, may encourage ecological customer behavior when it comes to packaging.

Similar to this, ideas regarding group activities may also encourage environmentally friendly behaviors that lead to environmentally friendly packaging. Communicating collective-level outcomes like climate justice might have an impact on promoting environmentally friendly behaviors since they have the special quality of demanding group action. Communication on the unequal distribution of harmful environmental risks and how the most vulnerable people experience them, in particular, might be particularly effective.

P15: Disseminating knowledge on climate justice might encourage environmentally conscious consumers to switch to environmentally friendly packaging.

Tangibility is also associated with collective activity. Anecdotally, highlighting the group's influence is a common strategy for encouraging eco-friendly behavior. collaborative effect framing draws attention to the issue with collaborative action, which may lead to a drop in sustainable activity. Conversely, it magnifies the apparent magnitude of the influence, perhaps promoting sustainable conduct regarding eco-packaging, as individuals are frequently indifferent to significant numerical variations in environmental consequences.

P16: Framing collective effect in a tangible rather than an ethereal way encourages environmental behavior towards eco-packaging.

A great deal of unsustainable behaviour has been learnt in a way that makes it automatic in nature as opposed to regulated. Hence, adopting sustainable consumption frequently entails (at least initially) substituting more deliberate new behavioural responses for more reflexive ones (like using one's own shopping bag). This difficulty may be linked to the development of habits. Remember that leveraging discontinuity—the idea that significant life events might facilitate the occurrence of other types of habit change—is one strategy for influencing habitual change. Beyond sporadic significant life events, it's also feasible that a certain attitude contributes to habit change. People with a "fresh start" mentality are more likely to be favorable about things that provide a new start and to have positive intentions when it comes to donating to charities that support these receivers of a fresh start. Seeing a new behavior as a "fresh start" might act as a type of irregularity that increases the likelihood of habit modification.

P17: People with a measured or controlled fresh start mentality are more likely to adopt environmentally friendly behavior patterns.

Tangibility may help in the process of adopting sustainable behavior, even if it frequently necessitates replacing an instinctive habit with a regulated one. People may analyze experiences more deeply when faced with concrete results because they are more immediate and vivid, which may encourage them to rely more heavily on feelings and intuition when making judgments.

P18: treatments that promote tangibility cause individuals to process information more experientially rather than analytically, which will reduce the efficacy of subsequent treatments.

The fact that environmentally friendly customer behaviors are frequently described as ambiguous, and challenging for the customer to understand presents a barrier to our efforts to promote them. While there may be varying degrees of risk and uncertainty associated with conventional customer behavior, decisions made in conventional customer contexts often have more defined and predictable results than those made in environmentally friendly customer contexts. One way to solve the abstractness issue is to take social impact into account. People are impacted by social issues in part because, in uncertain situations, we frequently look to the expectations and actions of others.

P19: Social elements such as the presence of others, their behaviors, and/or their expectations will have a greater influence on behavior when the environmentally friendly action or the result is unclear, unknown, or novel in some way.

This may be more noticeable in people who avoid uncertainty a lot. The development of habits may be significant in addressing the abstractness issue. Individual activities seem little and insignificant in comparison to the severe, ambiguous, and potentially large-scale repercussions of climate change and other crises. This might cause customers to become demotivated due to information overload and a lack of optimism for significant change, a condition known as "green fatigue." Celebrating tiny, tangible victories might be one way to encourage environmentally friendly behavior and maintain customer interest.

P20: By offering rewards for little achievements, eco-packaging will keep customers motivated to keep up their ecologically beneficial habits and prevent environmental fatigue.

The issue of being abstract has a personal component as well. Addressing the issue of vague and ambiguous results directly may include taking into account the potential effects on the individual. We've discovered that presenting sustainable impacts and results as personal, local, and relevant helps promote environmentally friendly customer behavior. Future studies, though, may look into different ways to make a more personal connection between sustainable results and the self. These researchers discovered that people are more inclined to contribute to retirement savings when they feel more connected to their future selves. It is feasible that customer behaviors towards environmentally friendly packaging would rise as a result of manipulations that establish a link between the present and future selves.

P21: Customers are more inclined to adopt eco-packaging practices if they are urged to think about their future selves.

Providing more tangible information about the present emotional advantages and costs associated with environmentally friendly behaviours might also help them feel less abstract. Subsequent research endeavours may investigate the optimal modalities of communication to elicit feelings in people that correspond with sustainable behaviours. Images are known to elicit feelings more quickly in some situations, such as discussing intergroup disputes. To evoke specific feelings, visual information may best convey how environmental concerns may affect others; also, visual communications may potentially have a stronger impact on individuals who visualise things.

P22: Compared to text, visual messages will be more successful in arousing feelings of love and empathy that are directed towards others, and they will also encourage people to take more sustainable action. Those who are visualizers will be more sensitive to this influence.

Emotions may have a role in the abstractness issue. Customers may feel more relevant and less abstract when they can comprehend the consequences of their choices. It has been demonstrated that emphasizing the impact of charity giving increases the emotional benefits associated with the action. However, the particular emotions connected to the influence of sustainable purchasing behaviors have not been examined in previous research. In contrast to other anticipated moods associated with sustainable activity, anticipatory pride may be more likely to arise when the prospective impact is made explicit and tangible.

P23: Increasing the certainty of the beneficial effects of ecological behavior towards eco-packaging now will boost self-esteem and increase the probability that such behaviors will continue in the future.

There is another approach to connect feelings to the abstractness issue. Social media's widespread use and sharing capabilities expose users to other people who may share their sustainable behaviours. People may post photos of their bike or carpool ride, for example, along with their feelings as they go. Positive emotions increase our sense of proximity, and as a result, we are more empathetic towards and sensitive to the sentiments of those who are near to us. Therefore, by strengthening the feelings we anticipate experiencing when we engage in the behaviour, close others sharing their emotions related to implementing sustainable behaviours towards environmentally friendly packaging should be more successful at minimising abstractness.

P24: When people share their emotional reactions to environmentally friendly packaging practices, social distance will cause emotional contagion. This means that when people who are close to you—as opposed to people who are far away—share their happy experiences with environmentally friendly packaging practices, the benefits of those practices will appear more tangible.

Lastly, tangibility and the abstractness issue are related. Using similarities is one strategy to help make knowledge less abstract and enhance the tangibility of actions and results. Since sustainability is an ethereal and abstract idea, it may be easier for consumers to connect with the notion by drawing comparisons between a sustainable action or result and a well-known instance or experience that has nothing to do with sustainability.

P25: Customer behavior is more likely to shift towards environmentally friendly packaging when similarities are used in conjunction with ecological actions or behaviors as opposed to traditional ones.

CONCLUDING THOUGHTS

Whether our theory can be extended to other behaviours, such as prosocial activities or health behaviours, or if the components are specific to environmentally friendly behaviours by customers towards environmentally friendly packaging, is a topic of both theoretical and practical relevance. We speculate that many of our framework's features could also apply to the other constructive behaviours. We do point out that some factors could be specific to the sustainable use of eco-packaged goods. For instance, the issue of group vs individual action does not confront health behaviours to the same extent as it does ecological behaviours. While prosocial and health behaviours also have tangibility issues, consumers' perceptions of sustainable practices and results are probably less palpable than those of health and prosocial behaviours about environmentally friendly packaging. It is up for future study to investigate this, however, there is theoretical and practical promise in extending the framework to other disciplines. After reviewing and classifying the literature on behavioural science, we have identified five major psychological pathways that can be used to promote sustainable consumer behaviour in the direction of environmentally friendly packaging change: social impact, developing habits, the self as an individual, emotions and thinking, and tangible. The SHIFT framework is expected to assist practitioners interested in encouraging ecological customer behavior towards eco-packaging in this inquiry. Expect this approach to also encourage further study in this crucial area and help scholars conceptualize various ways to influence sustainable consumer behavior. Ultimately, the framework will enable businesses that want to operate sustainably to do so in ways that may optimize both the environment and their strategic objectives. It will also assist in encouraging ecological customer behavior to shift towards eco-packaging. Shifting consumer behaviors towards sustainability through eco-packaging is increasingly influenced by a heightened environmental consciousness. Consumers are becoming more attuned to the ecological impact of packaging, demanding eco-friendly alternatives that minimize waste and promote recycling. Cost analysis reveals that initial investments in sustainable packaging may be higher, but companies are recognizing long-term benefits in reduced environmental footprint and enhanced brand loyalty. Global market trends underscore a growing preference for eco-packaging, with businesses adapting their strategies to align with the rising demand. The regulatory landscape is evolving to encourage sustainable practices, with governments worldwide implementing stricter guidelines and incentives for eco-friendly packaging solutions. Technological innovations play a pivotal role, driving the development of biodegradable materials, smart packaging, and efficient recycling processes, fostering a comprehensive shift towards sustainable packaging practices that resonate with the evolving values of conscious consumers.

REFERENCES

Adrita, U. W., & Mohiuddin, M. F. (2020). Impact of opportunity and ability to translate environmental attitude into ecologically conscious consumer behavior. *Journal of Marketing Theory and Practice*, *28*(2), 173–186. doi:10.1080/10696679.2020.1716629

Asim, Z., Shamsi, I. R. A., Wahaj, M., Raza, A., Abul Hasan, S., Siddiqui, S. A., Aladresi, A., Sorooshian, S., & Seng Teck, T. (2022). Significance of Sustainable Packaging: A Case-Study from a Supply Chain Perspective. *Applied System Innovation*, *5*(6), 117. doi:10.3390/asi5060117

Boz, Z., Korhonen, V., & Koelsch Sand, C. (2020). Consumer considerations for the implementation of sustainable packaging: A review. *Sustainability (Basel)*, *12*(6), 2192. doi:10.3390/su12062192

Branca, G., Resciniti, R., & Babin, B. J. (2023). Sustainable packaging design and the consumer perspective: a systematic literature review. *Italian Journal of Marketing*, 1-35.

Čapienė, A., Rūtelionė, A., & Krukowski, K. (2022). Engaging in Sustainable Consumption: Exploring the Influence of Environmental Attitudes, Values, Personal Norms, and Perceived Responsibility. *Sustainability (Basel)*, *14*(16), 10290. doi:10.3390/su141610290

Cheah, I., & Phau, I. (2011). Attitudes towards environmentally friendly products: The influence of ecoliteracy, interpersonal influence and value orientation. *Marketing Intelligence & Planning*, *29*(5), 452–472. doi:10.1108/02634501111153674

Corbett, J. B. (2005). Altruism, self-interest, and the reasonable person model of environmentally responsible behavior. *Science Communication*, *26*(4), 368–389. doi:10.1177/1075547005275425

De Bauw, M., De La Revilla, L. S., Poppe, V., Matthys, C., & Vranken, L. (2022). Digital nudges to stimulate healthy and pro-environmental food choices in E-groceries. *Appetite*, *172*, 105971. doi:10.1016/j.appet.2022.105971 PMID:35181380

Ding, L., Guo, Z., & Xue, Y. (2023). Dump or recycle? Consumer's environmental awareness and express package disposal based on an evolutionary game model. *Environment, Development and Sustainability*, *25*(7), 6963–6986. doi:10.1007/s10668-022-02343-1 PMID:35493767

Dinh, M. T. T., Su, D. N., Tran, K. T., Luu, T. T., Duong, T. H., & Johnson, L. W. (2022). Eco-designed retail packaging: The empirical conceptualization and measurement. *Journal of Cleaner Production*, *379*, 134717. doi:10.1016/j.jclepro.2022.134717

Gatersleben, B., Murtagh, N., Cherry, M., & Watkins, M. (2019). Moral, wasteful, frugal, or thrifty? Identifying consumer identities to understand and manage pro-environmental behavior. *Environment and Behavior*, *51*(1), 24–49. doi:10.1177/0013916517733782

Granato, G., Fischer, A. R., & van Trijp, H. C. (2022). The price of sustainability: How consumers trade-off conventional packaging benefits against sustainability. *Journal of Cleaner Production*, *365*, 132739. doi:10.1016/j.jclepro.2022.132739

Jóźwik-Pruska, J., Bobowicz, P., Hernández, C., & Szalczyńska, M. (2022). Consumer Awareness of the Eco-Labeling of Packaging. *Fibres & Textiles in Eastern Europe*, *30*(5), 39–46. doi:10.2478/ftee-2022-0042

Ketelsen, M., Janssen, M., & Hamm, U. (2020). Consumers' response to environmentally-friendly food packaging-A systematic review. *Journal of Cleaner Production*, *254*, 120123. doi:10.1016/j.jclepro.2020.120123

Koenig-Lewis, N., Palmer, A., Dermody, J., & Urbye, A. (2014). Consumers' evaluations of ecological packaging–Rational and emotional approaches. *Journal of Environmental Psychology*, *37*, 94–105. doi:10.1016/j.jenvp.2013.11.009

Korhonen, J., Koskivaara, A., & Toppinen, A. (2020). Riding a Trojan horse? Future pathways of the fiber-based packaging industry in the bioeconomy. *Forest Policy and Economics*, *110*, 101799. doi:10.1016/j.forpol.2018.08.010

Kurz, T., Gardner, B., Verplanken, B., & Abraham, C. (2015). Habitual behaviors or patterns of practice? Explaining and changing repetitive climate-relevant actions. *Wiley Interdisciplinary Reviews: Climate Change*, *6*(1), 113–128. doi:10.1002/wcc.327

Lan, B. T. H., Phuong, T. T. L., Dat, T. T., & Truong, D. D. (2023). Factors affecting the purchase intention of products with environmentally friendly packaging of urban residents in Ho Chi Minh City, Vietnam. *Sustainability (Basel)*, *15*(9), 7726. doi:10.3390/su15097726

Mahajan, Y., Hudnurkar, M., Ambekar, S., & Hiremath, R. (2023). The Effect of Sustainable Packaging Aesthetic on Consumer Behavior: A Case Study from India. Academic Press.

Minton, A. P., & Rose, R. L. (1997). The effects of environmental concern on environmentally friendly consumer behavior: An exploratory study. *Journal of Business Research*, *40*(1), 37–48. doi:10.1016/S0148-2963(96)00209-3

Nemat, B., Razzaghi, M., Bolton, K., & Rousta, K. (2019). The role of food packaging design in consumer recycling behavior—A literature review. *Sustainability (Basel)*, *11*(16), 4350. doi:10.3390/su11164350

. Nguyen, A. T., Yến-Khanh, N., & Thuan, N. H. (2021). Consumers' purchase intention and willingness to pay for eco-friendly packaging in Vietnam. *Sustainable Packaging*, 289-323.

Oliver, M. O., Jestratijevic, I., Uanhoro, J., & Knight, D. K. (2023). Investigation of a Consumer's Purchase Intentions and Behaviors towards Environmentally Friendly Grocery Packaging. *Sustainability (Basel)*, *15*(11), 8789. doi:10.3390/su15118789

Popovic, I., Bossink, B. A., & van der Sijde, P. C. (2019). Factors influencing consumers' decision to purchase food in environmentally friendly packaging: What do we know and where do we go from here? *Sustainability (Basel)*, *11*(24), 7197. doi:10.3390/su11247197

Purcărea, T., Ioan-Franc, V., Ionescu, Ş. A., Purcărea, I. M., Purcărea, V. L., Purcărea, I., Mateescu-Soare, M. C., Platon, O.-E., & Orzan, A. O. (2022). Major Shifts in Sustainable Consumer Behavior in Romania and Retailers' Priorities in Agilely Adapting to It. *Sustainability (Basel)*, *14*(3), 1627. doi:10.3390/su14031627

Roozen, I. T., & Pelsmacker, P. D. (1998). Attributes of environmentally friendly consumer behavior. *Journal of International Consumer Marketing, 10*(3), 21–41. doi:10.1300/J046v10n03_03

Rutitis, D., Smoca, A., Uvarova, I., Brizga, J., Atstaja, D., & Mavlutova, I. (2022). Sustainable value chain of industrial biocomposite consumption: Influence of COVID-19 and consumer behavior. *Energies, 15*(2), 466. doi:10.3390/en15020466

Sastre, R. M., de Paula, I. C., & Echeveste, M. E. S. (2022). A systematic literature review on packaging sustainability: Contents, opportunities, and guidelines. *Sustainability (Basel), 14*(11), 6727. doi:10.3390/su14116727

Sharma, M., & Mahlawat, S. (2021). Green Marketing: A Study Of Eco-Friendly Initiatives Towards Green Fmcg Products. *Webology, 18*(1).

Sharma, M., & Painuly, P. K. (2023). Did COVID-19 Support Sustainable Marketing?: Modelling the Enablers of E-Commerce–Online Shopping in the Pandemic. In Sustainable Marketing, Branding, and Reputation Management: Strategies for a Greener Future (pp. 522-537). IGI Global.

Sharma, N., Saha, R., Sreedharan, V. R., & Paul, J. (2020). Relating the role of green self-concepts and identity on green purchasing behaviour: An empirical analysis. *Business Strategy and the Environment, 29*(8), 3203–3219. doi:10.1002/bse.2567

Siddiqui, S. A., Zannou, O., Bahmid, N. A., Fidan, H., Alamou, A. F., Nagdalian, A. A., Hassoun, A., Fernando, I., Ibrahim, S. A., & Arsyad, M. (2022). Consumer behavior towards nanopackaging-A new trend in the food industry. *Future Foods : a Dedicated Journal for Sustainability in Food Science, 6*, 100191. doi:10.1016/j.fufo.2022.100191

Stern, P. C. (1999). Information, incentives, and proenvironmental consumer behavior. *Journal of Consumer Policy, 22*(4), 461–478. doi:10.1023/A:1006211709570

Taufique, K. M. R. (2022). Integrating environmental values and emotion in green marketing communications inducing sustainable consumer behaviour. *Journal of Marketing Communications, 28*(3), 272–290. doi:10.1080/13527266.2020.1866645

Taufique, K. M. R., Siwar, C., Chamhuri, N., & Sarah, F. H. (2016). Integrating general environmental knowledge and eco-label knowledge in understanding ecologically conscious consumer behavior. *Procedia Economics and Finance, 37*, 39–45. doi:10.1016/S2212-5671(16)30090-9

Van Birgelen, M., Semeijn, J., & Keicher, M. (2009). Packaging and proenvironmental consumption behavior: Investigating purchase and disposal decisions for beverages. *Environment and Behavior, 41*(1), 125–146. doi:10.1177/0013916507311140

Wandosell, G., Parra-Meroño, M. C., Alcayde, A., & Baños, R. (2021). Green packaging from consumer and business perspectives. *Sustainability (Basel), 13*(3), 1356. doi:10.3390/su13031356

Wang, Y., & Wang, Y. (2021, May). Research on the application of environmentally friendly packaging materials in the sustainable development of logistics. *IOP Conference Series. Earth and Environmental Science, 781*(3), 032025. doi:10.1088/1755-1315/781/3/032025

White, K., Habib, R., & Hardisty, D. J. (2019). How to SHIFT consumer behaviors to be more sustainable: A literature review and guiding framework. *Journal of Marketing*, *83*(3), 22–49. doi:10.1177/0022242919825649

Xu, Y., & Ward, P. S. (2023). Environmental Attitudes And Consumer Preference For Environmentally-Friendly Beverage Packaging: The Role Of Information Provision And Identity Labeling In Influencing Consumer Behavior. *Frontiers of Agricultural Science and Engineering*, *10*(1), 95–108.

Zaman, K., Iftikhar, U., Rehmani, M., & Irshad, H. (2023). Embracing biodegradable bags: Effects of ethical self-identity on consumer buying behavior. *Social Responsibility Journal*, *19*(3), 474–485. doi:10.1108/SRJ-03-2021-0099

Chapter 12
Unseen Motivators:
A study exploring the effect of subliminally priming known human faces Vs unknown human faces on consumers product selection decisions

Rabia Abhay
ⓘ https://orcid.org/0000-0002-2888-6523
Christ University, India

Sibin Mathew Nesin
ⓘ https://orcid.org/0000-0003-2216-6266
Christ University, India

ABSTRACT

The human mind is constantly being influenced by a vast number of external stimuli that are perceived consciously as well as unconsciously. The chapter attempts to explore how unconscious (subliminal) priming of known and unknown human faces could impact product selection and decision-making time of consumers. 2 (Known face X Unknown face) X 2 (Product selection X Decision-making time) within-subject design was used for the study. A pilot study was conducted to estimate the subliminal time threshold of the population. It was found to be 17ms. A stimulus-priming experiment designed in Opensesame software was used to subliminally expose the participants to both known and unknown human faces. They were then asked to select a product that they were willing to buy from an option of four products, of which one of the products was primed along with human face (known vs. unknown). The product selection rates as well as the time taken to select the product were recorded. A total of 100 participants falling in the age category of young adults (18-39) took part in the study.

DOI: 10.4018/979-8-3693-2367-0.ch012

INTRODUCTION

In the mid to late 19th century, while walking down a road it wasn't an uncommon sight to see big billboards advertising various products. In fact, the first billboard advertisement was done in 1830 by a person called Jarred Bell (Content,2019). The invention of the radio in the early 20th century paved the way for a paradigm shift in the mode of advertising. With its enlarged reach among the public, radios slowly became the preferred mode of advertising. The first radio advertisement aired in 1922 and it was done by WEAF in New York City (Hogdson,2021). Later around the mid-20th century, the invention of Television ushered in a new age of EVDS (Electronic Visual Display Systems). This paved the way for yet another paradigm shifts in the mode of marketing and advertisements. It presented an enlarged reach amongst the public as radio did but also engaged the people in visual form. This gave new impetus to advertisement and marketing campaigns. The first televised advertisement was aired in 1941 (Jay,2023). From then on EVDS has become the preferred mode that most marketing and advertisement campaigns prefer. The introduction of the first commercial computers in 1951 (Sinha & Sinha, 2023) and the launch of the World Wide Web in 1993 (History,2020) worked towards solidifying that status. In the current technological age, social media stands tall as the most preferred mode of marketing and advertising (Remi,2021).

Despite different iterations and variations, the core aim behind all the above-said examples was the need of an organization or a company to engage a potential consumer and create a positive inclination among them in favour of their products. Over time the methods used towards that end have evolved with the increasing complexity of technology, but the core aim has always remained the same. The current chapter explores the concept of consumer engagement through the lens of unconscious modalities, which yet again is an innovation that is seen to be on the rise, and is used by companies and organizations to influence consumers.

Consumers: Pseudo-Rational Entities

Engel et al., (1986) defined Consumer behaviour as to be the acts done by individuals with the motive of obtaining, using and disposing of economic goods and services. This also includes the decisional processes that precede these acts. The field of study that focused on consumer behaviour evolved around the 1960s and was dominated by two schools of thought, positivist and non-positivist. The positivist school of thought, also known as the traditional school of thought, was of the opinion that the world was a rational place where all the happenings happen in an orderly and predictable manner (Pachauri,2001). Extending this idea to the realm of marketing, they were of the belief that consumers were also rational entities who based their daily consumption decisions on sound logical foundations. This school of thought bases its arguments on the concept of the utilitarian aspect of consumer engagement i.e. consumers are rational beings who while engaging in consumption processes aim at increasing their utility trade-off. This school of thought still runs strong and has deep-rooted seats amongst the hearts of most market and consumer-oriented researchers.

Figure 1. Positivist approach towards consumer behaviour. The consumer is considered to be the focal point in which the needs, information regarding the product, and utility interact and then, using a rational filter, the consumer develops his consumption behaviour.

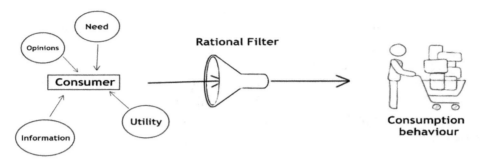

An opposing school of thought is the school of non-positivism. This is a relatively new school of thought that came into existence in the early 1980s (Pachauri,2001). This school came up as a critique of the positivist school of thought. The non-positive school of thought believed that its predecessor didn't account for the complex social and cultural world where the consumers find themselves in real-life scenarios and focused on a homogenous society and overemphasized the rational aspect of the consumers. The non-positivist approach emphasizes the importance of the symbolic and subjective experiences of an individual while they engage in a transactional process such as buying a product. They felt consumers were free to create meaning based on their cultural and ethnic background when they indulged in such activities. They, unlike the positivist approach which saw consumers as rational entities, believed that consumers as emotional entities and based their consumption choices on the emotional valence of the transactions.

Figure 2. Non-positivist approach towards consumer behaviour. The consumer is considered to be an integral part of society, and is influenced by opinions, needs, etc. and ultimately develops their consumption behaviour. In this approach, the consumer bases their behaviour on their emotional reasoning.

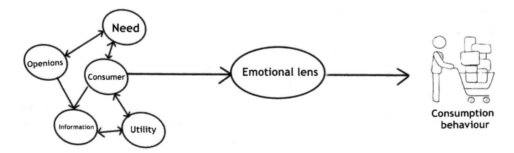

They placed greater emphasis on the symbolic aspect of the choice than the rational aspect. For example, crossing a bakery shop will make you feel like going in a buying the baked items despite being not hungry. It is because of the aroma that lingers outside the shop that makes you act impulsively to momentarily satisfy a symbolic urge to consume the commodity despite lacking any rational impetus to do the same.

In the current world scenario, the non-positivist approach appears to have garnered more credence than its predecessor. A plethora of studies have found that consumers largely base their decisions on momentary impulses fuelled majorly by the emotional valence of the circumstance. The lens model proposed by Parikshat S. Manhas (2012) states the view that consumer preferences are formed after considering the view held by the outside world which then leads them to assign an affective valence to their decision-making processes. Studies have found that various intrinsic characteristics of a consumer such as personality (Egan & Taylor, 2010; Lin 2010; Ranjibarian & Kia, 2010), cultural background, materialistic nature, etc. prompt them to act based on non-rational tendencies. This further authenticates the non-positivistic take on consumer behaviour.

Consumer Engagement: An Overview

The billboards of the 1800s, the audio and video advertisement telecasts of the early and mid1900s, and in the current scenario, the screens of your mobile phones and laptops, all of these, despite varying in their forms were outlets through which companies and organizations attempted to engage potential consumers with their products and services. The success of any company lies in its ability to effectively engage its consumers with its products, creating a positive attitudinal change in them towards the product. Over time, many methods have been used towards this goal. The examples talked about in the earlier paragraphs (billboards, televisions etc) are a few of its manifestations. With the fast advent of new and improved technologies, methods used towards consumer engagement have also evolved accordingly. We shall focus primarily on one major way that has been constantly employed by companies and organizations in increasing the efficacy of consumer engagement, namely 'Priming' and its evolution over time.

Priming

The constant interruption of a movie that you might be watching online by an advertisement showcasing a product or a popup which keeps coming again and again while you are browsing some websites, urging you to try out some new product or service is a common sight these days. These are modern-day examples of priming. Priming is defined to be "The change in the ability to identify or produce an item due to the prior exposure to the same item" (Tulvig & Schacter,1990). In short, the circumstances in which an object was previously viewed by an individual have the potential to influence their perception regarding the same object when viewed later on. Advertising is perhaps the most famous manifestation of this process in the world of marketing. One is constantly exposed to multiple products and services frequently through their constant exposure to such advertisements, whether in a magazine that they read or in a website that they are browsing. Advertisements have virtually invaded almost all aspects of an individual's everyday life. This frequent exposure to products and services through such advertisements that portray them in a good light has been seen to positively influence the individual's perspective regarding the advertised product, proving the impact of priming on consumer behaviour (Sagal,2015; Fatima & Lodhi,2015; Arshad & Aslam, 2015).

The spreading activation theory is one of the major theories that attempts to explain the effectiveness of priming. It states that the strength of the mediating semantic links between a prime (mostly an emotion) and a target (product) is what enhances the amount of activation that spreads between them.

Advertisements are created in such a manner that they give a background narrative that links the prime (emotion) with the target (Product) in a meaningful way. A suitable example to elucidate this connection would be an advertisement created in such a way that the product advertised evokes a particular type of emotion within the consumer, then the consumer, in future exposure to the same object will feel the same emotion that he or she felt thus increasing the chance of the product being selected for purchase depending on what emotion it evoked. Recent trends in marketing show an increase in such affective (Emotional) priming strategies. Studies have shown such marketing strategies have been successful in creating a good first impression for their product, increasing the memorability of their products and also having a significant impact on the purchase intention of the consumer towards that product (Nair,2020). An increase of sales by 31% induced by emotion-evoking advertisements is a clear testimony to the impact affective priming has on consumer behaviour (Pringle,2008). Emotions primed by the advertisements on the products are seen to be antecedents of attitudinal change an individual has towards the product and the change is usually positive (Batra et al., 1986).

All these examples show the importance of affective priming techniques used in current-day marketing campaigns in instilling positive attitudinal change towards the marketed product. Let us go a little further into the realm of priming and discuss about a novel field that is emerging in that area that taps into the unconscious mind of the consumer.

Subliminal: The Realm of the Unconscious

Since birth, a person is constantly in exposure to a vast multitude of external stimuli which goes a long way in influencing their perception of the world. All these external factors need not be consciously perceived. Most of the external stimuli to which an individual is exposed are processed unconsciously by them. It's proven that unconscious activation precedes any conscious action done by an individual (Bargh & Morsella,2008).

The overflow hypothesis is one of the major proponents that attempt to explain how subliminal stimuli can influence conscious decisions. It states that any stimulus that is rich in details and emotional valence has the potential to 'overflow' from the cognitive consciousness into the other facets of consciousness including the unconscious (Block,1995; Lamme,2003). Thus, Subliminal influence could also play a pivotal role in molding the decision-making processes of an individual in almost all aspects of their daily life (Marzuki et al.,2010; Strahan et al.,2002; Borovak et al.,2022)

The involvement of subliminal priming techniques in the field of marketing began in the late 1950s. In the infamous Vicary experiment of 1957, a businessman named James Vicary exposed the audience of a movie theatre to subliminal cues prompting them to consume more Coca-Cola and popcorn. It was seen to have increased the sales of the mentioned items by 18.1% and 57.5% respectively (O'Barr, 2005). Though this was an example of non-affective subliminal priming, results did show promising results that fueled an interest in the realm of the unconscious and its potential usage in influencing consumer decisions. Later on, Vicary retracted his claims on the efficacy of subliminal cues in instilling an attitudinal change in the movie audience, but by then the seeds of subliminal underpinnings of consumer decision-making were already sowed (O'Barr, 2005). Extensive studies have indeed shown that stimuli that are presented below the conscious threshold of an individual could indeed influence their decision-making and behaviour. For instance, the study done by Treburg et al., (2011) found evidence for human gaze direction being influenced by subliminal cues. The affective valence of the stimuli presented below the conscious threshold impacted the gaze direction and time. Even words presented to participants in a subliminal modality were seen to evoke a significant change in the emotional attributes of trustworthiness and belief that the participants held towards an external stimulus (Legale et al., 2011). Conclusive evidence regarding the impact subliminal stimulus has on cognitive processes based on biological underpinnings was demonstrated by a study conducted by Gaillard et al., (2007) showed intracranial readings done on epileptic patients were sensitive to stimulus presented beneath the conscious level. fMRI studies further provide evidence to the same by findings such as BOLD-dependent activities in brain regions that governed attentional control such as bilateral interparietal sulcus were suppressed when subliminal stimuli were shown in a repeated manner, giving proof to the fact that human attention can indeed be influenced using subliminal methods (Kristjansson et al., 2006). Advertisements are only as impactful as the duration of time they hold influence over the behaviour of a consumer. Subliminal priming was also seen as impactful in this aspect. It has been found that subliminal messages have a long-lasting impact, up to almost a month (Levnison,1965).

Affective priming is also found to be effective when done in subliminal modalities (Herman et al., 2003). Affective primes that evoke deeply ingrained evolutionary emotions such as fear or anger have been seen to increase the subliminal impact of a stimulus (Kirdar, 2012). This could be used to instill an attitudinal change in the minds of consumers which is mostly positive towards the advertised product. One interesting study showed that hotel advertisements that were subliminally primed with affective stimuli (in this case emoticons) had a positive impact on the consumer's perception towards the hotel rooms (Hsu & Chen,2020). In general hotel advertisements which were primed with emoticons of a positive affective valence were seen to have more attractive hotel rooms in comparison to a control group where no priming was done. Another interesting subliminal priming study found that when non-abstract stimuli such as common day objects were coupled with negative subliminal stimuli, they were perceived to be more aesthetically good than when they were subliminally primed with positive affect stimuli (Era et al., 2015). In line with this study, it was found subliminal primes had the opposite effect on the aesthetic perception of abstract items. It was seen that abstract items (i.e. abstract art) were seen to be more aesthetically pleasing when subliminally primed with positive affect stimuli than when primed with negative affect stimuli (Flexas et al.,2013). This seeming misattribution of affect depending on the affective valence of the subliminal stimuli suggests that subliminal stimuli could have varying affective impacts on individuals depending on the context in which they are shown.

The study discussed in this book chapter also attempts to assess the impact of affective subliminal priming on purchase intentions. The efficacy of subliminally priming known and unknown faces on purchase intentions has been explored in this study through a priming experiment.

Study Overview

The Study attempts to explore the affective influence of subliminally priming known and unknown faces on consumer product selection decisions and the time taken for them to arrive at that decision. For the study, the 'young adult' (individuals with age between 18-39 years of age (Baack et al., 2021)) population was selected as it's the age group which is more in tune to indulge in increased economic activities. The study comprised of 100 participants (19 = Male). It was made sure that they didn't have any underlying ailments such as impaired mental health that could impact their decision-making skills. They were screened using a General Health Questionnaire (GHQ). The participants were asked to provide a standardized picture of a person whom they were close with. Their interpersonal closeness to that person was assessed using the Relationship Closeness Inventory (RCI). The study paradigm was created in E-

Prime, which is a psychology experiment creator with an extensive history of usage in similar settings (Richard et al., 2009; Taylor et al., 2017). The study followed a 2 (Unknown Face Vs known Face) X 2 (product selection Vs Decision Time) within subject design. Special care was given to standardizing the facial stimulus. All the facial stimuli were converted to monochromatic versions and normalized for characteristics such as contrast, hue etc. They were standardized to 512 X 720 pixels.

Setup

The priming study comprised 20 trials per person which will be divided into four groups of five trials each. The first three groups will deal with 3 different products (a male-inclined product, a female-inclined product and a neutral-inclined product) to reduce the noise and increase the efficiency in detecting the effect of priming in product selection by considering the bias that product stereotypes could create (Selecting a single product and limiting the number of trials could lead to biases). The fourth group will undergo trials without any priming procedure which shall act as the baseline on which the other three groups will be compared.

Each Trial will comprise 24 slides which will be a series of tasks in which the subjects will be shown slides with a shaded rectangle in either the left or right visual field. The subjects will be instructed to press the corresponding cursor key to the visual field where they find the shaded rectangle. The priming procedure happens between the presentation of these slides. There shall be priming slides placed between the task slides for a duration below the conscious threshold (17ms), thus escaping the conscious detection of the subject. This time threshold for subliminal stimulus presentation was deduced from a pilot study conducted on 24 Participants.

A single block shall thus comprise 3 slides, a slide with a cross in the middle to attract attention, shown for 100ms, followed by the priming slide. This slide shall comprise the human face (Unknown vs. known) along with the product that is being primed. It shall be shown for 200 ms (17 ms – duration time and 183 ms - interstimulus interval). Finally, the block ends with the target slide showing the target as a shaded rectangle, in either of the visual fields and the participants respond by pressing the corresponding cursor key.

Figure 3. Pictorial representation of a single block. A priming block is repeated 8 times for the priming process to take place. It's followed by a product selection block repeated four 4 times making the mean chance levels for selecting the primed product 25%.

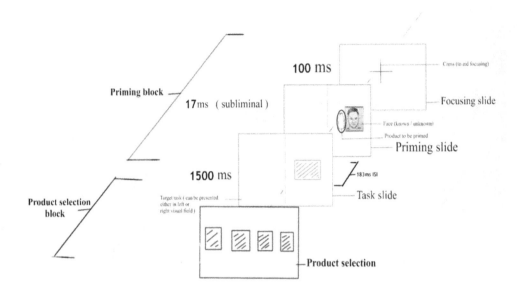

The subjects were made to do the trials without any priming at the beginning to minimise the contamination of their responses through the spillover of the priming effects from the other sets of trials which have priming slides. The results will be taken as the baseline on which the results from the other trials will be compared. The pictorial representation of the entire procedure is as follows.

Figure 4. Representation of an entire trial (8 blocks of 3 slides each). At the end of the trial product selection slide is shown for 4 times.

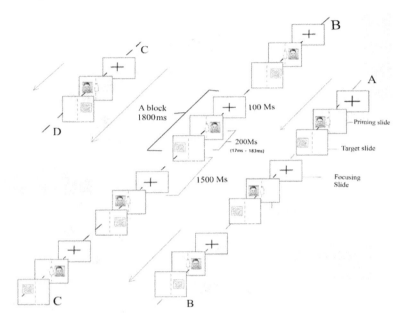

After each trial, the participants were given the option of four products of which one of the products was primed. Special care was given to standardising the three other products shown with the primed product so that elements like colour, shape etc don't influence the product selection. They were asked to select the product they would be willing to buy. Their product selection rate and the time taken by them to arrive at the decision were recorded for analysis.

During the course of the experiment, the participants needed to undergo the above-mentioned procedure twice, once for both known and unknown facial conditions. Care was taken to give ample amount of time between these sessions (average of 2-3 days) to reduce the spillover of the earlier session into the next and influence the decision making.

RESULTS AND INSIGHTS

General Results

The Results reflect the product selection pattern and decision-making times from the responses given by the participants. It was seen that there was a significant difference between the product selection percentage under primed conditions in comparison to mean chance levels of product selection ($f (1,198) =29.63$, $P<0.001$ (Known Vs mean chance levels) & $f (1,198) =29.344$, $P<0.001$ (Unknown Vs Mean Chance levels))

Figure 5. Seen product selection % rates vs. mean chance levels rates when subliminally primed with known and unknown faces

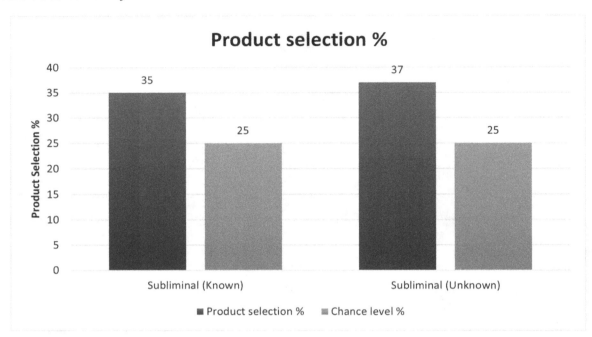

When subliminally primed with the face of a known individual it was seen that the participants selected the primed product around 35% of the time, which is 10% more than the chance levels of selection. When subliminally primed with the face of an unknown individual the primed product was seen to be selected around 37% of the time. That is 12% more than the chance level of 25%.

There was no significant difference in product selection rates amongst Known Vs unknown facial priming groups (f (1,198) =0.420, P=0.518). correlation analysis showed an overall mild negative correlation between the familiarity of the face (Assessed by RCI questionnaire) and Product selection and response time taken by the participants (-0.051 & -0.026 respectively)

Comparing the response times of the participants, A significant trend was seen. It was found that participants took more to arrive at the product selection decision when they were subliminally primed with known faces than when they were primed with unknown faces (f(1,198)=42.304, P<0.001).

Figure 6. Seen decision-making time (response times) when subliminally primed known vs unknown faces

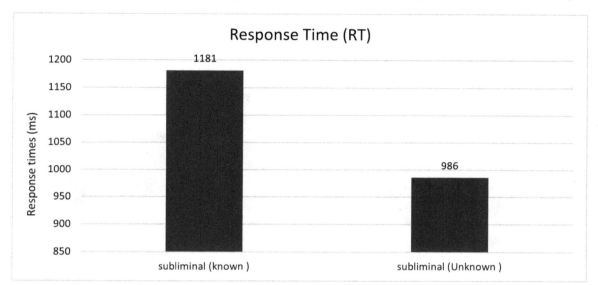

When subliminally primed with known faces, participants on average took around 1181 ms to decide on what products they wanted to buy. On the other hand, when primed with unknown faces on average they took only 986 ms to decide on what product to buy.

Gender Difference in Results

The gender of the participants, despite lacking significant levels of difference, showed a distinct trend. It was seen that males in general were more susceptible towards priming. This fact was reflected in their product selection rates. They in general, under both conditions (Unknown vs. known) had higher product selection rates (40% & 39% respectively) in comparison to female participants (36% & 34% respectively).

Figure 7. Trends seen in the influence of gender in product selection when subliminally primed with human faces (unknown vs. known)

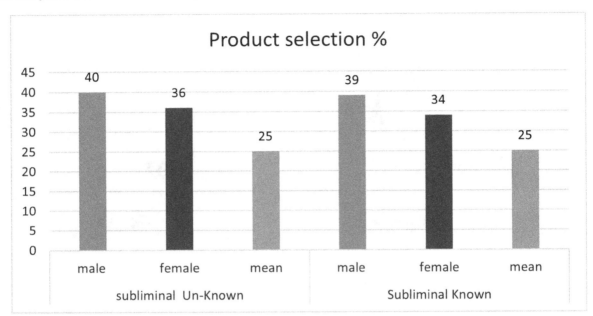

Comparing the response times, No significant difference was seen (f (1,98) = 0.009, P =0.924 (Known faces) & f (1,98) = 1.356, P=247 (Unknown faces)). Despite that, a trend was evident between the sexes. It was seen male participants had faster response timings for both conditions. This trend was evident in Unknown face priming conditions. Male participants on average took 920ms to respond when primed with an unknown face in comparison to 989ms for female participants. Under the known face priming condition, there wasn't much of a difference between male and female participants in their responses (1166ms & 1170ms respectively).

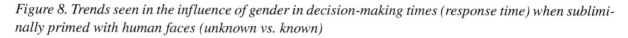

Figure 8. Trends seen in the influence of gender in decision-making times (response time) when subliminally primed with human faces (unknown vs. known)

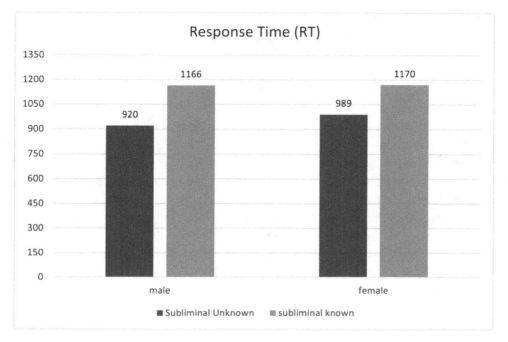

The correlational analysis found a mild positive correlation between the familiarity of the face in the known facial category and between the product selection percentage and decision-making time by male participants (0.030 & 0.168 respectively). The contrary was found for the female participants who showed a weak negative correlation between the familiarity of the faces and the product selection rates and decision-making times (-0.131 & -0.041 respectively).

DISCUSSION

General

The current study attempts to find the influence of subliminal exposure to known faces on consumers' buying decisions when compared to unknown faces. The emotional salience of known faces in comparison to unknown faces is hypothesized to overflow into the primed product thus inclining the consumer towards buying the primed object. The participant's product selection percentage and decision-making time results are discussed below.

Regarding the product selection made by the participants, a significant difference was seen when they were primed in comparison to when they were not. Irrespective of the familiarity of the face (Known vs. unknown) products primed with faces were selected at a much higher rate than the chance levels of 25%. For instance, Products primed with a known human face were selected 35% of the time and the products primed with unknown human faces were selected 37% of the time. Each has a selection rate higher than mean chance levels, showing that subliminal priming has an effect. Although the effect of subliminal priming is seen, there doesn't seem to be much of a significant difference in the product selection rates depending on the familiarity of the face primed. There was only a 2% difference between the product selection rate when primed with known and unknown faces. Thus, it is seen that the process of subliminal priming with human faces is effective in influencing consumer decisions albeit the familiarity of the face doesn't have much of a role in it.

Human beings are social creatures and faces are considered to be one of the prominent sources through which nonverbal communication takes place. Human faces are also highly efficient in conveying emotions. It has been found that scary/threatening facial stimuli evoked more responses in the amygdala in comparison to scary/threatening non-facial stimuli. Owing to the social salience human faces hold and their increased capacity to convey affective responses, the products subliminally primed alongside a human face will gain more salience than unprimed objects. This could be the reason why in this study it can be seen that products primed with human faces (irrespective of familiarity) were selected significantly more than mean chance levels. The result could also be because human faces are more efficient in engaging attention. It has been found that human faces are efficient at engaging attention by attracting the first saccade fixation of the eyes (Morrisey, Hofrichter and Rutherford, 2019). This could even happen even if the stimuli are not consciously seen (Meichen, Wei and Zhang, 2015). This increased efficiency in human attention engagement through subliminal facial cues could be one of the reasons why, products primed along with human faces are positively preferred by the participants. The initial assumption that was held regarding the familiarity of the faces primed influencing the product selection was not seen significantly in this instance. However, there was a slight (2%) increase in product selection when it was primed with an unknown human face.

The decision-making times of the participants reflect the amount of time that they took to reach a decision on which product they wanted to buy. There was a significant difference in the response time taken by the participants when they were primed with known Vs unknown faces. On an average participants took more time to decide what product they wanted to buy when they were primed with known human faces (1181ms) than when they were primed with unknown faces (986ms). There could be two possible explanations for this trend. Familiarity of human faces could influence decision-making time as a function of the 'cognitive space' that they occupy. Known human faces would take up more 'cognitive space', in the form of associated memories, affective salience etc. than unknown faces. when a known human face is seen (even unconsciously) it could evoke underlying memories and emotions associated with that face. This in turn leads to the utilisation of increased mental resources which manifests itself in increased decision-making times. In comparison, an unknown face won't have a large 'cognitive space' as there won't be any memories or emotions associated with that face.

Another possible explanation is the fact that an unknown face is perceived as a threat and is processed faster than known faces. Any novel stimulus that is not common in an individual's immediate surroundings has a high probability of being perceived as a threat. Evolutionarily it gives the advantage for an organism to mobilise its mental and physical resources when a threat stimulus is identified at the earliest. Since the face of an unknown individual could act as a potential threat, the human brain would process it much faster than a known face. This could manifest itself in the form of reduced decision-making time when primed with an unknown human face. Studies have shown that fear as a stimulus has a much stronger impact on creating an attitude change in an individual when presented subliminally (Kirdar, 2012). The faster decision-making times seen when products were primed with unknown faces in comparison to known faces could be seen to give credence to this fact.

The slight (2%) increases in product selection seen in participants when primed with unknown human faces when compared to being primed with known human faces, could also be explained by the fact that unknown faces are seen as a threat. Fear stimulus being more potent in creating an attitudinal change, could have inclined the participants more towards the primed product more than when it was primed with a known face as it held less fear quotient.

Gender Influence on Results

The participants' gender was also seen to play a role in determining the impact priming had on their product preference and decision-making times although there were no significant differences between the sexes. The results provide interesting insights into the possibility there might be gender differences in perceiving subliminal stimulus. From the results, it seems males are more inclined to be influenced by subliminal stimuli. Males in general were more susceptible to priming and were faster to respond across conditions (Known vs. unknown). Males were seen to select the products subliminally primed with human faces more than their female counterparts.

When primed with unknown faces subliminally A distinct trend emerged based on the participant's gender. Males were seen to choose the primed product 40% (15% above mean chance levels) of the time in comparison to 36% (11% above mean chance levels) of females. When it was known faces that they were primed with the product selection rate was 39% (14% above mean chance levels) in comparison to 34% (9% above mean chance levels) by females. The increased inclination of males to be influenced by subliminal stimuli could be because they are evolutionarily fine-tuned to pick up stimuli from the environment at a faster rate. From the time of hunter-gatherers, males were usually the ones who went hunting (Ember,1978) and in other life-threatening situations where fast assessment of the surroundings meant life and death. This could have sharpened their senses more than their female counterparts. This could enhance the processing of the unconscious stimuli too. This fact is also reflected in their faster response times, especially seen when subliminally primed with unknown faces. On an average males took 920ms to respond in comparison to 989ms by females when subliminally primed with an unknown face.

Earlier in the discussion, it was argued that unknown faces could act as potential threatening stimuli and thus elicit faster response times. In such a scenario it gives further credence to the earlier stated fact of males having more sharpened senses due to their evolutionary past. In such the past, any stimuli that could be threatening would have to be processed fast to ensure the safety of the individual. Males in that sense could have an enhanced capacity to perceive threat-like stimuli faster than females. Thus, explaining their faster response times.

When primed with known faces both male and female response times didn't show much of a variance (1166ms and 1170ms respectively). This could be because a known face is not perceived to be a threat and thus does not elicit a threat response. Since the faces used as known facial primes were close to the participant (irrespective of the gender), could have played a role in normalising the response time across the genders.

Another interesting result that potentially highlights the underlying gender difference in subliminal perception is the correlation result between the familiarity of the face shown in the known facial priming category and the product selection rates and decision-making time of the participants. Despite the lack of significant difference, a distinct trend was seen. Interestingly it was found that familiarity with the face had a mild positive correlation with the above-mentioned factors amongst male participants and a mild negative correlation amongst the female participants. That meant amongst the male participants, the more the face was familiar to them more inclined they were to buy the product primed alongside the face and more the time they took to reach that decision. In the case of female participants, the more familiar they were with the shown face, the less they selected the product alongside that face and the faster they were in arriving at the decision. Why did gender instil a contradictory consumption behavioural pattern amongst the participants when primed subliminally with known faces? The Positive correlation shown by men in comparison to females could be due to the earlier stated fact that men are typically sensitive to subliminal stimuli i.e. even to the emotional salience of the stimulus. Thus, exposure to a known face subliminally could evoke a more prominent response in males. This is given credence by the results. The fact that they took more time to decide on what product to select when the familiarity of the shown face was greater, could be due to the increased cognitive arousal it caused thus increasing the mental time needed to arrive at the concerned decision.

Read together, the data from product selection rates and subsequent decision-making times point fingers toward the fact that human faces even when shown subliminally influence decision-making enough to alter it from mean chance levels. Despite the familiarity of the face being discerned even in unconscious modality (seen in reduced response times for unknown faces) it doesn't cause much impact in altering the human decisions. This goes against the assumption that emotional salience attached to known faces could increase the impact each of them has on human cognition. Human faces irrespective of their familiarity are seen to influence human cognition.

Scope and Limitations

The study focused on evaluating the impact of subliminally priming human faces (Known vs. Unknown) on consumer decision-making process and decision-making time. The familiarity of the face was expected to be a mediating factor in increasing the efficacy of the priming process, with products primed with known human faces being selected more often, owing to the positive emotional salience held by them in comparison to unknown faces.

The face of a male was used as the unknown facial prime. This marks one of the limitations of the study as a male unknown face could potentially evoke different emotions between male and female participants. Despite steps taken to reduce the gender bias that could arise from stereotypes surrounding certain products (e.g. Lipstick = female, shaving blade = male) by exposing participants to products falling in both the stereotypes equally, along with neutral products (refer methodology section), gender of the participants can influence their reaction to product primed with unknown 'male' face differently. Future studies could study facial priming by devising a paradigm which addresses this limitation by looking into the impact of subliminally priming an unknown female Vs male face.

On similar grounds, the facial primes used under known conditions were also gender diverse i.e. participants were free to provide the picture of any individual to be used as the known facial prime irrespective of the individual's gender provided that they were emotionally close with that individual. This could also potentially hamper the efficiency of the study. Future studies could overcome this limitation by designing a paradigm in which they ask the participant to provide pictures of individuals that they are close to who are of the same gender i.e. providing the image of a male individual that they are close with. This could help in standardising the stimulus used in known priming conditions too.

Owing to the decreased representation of males (close to 20% of the sample) the difference in subliminal impact based on gender influences of the participants can't be generalised. Future studies could enlist a more gender-equal sample to further probe into the gender-based differences arising from subliminal priming.

CONCLUSION

The subliminal mode of marketing has always been under scrutiny regarding its efficiency in influencing consumer decisions. Since the infamous vicary experiment of 1957 and the subsequent claims of its falsification, the area of subliminal marketing has always been considered a pseudo-science topic. What most of the critics seem to forget is the fact that most of the human perception and cognitive processes are unconscious. It's a fact that unconscious activation precedes conscious action. Just because something is not consciously registered in attention doesn't mean it has failed to be registered in the human mind. Human consumption, in that sense also comes under the overarching influence of unconsciousness. It's seen that the underlying emotions associated with a product greatly influence consumer preferences towards that product even if the consumer is not consciously aware of it. This points fingers to the increased possibility of marketing stimulus shown to the consumer below their conscious perception threshold, which could indeed influence their consumption behaviour.

The results of the present study showed that human faces when used to prime a product subliminally, increased the probability of them being selected by the participants by 10% - 12% more than mean chance levels on average. The familiarity (Known vs. unknown) of the face despite significantly influencing the decision-making time of the participants, was not seen to exert any significant influence on the product selection rates other than increasing it from mean chance levels. Gender differences among the participants (Male VS female) were also seen to influence the impact of subliminal priming. Males in general were more susceptible towards being primed as seen from their increased product selection rates towards the primed product in both conditions (Known Vs unknown). They were also seen to have a faster response time towards product selection when subliminally primed with unknown faces. These results show promising effects that subliminal influence holds over influencing the consumption behaviour of an individual.

The present study aims to contribute to the existing literature reflecting the usage of subliminal methods in marketing strategies and show that subliminal methods could efficiently influence consumer behaviour. In this era of consumerism, which is defined by cutthroat competition, innovations are the need of the hour to find creative and effective methods to enhance consumer engagement. Tapping into the unconscious realm through subliminal methods could just do the job.

Ethical Approval

Concerned ethical approval to conduct this study was obtained from the ethics committee of the researcher's institution.

REFERENCES

ArshadM. S.AslamT. (2015). The impact of advertisement on consumer's purchase intentions. doi:10.2139/ssrn.2636927

Baack, B. N., Abad, N., Yankey, D., Kahn, K. E., Razzaghi, H., Brookmeyer, K., Kolis, J., Wilhelm, E., Nguyen, K. H., & Singleton, J. A. (2021). COVID-19 vaccination coverage and intent among adults aged 18–39 years—United States, March–May 2021. *MMWR. Morbidity and Mortality Weekly Report*, *70*(25), 928–933. doi:10.15585/mmwr.mm7025e2 PMID:34166337

Bargh, J. A., & Morsella, E. (2008). The unconscious mind. *Perspectives on Psychological Science*, *3*(1), 73–79. doi:10.1111/j.1745-6916.2008.00064.x PMID:18584056

Batra, R., & Stayman, D. M. (1990). The role of mood in advertising effectiveness. *The Journal of Consumer Research*, *17*(2), 203–214. doi:10.1086/208550

Block, N. (1995). On a confusion about a function of consciousness. *Behavioral and Brain Sciences*, *18*(2), 227–247. doi:10.1017/S0140525X00038188

Borovac Zekan, S., & Zekan, I. (2022, February). Subliminal messages in advertising: do they really work? In DIEM: Dubrovnik International Economic Meeting (Vol. 7, No. 1, pp. 102-113). Sveučilište u Dubrovniku.

Content. (2019). History of Billboard Advertising | Evolution of Outdoor Media. https://www.bmedia-group.com/news/history-of-billboard-advertising/

Egan, V., & Taylor, D. (2010). Shoplifting, unethical consumer behaviour, and personality. *Personality and Individual Differences*, *48*(8), 878–883. doi:10.1016/j.paid.2010.02.014

Ember, C. R. (1978). Myths about hunter-gatherers. *Ethnology*, *17*(4), 439–448. doi:10.2307/3773193

Engel, J. F., Blackwell, R. D., & Miniard, P. W. (1986). *Consumer behavior*. Dryden Press.

Era, V., Candidi, M., & Aglioti, S. M. (2015). Subliminal presentation of emotionally negative vs positive primes increases the perceived beauty of target stimuli. *Experimental Brain Research*, *233*(11), 3271–3281. doi:10.1007/s00221-015-4395-5 PMID:26238406

Fatima, S. & Lodhi, S. (2015). Impact of Advertisement on Buying Behaviours of the Consumers: Study of Cosmetic Industry in Karachi City. International Journal of Management Sciences and Business Research.

Flexas, A., Rosselló, J., Christensen, J. F., Nadal, M., Olivera La Rosa, A., & Munar, E. (2013). Affective priming using facial expressions modulates liking for abstract art. *PLoS One*, *8*(11), e80154. doi:10.1371/journal.pone.0080154 PMID:24260350

Gaillard, R., Cohen, L., Adam, C., Clemenceau, S., Hasboun, D., Baulac, M., Willer, J. C., Dehaene, S., & Naccache, L. (2007). Subliminal words durably affect neuronal activity. *Neuroreport*, *18*(15), 1527–1531. doi:10.1097/WNR.0b013e3282f0b6cd PMID:17885595

Hermans, D., Spruyt, A., De Houwer, J. & Eelen, P., 2003. Affective priming with subliminally presented pictures. Canadian Journal of Experimental Psychology/Revue canadienne de psychologie expérimentale, 57(2), 97.

History. (2020). World Wide Web (WWW) launches in the public domain,. https://www.history.com/this-day-in-history/world-wide-web-launches-in-public-domain

Hsu, L., & Chen, Y. J. (2020). Neuromarketing, subliminal advertising, and hotel selection: An EEG study. *Australasian Marketing Journal*, *28*(4), 200–208. doi:10.1016/j.ausmj.2020.04.009

Jay. (2023). The Fascinating History Of Television Commercials: How They've Changed Over The Years. https://allabouttelevision.com/history-of-television-commercials/

Kırdar, Y. (2012). Mysticism in subliminal advertising. JAMMO, 4(15), 222-239.

Kristjánsson, Á., Vuilleumier, P., Schwartz, S., Macaluso, E., & Driver, J. (2007). Neural basis for priming of pop-out during visual search revealed with fMRI. *Cerebral Cortex (New York, N.Y.)*, *17*(7), 1612–1624. doi:10.1093/cercor/bhl072 PMID:16959868

Lamme, V. A. (2003). Why visual attention and awareness are different. *Trends in Cognitive Sciences*, *7*(1), 12–18. doi:10.1016/S1364-6613(02)00013-X PMID:12517353

Légal, J. B., Chappé, J., Coiffard, V., & Villard-Forest, A. (2012). Don't you know that you want to trust me? Subliminal goal priming and persuasion. *Journal of Experimental Social Psychology*, *48*(1), 358–360. doi:10.1016/j.jesp.2011.06.006

Levinson, B. W. (1965). States of awareness during general anaesthesia: Preliminary communication. *British Journal of Anaesthesia*, *37*(7), 544–546. doi:10.1093/bja/37.7.544 PMID:5829165

Lin, L. Y. (2010). The relationship of consumer personality trait, brand personality and brand loyalty: An empirical study of toys and video games buyers. *Journal of Product and Brand Management*, *19*(1), 4–17. doi:10.1108/10610421011018347

Manhas, P. S., & Gulzar, F. (2012). A review and a conceptual framework of 'Irrational influences' on consumer purchase behavior (CPB). Pranjana. *The Journal of Management Awareness*, *15*(1), 47–53.

Morrisey, M. N., Hofrichter, R., & Rutherford, M. D. (2019). Human faces capture attention and attract first saccades without longer fixation. *Visual Cognition*, *27*(2), 158–170. doi:10.1080/13506285.2019.1631925

Nair, D. (2020). Affective Priming Technique in Advertising–An Empirical Study With Reference to Fast Moving Consumer Goods Sector. Academic Press.

O'Barr, W. M. (2013). Subliminal" advertising. *Advertising & Society Review*, *13*(4). Advance online publication. doi:10.1353/asr.2013.a497057

Pachauri, M. (2001). Consumer behaviour: A literature review. *The Marketing Review*, *2*(3), 319–355. doi:10.1362/1469347012569896

Pringle, H. (2008). *Brand immortality: How brands can live long and prosper*. Kogan Page Publishers.

Ranjbarian, M. K. N. (2010). The Influence of Personality Traits on Consideration Set Size. *European Journal of Soil Science*, *15*(2), 124–136.

Richard, L., & Charbonneau, D. (2009). An introduction to E-Prime. *Tutorials in Quantitative Methods for Psychology*, *5*(2), 68–76. doi:10.20982/tqmp.05.2.p068

Sagal, L. O. 2015. The impact of advertisement on sales: Case study in some selected telecommunication companies in Somalia. European Journal of Business and Management, 7(36).

Sinha, S., & Sinha, S. (2023). Unveiling the legacy of UNIVAC 1: The first commercial computer - computer skills. Computer Skills. https://computerskills.in/univac1/

Skandrani-Marzouki, I., & Marzouki, Y. (2010). Subliminal emotional priming and decision making in a simulated hiring situation. *Swiss Journal of Psychology*, *69*(4), 213–219. doi:10.1024/1421-0185/a000025

Strahan, E. J., Spencer, S. J., & Zanna, M. P. (2002). Subliminal priming and persuasion: Striking while the iron is hot. *Journal of Experimental Social Psychology*, *38*(6), 556–568. doi:10.1016/S0022-1031(02)00502-4

Taylor, P. J., & Marsh, J. E. (2017). E-Prime (Software). The international encyclopedia of communication research methods, 1-3.

Terburg, D., Hooiveld, N., Aarts, H., Kenemans, J. L., & van Honk, J. (2011). Eye tracking unconscious face-to-face confrontations: Dominance motives prolong gaze to masked angry faces. *Psychological Science*, *22*(3), 314–319. doi:10.1177/0956797611398492 PMID:21303993

Tulving, E., & Schacter, D. L. (1990). Priming and human memory systems. *Science*, *247*(4940), 301–306. doi:10.1126/science.2296719 PMID:2296719

Zhang, M., Wei, P., & Zhang, Q. (2015). The impact of supra-and sub-liminal facial expressions on the gaze-cueing effect. *Acta Psychologica Sinica*, *47*(11), 1309. doi:10.3724/SP.J.1041.2015.01309

Chapter 13
Relational Marketing Applied to the Banking Sector in Portuguese Context

Cátia Rodrigues
Polytechnic Institute of Cávado and Ave, Portugal

Bruno Barbosa Sousa
https://orcid.org/0000-0002-8588-2422
Polytechnic Institute of Cávado and Ave, Portugal & UNIAG, Portugal & CiTUR, Portugal

Alexandrino Ribeiro
Polytechnic Institute of Cávado and Ave, Portugal & UNIAG, Portugal

Manuel José Fonseca
https://orcid.org/0000-0002-3290-8449
Polytechnic Institute of Cávado and Ave, Portugal & UNIAG, Portugal

ABSTRACT

Banks were forced to modernize their action plans and strategies in banking relationships so as not to lose their place in an increasingly competitive market due to the use of the internet. Relationship marketing arises in the banking context, due to the need to retain customers and not just because of the concern with attracting new customers. The sudden changes which affects society and the national and global economy mean that we must attribute increasing importance to relationships, loyalty and fidelity, and in the banking sector, the manager-client relationship requires some determinants such as loyalty, satisfaction, quality, and trust. The aim of this topic is to understand how the paradigm of relationship marketing in the banking sector has changed nowadays, considering the drastic change in the practices used by banks regarding their marketing and communication strategies, resulting of technological evolution. In order to achieve the proposed objectives, a qualitative methodology was used with semi-structured interviews.

DOI: 10.4018/979-8-3693-2367-0.ch013

INTRODUCTION

With the advent of social media, banks have found new ways to engage and boost their offerings with customers. Platforms such as Facebook, Twitter and LinkedIn and Instagram allow you to create an engaging online presence, capable of creating curiosity, interest and later making there a need to know more about a certain subject or product that is advertised there. Not only do these interactions provide an additional channel for customer service, but they also offer the opportunity to broadcast messages, promote events, and get instant feedback.

The term marketing is commonly used by several organizations to synthesize a series of strategic actions, often focused simply on communication and advertising issues. (Maçães, 2017) states that Marketing should be seen as a management function in which all activities carried out are developed outside the limits of organizations, and that it is not limited only to Marketing managers, but related to all functional areas of companies. It also states that taking into account globalization and the constant change of the world, where selling and fixing goods is a task in which the difficulty progressively increases, Marketing is an extremely important discipline for organizations (Maçães, 2017).

Marketing turns out to be a management philosophy and a way of generating exchange relationships, in which companies have the duty to focus on the market, in order to satisfy their needs as much as possible, while allowing it to meet its objectives. This technique aims to achieve customer satisfaction to enhance consumption through an exchange relationship.

The banking sector has undergone a significant transformation in recent decades, driven by technological advancement and changes in consumer demands and expectations, as well as, more recently, the more massive and widespread use of online banking driven by the Covid19 pandemic. In this context, relationship marketing has emerged as a key strategy for banks, seeking to build deeper and more meaningful relationships with customers. This study explores the impact of relationship marketing on the banking industry, analyzing how this approach has shaped the customer experience across two distinct generations – Generation Y and Generation X, driving loyalty and influencing business practices.

While traditional or transactional marketing was considered a short-term approach, where the focus was only on the transaction at hand, the constant and permanent evolution gave rise to new strategies and models that met the needs of consumers (Simi et al., 2022). Since the banking sector consists of many specificities, and the marketing area is the basis for commercial action, the theme of relational marketing applied to the banking sector fits perfectly with the surrounding themes.

Relational marketing arises, in the banking context, from the need to retain customers and not only from the concern of attracting new customers. The sudden changes that infect society, the national and world economy, force us to give more and more importance to the relationship, loyalty, and fidelity, and in the banking sector, the manager-customer relationship requires some determinants such as loyalty, satisfaction, quality and trust. The competitiveness of the market and the accessibility of information have caused changes in the behavior of consumers who become increasingly demanding and less loyal to companies. For businesses, on the other hand, attracting new customers can be very expensive, which leads them to try to retain the customers they already have.

One of the changes that created the most impact and that has been shaping our daily lives since then, was technological evolution. Technology has given us the opportunity to grow and improve in all strategies. It is up to us, as a society, to follow this development and adapt to the new reality, learning how to apply these new strategies and what means to use. In a world increasingly driven by technology and with digital evolution occurring at a rapid pace, we must use all means to keep up.

When we talk about advances in technology, more specifically at the level of the internet, loyalty may not be the first thing that comes to mind (Reichheld and Schefter 2000), however, and according to the authors, loyalty should be on a fast path to extinction. As such, relationship marketing is now a prominent topic in the marketing literature. It relates to all marketing activities aimed at establishing, developing, and maintaining successful relationships (Morgan & Hunt, 1994). However, there is still a high concern about maintaining the long-lasting relationship with customers, as it is understood that this is where the future of an organization comes from.

In the past, banks often took a purely transactional approach, focusing primarily on basic financial services. However, as competition has increased and customer expectations and demands have evolved, banks have begun to recognize the importance of having to go beyond simple financial transactions. Relationship marketing has become a strategic response to this shift, focusing on building lasting relationships based on trust, personalization, and ongoing communication.

Context

One of the key contributions of relationship marketing in the banking industry is the ability to tailor offers to individual customer needs. Through data analytics, banks can better understand spending patterns, financial goals, and customer preferences. This personalization not only improves the customer experience, but also increases the relevance of the offers, resulting in greater satisfaction and loyalty and consequently trust in the institution, which can lead to future business.

With the increase in the level of competition in the banking sector in recent years, brought about by globalisation and development, financial systems have been forced to undergo numerous adaptations (Hasan, 2019; Simi et al., 2022). In the case of financial services, in particular, in the relationship between a bank and a customer, when the latter intends to invest his money, the latter is concerned with knowing, through an interactive process, his profile. Thus, the service offered will depend directly on the customer's performance. In today's economic model, customer loyalty has become a crucial issue for the future success of several financial institutions, which has led to them also having to resort to optimal marketing strategies to establish long-term relationships with their customers (Simi et al., 2022).

Customers are looking for more than a place to store money or buy products, they are also looking for a personalized relationship, based on trust (Hasan, 2019).

Several previous studies have demonstrated the positive impact of relational marketing guidelines, fundamentals, and practices as an important tool for meeting the goals of retaining and retaining customers with the highest value (Simi et al., 2022). It was also found to be more valuable for a financial institution to direct marketing towards intangible elements, such as quality of service and customer satisfaction, as this type of marketing is more appropriate when the customer wants a personalized service, as is the case with a set of complex banking products and services, where most customers prefer their decisions to be informed by the knowledge that bank employees have about the products and available services and thus, seek to maintain long-lasting relationships with customers in order to maintain them (Hasan, 2019; Unes et al., 2019).

Some studies show that the higher profitability of banks is associated with relational marketing practices (Martins, 2006). However, relational marketing has been referenced as an indispensable strategy for bank branches to be able to keep up with the rapid growth that occurs in the environment, since the domain of relational marketing is directly related to the key elements of banks. It is thus an important tool for meeting the objectives of retaining and retaining customers with greater value.

Banks must interact with their customers on a constant basis, in order to understand, in the most correct way possible, what kind of products and services they are looking for (EY, 2010). All customer interactions with the company are made through the company's employees, so they must be properly prepared and motivated to enhance the value of the relationship. Whenever a customer interacts with the banking institution (by phone, email, or in person), the customer absorbs a certain image of the institution, each of which contributes to their overall satisfaction (Al-alak and Alnawas, 2010). Menon and O'Connor (2007) indicate that, in the financial sector, whenever a customer interacts with the company, he has the opportunity to evaluate, re-evaluate or confirm his expectations about the relationship with the company. The customer's perspective on the bank is the last area. Every interaction between the client and the institution should be seen by the latter as an action that "added value". Al-alak and Alnawas (2010) demonstrated that relationship marketing activities conducted by financial institutions create and add value to their customers, resulting in both increased customer satisfaction and trust, as well as the temporal extension of the relationship and positive word-of-mouth. The bank must therefore, be concerned with the valuation of its customers.

Previous studies have identified that some personal characteristics such as the age of the account holder, the length of the account, the profile of the investor/beneficiary, the internal relationship, the long-term asset contracts, the risks in other banks, the number of products, the cancellation of the product, the average amount of the inflows and the existence of a joint customer are the variables that best identify the propensity of customers to end their relationship with a bank. They also concluded that customers who place more importance on growth and fulfillment as personal values are less loyal to their bank, with this evidence being more evident in women, the elderly, and high-income consumers (Unes et al., 2019). In addition, it was possible to verify that the most important characteristics for consumer satisfaction are: the perception of the service provided by the agencies, security, self-services, accessibility, coverage and speed (Unes et al., 2019). The application of relational marketing techniques in the banking sector emerges as a competitive advantage, and the main role being the responsibility of the Account Manager, since he knows the Bank's offer and the customer's needs, wich is why he is responsible for promoting proximity and improvement of the relationship between the bank and the customer. The relationship with the customer is an asset that has to be managed, as it has strong possibilities of being profitable for the Banking Institution. A successful relationship involves mutual trust and loyalty, interaction and dialogue, commitment, empathy and a satisfactory performance of the role of each party in the relationship. These are key elements of a relationship marketing strategy that differ from traditional marketing.

From a more modern point of view, we cannot overlook the fact that banking is increasingly being used online. In this environment, relationships between customers and financial service providers may be increasingly absent, as interpersonal encounters are replaced by online interactions (Hasan, 2019). According to a study by Ernst & Young (2010), the current economic crisis has had, and has, a profound and lasting impact on the way customers interact with their banks and has had a negative or very negative impact on their trust in the banking sector (EY, 2010), a key feature for establishing strong, long-term relationships. This is one of the main factors that leads customers to leave the institution. Moreover, certain types of products, such as banking products, require support from customers when making a decision, so that it is carried out with the necessary wisdom about the product or service involved in the transaction (Dibb and Maeadows, 2001).

Relational Marketing in the Banking Sector

Despite the evident benefits of relationship marketing in the banking industry, there are challenges and ethical considerations that deserve attention. The use of sensitive data requires a responsible approach, ensuring customer privacy and security. Additionally, excessive personalization can raise concerns about manipulating customer behavior, requiring balance in the implementation of relationship marketing strategies.

The COVID-19 pandemic has further highlighted the importance of relationship marketing in the banking industry. Rapid adaptation to emerging customer needs, transparent communication on relief measures, and emphasis on financial assistance have solidified customer confidence during these difficult times. Financial institutions that have demonstrated empathy and agility in how they have faced the challenges of the COVID-19 pandemic have seen significant benefits in terms of reputation, security, and customer loyalty.

The so-called "communications boom", technological innovation and the revolution in information and the possibility of enabling interactive communication, have forced companies to provide quick responses, namely: knowing the customer, in order to provide quality products and/or services at a fair price, according to the various needs of the customer. The marketing philosophy places the acquisition of new customers as being only the first step in the marketing process. Cementing the relationship, turning indifferent customers into loyal customers, and serving consumers as customers is also marketing" (Berry, 1983). This author also adds that relational marketing used to attract, maintain and increase consumer relationships usually generates loyalty, which subsequently generates profits (Berry, 1983). Relationship marketing strategy, in addition to its ability to help understand customer needs and act towards satisfying their wants and needs by understanding their motivations and behavior patterns, can also lead to customer loyalty and retention and cost reduction (Hasan, 2019; Unes et al., 2019). It is considered a long-term marketing strategy, aimed at developing and maintaining lasting relationships with customers, through personalized communication, new forms of market segmentation, multiple touchpoints, and real-time measurement of customer satisfaction (Simi et al., 2022). Relationship marketing has been regarded as a crucial strategy for the financial services industry, especially the banking sector, due to the rising cost of acquiring new customers, rising customer expectations, and the high rate of customer defections (Hasan, 2019). For Lindon et al. (2004), relational marketing "presupposes the creation of differentiated strategies for differentiated customers that go far beyond direct contact, based on the knowledge of these customers' needs and their perception of service". According to Zeithmal and Bitner, relationship marketing is a new philosophy of doing business, with its strategic orientation being based on maintaining and developing relationships with current customers, as opposed to attracting new customers. The very philosophy of relationship marketing assumes that customers give preference to continued relationships with companies, to the detriment of constant change of supplier (Simi et al., 2022). With this relationship, the company and the customer gain knowledge, trust, and commitment to each other, which allows them to act more securely in subsequent contacts (Simi et al., 2022). According to Arnett, German & Hunt (2003), there are six main success factors of relationship marketing, which involve: trust, commitment, cooperation, keeping promises, shared values, and communication (Unes et al., 2019).

Customer Loyalty and Retention as a Source of Value

Data collection and analysis play an important and decisive role in banking relationship marketing. Modern banks use advanced algorithms to understand customer behavior, identify needs and trends, and anticipate needs. Not only does this analysis facilitate personalization, it also enables financial institutions to make more targeted and informed decisions about developing differentiated products and marketing strategies.

Relationship marketing redefines the meaning of customer loyalty in banking. It's not just about ensuring that customers carry out recurring transactions, but also about building an ongoing, binding relationship that transcends the most basic and routine financial operations. Rewards programs, personalized services or proactive communication are key tools to cultivate loyalty, turning customers into true brand advocates.

With trust being a central and crucial element in the banking industry, relational marketing plays a key role in building and maintaining this attribute. Transparency in business practices, open communication and efficient resolution of transactions or problems contribute to building trust on the part of the customer. In this sense, trust is one of the main drivers of customer loyalty in the banking sector.

In a market as competitive as the current one, there are some factors that make the difference and that make a company a market leader to the detriment of others. One of the best and most operational tools to have a more correct perception of the market is the preparation of a marketing plan, which is essential to achieve the pre-established goals. In this way, the entrepreneur plans the entire product environment, in order to obtain the best results, managing resources better, measuring expectations better, without ever losing sight of the diversity of perceptions, communication processes and cultural paradigms.

The purpose of developing a marketing plan is to be aware of the market, to innovate for the customer, to bring people what they identify with. Therefore, when drawing up a marketing plan, it is essential to take into account the population or target audience to whom such a plan is addressed. Marketing starts even before the product exists, it is present in the creation phase, the transaction, and after the product is sold. In other words, marketing involves all phases of the life of a product or service, being a fundamental element for its success. And it is also always present in the company's relationship with the customer. The main objective of companies should always be to please consumers, in order to build customer loyalty, while meeting the needs of the company itself and allowing the continuous improvement of its production and commercial processes, in constant interaction. However, it is important to highlight that involving people is not the same as making several offers, but rather providing valuable content. The idea is to get them to keep in touch with the business and, consequently, offer a greater degree of permission for your company. In this way, customer loyalty has thus become a motto for companies. According to Bogmann (2000), the concept of fidelity is defined as "the quality of one who is loyal, true, present". The same author considers that this should be a quality that the client should possess (Kumar et al., 2018). Loyalty is a behavioural response (purchase), expressed over time, in a non-random way from a decision-making process, regarding one or more brand alternatives, and is also a psychological process of decision and evaluation. It can be seen as the existence of a consistent repurchase pattern over time, which is indicative of the existence of loyalty, and which can be evaluated in data collection (Kumar et al., 2018). According to many researches, a loyal customer is beneficial for an organization with regard to increasing the growth rate as well as improving organizational stability, as loyalty has been found to affect the productivity of the company, as higher customer retention leads to cost reduction, sales growth, market share, reduction of acquisition costs and customer service. It is also considered important for companies, as it is a constant source of income that does not generate funding expenses (Gopalsamy & Gokulapadmanaban, 2020; Hasan, 2019; Kumar et al., 2018). E-banking is more accessible and convenient than traditional banking (physical branches). Customers get the fastest and most efficient services, and banks save costs. However, e-banking makes the market more transparent, makes it more difficult to differentiate services, increases competition, decreases the cost of switching from one bank to another. Thus, banks must foster a long and deep relationship with their customers, and trust is very important (Unes et al., 2019). It is important to distinguish between what is just customer retention, and the true meaning of the term loyalty and loyalty does not guarantee retention. Customer retention is concerned with maintaining the business relationship established between a company and a customer. Customer loyalty can be defined both in terms of customer behavior, which has been synonymous with customer retention, and in terms of customer attitudes. Understanding how to build customer loyalty in banks has become a real challenge that requires daily attention in order to prevent and prevent customers from moving to the competition.

Costumer Relationship Management (CRM)

The growth of digital banks has changed the behavior pattern of users, through the inclusion of advantage clubs, which offer personalized benefits aimed at the needs of the institution's customer profile, assisting in the process of customer retention and satisfaction. The most common strategy is CRM (Customer Relationship Management), which in Portuguese stands for "Customer Relationship Management". It is, therefore, a tool to support and improve business processes, through the use of technology and software solutions that not only coordinate the multiple functions of the business, but also the means of communication with the customer, for example, call center or eventually through the web and integrates the operations of Sales, Marketing, Call Center, Help Desk, Inventory, Field Services, and Quality (Moon et al., 2020). In the banking system, we can draw a quantitative profile built with several variables such as region/location, income, age, history of products and services used for payment, etc. However, it is not enough, because in terms of loyalty, it only reflects a comparison considered misleading for a pattern of repeated purchase, lacking a psychological component or customer preference towards the bank (Moon et al., 2020). The CRM should allow for a complete customer profile, but it should also support marketing activity and the launch of specific campaigns. The benefits of this new strategy are: increased revenues from sales, new product developments, a good customer base, a higher degree of customer satisfaction, reduced management and marketing costs, customer loyalty and retention, among others (Moon et al., 2020). Several studies have explained that satisfaction mediates between relationship management and retention rate in the banking sector and that satisfaction among customers was achieved through CRM that recognized customer expectations, needs, behavior and preferences.

Developing and implementing a CRM in the banking system leads to greater efficiency in terms of customers and bank flow (Moon et al., 2020). In 2010, the comprehensive definition of CRM allows us to have a more complete view of its meaning, implying that the customer is seen as the key element, towards which all the processes of an organization are oriented and improved, in order to interact with its customers. Peppers and Rogers consider that marketing strategies are personalized and developed in four fundamental stages, which correspond to the phases of the CRM model (Peppers and Rogers, 1999).

CRM plays a significant role in relationship marketing in the banking industry. Marketing campaigns are increasingly tailored to each customer's individual preferences, transactional history, and specific financial needs. CRM systems centralize customer data, collect, store, and manage data in a detailed way about the different customers. This allows for a comprehensive understanding of each individual's individual profile, transactional histories, and preferences, making it easy to personalize interactions. Based on the data collected, banking systems can segment customers in a more efficient way, which allows them to create targeted marketing campaigns that are tailored to the specific needs of different demographic groups. Once they have all the information from the CRM, banks can send personalized communications, with special offers, financial product recommendations, or relevant updates according to the profile. This personalized approach connects and strengthens bonds with customers, building close relationships and loyalty.

CRM assists in all stages of customer contacts, ensuring a cohesive experience at all points of communication, such as online interactions, customer service, physical branches, among others, providing an integrated and consistent experience. In this way, by analyzing behavior patterns and transactions, CRM systems help banks anticipate customer needs, enabling them to proactively offer financial services and solutions, demonstrating an appropriate and genuine commitment that meets customer satisfaction.

CRM makes it easy to continuously collect customer feedback, allowing for quick adjustments to marketing strategies, and a constant improvement in the bank's approach based on the preferences and demands that evolution requires.

In summary, CRM plays a key role in relational marketing in the banking sector, enabling institutions to cultivate stronger and more personalized relationships with their customers, especially in younger generations, who value experiences that are more adapted to their needs and expectations, as these are increasingly demanding.

As CRM is a business strategy and a very important technological component, it is essential that its epicenter is the knowledge about the customer and the existing information about them, such as: understanding who they are, why they buy, what they buy, what motivates them, how they react, that is, segmenting customers, thus crossing All the information, in order to provide a complete profile of the (potential) customer. Only after this step is completed, CRM can be defined as a strategy, enabling, based on the data obtained, a better management of these, making an evaluation that allows to retain and retain them, in favor of the organization (Raquel & Cunha, 2012). The understanding of CRM functionalities is important for all companies that have a direct or indirect relationship with their customers, allowing them to understand and understand that the functionalities of a software help in the processes of an organization, leading to all being interconnected, starting to be based on each other, clarifying and defining processes and procedures well.

DISCUSSION OF RESULTS

Technological advancement and the increasing prevalence of online banking have drastically altered the way customers interact with financial institutions. Millennials and Gen X, in particular, prefer digital solutions and online experiences. In this context, relational marketing in banking now focuses on offering intuitive platforms and mobile apps, streamlined online onboarding processes, and effective customer service through digital channels.

The traditional approach to banking is giving way to more personalized, customer-centric strategies, with relationship marketing playing an extremely important role in this process.

Trust is key in banking, and relationship marketing plays an essential role in building and maintaining that trust. Banks invest in transparent communication, providing clear information about products, policies, and fees. This clarity is of utmost importance to millennials and Gen X, who value authenticity and corporate responsibility.

The importance of relationship marketing in banking for millennials lies in the emphasis this generation places on customer experience, personalization, and digital interaction. Banks that implement effective relationship marketing strategies for millennials can build stronger, longer-lasting relationships by offering intuitive online services, proactive customer service, transparency in communications, and financial solutions that are better tailored to the specific needs of millennials. Personalization, both in terms of offers and interactions, is key to attracting and retaining millennial customers, who value convenience and authenticity in relationships with financial institutions.

In turn, the importance of relationship marketing in the banking sector for Gen X is crucial due to the specific characteristics of this generation. Gen X values personalized experiences, digital convenience, and authenticity. Banks that implement effective relationship marketing strategies for Gen X can establish deeper, more lasting connections.

For Gen X, it is essential to offer innovative financial solutions, intuitive user interfaces on digital platforms, transparent communication, and a strong social media presence. This generation is highly inclined to online, to technology in general and relies on digital channels for their transactions and interactions. The inclusion of ethical values and sustainable practices, social and environmental responsibility. they are also a trait appreciated by these individuals, as Gen X tends to value companies aligned with social and environmental causes. In summary, successful relationship marketing in banking for Gen X requires an approach centered on digital experience, transparency, and values.

Despite advancements, the banking industry faces ongoing challenges in the field of relationship marketing. Rapid technological evolution requires constant adaptation of marketing strategies. Additionally, ensuring the security and privacy of customer data has become a top priority.

In summary, the current context of relationship marketing in banking reflects a significant shift towards more personalized, customer-centric, and technology-driven strategies. Understanding the characteristics and preferences of millennials and Gen X is critical, and banks are continually looking for ways to innovate and meet the growing expectations and needs of these customer segments. Success in relationship banking marketing depends on the ability to adapt to these dynamic changes, providing exceptional, credible, transparent and satisfying financial experiences, building strong and long-term relationships with customers.

CONCLUSION

As the banking industry continues to evolve in tandem with the rapid advancement of technology, relationship marketing remains at the forefront of customer acquisition strategies. The integration of emerging technologies, such as artificial intelligence, promises to further enhance the personalization and effectiveness of relationship marketing initiatives. However, it is critical that banks continue to balance innovation with ethical considerations, ensuring that the benefits extend to both institutions and customers.

In a short period of time, banking has seen the exponential growth of the market and competition, which has led to an extremely rapid adaptation, in order to keep up not only with this evolution, but also to develop and implement procedures that build loyalty among existing customers.

It is concluded that relationship marketing is still a factor that brings confidence to banking customers. It is a set of marketing activities aimed at establishing long-term relationships.

As much as several institutions are sought in order to perceive the existence of better conditions, the issue of security that the relationship transmits is still a point in favor that weighs on the decision of customers at the time of choice.

In summary, relationship marketing has revolutionized the way banks approach customer interaction. By prioritizing long-lasting relationship building, personalization, and transparency, financial institutions are able to not only meet customer expectations, but also anticipate customer needs. The impact of relational marketing in the banking industry is evident not only in improving the customer experience, but also in building trust, loyalty, and effectively adapting to emerging challenges. As we move forward, the seamless integration of these strategies is essential to the successful evolution of banking in the age of relationship.

Main Limitations and Suggestions for Future Investigations

By focusing exclusively on generations X and Y in the analysis of the impact of relationship marketing in the banking sector, we can have as limitations a significant diversity within each generation, with variables such as socioeconomic background, individual values and consumption preferences. An overly generalized approach runs the risk of not containing this diversity, thus resulting in marketing strategies that do not fully correspond to the needs and characteristics of all members of these generations, as there is significant diversity within each one. Individual differences can be substantial, making it difficult to apply broad conclusions to all members of these generations.

In addition, rapid technological advancement can lead to rapid changes in the preferences and behaviors of these generations, i.e., what is relevant today may not be relevant in a few years or even months. What's relevant today can become obsolete in short periods, making it challenging to keep marketing strategies up-to-date.

The preferences and behaviors of these generations can evolve rapidly due to the influence of technological and cultural changes.

Attitudes towards relationship marketing can vary significantly based on cultural and regional context. What works in one region may not be effective in another, requiring further analysis of these factors. As such, a broader analysis that includes a broader view and considering other demographic factors can provide a more complete understanding of the relationship marketing landscape in the banking industry.

The too rapid advancement of technology can also create challenges for researchers, as digital trends can change before they are even fully understood. This requires constant adaptation of research strategies.

By addressing these limitations, researchers can improve the quality and relevance of future studies, which can provide a more complete analysis and understanding of the impact of relationship marketing on millennials and X.

Although the methodology applied allowed us to achieve the objectives initially proposed, it is important to reflect on the limitations that were part of it. The methodology chosen to carry out the study was the interview and the focus groups, and the reason for this choice was mainly with the objective of understanding the form and vision of relational marketing in the generations, resulting in richer feedbacks. However, the fact that we only used two generations meant that the age range was more restricted. It would be interesting to use a wider range of ages in the future, or even, if possible, to analyze all generations, in order to make a broader comparative study. We consider this to be a point of improvement in a future study.

REFERENCES

Al-alak, B., & Alnawas, I. (2010). Evaluating the Effect of Marketing Activities on Relationship Quality in the Banking Sector: The Case of Private Commercial Banks in Jordan. *International Journal of Marketing Studies*, *2*(1). Advance online publication. doi:10.5539/ijms.v2n1p78

Arnett, D., German, S., & Hunt, S. (2003). The identity salience model of relationship marketing success: The case of nonprofit marketing. *Journal of Marketing*, *67*(2), 89–105. doi:10.1509/jmkg.67.2.89.18614

Berry, L. (1983). *Relationship Marketing*. American Marketing Association.

Bogmann, I. M. (2000). *Marketing de relacionamento - Estratégias de fidelização e suas implicações financeiras*. Livraria Nobel S.A.

Dibb, S., & Meadows, M. (2001). The Application of a Relationship Marketing Perspective in Retail Banking. *Service Industries Journal*, *21*(1), 169–194. doi:10.1080/714005011

Ernst & Young. (2010). *Understanding Customer Behaviour in Retail Banking*. Ernst & Young.

Hasan, M. (2019). Relationship Marketing and Customer Loyalty: Experience from Banking Industry of Bangladesh. Journal of Organisational Studies and Innovation, 6(1).

Lindon, D., Lendrevie, J., Levy, J., Dionísio, P., & Rodrigues, J. V. (2004). *Teoria e Prática do Marketing*. Lisboa: Publicações Dom Quixote.

Maçães, M. (2017). *Marketing e Gestão da Relação com o Cliente*. Actual.

Martins, E. (2006). *Marketing relacional na Banca: A Fidelização e a Venda Cruzada*. Editor Vida Económica.

Menon, K. & O'Connor, A. (2007). Building Customers' Affective Commitment Towards Retail Banks: The Role of CRM in Each Moment of Truth. *Journal of Financial Services Marketing*, 12(2), 157.

Moon, M. A., Commer, P. J., Sci, S., & Farooq, A. (2020). Service Fairness, Relationship Quality and Customer Loyalty in the Banking Sector of Pakistan. *Pakistan Journal of Commerce and Social Sciences*, *2020*(2).

Morgan, R. M., & Hunt, S. D. (1994). The Commitment-Trust Theory of Relationship Marketing. *Journal of Marketing*, *58*(3), 20–38. doi:10.1177/002224299405800302

Raquel, S. & Cunha, R. (2012). *CRM - Customer Relationship Management – Uma Estratégia – Estudo de Caso Osvaldo Matos* Universidade do Porto (Portugal).

Reichheld, F., & Schefter, P. (2000). E-Loyalty: Your Secret Weapon on the Web. *Harvard Business Review*, 105–113.

Simi, S., Santos, D., Carvalho, C. E., & Begnini, S. (2022). Marketing de relacionamento e reputação corporativa: Estudo do setor bancário. *Revista de Administração Unimep*, *19*(7), 223–246.

Unes, B. V. J., Camioto, F. C., & Guerreiro, E. D. R. (2019). Fatores relevantes para a fidelização de clientes no setor bancário. *Gestão & Produção*, *26*(2), e2828. doi:10.1590/0104-530x2828-19

Zeithaml, V. A., & Bitner, M. J. (2000). *Services Marketing: Integrating Customer Focus across the Firm*. Irwin McGraw-Hill.

About the Contributors

Mudita Sinha is currently associated with Christ University as an Associate Professor of Marketing. She has completed her Ph.D., Masters in Marketing Management, and MBA. Dr. Sinha is an experienced researcher, faculty, and salesperson with proven abilities. She is a competent professional with over 12 years of combined experience in Industry, Business Education, Institutional Affairs & administrative functions. Dr. Sinha has published several articles in various National and International Journals of repute in Marketing and General Management. To keep her knowledge updated and deliver the best quality she participates and presents research articles at different National and international conferences.

Arabinda Bhandari is presently working as an Associate Professor in Strategic Management area in School of Management, Presidency University, Bangalore, India. He is an author of "Strategic Management - A conceptual Framework", published from McGraw Hill India. He has more than 20 years of experience in industry and academics.

Samant Shant Priya is an Associate Professor at Lal Bahadur Shastri Institute of Management (LBSIM), New Delhi. Prior to joining LBSIM, he had served as HOD (MBA and Marketing) with SIBACA, Lonavala. He did his MBA with first class distinction in 2001 from Shivaji University and Ph.D. in 2013 from MANIT, Bhopal, an institute of National Importance. He has served as Member Syllabus Revision Committee, Chairman Viva- Voce of Projects, Chairman Paper Setters at SPPU, Pune. He has eleven and half years of teaching experience and even brings around eight years of corporate experience in sales and marketing functions. He has attended, presented, delivered and chaired sessions in many conferences including one at the Indian Institute of Management, Ahemdabad wherein he has also chaired one session. To his credit, he has 17 research papers; one of them is Thomson Reuters indexed, three of them are SCOPUS Indexed and ABDC listed.

Sajal Kabiraj specialises in supply chain management consulting for retail companies and innovation-based market research studies. He has strong international practice area and research experience in multinational corporations such as Datamatics, IndoRama and NOCIL (Petrochemicals), a JV of Royal Dutch Shell-AMG, iCRM (KL, Malaysia), and MMT Center (JIBS, Sweden). He has spent time as a Researcher with Volkswagen Consulting AG, Germany, Schenker Logistics AB, Sweden and Center for Industrial Production, Aalborg, Denmark. He has been actively involved in research studies with Datamatics Inc, Panasonic, Telekom Malaysia, The Coca Cola Company, SIDBI, Jasubhai Media, CIDCO, ONREC (Canada) and Schenker Logistics AB. Dr Kabiraj presently teaches at the School of Entrepreneurship and Business at Häme University of Applied Sciences (HAMK), Finland. Through his teaching career in China as a tenured Full Professor and elsewhere, he has been awarded the Best Teacher Awards in 2008, 2011, 2014 and 2018 for academic research and teaching excellence. His research interests lie in strategic management, organization science, innovation, entrepreneurship and technology management.

* * *

Nilesh Arora is an academician with 21 years of Industry, teaching, and research experience. He has MBA in Marketing and Ph.D. in Management. He has been in academic leadership roles for the last 10 years and has 6 years of experience in the industry. He is presently working as Professor in Marketing area and Director, University School of Business, Chandigarh University, Mohali, Punjab, India. He has been teaching courses like Marketing Management, Consumer Behavior and Advertising. He is an avid researcher, prolific writer, and an academician of repute. He has attended and presented research papers in various National and International Conferences and Seminars in leading Universities and has several publications in national and international journals of repute. He has published research papers in various journals like Journal of Consumer Marketing, Marketing Intelligence and Planning, Journal of Global Scholars of Marketing Science, Journal of Global Marketing, Asian Academy of Management Journal, Decision, International Journal of Business and Globalisation. Dr. Arora's research interests include Consumer Behavior, Celebrity Endorsement, Social Media Advertising, and Retail.

Nitesh Behare is an accomplished author with a wealth of knowledge and 15 years of experience in the academic field. He currently holds the position of Associate Professor at the Balaji Institute of International Business (BIIB), Sri Balaji University Pune (SBUP). Throughout his career, Dr. Behare has made significant contributions to the academic world through the publication of numerous research papers and book chapters, establishing himself as a recognized authority in his field.

Shubhada Behare is a promising independent author, whose interest for writing extends across various forms including Chapters in edited Books, research papers, and journal articles. With a keen eye for detail and a relentless pursuit of excellence, Shubhada is dedicated to honing her craft and refining her skills as a writer. Born with a natural inclination towards storytelling and a profound curiosity about the world, Shubhada embarked on her writing journey with a determination to explore diverse topics and share her insights with the world. She believes in the power of words to transform lives and is determined to make a difference through her writing.

Shikha Bhagat is an Assistant Professor in the School of Business and Management at Christ (Deemed to be University) Bengaluru. She graduated from Guru Nanak Dev University, Amritsar, and was awarded a gold medal for her outstanding performance. Her doctoral degree was conferred by Noida International University Greater Noida, Uttar Pradesh and her research focus encompasses marketing, international marketing, and global business. She boasts 13 years of experience in both teaching and research fields. Additionally, she has authored numerous papers and book chapters published in reputable international and Indian journals indexed in Scopus and Web of Science. She has actively engaged in academia and participated in various forums addressing consumer behavior, global business and international business marketing techniques. Significantly, she was honored with the Best Paper Award at the 2023 international conference organized by Jain University. Her work demonstrates a commitment to advancing knowledge in her expertise and contributing to the academic discourse.

Abhay Grover is a research scholar at Chandigarh University's - University School of Business in Punjab, India, and an Assistant Professor at Lovely Professional University's Mittal School of Business in Phagwara, Punjab. He is a passionate academician with over ten years of teaching experience and two years of industry experience. He is interested in teaching subjects such as GST, Accounting, Law, and research in marketing, social commerce, etc.

Zhang Jieyao is a senior lecturer in the School of Management and Economics, Chuxiong Normal University, China. Her doctorate is from the Taylor's University in Hospitality and Tourism with research on Pro-environmental Behavioural Intention towards Ecotourism in China. She has two postgraduate degrees; master's in International Hospitality Management from the Taylor's University and Hospitality Management from University of Toulouse, France. Her research areas include natural tourism, eco-tourism, and behavioural studies.

Uttam Kaur is a research scholar of University School of Business, Chandigarh University, Mohali. Her area of interest is general management. She is currently in the final year of her Ph.D. program, specializing in marketing research. As a seasoned researcher, she possesses expertise in utilizing software such as PLS-SEM, SPSS, and AMOS. She has contributed to the academic community with the publication of a book chapter titled "A Typology of Digital Marketing Channels with a Special Reference to India," indexed in Scopus. Her ongoing research focuses on understanding consumer behaviors related to sustainability, with her primary research area centered around sustainability. Uttam Kaur is the corresponding author.

Jeetesh Kumar is a senior lecturer in the School of Hospitality, Tourism and Events, Taylor's University, Malaysia. His doctorate is from the Taylor's University in Hospitality and Tourism with research on Economic Impacts of Business Events in Malaysia. He has two postgraduate degrees; professional master's in Hospitality Management and International Tourism from University of Toulouse, France and the other in Business Administration (MBA—Marketing) from Hamdard University, Pakistan. His research areas include economic impacts, economic modeling, MICE, medical tourism, and behavioral studies. He has worked on consultancy and research projects at the national level and authored 35+ publications including research articles and book chapters.

Sunita Kumar is a passionate educationist with 19+ years of experience (Industry: 5+ years and Teaching: 14+ years) experience. My area of expertise/ research includes advertising, branding, digital marketing, consumer behaviour, and Marketing Analytics. Over the last 12 years, I have published more than 20 papers in scopus-indexed journals/ chapters in a book, conference proceedings, and received positive evaluations for many marketing units, including Brand Management, Consumer Behaviour, Social Media and Digital Marketing, and Marketing Analytics. I am also actively supervising master's and PhD candidates from Christ University Bangalore, having a keen research interest and involvement in research and consultancies projects.

K. Lakshmypriya holds a doctoral degree in Management on the research area work life balance of women entrepreneurs. She has over 21 years of academic experience in UG and PG programs and two years of corporate experience. Currently, she is affiliated with Christ University, as an Associate Professor and is the actively engaged in entrepreneurship developmental activities. She is also the E cell coordinator and mentor at the University She is a Certified entrepreneurship educator from Stanford technological ventures and NEN. She has undergone Faculty training in entrepreneurship from EDII, Ahmadabad. Her area of expertise includes design thinking, social entrepreneurship, social innovations, Tech in education, Talent management and DEI. She has Curated courses on Innovation and Entrepreneurship for students and executive training programs in the capacity of coordinator for entrepreneurship specialization. Presented paper on Social entrepreneurship at IIM Trichy, INDAM conference,2020, Humanistic management conference at IIM Nagpur in 2023 and 150 papers in various national and international conferences. 42 publications in the domain of entrepreneurship, innovation and HRM in peer reviewed and Scopus indexed journals with Emerald, Springer, Taylor and Francis. She has served as Consultant at SHG and women empowerment program at KRRA, Trivandrum, Kerala 2016-2017, consultant in design thinking training for Tata electronics in 2021 and mobility services business plan consultant for a startup in Bangalore. She has three patents to her credit. Currently doing a University funded project on understanding succession planning and financial models and its impact on organizational sustainability of Nonprofit organizations.

Rashmi Mahajan is a triple post graduate and is a Masters of Computer Management, Post Graduate Diploma in Business Management [Marketing] & Masters of Business Studies [Marketing]. She has completed her PhD in Marketing Management and a Diploma in Training & Development from Indian Society for Training & Development, Pune Chapter. She has around 19+ years of experience teaching undergraduate as well as post graduate students and has 3 PhD scholars pursuing their PhD under her guidance. She has published various papers in National as well as International journals and has 2 patents and 1 copyright credited to her name. She also has 10 Chapters Published. She is a Professor, Head of Department of International Business & Dy. Director of BIIB in Sri Balaji University Pune (SBUP).

Mohammed Majeed (DBA, CBC) is a Senior Lecturer (PhD) at Tamale Technical University, Tamale-Ghana. He is the current Head of Department (HoD) of Marketing. His current research interest includes branding, social media in service organizations. Majeed holds Doctor of Business Administration (DBA), Certified Business Analyst and Consultant (ICBAC), MPhil and MBA Marketing. Majeed has published with good publishers such as Emerald, Taylor & Francis, Apply Academic Press, Asia-Pacific Management Accounting Association, Springer and Palgrave McMillan.

Anagha Nair is an individual currently pursuing Master's in Commerce (Mcom) at CHRIST (Deemed to be University) Bangalore, having an innate curiosity for the complexities of commerce and finance.

Dinesh Kumar R. is an Assistant Professor in Commerce, combines five years of corporate experience at Titan Company Limited and Legal Cliff Consultants Pvt Ltd with nine years of teaching at Christ University. His transition from corporate to academia seamlessly integrated his practical knowledge with academic insight, fostering a learner-centric approach. Passionate about emerging trends, he delves into digital marketing and technology, including augmented and virtual reality. His commitment to excellence is evident through his certifications as a Google Certified Educator and a Google Professional Career Certified Digital Marketer. Beyond his professional roles, he embodies the spirit of a lifelong learner, continually pushing the boundaries of teaching methodologies and Research.

Rashmi Rai is the Head of the Department of School of Business and Management, CHRIST (Deemed to be) University. An Associate Professor having 21 years of experience has done her double Masters in Marketing and HR and Phd in Management, her primary area of interest is Human Resources Management and Organisational Behaviour. Her Core Competencies are good communication and writing skills, profound knowledge of the subject areas, and teaching students using innovative pedagogy tools. Having a keen research interest has helped her develop around 52 research papers and several Book Chapters indexed in Scopus, published nationally and internationally in reputed journals and books, and the quest is still on. She has also published a book on "Quality of Life" by Routledge. She has conducted many workshops on various subjects in management and had an opportunity to present papers and serve as a session chair at several conferences.

Vinayak Shitole is a seasoned professional with a combined experience of 5 years in the corporate sector and two years in academia. He has demonstrated expertise in International Finance and Expenses and is currently affiliated with Assistant Professor, where he plays a pivotal role in the field. Academic Experience: Prof. Shitole has been imparting his knowledge to the academic community. He has been an Assistant Professor at Arihant Institute of Business Management since June 2023, teaching subjects like Financial Derivatives and Risk Management, International Business Environment, Marketing of Financial Services, and Corporate Financial Restructuring. His academic responsibilities also include supervisory roles, program coordination, and mentoring of MBA students. During his tenure at BVDU-IMRDA, Sangli, from June 2021 to June 2023, Prof. Shitole educated students on subjects such as International Financial Management, Corporate Finance, Financial Management, Enterprise Business Applications, and Investment Analysis & Portfolio Management. He actively contributed to the university examination paper setting, acted as a paper checker, and assisted with NAAC Assessment criteria for teaching and learning. Corporate Experience: Before his academic career, Prof. Shitole worked as an IT Expense Specialist at Optimas OE Solutions, Pune, from August 2019 to May 2023. He managed IT procurement processes for North America and Asia Pacific, tracked purchase expenses, and collaborated closely with the global finance team. Prof. Shitole also worked as an Outbound and RMA Executive at DHL Supply Chain - Dell Logistics, Pune, for a brief period, where he was responsible for processing orders, maintaining order records, and coordinating with customers. Before his academic journey, he served as a Purchasing Executive at New Bharat Diesels, Sangli, from May 2017 to May 2018. His responsibilities included negotiating prices with suppliers, maintaining records of goods ordered, and ensuring the timely fulfilment of orders. Education: Prof. Shitole is pursuing a PhD in Management Studies from BVDU-IMRDA, Sangli, with an expected completion date in June 2024. His research focuses on "A Study of Marketing Strategies for the Revival of the Wine Industry in Western Maharashtra, with Special Reference to Sangli District." His research contributions span areas such as economic growth, cultural heritage preservation, enhancing consumer satisfaction, ensuring regulatory compliance, fostering competitiveness, promoting sustainability, respecting regional nuances, and encouraging stakeholder collaboration. His research guide is Dr. Pratap Desai, Deputy Director, BVDU-IMRDA, Sangli. In addition to his PhD, Prof. Shitole holds a Diploma in Taxation Law from BVDU-IMRDA, Sangli, and an MBA in Finance and Production Management from the same institution. He also gained recognition for his RICO AUTO Industries Ltd., Gurugram, Delhi internship project. His educational journey began with a Bachelor of Engineering in Mechanical Engineering from PVPIT, Budhgaon, Sangli, and a Diploma in Mechanical Engineering from MSBTE-Shantiniketan Polytechnic, Sangli. Personal Interests: Prof. Vinayak is a dedicated and passionate educator committed to contributing to the academic and corporate domains. He brings his unique blend of experience and expertise to the subject matter of the book chapter, ensuring that it provides valuable insights and perspectives.

Rishi Prakash Shukla is a highly accomplished individual in the field of Artificial Intelligence (AI) and analytics. With 12 years of experience, he has made significant contributions to the field through his research and development work. He has 6 patents and has published 20 research papers, demonstrating his expertise and depth of knowledge in AI and analytics. Dr. Shukla has worked with institutions such as Symbiosis International University and has also contributed to projects at the Indian Institute of Management. He has a keen interest in new technologies, particularly in the area of metaverse. He is an IBM and SAS certified professional, further adding to his credentials in the field of AI and analytics. In addition to his work in AI and analytics, Dr. Shukla is also an author of 5 books on futuristic technologies. He is known for his friendly demeanor and love for travel, as well as his passion for social experimentation using technology. With his extensive experience, knowledge, and passion for technology, Dr. Rishi Prakash Shukla is a valuable asset to any organization.

Prashant Kumar Siddhey is presently working as Professor of Management in University School of Business, Chandigarh University, Mohali. He did his Ph.D on supply chain efficacy in manufacturing sectors of India from Devi Ahilya University, Indore, Madhya Pradesh, India. His area of specialization is Supply Chain Management and General Management and has teaching experience of 15 years.

Bruno Barbosa Sousa is Adjunct Professor of Marketing at Polytechnic Institute of Cávado and Ave (IPCA), Portugal and PhD in Marketing and Strategy in Universidade do Minho, Portugal. Head of Masters Program - Tourism Management and Marketing Tourism (IPCA); CiTUR – Center for Tourism Research, Development and Innovation and UNIAG research member. He has published in the Journal of Enterprising Communities, Tourism Management Perspectives, Current Issues in Tourism, Journal of Organizational Change Management, World Review of Entrepreneurship, Management and Sust. Development, among others. https://orcid.org/0000-0002-8588-2422.aac5d92a-6e64-4f88-8f01-362429bd4dc7

Muhammad Usman Tariq has more than 16+ year's experience in industry and academia. He has authored more than 200+ research articles, 100+ case studies, 50+ book chapters and several books other than 4 patents. He has been working as a consultant and trainer for industries representing six sigma, quality, health and safety, environmental systems, project management, and information security standards. His work has encompassed sectors in aviation, manufacturing, food, hospitality, education, finance, research, software and transportation. He has diverse and significant experience working with accreditation agencies of ABET, ACBSP, AACSB, WASC, CAA, EFQM and NCEAC. Additionally, Dr. Tariq has operational experience in incubators, research labs, government research projects, private sector startups, program creation and management at various industrial and academic levels. He is Certified Higher Education Teacher from Harvard University, USA, Certified Online Educator from HMBSU, Certified Six Sigma Master Black Belt, Lead Auditor ISO 9001 Certified, ISO 14001, IOSH MS, OSHA 30, and OSHA 48. He has been awarded Principal Fellowship from Advance HE UK & Chartered Fellowship of CIPD.

Shrikant Waghulkar is a seasoned educator with a wealth of experience spanning over 10 years in the field of management education. He holds a prestigious Doctorate degree in management faculty from Savitribai Phule Pune University, Pune, a testament to his dedication and scholarly achievements. Dr. Waghulkar's academic interests are diverse, with a particular focus on subjects such as Research Methodology, Personal Management, Rural Marketing, and Digital Marketing. Beyond his academic pursuits, Dr. Waghulkar is deeply committed to social causes, showcasing his passion for community upliftment. He is actively involved in philanthropic endeavors and serves as a leading figure in a charitable trust dedicated to advancing the educational prospects of farmer's children. Through this initiative, he aims to provide better educational opportunities to underserved communities, thereby contributing to their social elevation and empowerment. Driven by his passion for both academia and social welfare, Dr. Waghulkar also harbors a keen interest in marketing research. His multifaceted approach to academia, coupled with his altruistic endeavors, exemplifies his holistic commitment to education, research, and societal betterment.

Index

W

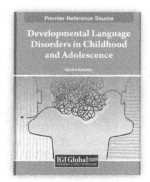

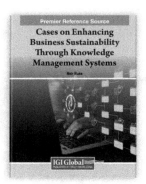

 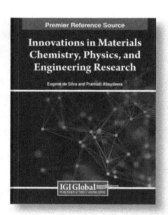 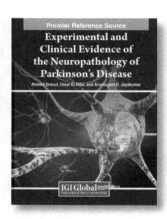 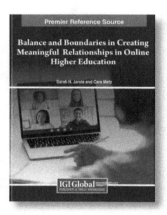

www.igi-global.com

Publishing Tomorrow's Research Today

IGI Global's Open Access Journal Program

Including Nearly 200 Peer-Reviewed, Gold (Full) Open Access Journals across IGI Global's Three Academic Subject Areas:
Business & Management; Scientific, Technical, and Medical (STM); and Education

Consider Submitting Your Manuscript to One of These Nearly 200 Open Access Journals for to Increase Their Discoverability & Citation Impact

Web of Science Impact Factor **6.5**	Web of Science Impact Factor **4.7**	Web of Science Impact Factor **3.2**	Web of Science Impact Factor **2.6**

JOURNAL OF
Organizational and End User Computing

JOURNAL OF
Global Information Management

INTERNATIONAL JOURNAL ON
Semantic Web and Information Systems

JOURNAL OF
Database Management

Choosing IGI Global's Open Access Journal Program Can Greatly Increase the Reach of Your Research

Higher Usage
Open access papers are 2-3 times more likely to be read than non-open access papers.

Higher Download Rates
Open access papers benefit from 89% higher download rates than non-open access papers.

Higher Citation Rates
Open access papers are 47% more likely to be cited than non-open access papers.

Submitting an article to a journal offers an invaluable opportunity for you to share your work with the broader academic community, fostering knowledge dissemination and constructive feedback.

Submit an Article and Browse the IGI Global Call for Papers Pages

We can work with you to find the journal most well-suited for your next research manuscript.
For open access publishing support, contact: journaleditor@igi-global.com

Individual Article & Chapter Downloads
US$ 37.50/each

9 798369 346389